C000300058

LONDON'S LOST TUBE SCHEMES

LONDON'S LOST TUBE SCHEMES

Antony Badsey-Ellis

Capital Transport

First published 2005
ISBN 185414 293 3
Published by Capital Transport Publishing
P.O. Box 250, Harrow, Middlesex
Printed by Thomson Press Ltd
Lyon Road, Harrow, Middlesex

Contents

Abbreviations

B&PCR	Brompton & Piccadilly Circus Railway
BoT	Board of Trade
BS&WR	Baker Street & Waterloo Railway
C&BR	City & Brixton Railway
C&CPERS	City & Crystal Palace Electric Railway Syndicate
C&CPR	City & Crystal Palace Railway
C&CS	Clapham & City Subway
C&NESER	City & North East Suburban Electric Railway
C&NLR	City & North of London Railway
C&OKRR	City & Old Kent Road Railway
C&SER	City & Surrey Electric Railway
C&SLR	City & South London Railway
C&WER	City & West-End Railway
CC&WER	Charing Cross & Waterloo Electric Railway
CCE&HR	Charing Cross, Euston & Hampstead Railway
CCH&DR	Charing Cross, Hammersmith & District Railway
CCS	Charing Cross Syndicate
CJ&PR	Clapham Junction & Paddington Railway
CL&SS	City of London & Southwark Subway
CLR	Central London Railway
CMR	Central Metropolitan Railway
CW&WR	City, Wandsworth & Wimbledon Railway
E&HR	Edgware & Hampstead Railway
E&SBR	Ealing & Shepherd's Bush Railway
ELR	East London Railway
ER&VR	Edgware Road & Victoria Railway
ERC	Electric Railways Company Ltd
GER	Great Eastern Railway
GN&CR	Great Northern & City Railway
GN&SR	Great Northern & Strand Railway
GNP&BR	Great Northern, Piccadilly & Brompton Railway
GNR	Great Northern Railway
GPO	General Post Office
GWR	Great Western Railway
H&CR	Hammersmith & City Railway
HC&NELR	Hammersmith, City & North East London Railway
I&ER	Islington & Euston Railway
SK&PS	South Kensington & Paddington Subway
KCCC&WS	King's Cross, Charing Cross & Waterloo Subway
KRR	King's Road Railway
L&GFC	London & Globe Finance Corporation
L&PECC	London & Provincial Electric Construction Company
LB&SCR	London, Brighton & South Coast Railway
LCC	London County Council
LC&DR	London, Chatham & Dover Railway

LCER	London Central Electric Railway
LCR	London Central Railway
LCS	London Central Subway
LCSR	London Central (Subway) Railway
LER	London Electric Railway Company
LNWR	London & North Western Railway
LSR	London Suburban Railway
LSWR	London & South Western Railway
LUER	London United Electric Railway
LUT	London United Tramways
LW&EFR	London, Walthamstow & Epping Forest Railway
MARC&CS	Marble Arch, Regent Circus & City Subway
MBW	Metropolitan Board of Works
MCC	Middlesex County Council
MDETC	Metropolitan District Electric Traction Company
MDR	Metropolitan District Railway
MLR	Mid-London Railway
MR	Metropolitan Railway
N&SLS	North & South London Subway
N&SWER	North & South Woolwich Electric Railway
N&SWS	North & South Woolwich Subway
NELR	North East London Railway
NER	North Eastern Railway
NETC	National Electric Traction Company
NLR	North London Railway
NW&CCR	North Western & Charing Cross Railway
OS&CR	Oxford Street & City Railway
NWLR	North West London Railway
P&CR	Piccadilly & City Railway
P&CCR	Paddington & Charing Cross Railway
PC&NELR	Piccadilly, City & North East London Railway
PDC	Pneumatic Despatch Company
SDR	South Devon Railway
SECR	South East & Chatham Railway
SER	South Eastern Railway
SKR	South Kensington Railway
SK&K&MAS	South Kensington & Knightsbridge & Marble Arch Subways
T&FGR	Tottenham & Forest Gate Railway
T&HJR	Tottenham & Hampstead Junction Railway
UERL	Underground Electric Railways of London, Ltd
VC&SER	Victoria, City & Southern Electric Railway
VK&GR	Victoria, Kennington & Greenwich Railway
W&CR	Waterloo & City Railway
W&ER	Watford & Edgware Railway
W&SLJR	West & South London Junction Railway
W&WR	Waterloo & Whitehall Railway

Introduction

There have been many books published about the underground railways of London. This book describes the tube railway schemes that might have happened, but for various reasons failed to be built, and covers the period from the birth of the tube railway up to the First World War. In order to provide a greater understanding of these schemes, the history of a few of the unbuilt cut-and-cover railways is included. I have not set out to describe these schemes in the same detail as for the tube proposals, and their full history must await another book.

Most of the existing histories of the London Underground make reference to a few of these unbuilt tubes in a sentence or two, but I have set out to provide fuller details of this neglected part of London's history. It would be impossible to describe the details of these railways without providing the context of the lines that were constructed, and so this is included as well, but I have not sought to provide the detailed story of these latter railways.

The idea for this book dates back to December 2001, when I began to investigate the records of some tube railway schemes held at the National Archives (then the Public Record Office) listed in *Railway Records*. What was intended to be a short article grew beyond my expectations.

Throughout the book I have indicated the names of stations in bold print. It should be noted, however, that station names are remarkably transient, especially before the line is constructed, and had the railways been built it is likely that many stations would have borne different names. I have tried to determine the names in use by the companies and promoters at the time of promotion wherever possible. In many cases this is from the transcripts of Parliamentary Committees, and a reference to "the station at Avonmore Road" may not actually mean that that name was intended. Where references are made to stations in existence, the name at the time is used, and an endnote will explain the subsequent changes.

Measurements are given in imperial units throughout the book, as these were the only units used in the many documents that I consulted. I have generally placed the metric equivalent in parentheses to an appropriate level of accuracy. No attempt has been made to refactor prices to modern equivalents, as there are so many factors that make any such comparison almost worthless.

I am very grateful to the staff of the National Archives (formerly the Public Record Office), the London Metropolitan Archive, the House of Lords Records Office, London's Transport Museum Reference Library, the Transport for London Archives, the Guildhall Library, the Law Society Library, and the Inner Temple Library for the assistance that they have provided over the three years that this book took to write. A list of references is included at the end of the book in case any reader wishes to pursue the facts about a particular scheme in more detail.

I am indebted to Mike Horne, Paul Hadley, and my wife Wendy, who have all read the manuscript and provided invaluable comments that have improved both the style and content. Unless otherwise credited, the new maps are the work of Mike Harris.

Antony Badsey-Ellis
Amersham
June 2005

Traffic Beneath the Streets

The First Underground Railway

On Friday 10 January 1863, the world's first underground railway opened. Of course, railway tunnels had been constructed before, but this was the first time a railway had been constructed almost entirely underground for the purposes of avoiding the congested streets of a city. The Metropolitan Railway (MR) was 3½ miles (5½ km) long, and ran between Paddington and Farringdon Street. It had been constructed through a process known as 'cut-and-cover': the streets above the line of the railway were cut open, a trench was dug, and the tunnel sides and roof were constructed, before being covered over with the street restored. As can be imagined, this was an immensely disruptive way to build a railway through a busy metropolis like London.

Despite a degree of scepticism in certain parts of the press,[1] Londoners flocked to their newest railway. Almost 9.5 million journeys were made in its first year, even with a disrupted service in August when the company had a dispute with the Great Western Railway, who provided the trains.

Cut-and-cover construction continued for a number of years, as the MR was extended eastwards to Moorgate Street, and southwards to South Kensington. Where possible the line was placed in a cutting between buildings, which allowed the noxious fumes from the locomotives to disperse. However, under the hills at Mount Pleasant (between King's Cross and Farringdon) and Campden (between Notting Hill Gate and High Street Kensington) tunnels were dug by conventional means.

The Rush for Railways

The immediate success of the MR in 1863 led to a rush to deposit plans for new railways across the capital. "We would as soon enter a Lunatic Asylum as attend a meeting of the Institute of Civil Engineers," noted *The City Press.*[2] The 1864 session of Parliament had some 33 schemes totalling 174 miles (280 km) of line to consider. Six failed to pay their deposits fully and were consequently dropped, and so a Joint Select Committee of both Houses of Parliament was convened to consider the remaining 27 plans. Few of them survived; those that did were principally connected with the desire to establish a circular route on the north bank of the Thames connecting many of the main line stations. To this end, the MR was successful in promoting lines from Paddington to South Kensington, and from Moorgate to Tower Hill.

John Fowler, the Metropolitan's engineer, proposed a railway along the north bank of the Thames to connect the two ends of the MR. This was to be the Metropolitan District Railway (MDR), a new and separate company from the MR, which was also approved by the Joint Committee. It constructed its own line between South

Kensington and Blackfriars using the cut and cover method, and to be operated by the well proven steam locomotive. The first section, from South Kensington to Westminster Bridge[3] was opened in 1868, and the line on to Blackfriars in 1870.

The Metropolitan was also the victim of its own success, and congestion between King's Cross and Farringdon caused it to construct a parallel route between these points. This was primarily for the use of the main line companies that connected to their route at each end (the Great Northern Railway at King's Cross, the Midland Railway at St Pancras, and the London, Chatham & Dover Railway at Farringdon). Following its authorization in the 1864 Metropolitan Railway Act, it was opened in early 1868. The duplicate tracks have ever since been known as the City Widened Lines.

The London Central Railway

Another of the successful schemes from the 1864 railway rush was the North Western & Charing Cross Railway (NW&CCR), which proposed a cut-and-cover railway linking Euston and St Pancras with Charing Cross. The plans were authorized by Parliament that year, and with the backing of the London & North Western Railway (LNWR – the owners of Euston) and the South Eastern Railway (SER – at Charing Cross) seemed to be certain of success. A further Act of 1866 allowed the company to form working agreements with both of these companies, and traffic agreements and fares were prepared with the aforementioned main line companies. The two companies would each be offered half of the shares in the line.

One of the problems facing the railways was the lack of money up front. With all of the difficulties in raising the large amounts of capital required, it made sense (from the viewpoint of the promoters) to pay their contractors in company shares. It was, in a way, an early form of risk-sharing. It gave the contractors an incentive to complete the line as quickly as possible, so that it could start to turn a profit. They would then receive the healthy dividends promised by the promoters, and the shares would hopefully rise in value as well.

Unfortunately, the contractors still needed to find cash to pay their workforce – share certificates would not be of any use to a workman looking to feed his family. Management of the cash flow was crucial, and in early 1866 a firm called Smith and Knight (which had constructed part of the MR) hit a problem, and failed. Three finance houses that had supported the contractors promptly collapsed as well. The crisis could have ended there, had Sir Samuel Morton Peto, another contractor, not run into difficulties and started to sell off the shares that he accepted from various railway companies. A major stock market crash ensued.

By May 1866 the financiers Overend, Gurney & Co failed, and interest rates soared to 10%. Another thirteen banks collapsed, and then their clients started to fail as well. Needless to say, this made the raising of capital nearly impossible for a time, and in 1867 the promoters of the NW&CCR deposited a Bill to extend the time permitted for them to construct the railway. The financial situation still did not improve, and this led to the abandonment of the NW&CCR. For most of the time the only money that they had raised was a mortgage of £330,000 – but nothing from shares. Even the attempt to abandon the line in 1868 was a failure: the Bill to enact this was not deposited with Parliament in time for the 1869 session.

Three years later, in 1871, the plans were dusted down and deposited again, under the new name of the Euston, St Pancras & Charing Cross Railway. In the north this would connect with the LNWR tracks north of Euston, near to the Hampstead Road bridge. Descending a 1 in 41 gradient, the line would pass beneath Drummond Street and Euston Street before curving to the south-west. A station giving passenger interchange with the MR would be provided at **Gower Street** (named to match the Metropolitan's station). It would be parallel to, and on the north side of the MR station, with possible cross platform interchange between the new westbound line and the eastbound MR.

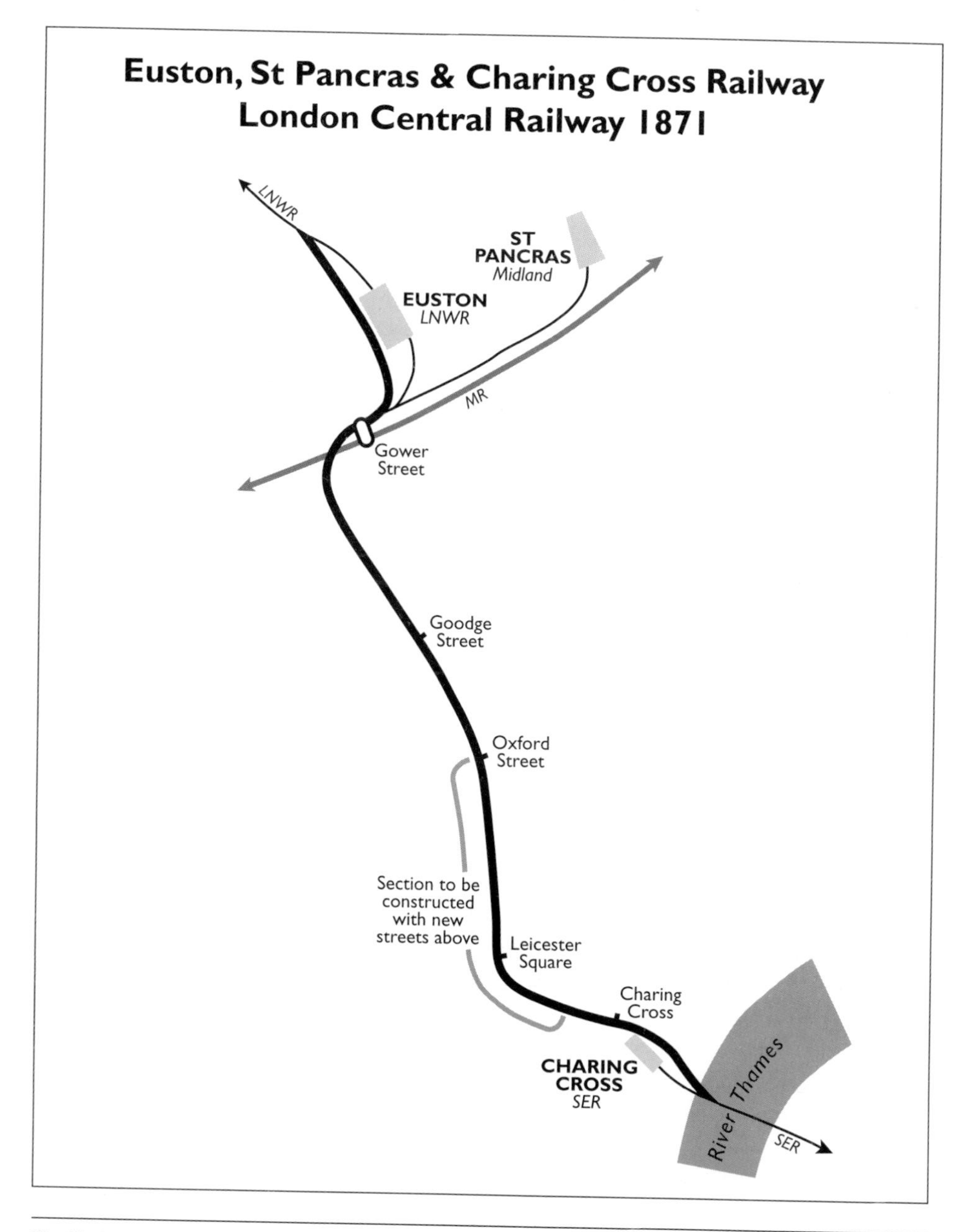

Two branches would lead east from this station, neither of which had been in the 1864 scheme. The first connected with the eastern side of **Euston** station, and would presumably allow passengers arriving at that station access to the underground railway. The second branch would lead to the **St Pancras** station of the Midland Railway, providing further service possibilities.

West of Gower Street the line would descend to curve below the MR at the junction with Tottenham Court Road, passing 18 feet (5.5 m) below the older railway. South of the Euston Road the line would be situated on the west side of Whitfield Street; all of the houses between Grafton and Goodge Streets would be bought by the railway to provide the necessary land. A station would be provided at **Goodge Street**.

Southwards the railway would continue in the same line as far as Oxford Street station. It would then curve slightly to the right, and follow a straight line to Leicester Square, where the station would be on the north side of the square. Curving to face south-east, the line would proceed towards the church of St Martin's-in-the-Fields, and pass to the north of the church under Chandos Street. The final station on the line would be on the north side of the Strand, opposite **Charing Cross** SER station. Coutts & Co Bank today occupies this site, which was known in the 1800s as the Lowther Arcade. The block of land on which the station would be sited was already occupied by houses, most of which would remain in place, with the station in the middle. To maximize the use of daylight a glass roof would be built over the station. The owner and builder of many of the houses was one William Herbert (who had recently died), and whose estate vigorously petitioned against the Bill, claiming that the noise, smoke, and steam would render the rear rooms of the houses unusable, and devalue the property. South of the Strand the line would rise to the surface between the main line station and Villiers Street, and ascend a viaduct (at 1 in 44.6) to join the SER on the Hungerford Railway Bridge. The connection would be close to the Middlesex Pier of the bridge.

The company did not intend to operate its own trains, but instead would allow the main line companies to operate their services through the tunnels. All three connected railways (LNWR, SER, and Midland Railway) were favourably disposed to the new railway. The tunnels would be 26 feet (7.9 m) wide and 14 feet (4.3 m) high, giving a fairly tight fit for main line rolling stock, and probably a fairly noxious atmosphere for the passengers given that steam locomotives would have been used. Ventilation holes were to be constructed along the route, as they were with the MR, to allow the smoke and steam to escape. The only definite location recorded for one of these was in Chandos Street, to the north of Charing Cross station.

As will be realized from the description of the route, there were no convenient roads between Oxford Street and Chandos Street beneath which the railway could pass. The company proposed constructing two new streets as part of the scheme, linking Leicester Square to Oxford Street northwards, and Castle Street southwards. Castle Street disappeared in 1887 when Charing Cross Road was constructed; in fact, the new streets proposed by the railway were an earlier plan for the new road. Both new roads would be 60 feet (18.3 m) wide, and sewers would be constructed under the roads. The Vestry of St James's Westminster[4] supported the new road, and let the Metropolitan Board of Works (MBW) know their opinion. However, the Vestry of St Martin-in-the-Fields took the opposite view.

In March the promoters wrote to the MBW asking if they would be willing to contribute half the cost of making the new road. This was considered carefully, and two months later the Board stated that it was prepared to contribute a maximum of £200,000. They stipulated that this was to include the road through Leicester Square.

At the southern end of the line, construction would result in the stopping-up, or closure, of York Place and Duke Street.[5] A correspondent to the MBW suggested that the north end of Buckingham Street (now Buckingham Arcade) be widened as far as the Strand, and a new street be made between Villiers Street and Buckingham Street to compensate for this closure. Unfortunately for the idea it was found that widening Buckingham Street would involve payment of at least £45,000 compensation to the owner of Allen's, a trunk-makers, which had already been moved once when Charing Cross station was constructed.

The railway received the Royal Assent on 14 August 1871, with £2 million of capital. Shortly after this the scheme was again renamed, becoming the London Central Railway (LCR). The cost of constructing the railway was estimated at just under £1.4 million, with the new roads another £280,000. The cost of acquiring property along the lines of the new roads was split equally between the railway and road totals.

A prospectus was issued on 2 December 1871 to encourage people to purchase shares; this did not prove a success. The lack of funds prevented construction, and in 1873 the promoters returned to Parliament and successfully gained a further Act extending their permitted time for the construction of the line. Other proposals in the same session were rejected: these included the eastward extension of the line from St Pancras to King's Cross, where the line was planned to rise to the surface and join the tracks at the eastern platforms. An east-facing link to the Metropolitan Railway in front of St Pancras formed part of this proposal. Further west a flying junction with the MR was planned. This would diverge northbound from the LCR at Grafton Street, and join the MR just east of Portland Road station.[6] All of these connections were rejected by Parliament after strong opposition from the MBW.

Even with the authorized extension of time, the finances of the LCR did not improve, and in 1874 the scheme was formally abandoned.

The Charing Cross & Euston Railway

A very similar cut-and-cover scheme was the Charing Cross & Euston Railway, which emerged in 1885. As with the LCR it was to branch from the LNWR at Hampstead Road, curving to pass to the west of Euston main line station. It would descend a 1 in 70 gradient to pass in a covered way beneath Cardington Street (which would be stopped up) and Drummond Street. A station providing interchange with **Euston** would be sited around this point.

South of here it would curve to the south-west, placing it parallel with the Euston Road. Next it would swing south, passing in a tunnel beneath the MR, at a depth of 45 ft 4 ins (13.8 m). There would not be any station or interchange between the two railways. The line would then follow Whitfield Street as far south as Howland Street, at which point it would pass in an S-curve beneath Howland Mews East to reach the line of Tottenham Court Road. The mews would be purchased by the company, and used for **Howland Street** station.

The railway would now follow Tottenham Court Road to the junction with **Oxford Street**. South of here it would be constructed in conjunction with the new Charing Cross Road planned by the MBW, and would follow this as far as St Martin's Place, with an intermediate station at **Cranbourn Street**. It would curve to the north of the church of St Martin-in-the-Fields, and then pass under the Lowther Arcade and the Strand. The line would split at Adelaide Street, with one branch staying below surface level and terminating parallel to Villiers Street – this would be **Charing Cross** station. The other branch would pass under the same street, which would be closed to allow the railway to rise to the surface, which it would achieve at Duke Street (now John Adam Street). It would continue to climb at a gradient of 1 in 70, onto a new railway bridge that would be on the north side of the existing Hungerford Bridge (taking the place of the footbridge, which would be replaced further north). The tracks would finally merge with those of the SER on the south bank, at Belvedere Road.

The closure of Villiers Street would cause some inconvenience (as was noticed by the LCR). To alleviate this it was proposed to widen the parallel Buckingham Street so that it would connect with the Strand at its north end. To the south a new piece of road would be constructed across the southern end of Victoria Embankment Gardens, passing over the MDR station. This road would link Buckingham Street to the Victoria Embankment.

The company would not have run its own trains, but rented rights of passage to the main line companies, who would operate their own steam trains across London through its tunnels. They never had the chance, though, as the promoters withdrew the Bill in late February.[7]

More Cut-and-Cover Proposals

We now go back to the early 1870s, to look at some of the schemes that proposed complete railways, rather than just the provision of the tunnel and tracks, to be leased to main line companies.

The Mid-London Railway

The Mid-London Railway (MLR) promoted its two Bills in the 1872 session of Parliament. It sought to alleviate the disruption caused by excavating the busy streets across the City by constructing a new road as an extension of Oxford Street running east, with the railway beneath.

> **Capital and Borrowing Powers**
>
> The Bills for railways have to declare the amount of money needed by the company to cover all of their costs of construction, equipment, and other items, such as parliamentary and legal expenses. Most of the total is raised through the issuing of shares to which the public can subscribe. An additional amount, up to one-third of the total share value, can be obtained by the company taking out a mortgage. Restrictions in the Bill usually prevent the mortgage being raised until a certain, large percentage of the shares have been subscribed to. The amount to be raised is inevitably more than the estimated costs, and this contingency is expected by Parliament. As shall be seen with some of the later schemes, it can be a difficult matter to decide when the surplus is too much and the scheme is being over-capitalized.

The first, and less contentious, Bill was for a railway starting at the LNWR at Willesden, and running for a distance of just over 3½ miles (5.7 km) to Marble Arch. Part of the route would be in tunnel. The line proposed in the second Bill was to start at Marble Arch as a continuation of the first, and run due east paralleling Oxford Street and High Holborn. To the east of Holborn Viaduct it would leave the line of the streets and be constructed under a new street through the City. At around St Martin's-le-Grand it would move to the north of Cheapside, still beneath a new street. It continued east and ended by connecting to the East London Railway at Commercial Road. This portion of the line would be 5½ miles long (8.9 km), including 1¼ miles (2 km) of new street. The railway would cost £2,596,616 to construct, and the road a further £1.4 million. Capital of £4.8 million was sought for the entire route from Willesden to Whitechapel, with further borrowing powers for £1.6 million. The Parliamentary deposit for the railway was a not inconsiderable £250,000.

Stations were to be provided at **Cumberland Gate** (Marble Arch), **Regent Street** (Oxford Circus), **Tottenham Court Road, Holborn, Charterhouse Street** (Holborn Circus), **Bank, Bishopsgate Street, Whitechapel,** and **Commercial Road.**

As can be imagined, this would have involved a vast amount of property demolition (in place of street excavation) followed by construction of the railway. The disruption to London, and especially the City, would have been enormous, although having a straight, wide road across the City would have been of huge benefit. However, it may be recalled that even after the Great Fire had destroyed much of the City, such an eminent person as Sir Christopher Wren could not push though his plans for creating wide streets across the City. The Metropolitan Board of Works opposed the scheme, but the Corporation of the City of London broadly welcomed it. The House of Commons was not convinced with either the finances or the belief that the new road would ever be constructed, and the Bill for the section between Marble Arch and Whitechapel was thrown out. This left the promoters with an authorized railway from Willesden to Marble Arch; the press thought that the promoters would not be in any great hurry to construct this, and felt the decision of Parliament to be unsatisfactory.[8]

On 15 May a meeting of the inhabitants of Kilburn voiced their support for the MLR, and encouraged the recommital of the Bill for the rejected eastern section. They noted that a Parliamentary deposit had been made, which demonstrated the good will and financial strength of the company. They went on to urge the LNWR to support the scheme, either in its authorized and truncated form to Marble Arch, or fully (presumably by backing a new Bill). Nothing came of this support, and the MLR disappeared.

The City & West-End Railway

The Metropolitan sought to link the West End with their station at Farringdon with a line promoted as the City & West End Railway, and deposited plans for this scheme with Parliament for consideration in the 1873 session. This was intended to branch off just north of Farringdon and curve west under Charterhouse Street to Holborn Circus. It would continue following the route of Holborn as far as New Oxford Street. Here it was intended to curve left, under the proposed new road that was eventually constructed between 1877 and 1886 as Shaftesbury Avenue – this would be followed to Piccadilly Circus. It was intended to continue the line west as far as South Kensington, thus forming a circular railway entirely controlled by the Metropolitan.

Parts of the railway would be in open cutting, roughly 20 feet (6.1 m) below street level. Under Shaftesbury Avenue in particular, the route would be in tunnel, descending to 50 feet (15.25 m) to pass under the authorized London Central Railway at Nassau Street (now disappeared, but formerly to the south of the route of Shaftesbury Avenue, and east of Macclesfield Street).

The MR offered running rights to its main line partners (suggesting that a junction at Farringdon with its City Widened Lines would be provided), but none was interested in the scheme; as a result of this the Bill was withdrawn, with no Parliamentary deposit having been made. It was explained shortly after, at a company meeting, that the C&WER was created to counter the threat of the Mid-London Railway. It had cost the company £1,200 to plan the line, and the collapse of the MLR scheme had meant that the MR had incurred very little cost for its opposition. The Board did not feel that the Metropolitan's shareholders should or would want to shoulder the burden of financing a new line at the same time as continuing to extend the railway to Liverpool Street.

The Central Metropolitan Railway

The Central Metropolitan Railway (not linked in any way with the MR) deposited its plans with Parliament in 1881, and planned to run from Parliament Square to St Pancras station. The intention was for it to follow Parliament Street and Whitehall into Trafalgar Square, and from there, north into St Martin's Lane, which would require widening. It was then to curve north-east under Long Acre (also to be widened in places) and Great Queen Street before swinging north again beneath Southampton Row. Following Gloucester Street, Queen Square, Brunswick Square, and Judd Street, the line would finally curve east under the roads and houses just south of the Euston Road, terminating at right angles to Liverpool Street (now Birkenhead Street).

The line was intended to be roughly 35 feet (10.7 m) below the street surface, and would have ventilators located at road junctions. Parcels, livestock, and freight were to be carried, as well as passengers, as shown by the carriage rates given by the company.

The CMR was incorporated on 6 December 1881, with capital of £800,000. The few initial subscribers – presumably the promoters – each paid for one share, providing a total investment of £70. Almost three months later the nominal capital was increased to £1 million, but still with no sign of anyone interested in buying the shares.

As could have been expected, the government was very concerned about the section along Whitehall. The Treasury in particular raised concerns about the effect of the shallow tunnelling on its massive and heavy buildings, and did not feel that reinforcing the underpinning clauses in the Bill would have enough effect. In the end it did not need to worry – the Government opposed the railway beyond Charing Cross, and this section was dropped from the Bill. The House of Commons then rejected the Bill at its second reading following strenuous opposition from W. H. Smith (the bookseller-turned-MP),[9] who made a number of allegations that the directors had not been appointed and the promoters were not known. One of the MPs in favour of the line refuted these allegations, accusing Smith of speaking "the reverse of the truth". The Speaker demanded that this comment be retracted; this was done, but replaced with the "reverse of correct".[10] However, the proponents of the Bill could not muster enough support in the Commons, and the Bill was lost.

The following week *The Railway Times* noted that Smith had been "acting in the capacity of guardian of the interests of the constituency of the city of Westminster", and that his chief opposition was due to the earth being carted through the streets. In their editorial they considered that this was a bad decision, as the railway would have provided a great deal of good in return for a little inconvenience during construction.[11] The company was wound up on 2 May 1884, and formally dissolved on 20 March 1906.

The Electric Railways

In the 1880s, the concept of electricity was still very new for most people. London's first electricity generating station was opened in 1889, so the concept of using electricity to move a train was little short of revolutionary at the start of the decade.

The first electric railway was actually demonstrated in May 1879 at the Berlin Trades Exhibition by Dr Werner von Siemens, using a small locomotive and three carriages on 900 yards (824 m) of track. Just over four years later, on 4 August 1883, Magnus Volk opened the first electric railway in Britain, along the seafront in Brighton.[12] Rebuilt several times, this line is still in operation today.

The deposition of a Bill in 1881 for an underground electric railway in London was therefore a rather daring and courageous act on the part of its promoters and engineers.

The Charing Cross & Waterloo Electric Railway

Another scheme that was to take a very similar route to the W&WR was deposited with Parliament at the end of 1881. The Charing Cross & Waterloo Electric Railway (CC&WER) proposed, as the name suggested, using electricity to move the trains through its tunnels, although pneumatic power was also a possibility.[13] It was promoted by John Read and Sir Henry Tyler, both of whom were directors of the Great Eastern Railway (amongst a number of other railway directorships).

Twin tracks would link **Trafalgar Square** to **Waterloo** main line station; beneath the Thames these would be in iron pipes sunk into a trench and connected to cut-and-cover tunnels under the roads. The company prospectus of 29 March 1883 alleged that a 60-feet (18.3 m) section of one of these tunnels had been constructed beneath Northumberland Avenue and the Victoria Embankment, and lined with white bricks. The covered way on the south side of the Thames would be similarly lined.

The northern station would be 20 feet (6.1 m) below street level, with the tracks falling at 1 in 42 under Northumberland Avenue. The line would then curve under the junction with Whitehall Place and the Victoria Embankment Gardens before crossing under the Thames. It would then rise at 1 in 33 under College Street and Vine Street (both now lost under the South Bank complex and Shell Centre). It would terminate on a block of land bounded to the south by Vine Street and to the west by York Road, which would be taken over entirely by the railway. Here the tunnels would rise to the surface for the Waterloo station, allowing the line to be directly connected with the LSWR platforms. The generating station for the line would also be sited here. Today this block of land is the north-west corner of Waterloo main line station, and faces the Shell Centre across York Road.

Capital of £100,000 was sought through a share issue, with additional borrowing powers of £33,000. The railway was backed by the electrical engineering company of Siemens Brothers (founded by Dr Werner von Siemens), with Dr C. W. Siemens as the electrical engineer. The civil engineers were Henry Law and George Chatterton. The firm of Kellett & Bentley was to construct the railway, and had estimated that this could be achieved for £80,000. Eighteen months was thought sufficient to construct the line.

Siemens would be paid £12,000 for the electrical equipment, and would also operate the line for the first five years. In return they would receive £5,000 per year, plus one-fifth of the receipts over £20,000. The promoters estimated the annual revenue at £24,000, assuming that 12,000 people would make the 3½-minute journey each day.

The MDR was concerned about the prospect of tunnels being constructed under its line, and succeeded in getting an onerous penalty clause added to the CC&WER Act. This would compel the latter company to pay £200 to the MDR for each obstruction to their trains that was caused, plus an additional £100 per hour for the duration of the stoppage.

The CC&WER was incorporated by an Act of 18 August 1882. In December of the same year it deposited a Bill to extend the line from Waterloo to the Royal Exchange, via Blackfriars, on a very similar route to that taken a decade later by the Waterloo & City Railway. The MBW opposed the extension, and prepared a petition. The Bill was read for the first time in the House of Commons on 20 February, and the next month the MBW sealed their petition and submitted it. They wanted to know what provision was being made by the railway for paying them an easement for the right to pass beneath the Victoria Embankment. However, 1883 was a difficult year for the company. They had trouble raising the finance required for the line, and Dr C. W. Siemens died. The extension Bill was withdrawn from Parliament in early May.

The association of Siemens with the line should have guaranteed success, but his death, in addition to all of the company's financial problems, killed it off without any construction having started. In 1885 a shorter northern extension a few hundred yards to Cockspur Street (on the western side of Trafalgar Square) was promoted, but sensing that the end was probably near, an abandonment Bill was also promoted. The extension Bill was withdrawn in late March, leaving the way clear for the process of abandoning the line. It was noted by *The Railway News* that the promoters were unable to raise the finance owing to the novelty of the line ("first project for an electrical railway in England").[14] The Committee considering the Bill were convinced by Henry Law that the CC&WER was impractical to construct under the terms of the 1882 Act, and approved the abandonment. The company was formally abandoned by Act of Parliament on 16 July 1885.

The London Central Electric Railway

In 1883 plans for the London Central Electric Railway (LCER) were deposited with Parliament. This line was intended to extend the CC&WER northwards from its Charing Cross terminus, across Trafalgar Square, and then along St Martin's Place and Castle Street to the south end of Dudley Street.[15] Stations would be sited at **Charing Cross**,[16] **Cranbourn Street**, and **Dudley Street** (roughly the site of Cambridge Circus). A separate branch would run east from **Regent Circus** and along Richmond Street and King Street also to Dudley Street, where it would join the main railway.[17] The combined line would then pass along under Dudley Street to its north end, before curving east. It then continued along **New Oxford Street** (with a station located where Bloomsbury Way joins today) and High Holborn (stations at **Little Queen Street**,[18] **Brownlow Street**, and **Grays Inn Road**) before reaching **Holborn Circus**. From here it would loop in a curve to the north-east under Charterhouse Street. It then swung back south-east under **Farringdon Street** and Snow Hill before passing **Old Bailey** and terminating a short way to the east at St Martin's-le-Grand, near to the new **Post Office**. The cost of this construction was to be covered by raising share capital of £500,000, and having borrowing powers of up to £166,666.

The line was generally about 25–30 feet (7.6 – 9.2 m) below street level, in a cut-and-cover built trench. This would provide a width of 15 feet (4.6 m) in which the two tracks would be positioned, and a height of just 8 ft 9 ins (2.67 m). The platforms would have been 10 feet (3.1 m) wide. At the terminal stations track traversers would be provided. These would allow complete trains to be slid sideways from one track to another, avoiding the need for any type of shunting.

The gradient was gently up hill from Trafalgar Square and Regent Circus to Southampton Row, then downhill to pass below the Fleet valley and the London, Chatham & Dover Railway at Snow Hill. The final run to Post Office was again uphill.

Electrically-propelled carriages were to be used, with five being coupled together to form peak hour trains, and groups of two or three running off-peak. Each carriage was to be motorized, and would travel at a speed of just 10 m.p.h. (16 km/h) to minimize the power that would be wasted by braking. Electricity would be supplied at 400 V by a single conductor rail, returning via the running rails, and the power station would be capable of generating 750 horsepower (560 kW).

The small size of the tunnels meant that the carriages would also be small; only 27

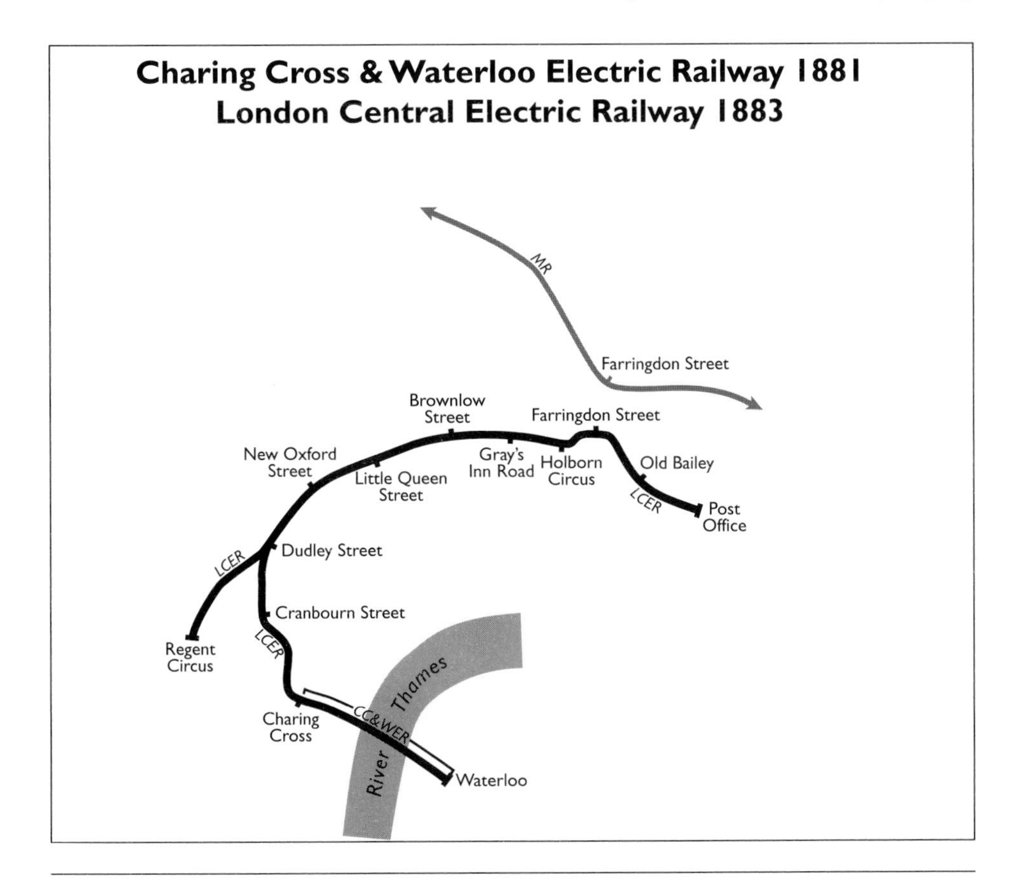

passengers, and one conductor, would fit into each, boarding via platforms at the end of each carriage rather than side doors. The passengers would reach the station platforms by descending stairs at each station; around 70 in the case of Old Bailey, some 36 feet (11 m) below street level. The promoters were questioned about this and declared that lifts were "too inconvenient" for passengers.

Siemens Brothers were involved in the promotion of the railway (as well as the CC&WER), and were to run it (supplying all staff) for five years after opening. In return, they would be paid £28,000 annually.

The Select Committee of the House of Commons decided to reject the Bill, stating that it had approved the CC&WER as an experimental line. They wished to see it prove itself before they sanctioned the type of extensive extension that the LCER promoters envisaged. Electricity was still very much an unknown quantity for London's railways. The MBW had also put up strong opposition to the line, noting that it would cause much interference with their sewers.

Concerns were also expressed about the small size of the tunnels, and that perhaps omnibuses would be able to provide a better service (and one without the need to walk up and down many tens of steps).

The London Central Subway

The London Central Subway (LCS) plans of 1885 were for a shallow railway between Charing Cross and King's Cross, a total distance of 2 miles 68 yards (3.28 km). At the latter station the line would commence in Gray's Inn Road, immediately south of the MR station.[19] Running east in two separate subways on the south side of the MR tunnel, the railway would undercut both the pavements and the gardens of the houses on the south side of Euston Road, with the rails around 16 feet (4.9 m) below ground level. The Skinners' Company, who were governors of the Tonbridge School on the Euston Road, objected to the railway company taking their grounds, but leaving the building: they wrote to the Charities Commissioners requesting their permission to petition against the Bill. A clause was prepared that would oblige the LCS to take all of the buildings and grounds, something that would be very much more expensive for the railway.[20]

At Gower Place the line would curve sharply south into Gower Street, and descend at 1 in 50, to a depth of about 40 feet (12.2 m) below the street. Passing beneath Bedford Square and Bloomsbury Street, it would curve southwards under Broad Street and into Great St Andrew Street. Crossing Seven Dials, it would follow Little St Andrew Street into Upper St Martin's Lane and then St Martin's Place, before crossing Trafalgar Square on the east side and terminating in Charing Cross, where the tunnel would be 18 ft 9 ins (5.7 m) below ground level.

It is not clear from the plans, but it is likely that the southbound line was to be placed under the northbound line for a distance between Broad Street and Upper St Martin's Lane, due to the narrowness of the streets. At Seven Dials the lines were 54 ft 6 ins and 35 ft 6 ins (16.6 and 10.8 m) deep respectively. Some steep gradients were present: on the southbound line, from Seven Dials to Long Acre the line descended at 1 in 20, and there was a 1 in 33 uphill gradient for northbound trains between Broad Street and New Oxford Street. The actual tunnels were to have a width of 10 feet (3.1 m) and a height of 11 feet (3.4 m).

Limits of Deviation

The plans that are created by the railway companies and deposited with Parliament show the streets and buildings along the route, and the centre line of the railway, as well as the limits of deviation. These are the boundaries of the land outside which the railway structures are not allowed to fall. They are included because it is impossible to build the line on an exact course, and so they show the margin of tolerance in construction.

In general, all buildings and land to be purchased by the railway are included with the limits; thus, reference to the plans can indicate where stations and other surface structures will be sited.

Section of a plan showing limits of deviation and centre line.

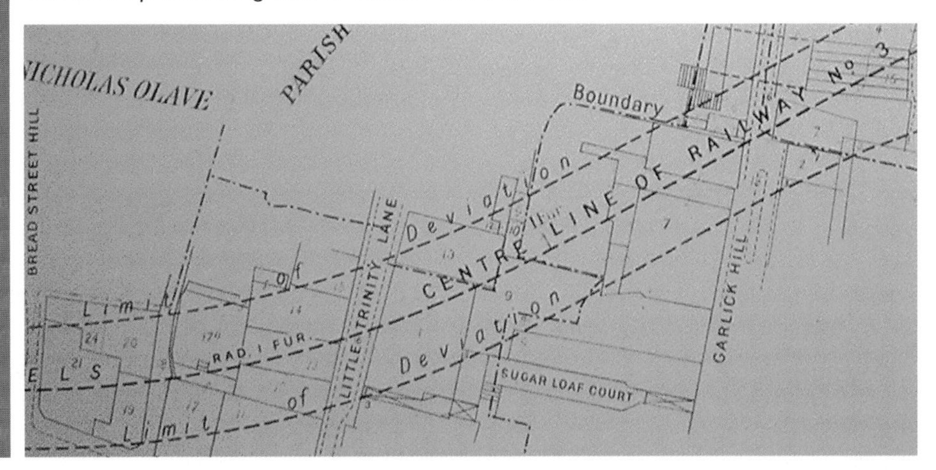

Stations were not clearly identified on the plans, but by noting where blocks of additional buildings were contained within the limits of deviation and adjacent to main roads crossing the line, a tentative list of stations may be compiled. From north to south, they are: **King's Cross**, **Endsleigh Gardens**, **Torrington Place**, **New Oxford Street**, **Seven Dials**, **St Martin's Place** (at the north end), and **Charing Cross**. Passengers would access the station platforms via staircases; lifts were not to be provided. One unexplained feature on the plans was the inclusion of an entire triangular block of buildings bounded by Great St Andrew Street, Queen Street,[21] and Neal Street within the limits of deviation.

The depôt for the railway would be located to the south of Euston Road, on a block of land occupied today by Flaxman Terrace (and in 1885 called North Crescent Mews). A tunnel 44 yards (40 m) long would diverge from the westbound subway and lead into the site, carrying a single track.

On 13 April 1885 the government's Office of Works informed the Treasury that their Consulting Surveyor had investigated the proposed route at the north side of Trafalgar Square and St Martin's Place. The surveyor felt that the National Gallery buildings were at serious risk of being made unstable by the shallow tunnels. The Office of Works wanted a clause inserted forbidding the railway from excavating to a depth of more than 25 feet (7.6 m) within 35 feet (10.7 m) of the south-eastern corner of the building. The standard clause that was added to all underground railway Bills concerning the need to underpin buildings was felt to be insufficient at this location.

The Office of Works recognized in their letter that the insertion of the clause would most likely force the promoters to abandon the route as proposed. However, the safety of the National Gallery was too important to be compromised.

Looking at a map of the area, it is difficult to see how the railway could be altered without introducing some very tight curves, or increasing the costs by passing beneath property. However, just three days later, on 16 April, a letter from the railway company informed the Office of Works that they had amended the route to avoid passing under any part of Trafalgar Square. Regrettably the plans of this change do not survive, nor does the letter give any details of the changes. It would appear that the changes were not sufficient though, as the Bill was withdrawn around 21 April by the promoters. No reason was given in the documents, although we may surmise that it relates to the difficulties of getting to their southern terminus, and the opposition from the Tonbridge School. The Skinners' Company certainly believed that their petition had a great deal to do with the decision of the promoters to withdraw.

The London Central (Subway) Railway

The final cut-and-cover proposal examined in this chapter is the London Central (Subway) Railway, which was not connected with the previously-mentioned plan of 1885. It was promoted in 1889 by an American, Colonel Rowland Hazard, who was Chairman and a large shareholder of the United States Subway Co of New York. The share capital for the line was £750,000, and borrowing powers of up to £248,000 were agreed.

The line was to start at the junction of **St James's Street** and Piccadilly, and run north-east under the latter road to **Piccadilly Circus**. It was then to follow Shaftesbury Avenue to **Cambridge Circus**, and High Holborn, with a station at the junction with New Oxford Street called **British Museum**. The railway would continue beneath High Holborn, via a station at **Chancery Lane**, to Holborn Circus, where it would terminate at **Holborn** station, 1⅔ miles (2.7 km) from its origin. The distances between the latter three stations are quite large, and it would seem likely that additional stations would be provided at Cambridge Circus and somewhere along High Holborn, although no documentary evidence for these has been found.

The line would closely resemble the New York subways as they were eventually built. The track bed, formed of concrete, would be just 12 feet (3.7 m) below the surface of the streets. Three lines of pillars would divide the space into four parallel galleries; the inner pair each 11 feet (3.4 m) wide for the two lines of railway, and the outer pair for services, such as gas, electricity, and water. Some streets would have four railway galleries, to allow express and local train operation at some future date. Initially only two would be equipped for the railway.

Wrought iron girders placed across the pillars at right angles would support a layer of concrete forming the tunnel roof and the roadway; this was to be 6–8 inches (15–20 cm) thick, and surfaced with asphalt. There would be clearance of 9 ft 6 ins (2.9 m) in the tunnels. The galleries would be separated from each other by boards of ferflax; this was an American invention, consisting of "steel wires interlaced with flax or vegetable fibre and oil compound, the whole pressed into a solid panel by hydraulic pressure."[22] It was supposed to be strong and fireproof.

The promoters evidently had big ideas. Hazard had presented a paper entitled *Underground Railway Communication in Great Cities* to the British Association for the Advancement of Science in 1888. This was reprinted as part of a booklet issued by the company and explained many of the details. This included their plans to expand the system

> . . . from about Aldgate through the City to the extreme West End of London, by two lines, via Holborn and Oxford Street on the North, and the Strand and Piccadilly on the South, with several connecting lines.[23]

The MBW was already constructing service subways beneath their new streets in London, such as Shaftesbury Avenue, and this gave the idea to the promoters. Service subways allowed the pipes and cables to be accessed without the need to dig up the road. The outer walls of the subways proposed by the LCS would be the cellar walls for the properties lining the streets above. At stations the service gallery would narrow behind the 12-feet (2.7 m) wide platforms. Only one platform would be constructed at each of the terminal stations; the additional space thus provided would allow for extra sidings where the trains would be maintained. Platforms were to be 250 feet (76.25 m) long.

Of course, the existing subway beneath Shaftesbury Avenue presented a problem for the railway company, who had no wish to re-excavate the street. Their solution was to cut a tube tunnel beneath the length of the road, placing Cambridge Circus station in tunnel as well, some 28 ft 6 ins (8.7 m) below the street. A 1 in 40 gradient would be used at each end to link the tube tunnels with the cut and cover parts. An original plan to dig up the avenue and construct the line with the service galleries to the side was dropped, probably on account of the disruption that it would cause.

Property would be purchased on both sides of the street to allow for access to station platforms. It is unlikely that sub-surface footbridges would have fitted into the diminutive tunnels, and the property purchase was probably necessary for station access rather than to save passengers from having to cross the road. Just twenty seven-inch (18 cm) steps would be required to gain platform access, although lifts were to be provided as well, which was rather extravagant for the time.

The trains were to be 212 feet (64.7 m) long, and would have five passenger cars of mixed first- and third-class accommodation. The cars would have riveted steel frames with ferflax body panels fitted; this, the promoters claimed, would make them virtually unbreakable.

There would be a motor car at each end, and a fully-laden train would weigh 145 tons. The floor of the cars would be just 36 inches (92 cm) above the rails, and the inside would be 7 ft 3 ins high by 7 ft 6 ins wide (2.2 (2.3 m). Each bogie would support the end of two adjacent cars,[24] and would have six wheels. Most interestingly of all, the current would be supplied through copper rails on the tunnel roof. Current would be collected by trolleys mounted on the car roofs, and returned via the running rails to the power station, which would be sited near the junction of Broad Street and High Holborn. Tunnel access would be located at the same site, although most maintenance would occur in the termini.

When the Bill appeared for its second reading before the Commons in March, it received a frosty reception. The MPs representing London constituencies were annoyed that the Bill was being put forward in the House of Commons by the MPs for Stoke-on-Trent and Wolverhampton. Gainsford Bruce, the MP for Finsbury, Holborn, wished that they had "tried it in their own districts before attempting to carry it out in the Metropolis." The fact that it would tunnel beneath some of the most prestigious streets in London, and that it did not connect to any other railway, made it too controversial. However, a vote was taken, and the Bill was referred to a Select Committee, in the usual way.

The proposal failed before the Select Committee, which listened to the promoters and petitioners between 9 and 23 May. The newly-formed London County Council (LCC), which took over from the MBW in 1889, was very much opposed to the railway interfering with the services under the streets. They also objected to a private company owning the railway (even though the other railways in London were privately-owned), and felt that it should "be in the hands of the Council as the central authority".[25]

One of the most famous petitioners against the line was Sir Joseph Bazalgette, the former Chief Engineer for the MBW, and the engineer for the new sewer system under the streets of London. He argued that the plans to lower the sewers to a position beneath the subway when they followed the same street would affect the careful levels and gradients that had been constructed; this could lead to blockages and other problems. He likewise objected to the disturbance of the service subways. He was paid a retainer of 10 guineas per day by the LCC for his expert evidence against the Shortlands & Nunhead Railway Bill;[26] this arrangement was extended for his work in connection with the LCSR. Benjamin Baker was also retained for evidence against the subway railway scheme. Baker's opposition was not entirely unexpected, as he was engineer to the Central London Railway, which would compete with the LCSR on the route east from Holborn. The CLR is described in more detail in a later chapter.

However, the basic failing for the company was commercial. The promoters estimated that they would need 22 million journeys per year to make the line viable; the MDR produced figures showing that over similar lengths of line they carried 1,145,178. Given that the size of the tunnels precluded any other railway from operating trains through it, it was doomed to failure.

One of the key limitations of all of these proposals was their reliance on cut-and-cover construction. As the MR had shown, this was a messy, disruptive, and time-consuming business that was tolerated less and less in the streets of the capital. The damage caused to property, congestion caused in the streets, and difficulties caused by re-routeing the pipes and cables underground made it impractical for future railways. An alternative was needed; otherwise, underground railways were going to be confined to the outskirts of the city.

The railway promoters were also carefully considering the method of propulsion for their new schemes. Steam was demonstrating itself to be the major cause of an unpleasant atmosphere on the Metropolitan and Metropolitan District Railways, and electricity was a novel and largely untested idea, but one that would eventually be the winner. In the meantime there was a third contender for powering London's underground railways.

The Pneumatic Railway

The use of pneumatic propulsion for railways became particularly fashionable in the mid-1800s. George Medhurst had proposed pneumatic tube railways in 1810, and the first patent was that of John Vallance in 1825. Vallance also constructed a demonstration line 150 feet (45.7 m) long near Brighton.

Two different pneumatic systems were developed. That promoted by Thomas Rammell involved trains being blown or sucked through tunnels. The carriages fitted closely into the tunnels to prevent the air from passing them, thus forcing the carriages to move.

The alternative system was called an atmospheric railway, and its foremost champion in Britain was Isambard Kingdom Brunel. He had seen a demonstration by the engineers Jacob and Joseph Samuda, who were looking to sell railway equipment based on their idea. A pipe was laid between the rails, and each train would have a piston that fitted into the pipe. A slot along the top of the pipe allowed the train to move along, and was sealed by a leather flap. The Samuda brothers patented improvements to the valves, which were the most troublesome part of the atmospheric system.

Brunel constructed the South Devon Railway between Exeter and Teignmouth on the atmospheric principle, and thus proved its complete inadequacy for main line railways. The leather flap valve continuously disintegrated, air leakage was high, and trains had to be moved by horses around junctions. This atmospheric system lasted less than two years, only running during 1847 and 1848.

The Pneumatic Despatch Company Railway

The Metropolitan was not the only underground railway to open in London in 1863. The other was the parcels line constructed by the Pneumatic Despatch Company (PDC) between the Parcels Office of the LNWR main line station at Euston (beneath platform 1), and the General Post Office (GPO) building in Eversholt Street (which housed the North West Division of the GPO). The choice of Euston was undoubtedly linked with the presence of a number of LNWR directors on the board of the PDC. It was also a short line intended to convince a sceptical GPO of the merits of the pneumatic railway.

The engineer was Thomas Webster Rammell, who had constructed a demonstration line on the surface in Battersea Park two years previously to prove that air pressure could be made to move small carriages through 30-inch (76 cm) diameter tunnels, if they fitted closely enough. The demonstration was a success, and the equipment was reused to lay the tunnel below the surface of the streets between Euston and the Post Office, a distance of 600 yards (549 m).

The line opened on 15 January 1863 for trials, and began to move parcels on 20 February. *The Times* foresaw the day "when the ponderous goods vans which now ply between station and station shall disappear for ever from the streets of London".[27]

The carriages travelled at around 25 m.p.h. (40 km/h), taking seventy seconds to make the journey. They had around an inch of clearance all around them, and rubber flanges were used to make a seal against the tunnel walls. The tunnels were made of cast-iron sections each 9 feet (2.74 m) long, and semicircular in section. The lower, flat part of the sections incorporated grooves which acted as 2 ft gauge rails.

The financial terms were not great for the PDC, which had originally asked the GPO to pay them £4,000 to operate a number of pneumatic lines across London. This had been refused, and the GPO also declined to give any commitments regarding their use of the line. They eventually agreed to pay 4s 11½d per day for the service, which ran six days a week. This amount was estimated to be half their saving from the use of the railway, but was nowhere near the actual operating cost of the line, which was £1 4s 5d per day. The hope was that once convinced of the line's utility, and with an expanded system, the GPO would pay a far greater sum that would lead them to profitability.

In September 1863 Rammell began to extend the railway beyond Euston, southwards under Tottenham Court Road,[28] and then curving eastwards under New Oxford Street and High Holborn to terminate at the GPO buildings in Cheapside. The main site on this route was the PDC offices at 245 High Holborn, at which trains would need to reversed. The steam engines required to pump the air through the tunnels would also be based here. This was a larger line, the tunnel being 4 feet (1.2 m) high and 4½ feet (1.4 m) wide, and the rails of 3 ft 8½ ins (1.1 m) gauge.

The failure of the GPO to commit to the PDC made the raising of capital very hard, and consequently to reduce costs the section between Euston and Holborn was completed first, and opened for use on 7 November 1865. The 1866 stock market failure (described earlier) caused a major problem. All of the contractors for the line had been paid in PDC shares, and the company became effectively bankrupt. It was making a loss on the whole line, and terminated its contract with the GPO in October 1866.

The PDC continued to raise money though, and persevered with its line from Holborn to the GPO in Cheapside. This was completed by the end of 1868, and four years of proving trials then commenced. Across the Fleet Valley the line had gradients of up to 1 in 15, leading to speeds of up to 60 m.p.h. (97 km/h) being reached as it passed over the subterranean river. However, the distances involved were pushing the steam engines and fans to the limits, and they eventually had to be upgraded; leakage of air from the tunnels did not help matters.

From 1 December 1873 a small flow of parcels and letters from Euston to the Cheapside office commenced, but by the end of October 1874 the PDC shut this down. The GPO was not paying enough for it to make it worthwhile, and also complained that water entering the tunnels was damaging the mail.

The PDC was finally liquidated in 1875, which would seem to end its story. However, in 1899 it was reformed, intending to repair the tunnels and operate the line electrically. The tunnels were surveyed and revealed to be in a very poor state though, and no work was ever done. The GPO purchased the tunnels in 1921 so that they could be used for telephone cables.[29] In 1928, a wiring fault in one of the tunnels ignited a build-up of coal gas; the surface of High Holborn was torn open for half a mile.[30]

The Oxford Street & City Railway

The PDC may have intended its railway to be for parcels use, but in its demonstration runs people had been transported along it. Rammell always intended that his pneumatic railway could be scaled up to a size that would allow conventional passenger traffic, and in the year that the original PDC line opened, he deposited another Bill with Parliament.

The Oxford Street & City Railway was designed by Rammell and John Fowler, who was engineer to the MR. The line was to run a distance of 2.4 miles (3.9 km) from the Marble Arch to Farringdon Street station on the MR. Running at an average depth of 20 feet (6.1 m) under the roadway until it reached Chancery Lane, it would then descend to a maximum of 35 feet (9.2 m) as it curved north-west under Leather Lane and Hatton Garden. Here it would not follow the line of the roads, but cut across them in a sinuous shape so that it aligned with Greville Street. This road would be followed down the side of the Fleet valley to the terminus of the railway on the west side of the MR station.

The scheme was rejected by the Parliamentary Committee that considered the 1864 railway Bills, along with plans for another pneumatic line from Victoria to Blackfriars via Westminster. Rammell was not defeated, however, and he carried out a trial in the grounds of the Crystal Palace, which carried passengers along a 600-yard (550 m) brick tunnel in a pneumatically-powered train. This proved that pneumatic propulsion could operate a railway, and spurred Rammell into planning for his next venture – the Waterloo & Whitehall Railway (W&WR).[31]

The Waterloo & Whitehall Railway

The W&WR proposed a line between York Road, alongside the main line station, and Great Scotland Yard on the other side of the Thames. It was to run parallel to and just to the south of the Hungerford bridge. It was to be ¾-mile (1.2 km) long.

The railway was to have carriages that fitted snugly inside the tunnels. Large fans at Waterloo would either blow or suck the carriage between the two stations, using air at a pressure of 2.5 oz/in^2 (10 g/cm^2) above atmospheric pressure. There were no severe curves or gradients planned, and the Crystal Palace trial seemed to show that the propulsion system would work in commercial service. Between the stations and the river the 12 ft 9 ins (3.89 m) diameter tunnel was to be brick-built, rather like a sewer, using cut-and-cover principles. A trench was to be dredged across the Thames, four cylindrical brick piers sunk into it, and five 200 ft (61 m) long prefabricated cast iron tubes 12 feet in diameter would be lowered into the trench and riveted together to form the under-river tunnel. These tubes would be cast by Samuda and Co. of Poplar (in east London), who had been heavily involved in the promotion of atmospheric railways in the 1830s. The gradients would be 1 in 80 downhill towards the river on the north bank, 1 in 26 in the tunnel (sloping down from the banks to mid-river), and 1 in 52 ascending from the river on the south bank.

Fifteen trains per hour were to run between 7 a.m. and midnight, conveying up to five first class passengers at 2d per head, and 20 second or third class passengers for 1½d or 1d each respectively. Each train was a single four-wheeled carriage with longitudinal seats either side of a central aisle, and they would be "as commodious, as well lighted, and as completely fitted for the comfort of the passenger, as those of the

Metropolitan Railway."[32] Three carriages would be used; at each station one would be loading or unloading, while the third would be in motion through the tunnel.

The original cost for the line was estimated at £87,000, although it rapidly became obvious that this figure was too low. Capital of £100,000 could be raised through the sale of shares, and an additional £33,000 could be borrowed.

Unfortunately, although the Bill was passed by Parliament on 5 July 1865, and construction started shortly afterwards, the company soon ran into financial trouble caused by the same crisis that had sunk the North Western & Charing Cross Railway (see page 1.). In 1867 it was determined that £42,170 had been raised, and £42,452 had been spent. Of this latter sum, £20,871 had gone on constructing the tunnel to the north of the river, and the rest on property purchases and other payments (including Rammell's £2,500 royalty).

At the sixth company meeting on 13 February 1868 the W&WR went into liquidation, although a W&WR Act of the same year authorized another £75,000 of capital and an extension of time for the completion of the line. With no more money raised, the company was finally wound up in 1885. The piers in the river were removed, and the only discernible trace of it now is the cellar of the National Liberal Club, which makes use of the brick construction on the north side of the Thames. According to *The Railway News*, some of the iron tubes were actually sunk in the river bed;[33] if so then the tubes would probably have been removed for scrap (or reuse) when the piers were demolished.

The Hyde Park Railway

In the year that the W&WR liquidated, Rammell put forward another proposal for a short pneumatic railway, this time across Hyde Park. Running north to south, the line would connect Cumberland Gate (the park entrance at Marble Arch, on Oxford Street) to Albert Gate, on Knightsbridge. Both stations would be outside the park boundaries; that at **Oxford Street** would be opposite the end of Park Lane, and that at **Knightsbridge** opposite the end of Sloane Street. The single running tunnel would be 8 feet wide by 10 ft 6 ins high (2.4 m x 3.2 m), and 4,450 feet (1.4 km) long. Construction would take place from two points other than the station sites. The first was a shaft about one-third of the way south from Oxford Street, and the second was via a disused sewer, which had been the main line of the Ranelagh sewer from Albion Street through the park.

The scheme was then modified to incorporate a 700-yard (640 m) length of the disused sewer. The sewer would have to be enlarged, but this would still save tunnelling for over one-third of the length of the line. The vents for the sewer would be closed up, and provision made for the drainage of any surface water that entered the tunnel. The site for the station at the north end was moved west, and placed on the south side of Oxford Street opposite the end of the Edgware Road. Knightsbridge station site was moved east to a point on the north side of Knightsbridge half way between Albert Gate and Wilton Place.

Both stations would have two side platforms, and three carriages would operate: at any one time there would one at each station, loading and unloading with passengers, and one would be in transit between the stations.

The station at Oxford Street would be at a higher level than that to the south, allowing trains to be blown northbound, and return under the influence of gravity, mostly on a 1 in 56 gradient. The engine and fan would therefore be contained at the Knightsbridge station, in a large chamber below the southern end of the platforms. The latter station would have a building at street level, sited above the platforms, whilst the northern station would be covered with a glass roof at its north end and would be accessed via a flight of steps to the east. No building would be erected, so as not to interfere with the site unduly.

The line would not have been very useful, and as Peter Bancroft states in his article on the railway "It might therefore be described as little more than a 'novelty' line."[34]

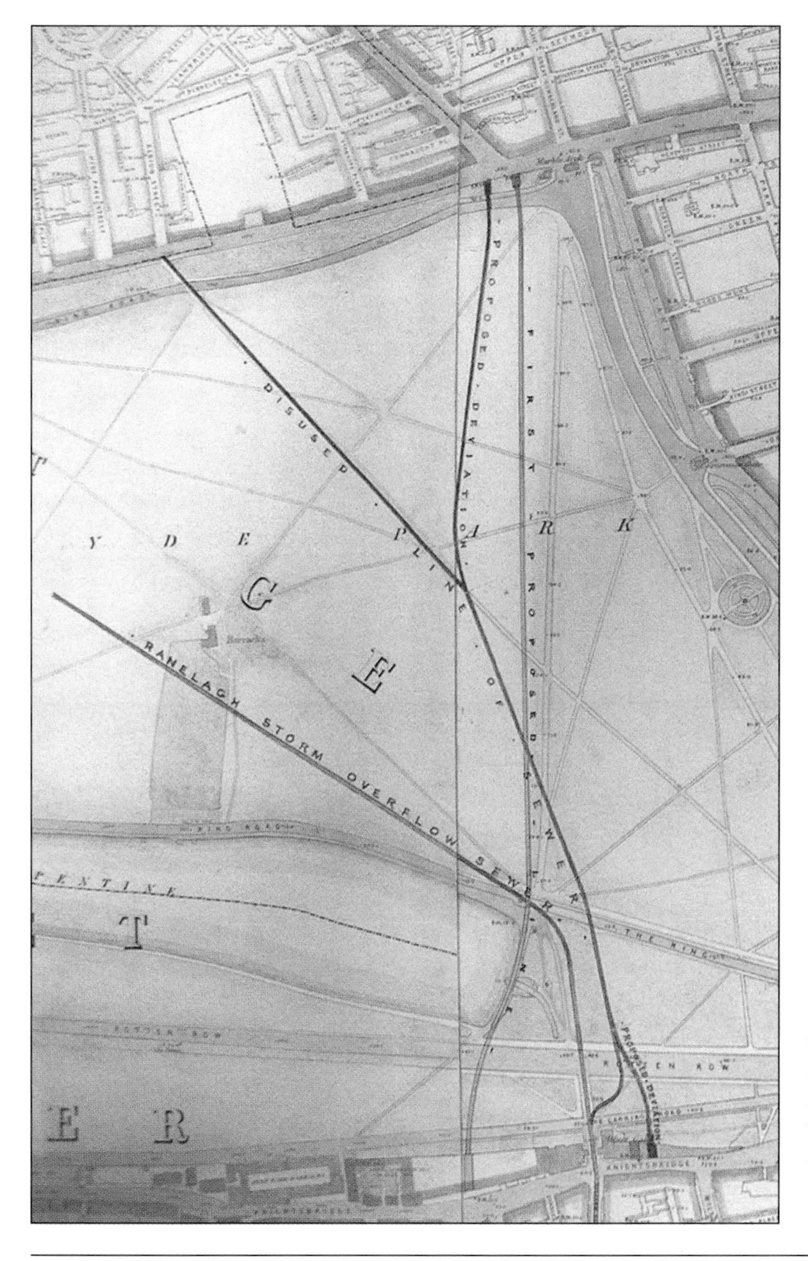

Plan of the 1868 Hyde Park Railway with the original route shown in yellow and the second version in green and brown.

The South Kensington Railway

Rammell kept himself busy looking for opportunities to promote his pneumatic railway. In 1872 he concocted a scheme that seemed to have a greater chance of success, because both the Metropolitan and the Metropolitan District Railways backed it.[35]

One of the areas of London that, to this day, is poorly served by the Underground, is along the south side of Hyde Park. Given the number of people who attend events at the Albert Hall, it remains surprising that no railway link has ever been constructed. The South Kensington Railway (SKR) was Rammell's attempt to fix this problem.

The SKR was to link the joint MR and MDR station at **South Kensington** with the Albert Hall. It would have a running connection with the MDR to the east of the station, and the line was to curve back to an alignment allowing it to run under Exhibition Road. It would follow this north to the junction with Kensington Road, and a station at the north end would serve the **Albert Hall**. An intermediate station serving the new **Natural History Museum** and the forerunner of the Science Museum was also proposed.

Around the beginning of 1872 the MR and MDR agreed that Rammell could be granted appropriate land and easements for 99 years, either free of charge or for a nominal rent. They also agreed to provide every facility to help construct the line, and once opened, provide interchange facilities. It must be assumed that the running connection was only for the transfer of rolling stock, as the stock would be completely different from that of the steam-hauled MDR.

Rammell continued with his designs for the railway, and in January 1873 the cost was estimated to be £57,000. The SKR Bill would permit the company to raise £60,000 through shares, and borrow a further £20,000 on mortgage. However, just two weeks later a more detailed estimate reckoned the cost at £70,000. This document also provided a traffic estimate of 5,460,000 passengers per year, providing an income of £10,413. After estimated running costs of £3,000 this would leave a profit of £7,413, giving shareholders a healthy dividend of 11%.

The MDR agreed to guarantee a loan of £50,000 to Rammell (with certain conditions imposed), but the MR was less forthcoming. However, they still signed up to a Heads of Agreement document at the end of 1873, in which they agreed to sell Rammell a triangle of land bounded by the north side of South Kensington station and Alfred Place West (since renamed Thurloe Place). This land is occupied today by the north end of the station arcade. Rammell agreed that the SKR would be responsible for the construction, equipping, and staffing of its line. Fares were set at 3d single/4d return in first class, and 2d single/3d return in 2nd and 3rd class (raising the question of why anyone would travel in 3rd class if 2nd class cost the same).

The sticking point was capital. Even with the proposed loan from the District Railway, no one would invest in such a speculative venture without some level of guarantee. The MDR had helped to a certain extent, but the failure of the MR to provide a similar level of support was noticeable. The rows rumbled on through into 1875, when a letter from the SKR to Sir Edward Watkin, Chairman of the MR, pointed out that Rammell could not raise the capital whilst the guarantee is absent. Watkin was reminded of the large amount of traffic that would accrue to his company from having a station in the Albert Hall/Kensington Road area. The letter was obviously to no avail, as a year later the scheme had not progressed.

The press published a few articles in the summer of 1876, describing how the SKR was almost ready to start construction. The accuracy of the articles was somewhat dubious: *The Standard* reported that the MR had subscribed "very liberally" to the railway, whilst *The Echo* noted that the MDR had already subscribed £10,000.[36] This provoked a letter from Myles Fenton, General Manager of the MR, to James Forbes of the MDR asking if the report was true. Forbes denied it, and Rammell too insisted that he had nothing to do with the article.

The end came for the SKR in 1877. Tiring of the scheme, the MR wrote to Rammell on 19 July to state that they could not consent to him issuing a prospectus for the line. They were also breaking all connections with the SKR, and no further negotiations were to be held. At the end of the year the MDR consented to Parliament releasing the £2,250 that had been deposited as part of the SKR Act.

The Mid-Metropolitan Railway

It was four years later, in 1881, that Rammell returned with a plan for a London railway. It was still to be pneumatic, but the Mid-Metropolitan Railway was a far more extensive scheme (and had nothing to do with the MR). It proposed three lines, the first from Shepherd's Bush, along Oxford Street, High Holborn, Cheapside, Cornhill, and Leadenhall Street to Aldgate. The second was to run from Eastbourne Terrace, Paddington, south-east to the Bayswater Road, at Clarendon Place, and then continue under Hyde Park, curving east to Hyde Park Corner, under Constitution Hill and St James's Park, to Bridge Street in Westminster. The third line would cut across Hyde Park in the opposite direction as it passed from Cromwell Road, in South Kensington, to the Marble Arch.

The Metropolitan Board of Works decided to oppose the scheme, because of the disruption it would cause. Their surveyor determined that it would interfere with the sewers and other MBW property 36 times.

The Railway News[37] estimated that the Parliamentary deposit would be £103,750. Over 3 acres of land was required, costing £750,000. The 4 miles 5 furlongs of line would have cost £1,703,000 for the tunnel or covered way, and the total cost for the railway would have been £2,075,000 (presumably this excludes land, but includes electrical equipment and rolling stock). Unfortunately, but probably not surprisingly in the light of the first of the costs above, after depositing the Bill with Parliament around the start of December, the promoters failed to pay the necessary deposit to Parliament. This was due by 14 January 1882, the last possible date for completing this. This was a serious breach of Parliamentary protocol, and the Bill was withdrawn by mid-February.

The scheme was redeposited for the 1883 session on 1 December 1882. The MBW raised the same objections as before, and the Board of Works for the Strand wrote to the MBW asking them to oppose on account of the inevitable disruption to Oxford Street. The opposition was not necessary though: the deposit was again not paid, and the Bill was withdrawn by the end of January.

The South Kensington & Knightsbridge & Marble Arch Subways

Rammell's final proposal was in 1885, with the South Kensington & Knightsbridge & Marble Arch Subways. This was again a pneumatic railway, presumably of a small size given the 3 ft 9 ins (1.14 m) gauge track (although the Bill permitted this to be altered to whatever the Board of Trade permitted. The Board was also given the power to change the means of locomotion, except to steam).

It was to run from a station at **Cromwell Road**, situated on Exhibition Road halfway between Cromwell Road and the Old Brompton Road. A short pedestrian subway would take passengers to the platforms, which would be sited 25 ft 6 ins (7.8 m) below the junction of Cromwell and Exhibition Roads. Trains would run eastward under Brompton Road, to **Knightsbridge**. The station would be on the apex of the corner between Knightsbridge and Brompton Roads. It would then continue in a north-easterly direction across Hyde Park to terminate on Oxford Street on the north side of the **Marble Arch**, opposite Park Lane. This would be the deepest station, 36 feet (11 m) below the surface, and like the others would be provided with lifts.

The railway would consist of a single tunnel 10 feet (3.1 m) wide, and 11 ft 6 ins (3.5 m) high for most of its length. For a distance of 100 feet (30.5 m) either side of Knightsbridge station it would widen to 22 feet (6.7 m), presumably to allow two carriages to pass at this point. The total length of the line was 1 mile 4 furlongs 2.6 chains (2.5 km), and the cost of construction was estimated at £198,000. An additional £71,000 was needed for the street improvement works.

As well as the railway works, *The Railway News* in a short article noted that "The scheme embraces certain street improvements"[38] – notably the widening of Knightsbridge Road between Hyde Park Barracks and Brompton Road, and the construction of a new road between Brompton Road and South Carriage Drive. This new road would take the alignment of Knightsbridge Green and Park Place, but widen and straighten them.

The Bill was deposited in November 1885, and two months later the MBW decided to petition against it. The residents of Brompton Road wrote to the Board as well, asking them not to sanction the subway. Their concerns were probably more about the construction work and the risk of damage to their houses, rather than the operation of the railway.

The South Kensington & Knightsbridge & Marble Arch Subways were as unsuccessful before Parliament as all of Rammell's previous schemes, and disappeared without trace in early 1886.

The Birth of the Tube Railway

One of the key innovations that was necessary to construct tube railways was patented on 20 January 1818, by Marc Brunel. This invention was the tunnelling shield. Inspired by watching a ship worm, *Teredo navalis*, which cuts through wood using bony plates and shores up the tunnel behind by lining it with its excreta, he perceived that a similar solid structure could protect miners and allow for the simultaneous construction of a tunnel lining.

His first patent was for a cylindrical shield, but when he was approached in connection with the construction of tunnel between Wapping and Rotherhithe, in east London, he replaced this with a rectangular shield. This would allow two roadways through the tunnel to be made. Within the shield, thirty-six miners would work in twelve columns of three 'cells', each carefully removing wooden boards facing the mud, excavating a few inches depth, and replacing the boards. Once all of the mud had been cleared behind all of the boards for three cells in the same column, the column would be pushed forward using jacks, and the mining would start again. Good progress was two to three feet (60–90 cm) per week.

The construction of the tunnel has been well documented elsewhere. Suffice to say that it took six times longer than the original estimate of three years to complete, and in 1869 it became part of the East London Railway. Today trains on the East London Line of the London Underground operate through it.

The Tower Subway

Peter Barlow was the engineer responsible for the construction of the Lambeth suspension bridge in London, which opened in 1862. Barlow had a flash of inspiration: the cast iron cylinders that he was sinking vertically into the London clay to form the bridge piers would, if pushed horizontally, form a tunnel that could run beneath a river. Five years after the bridge opened, Barlow received permission to construct such a tunnel beneath the Thames in the vicinity of the Tower of London. One of Barlow's former pupils, James Greathead, agreed to be the contractor, and took less than one year to complete it, at a cost of less than £20,000. On 2 August 1870 the Tower Subway was formally opened. It was rather claustrophobic, with an internal diameter of 7 ft 6¾ ins (2.3 m).

A small, cable-hauled carriage took up to twelve passengers at a time though the 1,340 ft (409 m) long tunnel, on a single 2 ft 6 ins (76 cm) gauge track. Passenger access was via lifts installed in the shafts on each side of the river. These arrangements proved to be less than satisfactory, and four months later the carriage and lifts were removed.

The basic problem was the low speed of the carriage, resulting in few people using the tunnel, and so very little revenue. The lifts were replaced by staircases, and the carriage by a walkway. For the next twenty-five years around one million people used the tunnel per annum. The nearby Tower Bridge, opened in 1894, proved to be a simpler means of crossing the river, and the tunnel closed in the same year. It still exists, having since been used for hydraulic power and water mains, and more recently communications cables.

The North & South Woolwich Subway

The N&SWS was the second tube tunnel on which construction actually started. Connecting Bell Water Gate in South Woolwich to a site immediately west of North Woolwich station, it was to be a short pedestrian thoroughfare that would save the residents of Woolwich from queuing for the ferry service. In their Act of 3 June 1874 the promoters sought to raise £60,000 in share capital, with an additional £20,000 permitted borrowing on a mortgage. In order to satisfy the river authorities the tunnel would have to pass deep below the Thames; a minimum of 60 feet (18.3 m) below the Trinity High Water mark.

The public would pay 1d to use the tunnel, with the toll being collected at the entrance to the tunnel. Anyone evading the toll would be subject to a fine of up to 40 shillings, with the same penalty being imposed for a variety of misdemeanours.

Greathead had invented new tunnelling equipment that would allow construction to take place through the waterlogged sands and gravel beneath the Thames at this point by using compressed air. A new hydraulic segment lifter would assist erection of the tunnel segments.

The land required for the tunnel was soon purchased, and construction started in 1876. However, it would appear that the contractor chose not to use Greathead's new equipment and swiftly ran into difficulties. By 1879 the company was back in Parliament seeking an extension of time for the completion of the tunnel, which had originally been set for 1 July of that year. The new Act received Royal Assent on 23 May, and gave the company another two years.

No progress was made, and in 1881 a further extension of time was granted, giving the company until the beginning of July 1884 to finish their tunnel. Still nothing happened, and in 1884 the powers to build the tunnel expired.

The Southwark & City Subway

One year before the Tower Subway opened, Barlow and Greathead submitted plans for a more ambitious scheme – a tube railway between Southwark and the north side of London Bridge in the City of London, to be known as the Southwark & City Subway. Two parallel cast iron tubes, constructed in the same way as the Tower Subway were to be provided, but with a slightly larger diameter of 8 feet (2.4 m). Between the stations, for the entire length of the line, the tunnels would be placed one above the other.

The line would commence near to St George's Church, at the junction of Borough High Street and Great Dover Street, and follow the High Street north, falling on a gradient of 1 in 36, and then 1 in 40 to the junction with Southwark Street. It then levelled off until it reached the Thames, just upstream of London Bridge, a depth of 82 ft 4 ins (25.1 m). Climbing at a gradient of 1 in 40 it passed under the river, and then followed

Swan Lane to Arthur Street West, under which it would terminate near to Martin Lane. Both stations were to be 47 ft 6 ins (14.5 m) below the surface, with passengers accessing the platforms by lift.

Parliament approved the scheme on 14 July 1870, primarily based on the success in constructing the earlier tunnel. However, it proved impossible to raise the money, given the poor returns on the Tower Subway. Barlow continued to promote the scheme for another three years, even publishing a pamphlet in 1873 demonstrating the beneficial effect that the subway would have on the traffic crossing London Bridge. Later that same year, however, he abandoned the scheme.

The City of London & Southwark Subway

Another tube railway Act came into being in 1884, again promoted by Greathead. On 28 July Royal Assent was given to a Bill for a short railway between **Elephant & Castle** south of the Thames, and **King William Street** in the City; it was named the City of London & Southwark Subway (CL&SS). An intermediate station was at **Borough**.[39] Twin tubes of 10 ft 2 ins (3.1 m) diameter were constructed, and the line was to be cable-hauled. Capital of £300,000 was sought, and this was doubled three years later when an extension of the original route southwards to **Stockwell** was authorized, via **Kennington** and **Oval**. This southern section used tunnels 10 ft 6 ins (3.2 m) in diameter.

Construction on the original line had just started, and this extension was completed prior to the opening of the line. A further southward extension to **Clapham Common** (with an intermediate station at **Clapham Road**[40]) was authorized on 25 July 1890, also to use the larger tunnel size. This Act also changed the name of the company to the City & South London Railway (C&SLR), a name more in keeping with its extended route. Almost five months later, on 18 December, the railway finally opened to the public between Stockwell and King William Street stations.

The railway was not permitted to pass beneath buildings unless the agreement of the owner had been obtained. To avoid purchasing such agreements (as most owners would charge) the railway followed the course of the public roads. Bridges counted the same as buildings in the eyes of the law. The only way that they could gain access to the City was by following the path of Swan Lane and Arthur Street West. The former lane is so narrow that it was not possible to place the tunnels side-by-side without them passing beneath the buildings that lined the road, so instead, they were placed one above the other. Beneath the Thames the tunnels were constructed to 'roll' into this position; below Arthur Street West they rolled back so that they were at the same level at the terminal station of King William Street.

The tunnels of the C&SLR were made of cast iron rings which comprised bolted-together segments.[41] The stations were built of brick, and were not of circular cross section to minimize the amount of clay that needed to be excavated: instead, they were flattened at the base. This proved to be a false economy, as the brick tunnels did not withstand the pressures of the clay nearly as well as the iron tunnels, and subsidence of surface buildings and roads occurred in the region of all of the stations. This led to Parliament insisting on new railways continuing to follow the pattern of the streets above.

The other change made by the C&SLR that was to be of great significance for the development of London's underground railways was the adoption of electric power for the trains. The line was originally planned to be operated using cable-haulage of the trains, but in 1888 the Patent Cable Tramway Corporation, which had backed the railway, collapsed. Combined with the scepticism of the C&SLR's Chairman towards cable haulage, this led the railway to investigate the possibility of running electric trains.[42] The company Mather & Platt equipped the entire line with current rails, fourteen small electric locomotives, and a power station at the Stockwell depôt.

Passengers gained access to the railway via hydraulic lifts, which were generally in the shafts that had been sunk as part of the construction of the tunnels. Between Stockwell and King William Street (with the exception of Elephant & Castle[43]) the platforms were at different levels, with 9 ft 6 ins (2.9 m) height difference. The lifts descended to a level between the two platforms, and ramps connected the lower lift landings to the platforms. This was done to reduce the amount of walking required by passengers.

In spite of all of the opposition to the construction of the C&SLR, and the fears that the line would be a commercial failure, passengers took to the railway in numbers far greater than expected. Fares were constantly being changed in an effort to spread the rush-hour loadings. In the first year alone, over 5 million people used the line, and a Bill for a further extension to Islington was deposited with Parliament – more of which in a later chapter.

Between them, the Tower Subway and the C&SLR established a lot of the principles for the London Underground for many years to come: cast iron tubes, cut through the London clay with the use of a tunnelling shield; underground railways not passing beneath buildings or bridges, but following the pattern of streets above; electrically-operated trains; and passengers accessing the platforms via lifts.

Another unusual precedent set by the C&SLR was the term *subway*. This had been used in the original CL&SS Bill in a feeble attempt to make the scheme seem less like a railway to Parliament and the Board of Trade. The fact that they reverted to the term 'railway' in 1890 did not prevent a number of schemes using the subway title in their names. The Glasgow Subway is the only remaining example in the UK of the term still applying to a railway, but the most famous example of this is not found in the UK, but in the USA, where many of their underground railways are known as subways. This was no coincidence, since the Americans had been taking a strong interest in the developments in London, and decided to adopt the term subway for their own lines back in the USA.

And so it was that the scene was set for more engineers and businessmen to promote tube railways across London. A number of these were built and form the core of today's Underground; their histories are told in detail elsewhere.[44] This book deals mostly with railways that were planned but never built.

The core of the story lies in the tube railway battles of 1901 and 1902, in which the two most ambitious schemes fought to control the traffic across London. But first, the forerunners of those railways must be examined.

Early Plans: Tube Proposals in the 1880s

Aside from the CL&SS, none of the new underground railways that had plans deposited with Parliament in the 1880s came to fruition. The various cut-and-cover schemes described in the first chapter all came to nought, and this chapter will take a look at the proposals for tube railways, based on the design of the C&SLR.

The Clapham & City Subway

Once the C&SLR received Royal Assent from Parliament, Robert Meyer, one of its original directors resigned. He immediately bid for the construction work – and nothing happened. He was replaced some six months later, and then deposited a Bill for a new tube railway that was to extend the C&SLR southwards. Unsurprisingly, the engineer for this railway was James Greathead.

The Clapham & City Subway (C&CS) was to be cable-hauled and run in twin cast iron tunnels, as with the C&SLR. These would be slightly smaller, with diameters of 10 feet (3.1 m). Unlike the C&SLR however, the stations were presumably to be built using the cut-and-cover technique, as they were placed just beneath the surface with the tubes rising to meet them. Station boxes 67 yards (61.3 m) long would be constructed immediately below the streets to house the platforms, which would be one above the other at depths of 14 ft 6 ins (4.4 m) and 28 feet (8.5 m). On leaving the stations the tunnels would usually descend at 1 in 20; this would aid acceleration on departure, and assist braking on arrival.

The railway would start at **Elephant & Castle**, with a running connection to the City of London & Southwark Subway. Rather strangely it would have its own platforms immediately to the south of those on the CL&SS – perhaps this was to allow for the trains to be transferred from one cable to another. This was to be the deepest station on the railway, at 47 ft 2 ins (14.4 m), simply because it had to connect to the C&SLR at this depth. All subsequent stations were built on the cut-and-cover principle described above.

The next station, at **Kennington Lane**, was to be sited in the apex of the junction. **Kennington Road** station would have been on the western corner of the junction between that road and Kennington Park Road. Further south, with accesses from both sides of the Clapham Road, would be stations at **Dorset Road** and **Stockwell** – the latter at the same place as the current station of that name. **Clapham Road** station would be at the junction with Bedford Road, where today's Clapham North station is to be found. The terminus for the line would have been at **Clapham Park Road**, with its station building on the east corner of the road junction at that point. The platforms at this station would be on the same level, 15 feet (4.6 m) below the street.

Capital of £600,000 was sought for the scheme, with borrowing powers of £150,000. The costs of constructing the 2 miles 6 furlongs 4 chains (4.5 km) of line were put at £391,850.

The London, Chatham & Dover Railway were concerned about the line, both because it passed beneath their railway, and because it was in competition with them. They instructed their Counsel to oppose the line before Parliament, for both of these reasons. Their notes to Counsel suggest they did not expect either the CL&SS or the C&CS to succeed.

The C&SLR were not interested in being associated with the new scheme, probably because of their experience of the promoter. Holman, in *The Amazing Electric Tube*, states that there was one chance of linking the two companies – a man called Joseph Browne Martin, who was a director of both. He was also a director of the Patent Cable Tramway Corporation, which was heavily involved in promoting both railways. Before he could achieve any sort of reconciliation, the Chairman of the CL&SS was changed, and Martin resigned. This was effectively the end for the C&CS, which withdrew its Bill in April 1885.

The King's Cross, Charing Cross & Waterloo Subway

As well as his involvement with the Clapham & City Subway, James Greathead deposited plans for another subway railway for the 1885 session of Parliament. The King's Cross, Charing Cross & Waterloo Subway (KCCC&WS) was very similar to the C&SLR, in that it was to run small trains through shield-driven tunnels 10 feet (3.1 m) in diameter, and would again pass below the Thames.

The line was to start at **Waterloo**, below the main line station, and head west below Vine Street and College Street to the river. Crossing at a slight diagonal, and at a maximum depth of 72 ft 5 ins (22.1 m) below the high water mark, it would reach the Victoria Embankment at the end of Northumberland Avenue. Taking a curve into the Avenue (and taking care to avoid the government buildings on the corner with Whitehall Place), a station would be sited at the junction with **Northumberland Street**. After Trafalgar Square would be a station at **St Martin's Place**; the line would continue north up St Martin's Lane, and then curve east under **Long Acre**, where the station would be at James Street, opposite the Covent Garden station of today.

Further to the north-east, after following Great and Little Queen Streets, the next station would be at **Southampton Row**, with the buildings on the north side of High Holborn. Curving east again under Theobald's Road, the line would proceed to a station at the junction with **Gray's Inn Road**, probably sited on the north-west corner. This latter road would then form the line of route northwards to the terminus at **King's Cross**. The total length was 2 miles 5 furlongs 3.8 chains (3.2 km).

In common with the C&CS of the same year, the intermediate stations were to be constructed in shallow covered ways directly below the surface of the streets. The tracks would be superimposed with a 13 feet (4 m) vertical difference between them. Northumberland Street and Southampton Row stations were around 10 feet (3.1 m) deeper than the other stations, probably to allow the railway to pass below sewers and service subways.

The termini had the tracks on the same level, and were slightly longer: 75 feet (22.9 m) at Waterloo, and 78 feet (23.8 m) at King's Cross. Obviously there was no point constructing the tunnels using shields at this depth, and in fact the running tunnels were to be around 20–40 feet (6.1–12.2 m) below street level. Gradients similar to those at either side of the stations were used either side of the Thames, except on the north side where one tunnel was at the even steeper gradient of 1 in 15. For the entire distance of the line between the termini the running tunnels were placed one above the other (not always the same way). It was only on the approaches to the termini that they moved apart laterally to come up beside each other.

Working agreements were sought with the main line companies of the GNR, the Midland, and the LSWR, as well as with the MR. Given the size of the tunnels these would not have been for through running, but instead to allow passenger interchange, and possibly for the operation of the line to be managed by one or more of these companies.

The Metropolitan Board of Works was preparing to oppose the Bill before the Parliamentary Committee in May when, as with the C&CS, the promoters withdrew their Bill.

The Islington (Angel) & City Subway

A further scheme for the 1885 session of Parliament was the Islington (Angel) & City Subway. It was another scheme from the fertile mind of James Greathead, and proposed a tube railway between the Angel in Islington and Moorgate Street in the City of London.

As with the KCCC&WS, the line was to use twin running tunnels 10 feet (3.1 m) in diameter, rising to the surface at the stations, which would be constructed on the cut-and-cover principle. Gradients and station dimensions were to be the same for both schemes. The first station on the IA&CS would have been located at **Islington (Angel)**, on the north side of City Road between Islington High Street and Torrens Street. Another building may have been placed diagonally across the road from this one, on the corner of Pentonville Road and St John Street. The next stations would be at **Pickard Street** and **Nelson Street** (now Mora Street), with buildings on both sides of the City Road. **Old Street** station would be the only intermediate station with platforms on the same level, and would be sited between Old Street and Cowper Street.

Further south, at Ropemaker Street and South Place, the station at **Finsbury Pavement** would revert to the usual two-level structure. The terminus, at **Moorgate Street**, would be at the south end of the road of that name, with its building on the west side north of Lothbury.

The 1 mile 5 furlongs 6.8 chains (2.75 km) of line was estimated to cost £370,089 to construct. As with the other Greathead railways the intention was that the trains would be cable-hauled, with passengers accessing the platforms via stairs and hydraulic lifts.

In February 1885 it was reported as non-compliant with Standing Orders in Parliament, but the House of Commons Standing Orders Committee permitted it to proceed. The corresponding House of Lords committee were not so generous, and on 10 March they rejected it entirely.

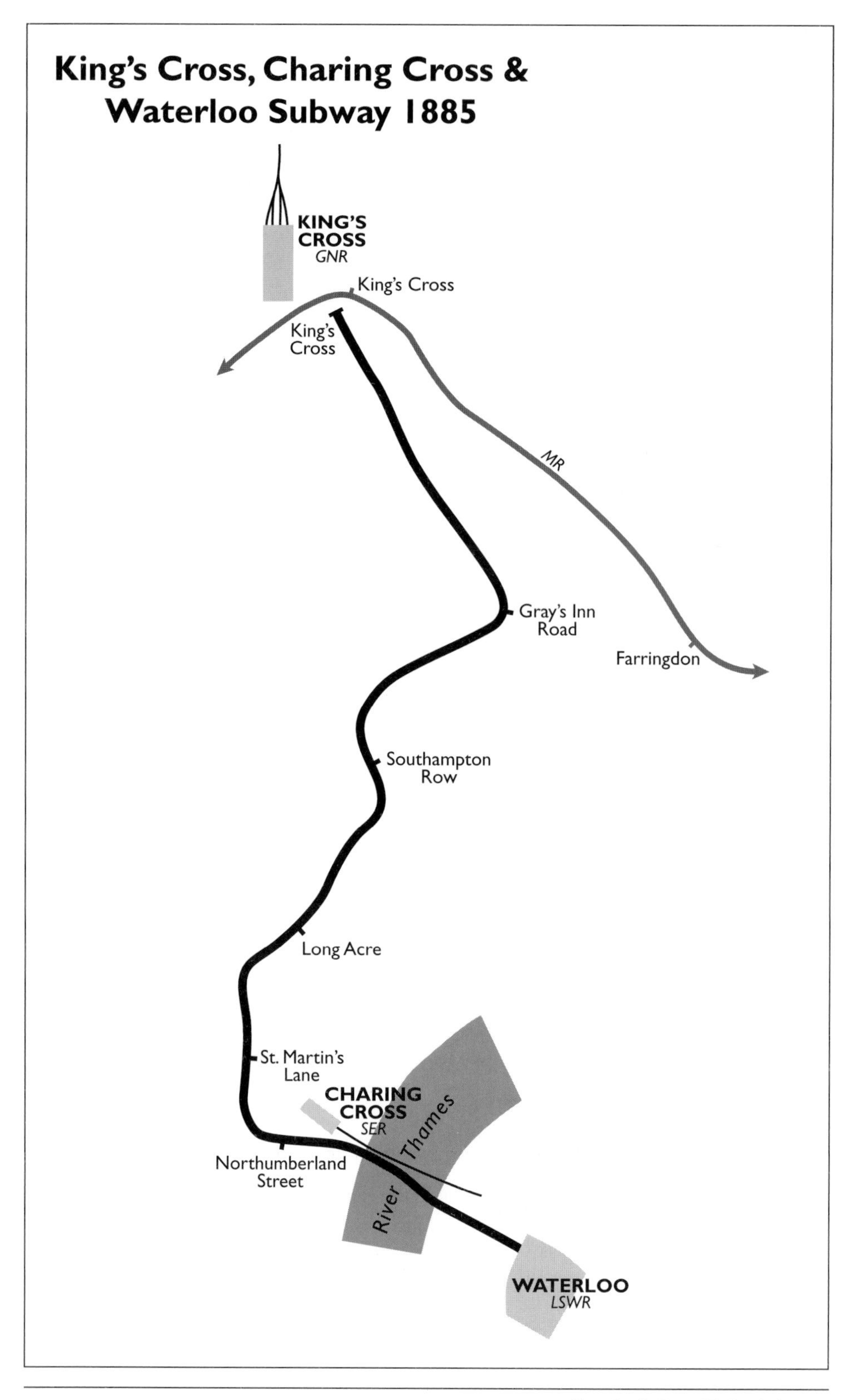
King's Cross, Charing Cross & Waterloo Subway 1885
KING'S CROSS
GNR
King's Cross
King's Cross
MR
Gray's Inn Road
Farringdon
Southampton Row
Long Acre
St. Martin's Lane
CHARING CROSS
SER
River Thames
Northumberland Street
WATERLOO
LSWR

Parliamentary Standing Orders

Standing Orders are a set of rules that apply to Private Bills that are before Parliament. They were first created in 1836, and are published at the end of each Parliamentary session. This is because each session may amend the Orders. Bills not complying with the Orders risk rejection, although the Standing Order Committee, comprising members of Parliament, has the authority to dispense with Orders if they see fit. By 1914 the Standing Orders occupied a volume of about 350 pages.

- Some of the requirements for railways during the period covered in this book include:
- Notice must be given of the intention to introduce a Private Bill. This must be published in November preceding the application, in the *London Gazette* and local press.
- Maps, plans, sections, and books of reference must be deposited with Parliament, the Board of Trade, clerks of affected parishes, and others, by 30 November.
- Notices must be served on affected property owners by 15 December.
- Estimates of expense, and lists of affected owners and occupiers must be with Parliament and the Board of Trade by 31 December.
- Plans must be at the horizontal scale of not less than 4 inches to the mile, and vertical scale of not less than 1 inch per 100 feet.
- A sum of not less than 5% of the estimate of expense must be deposited with the Court of Chancery by 15 January.

An Unusual Design of Railway

It is intriguing that having designed the CL&SS as a deep-tube railway, all of the tube railways promoted in 1885 (including the Marble Arch, Regent Circus & City Subway – see next section) had a similar design, namely tubular running tunnels 10 feet in diameter connecting stations constructed using traditional cut-and-cover techniques. Greathead was the engineer for all of them, and so the identical tunnel size is easy to explain: it was similar to the C&SLR, which had been authorized in the previous year. The fact that this was really too small for a serious railway would not be discovered for over five years.

The unusual station design allowed the more complex parts of the tunnels to be created from the surface downwards using techniques that were well-established. This would reduce the risk to the railway companies. The stacked nature of the stations, with one line above the other, served two purposes. Firstly, it allowed a narrower opening in the street, preventing the roadway from being closed completely for the duration of the works. Secondly, it allowed the running tunnels to be similarly superimposed, which meant that the limits of deviation would be less likely to pass under the private property bordering London's narrow streets, thus keeping the costs down.

It did, of course, mean that there would be some very steep gradients on the railways, in some cases over twice as steep as the steepest gradient used by passenger trains on the Underground today. However, with cable haulage the gradients would not be the problem that they were discovered to be for electrically-powered trains. When the C&SLR opened with electric traction in tunnels designed for cable haulage, they found severe problems with their steep approach to King William Street. Trains were taking multiple runs at the final hill, the electric lamps in each carriage dimming to a dull red glow as the electric motors drew all of the current they possibly could from the conductor rails. This was five years in the future for Greathead, and even he could not have foreseen in 1885 the rapid progress in electrical knowledge, and the different type of railway design that it would require. It is probably for the best that his proposals of 1885 remained firmly on the drawing board.

The question must be asked: why had Greathead changed from railways entirely in bored tube to the mixture of cut-and-cover and bored tube for this 1885 schemes? Construction work on the CL&SS did not start until 1886, so it could not be as a direct result of the happenings on that railway (although, as noted previously, the station design on the CL&SS caused noticeable damage to surface structures). The cost of construction was reduced, but so significantly that it would seem to demand a new design of railway.

Splitting the Circle

In 1884 the MR and MDR had finally completed the Inner Circle by joining their termini at Mansion House and Aldgate. They had previously spent much time extending their railways in seemingly any other direction. In part this was due to a fierce rivalry between their chairmen; another very valid reason was the cost of tunnelling beneath some of the most expensive property in the City of London. Having spent around £2.5 million on constructing just over 1 mile (1.6 km) of railway, they were determined not to lose out to any competitors. But in the same year, a scheme was deposited with Parliament that threatened the Circle.

The Marble Arch, Regent Circus & City Subway

Also deposited for the 1885 session of Parliament, the Marble Arch, Regent Circus & City Subway (MARC&CS) was a Bill for the construction of a railway along Oxford Street. This was the obvious east-west traffic artery across London, and the most lucrative along which to operate an underground railway. Designed by Greathead, the line was to start at **Marble Arch**, and progress east via intermediate stations at **Regent Circus**,[45] **Tottenham Court Road**, **Southampton Row**, **Chancery Lane**, **Holborn Circus**, and **St Martin's-le-Grand**, before terminating in **Cornhill** alongside the Royal Exchange. It would be just over 3⅕ miles (5.15 km) long, and like the other Greathead schemes of 1885 was to be a hybrid between a tube and a cut-and-cover railway. All of the stations except Southampton Row were to be constructed just below the surface of the street, as with the KCCC&WS. From these, twin tubes 10 feet (3.1 m) in diameter would descend at a 1 in 20 gradient[46] to run at depths of 35–68.5 feet (10.7–20.9 m).

The stations would be 67 ft (20.4 m) long, except for the termini, at 77 ft (23.5 m). All of the intermediate stations would have the platforms at different levels, with the upper one having its tracks 14 ft 6 ins (4.4 m) below the surface, and the lower one at 30 feet (9.1 m). Between Tottenham Court Road and Cornhill the running tunnels would remain one above the other as well, only swinging to the same depth on the final approach to the terminus. Southampton Row station would have been constructed as a proper tube station; the reasons for this variation from the standard are not documented. Passengers would access the stations via stairs or hydraulic lifts.

There was some local support for the railway. Mr L. H. Isaacs, the surveyor to the Holborn Board of Works noted that cable traction was not likely to be looked upon favourably. However, if the promoters proposed electrical working then this would be "a great boon to Londoners generally as freedom from the mephitic vapours which tend much to destroy the comfort of those travelling by the underground railways".[47] He was, however, concerned about the disruption to roads, sewers, and utilities.

The Bill had very little luck in Parliament. It was noted early in 1885 that, along with the Islington (Angel) & City Subway, it did not comply with certain Standing Orders. It was therefore referred to the Standing Orders Committee which, on 3 May, decided that the relevant Orders could not be ignored. This effectively killed the Bill.

The Central London Railway

The Central London Railway (CLR) of 1890 proposed to construct a line from just west of the junction of Bayswater Road and Queen's Road to King William Street in the City, a little under 4½ miles (7.2 km). Beyond this point the line would curve south to a junction with the C&SLR beneath Arthur Street West, allowing trains to run through to south of the Thames.

Stations were to be provided at **Queen's Road**, **Westbourne** (located at Stanhope Terrace, just east of today's Lancaster Gate station), **Marble Arch**, **Oxford Circus** (at Princes Street, west of the Circus), **Tottenham Court Road** (immediately west of St Giles Circus), **Southampton Row** (also called Holborn Restaurant), **Holborn Circus** (west of the Circus, at Fetter Lane), **Post Office** (the current location of St Paul's), and **King William Street** (also called Mansion House). The stations at Westbourne, Oxford Circus, Tottenham Court Road, Southampton Row, and Post Office would have the tunnels at different depths, with typically a 12 feet (3.7 m) difference in level. This allowed the platforms to be on the same side, and so the passageways could lead off from both platforms in the same direction. The lift shafts were to be on the same side of the street, and so the same shaft could serve both platforms with a minimum length of passageway. A similar arrangement exists on the Central Line today at Chancery Lane and St Paul's stations. All of the stations would have entrances on both sides of the street, except for Westbourne, where it would be only on the north side (probably because of the reluctance of the Crown to allow construction in Hyde Park), and at Post Office, where it was on the south side of the road.

At Tottenham Court Road, the company proposed clearing Bozier's Court, a block of buildings on the north-west corner of St Giles Circus. This would give them a site for their station. The Vestry of St Pancras had been asking for this block to be removed since 1886, on the grounds that it would improve the line of the street and the flow of traffic between Charing Cross Road and Tottenham Court Road. The LCC, to whom the request for permission was made, prevaricated. Their valuer recommended allowing the demolition, and suggested that the Council contribute to the cost of the work, noting the improvement to the corner that would result. However, the LCC Board maintained a high level of indecision, and the railway abandoned the idea in July 1890.

Hydraulic lifts would be located in the shafts at each station, two to a shaft. The Mansion House station was to be the only station with four lifts; the others would each have just two. All stations would have an additional shaft containing a spiral staircase, made of stone steps according to the evidence.

Hydraulic power for the lifts would be generated at the company's power station, to be located just west of Queen's Road on a 1½-acre (0.6 ha) site shared with the depôt. This would also generate the electricity for the line, which was to be supplied to the trains at 500 V DC via a single conductor rail located centrally between the running rails. Fifteen sidings on site would provide ample storage space for the trains, and an inclined tunnel (at 1 in 20) would provide access to the railway.

The trains would be 300 feet (92 m) long, comprising seven cars, with a locomotive at each end. They would carry a maximum of 300 passengers, and weigh roughly 80 tons. It was intended to run trains at 2-minute intervals. Their speed between stations would reach 25 m.p.h. (40 km/h), but with station stops the average speed on the line would be in the order of 15 m.p.h. (24 km/h).

The cast iron tunnels were to be slightly larger than those on the C&SLR, being 11 feet (3.4 m) in diameter, and would be at an average depth of 50 feet (15.25 m). Station tunnels would have a length of 300 feet and a diameter of 22 feet when on different levels, and 29 feet when on the same level. It is presumed that the stations on the same level would have a single tunnel containing an island platform with tracks either side – this would certainly be consistent with the measurements given, and with the C&SLR. After the tunnels were constructed a grout of blue lias lime would be injected behind the tunnel segments to fill any voids. This would set hard, helping to protect the tunnel.

The promoters were exasperated, and probably a little amused, by a report in one of the London newspapers, which assumed that their line was to be on the surface of Oxford Street:

> It would be absolutely intolerable if through this complicated throng of busy humanity, already rendered chaotic enough by multitudinous carriages, cabs, omnibuses, and wagons, there ran a line of Electric Railway; swift, silent, but under such circumstances, perhaps not wholly safe.[48]

In December 1889 the promoters issued a statement, in the form of a small booklet, which corrected this assumption and described the scheme in detail, after first quoting the article.

The scheme was examined by a Select Committee of the House of Commons between 21 April and 13 May 1890. Many petitions were submitted by property owners along the route, who were very concerned about the damage that the C&SLR was causing to property along its route. They argued that tunnelling under one of London's most prestigious streets and some of its most expensive property was a recipe for disaster; one estimated the potential compensation bill running into millions of pounds – a serious concern for a company with capital of £2.5 million. With C&SLR still months away from opening the view was also expressed that this was an experimental scheme, with no guarantees of success. The Committee modified the Bill as a result of this, stating that no prospectus was to be issued or capital raised until the C&SLR had been opened and carrying the public for three months.

The MR and MDR petitioned hard against the line. They claimed that Parliament had declared that the area inside their Inner Circle should remain free of railways, and that buses would be able to handle traffic in this area. The C&SLR objected to the junction with their line, and this was dropped from the Bill.

Bazalgette appeared in opposition as well, claiming that the line would seriously harm the sewers. The Dean and Chapter of St Paul's Cathedral lodged a petition, concerned at the effect tunnelling would have on their heavy building. The Bishop of London, a member of the House of Lords, put forward a motion opposing the Bill, in order to protect the cathedral. This was itself opposed by Lord Sudely, who spoke in favour of the tube railway. Sudely had been involved in promoting the South Kensington & Paddington Subway earlier in the year (see next chapter for the SK&PS), so his position was understandable. The debate ended with the Bishop withdrawing his motion.

The promoters compared their railway favourably to the earlier Mid-London Railway, and the competing London Central Subway, both of which were cut-and-cover schemes, and would have caused far greater disruption and damage. The Committee was obviously convinced, because on 13 May it approved the Bill to proceed.

A Select Committee of the House of Lords then considered the Bill. Similar evidence was given between 30 June and 16 July, but it arrived at a different conclusion, and the Bill was rejected. No specific reasoning was given, and it must be assumed that the Lords placed greater weight upon the concerns of the property owners and existing railways. The *Railway Times* discussed the ruling at length, feeling that the Lords had not taken the view of the Commons into account; nor had they considered the wider convenience for London that a tube railway would bring:

> Whether the decision was arrived at in the interest of the traders of Oxford Street, from which thoroughfare many pedestrians would doubtless have been drawn, in the interest of the Dean and Chapter of St Paul's, of the freeholders under whose property it was proposed that the line should pass, or of the British capitalists who would be asked to find the money for the undertaking, we know not; but inasmuch as both in the matter of evidence and arguments the same weapons were used by the same people on both occasions, it is clear that their weight and bearing must have influenced the two committees in different ways, and therefore the greater the necessity for some explanation as to the means that have brought about the end.[49]

The Lords concluded by recommending that the C&SLR should open to the public and be assessed before the CLR scheme should be returned to Parliament.

The London Central Subway

The second scheme deposited with Parliament in late 1889 was that of the London Central Subway, which had been rejected earlier that year (under the name of the London Central (Subway) Railway). The promoters had reassessed their route, and decided, like the CLR, that the Oxford Street axis would be more remunerative than their original plan from St James's Street to Holborn Circus. This time their route was from Shepherd's Bush, along the Bayswater Road and Oxford Street, to New Oxford Street and the junction with Bloomsbury Street. In all other respects the Bill was identical to that of the previous year.

The Bill disappeared, almost without trace. It was mentioned in the railway press as being one of the 1890 Bills in January of that year, but by mid-February mention of it had ceased. Charles Mott, the Chairman of the C&SLR, noted in that company's General Meeting of 18 February that all of the tube railway Bills other than their own and that of the CLR had been withdrawn for financial reasons.

The City & North of London Railway

One final railway that was proposed for consideration in the Parliamentary session of 1890 should be mentioned. The City & North of London Railway (C&NLR) was planned to extend the C&SLR northwards to the Angel in Islington, a distance of 2 miles 5.7 chains (3⅓ km). This would probably explain the similarity in name, as well as the engineer being Greathead.

Between the Thames and its terminus at King William Street, the tunnels of the C&SLR were positioned one above the other, allowing them to pass beneath the narrow Swan Lane and Arthur Street West. This fact would make it easy for the C&NLR to connect its running tunnels to those of the C&SLR without the need for complicated junctions: both would branch off to the left as the original tunnels curved right to King William Street station, approximately under Upper Thames Street. The northbound line was around 17 feet (5.2 m) above the southbound. Following Martin's Lane northwards into King William Street, this situation reversed, with the northbound line descending very slightly, and the southbound line ascending steeply on a gradient of 1 in 17. Of course, this being the southbound line the gradient would serve to accelerate the trains as they headed for the junction with the C&SLR; perhaps a slightly worrying piece of engineering!

At the north end of King William Street the line would curve right under Princes Street, entering the first station on the line at **Moorgate Street**. The station buildings would be on the north-west corner of the junction with Lothbury, and the platforms would be at the same level, the difference in depth between the tunnels having diminished under Princes Street.

The only other station on the line would be at **Angel**, the railway having followed the course of Finsbury Pavement and City Road since Moorgate. This would be over 1½ miles of line with no intermediate stations. Several sites are identified on the plan, which were perhaps required for digging shafts so that tunnelling could proceed at multiple points. These sites were (from south to north) adjacent to the City Road Basin, at Wharf Road; at Old Street; at Finsbury Pavement; between King William Street and Mansion House Place; and between King William Street and Cannon Street.

Perhaps if the railway had come to fruition one or more of these sites would have been used to add stations to the original plans. However, although the line was deposited with Parliament in good time it would appear to have made no progress. It received no mentions in the railway press of the time, and so it must be assumed that its promoters decided not to proceed with it at a very early stage.

Building on Success: The 1890s

Central London Success

The C&SLR had proved that a deep level tube railway could be powered electrically, and would be patronized and popular. It is certainly this success that allowed the promoters of the Central London Railway to emerge victorious from the 1891 session of Parliament.

By combining their original scheme with that of the London Central Subway (although without the involvement of the LCS) the promoters expounded a railway from Shepherd's Bush through to Cornhill, in the City of London. No connection with the C&SLR was sought, and at the other end of the line a depôt and power station were to be sited on land to the east of Wood Lane. The tunnels were increased in size slightly to have a diameter of 11 ft 6 ins (3.5 m).

Once again, the plans were approved by the Commons, but this time the Select Committee of the House of Lords was also in agreement after only two days of hearings. Many clauses were added to the Bill to protect the interests of those who would (or might) be affected by the construction and operation of the line, but at least it was approved. Royal Assent was received on 5 August 1891.

The following year a further CLR Bill sought to extend eastwards to the Great Eastern Railway (GER) station at Liverpool Street, and to replace Cornhill station with one at Bank, under the road junction. This met with the same success as their previous Bill, and received Royal Assent on 28 June 1892. One unfortunate side effect of the new route was a sharp curve in the line at Bank; this remains today, causing trains to generate ear-piercing squeals as they traverse the rails, and leaving large gaps between the train and the platform. The platform at Liverpool Street would have been straight, and located 54 feet (16.5 m) beneath the concourse of the main line station.

The story of the construction and equipment of the CLR will not be related in any more detail in these pages, as many other authors have recounted its history. Suffice to say that the line was constructed from Shepherd's Bush to Bank, and opened to the public on 30 July 1900.[50] The section to Liverpool Street was not constructed because of a dispute with the GER, although the powers were used to construct a pair of reversing sidings along part of the route between Bank and the junction of Old Broad Street and Throgmorton Street.

Other Plans Fall by the Wayside

The C&SLR prompted a number of schemes to be deposited with Parliament, of which the CLR was the only one to be successful in 1891.

The City & South London Railway Extension

The C&SLR proposed a new railway from King William Street to Islington. Unfortunately it was not to connect to the awkwardly-sited terminus at King William Street, but would be an independent line passing beneath Moorgate, Finsbury Pavement, and City Road. It was remarkably similar to the City & North of London Railway proposal of the previous year, except that its southern end continued to a point nearer to King William Street station.

One of the problems that had beset the C&SLR was that in order to reach the City with minimum tunnelling beneath property (including London Bridge), the line had been brought under Arthur Street West. This is a narrow road curving through 90° ending at King William Street, where the station tunnel lies at right angles to the main road. The railway ascended a steep gradient into the station, which caused the tiny locomotives great difficulties; of course, this would not have been a problem had the line been cable-hauled, as was originally intended. Finally, the siting prevented any extension of the line other than towards Tower Hill.

So it was that the 'extension' was to have a separate station at King William Street, with about 150 yards (137 m) of passageway connecting the two. Passengers from south of the Thames would need to leave their train and traipse through this passage to board another train to Islington. This train would run through larger, 11 feet (3.36 m) diameter tunnels, allowing the Islington line to have larger rolling stock. The tunnels of the original line had shown themselves to be too small from the outset, but joining them to larger tunnels would not allow larger trains to be operated along the route.

Greathead explained to the Select Committee examining the Bill that the only alternative to this plan was to create a new pair of tunnels under the Thames (increasing the expense, and resulting in the waste of the original tunnels). However, the main reason for the Bill was explained by one of the other engineers for the company, Sir John Fowler. It was to prevent a repeat of the previous year, when the CLR had proposed a connection. If they had a line running northwards, they reasoned, it would prevent the CLR or any other company from blocking them. This was just a temporary measure until a better way could be found of connecting the lines.

Their arguments were to no avail, and on 16 March the Committee rejected the proposal, the Chairman stating that he believed that the Bill's weak point was the failure to connect to the existing line.

The North & South London Subway

The promoters of the North & South London Subway (N&SLS) in the 1890 session of Parliament planned a line running from Camden Town southwards to Elephant & Castle. Trains were to be conveyed in separate tunnels 12 ft 3 ins (3.7 m) wide, and the same height; the plans do not state if they were to be circular or square in cross-section.

The depôt for the line was to be in Camden Town, on the same site currently occupied by the Northern line station. From the southern apex it would extend north as far as Buck Street on the western side, and Hawley Crescent on the eastern. The site would excavated to about 30 feet (9.1 m) deep for the tracks. It is possible that a power station would have been on the same site.

The actual running lines would head south from the depôt to the first station at

Mornington Crescent. (These are indicative names, as none is provided on the plans). Following the course of the Hampstead Road, and passing under the LNWR tracks from Euston, the next station would be at **Ampthill Square**. At **Euston Road** the station would be on the north-east corner of the junction, with the Hampstead Road being widened outside.

Continuing south beneath Tottenham Court Road, a station would be sited opposite **Francis Street** (now Torrington Place). The main road would be widened further south at **New Oxford Street** to accommodate the station on the north-west corner. The line would pass over the Middle Level Sewer under this road. Charing Cross Road charted the course of the line further southwards. At Cambridge Circus the subway would cross under the Piccadilly branch of the Middle Level Sewer. At the curve into **St Martin's Place** a station would be positioned behind the National Gallery, just north of Green Street. This would presumably be the station to use for Trafalgar Square, as no other station would be closer.

The line passed under the east side of the square and into Whitehall. At the junction with **Charles Street** a station would have access from both sides of the road. Parliament Square would be undercut on its east side as the line curved gently to the west of the Palace of Westminster and into Abingdon Street, where a station would be sited on the corner with **Great College Street**. South of this station the line would have curved to the east and passed under the Thames, reaching the other side at the junction of **Lambeth Palace Road** and Lambeth Road, with the station on the south. It would progress east below the latter street, with the tunnels briefly diverging to pass under the LSWR bridge. An intermediate station at **Kennington Road**, with the buildings again on the south side, would be passed before following St George's Road to the terminus at **Elephant & Castle**. A foot subway would take passengers from the east end of the N&SLS platforms to a point slightly south of the centre of the C&SLR platforms, descending a 1 in 9 gradient as they did so.

The line was remarkably level, compared with some of the previous plans. The steepest gradients used were 1 in 60, for a short stretch between the Thames and Lambeth Palace Road, and also the section beneath Whitehall.

From the press reports of the time, and the absence of the Bill in the Parliamentary record, it must be assumed that the Bill was never deposited.

The (South) Kensington & Paddington Subway

Cut-and-cover schemes had not vanished, in spite of the enthusiasm for tube railways. The Kensington & Paddington Subway scheme of 1890 was for a shallow electrically-powered railway linking those two locations, to be constructed at a cost of £376,637. No reasons were given, but the Bill was dropped by 28 February 1890.

The following year it returned, in a very similar form, although called the South Kensington & Paddington Subway (SK&PS). It was to commence at **South Kensington**, to the north of the MDR station in Alfred Place West. Running due north under Exhibition Road, moving to the west side as it passed north of Cromwell Road, the next station would be at **Imperial Institute Road**. Shifting a little further west it would continue north between the Imperial Institute and the Technical Institute, before curving west to a station immediately adjacent to the **Royal Albert Hall**. This station was to be sited under the courtyard to the south-east of the hall, and would include sidings as well. The line would depart this station due north, cross Kensington Gore, and pass into Kensington Gardens a little to the east of the Albert Memorial. At the centre of the gardens it would curve slightly to the east, then passing the end of the Serpentine (now called The Long Water) to a station under the **Uxbridge Road** (since renamed Bayswater Road). From here it would follow Lancaster Terrace, and then curve left into Spring Street. The railway would take the entire block of houses to the south of the MR station at **Praed Street**, east of Spring Street, for its passenger terminus. The railway would continue under Spring Street and Eastbourne Terrace to a connection with the GWR at the west end of Bishop's Road Bridge (today's Bishops Bridge).

In fact, there is already a subway in existence between South Kensington and the Imperial Institute. It was constructed by the District Railway and allowed passengers conveniently to access the museums and other important buildings along Exhibition

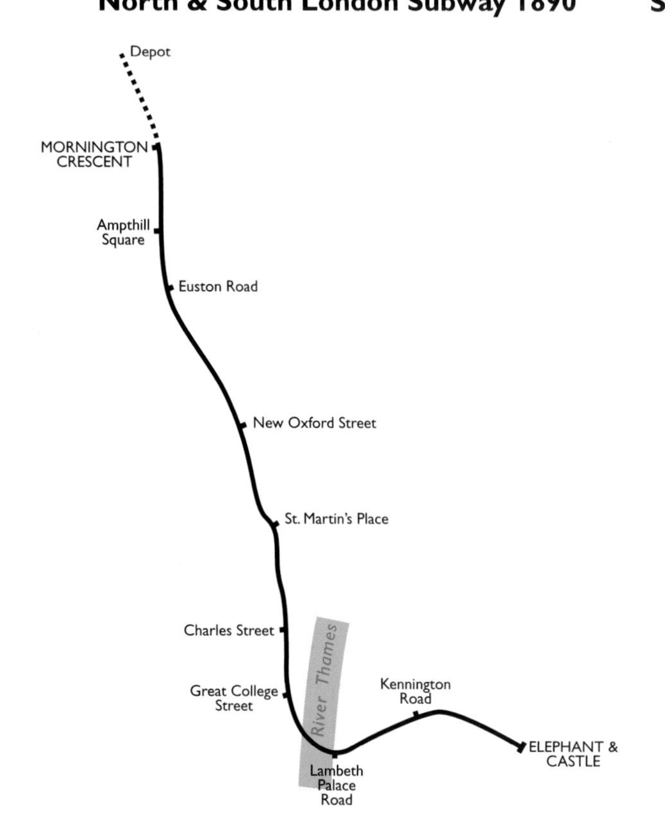

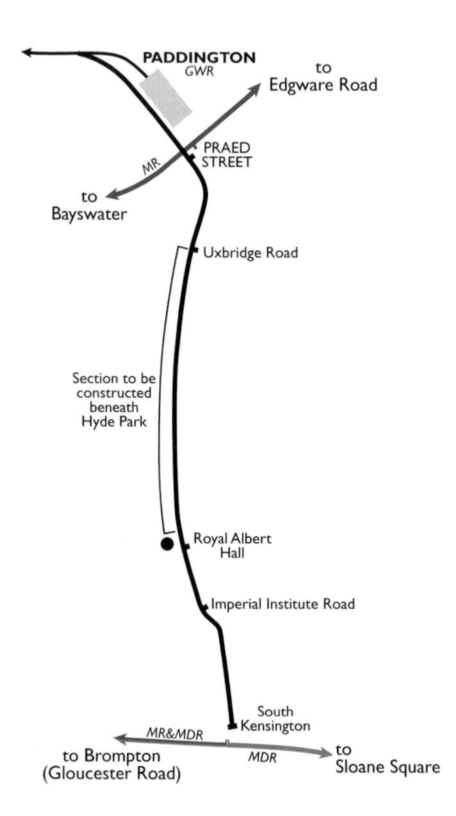

Road.[51] A toll of 1d was charged to walk through the subway, which was opened on 4 May 1885 to coincide with the Inventions Exhibition. A series of exhibitions continued to run until 10 November 1886, when the subway closed. Thereafter it was occasionally opened for special events. This lack of use was undoubtedly what spurred the SK&PS to reuse the infrastructure. With a width of approximately 18 feet (5.5 m) there was adequate room for two lines of railway track, and the height of 11 feet (3.4 m) was also no impediment. The subway was to be purchased from the MDR for £33,000; not a bad price given that it had cost the MDR £42,614 to construct just six years previously.

The other costs for the line included £102,000 for the other tunnels and stations, and £14,000 to make good roads, sewers, and other subterranean services. Capital for the railway was set at £276,000, with additional borrowing powers of £92,000.

Although the line was intended to be electrically operated, the Bill also permitted it to be cable-hauled; this was a sensible measure when the success of electricity for railway traction was still in doubt (although the C&SLR was proving the ability of electricity). The fares were to be 3d for the 1st class passengers, and 2d for 3rd class. The carriage of small parcels was permitted, and the Bill gave a scale of charges, broken down by weight.

Of all of the railways considered here, this is one of the smallest in terms of tunnel size. Through Kensington Gardens the railway was to run in twin tunnels 9 feet (2.75 m) wide and high – 1 ft 2 ins (36 cm) smaller than the smallest C&SLR tunnels.

The most controversial part of the proposal was the section through Kensington Gardens. This section was to be constructed as a trench 25-feet (7.6 m) wide and at least 17-feet (5.2 m) deep. Twin tubes were to be made in the trench, which would then be filled with mass concrete. At least 3 feet (0.9 m) of soil and grass would then overlie this massive block.

The Office of Woods was favourably disposed towards the scheme, subject to payment of an easement for passing through Kensington Gardens. For this right, they set a fee of £8,500. Surprisingly, the Office also suggested that a station in the middle of the Gardens would be a useful feature for the line. This would be the only acceptable reason for any surface openings to the railway in the Gardens.

Unsurprisingly great opposition was raised to the line. It was felt that the sole purpose of the railway was to "stimulate the declining fortunes of the Albert Hall",[52] at the expense of the amenity of the Gardens. The Bill allowed five years for construction, and some local residents assumed that this meant that Kensington Gardens would be dug up for a similar period. The MP Arthur Baumann wrote stridently to *The Times*:

> Nor did the First Commissioner of Works deny the statement publicly made that a station ("kiosque" the wise call it), with all its charming concomitants of a ticket collector, a policeman, an applewoman, and a newsboy, is to be erected in the heart of that beautiful park, where now children play in peace and safety and those in search of rest and solitude ramble undisturbed. And why is this thing to be done? The truth is that the Albert Hall has been a financial fiasco, and the seatholders, amongst whom are some very influential persons, are making this last deperate effort to bring the public to their doors, within which, I am told, the entertainments in future are more likely to be of the Wild West or Hengler's Circus order than classical concerts.[53]

Baumann went on to give details of a committee being created to preserve the gardens and repel the railway, and asking people to contact him if they wished to join. Five days later *The Times* published a follow up letter from Baumann, in which he stated that over 150 residents had contacted him to complain about the subway.

On 11 March *The Times* published a letter from Major-General Charles E. Webber[54] (one of the promoters), claiming that the protesters were unrepresentative of the population of London; all probably had private transport, and would most likely never use the subway. He noted the lack of concern from the park authorities and Office of Works, and pointed out that "barely a dozen trees and comparatively few shrubs" would be removed, and most of the trees were decayed anyhow. The construction would not take five years; it could be completed in six months, and would involve a length of one or two hundred yards (90–180 m) being constructed at a time.

He went on to explain that the station in the park was not essential. The travel time from Paddington to South Kensington would be 7 minutes, enabling easy access to the museums.

By way of riposte, Basil Holmes, secretary of the Metropolitan Public Gardens Association, claimed that the railway would "act as a vast drain to the soil for killing a further indefinite number [of trees] on either side".

The LCC was opposed to the subway, on the grounds that it would interfere with their sewers, both existing and proposed. It would also cause a great inconvenience whilst it was being constructed. They resolved to petition against the line, again retaining the services of Benjamin Baker as an expert witness.

In August 1890 the railway published a promotional booklet written by Webber, which included a beautifully detailed map of the subway. It described the route of the subway, which was to be constructed "in accordance with the patents of Colonel Hazard", the promoter of the London Central (Subway) Railway in 1889.

It was noted that at the south end of the line it might be possible to extend the subway south across the MDR to Chelsea. At South Kensington station, sidings were to be located in Alfred Place, next to the MDR station and west of the subway.

Two different lengths of subway car were described, as the promoters were still undecided as to which they preferred:

	Short Car	**Long Car**
Length	19 ft (5.8 m)	26 ft (7.9 m)
Width	6 ft 3 ins (1.9 m)	6 ft 3 ins (1.9 m)
Weight	6 tons	9 tons
Seats	18	24
Standing	12	16
Number of lamps	6	8

The bodies of the cars would be suspended between bogies, with the floor one step (presumably about six inches) above rail level. Access would be through sliding doors on each side of cars. Doors at the end of each car would allow the conductor to pass between cars. Interior lighting would be provided using lamps of eight-candlepower in each car. Every car would have electric motors, and the maximum speed would be 20 m.p.h. (32 km/h).

The cars would run singly or in groups of two or three, depending on passenger demand. One driver and conductor would be required for each train. The promoters calculated that 18 cars were required for a 1-minute service; allowing for maintenance, 22 were to be ordered.

Electricity would be supplied to the cars through an overhead wire in the tunnels, with the current returning through the rails. The voltage was not yet decided, but 500V would be the maximum.

The 60 lb/yd (29.8 kg/m) rails would be flush with the floor of the tunnels, and cross passages between the tunnels would be provided to reduce air resistance. Eight-candlepower lamps suspended from the roof would illuminate the stations and tunnels. Those in the tunnels would be spaced no closer than 50 feet (15.25 m), and lit in emergencies only.

One remarkable feature of the plans was the power station. The promoters were considering making a subterranean space south of the Albert Hall for this facility, with chimneys inside new mansions being erected (presumably those on the north side of the new Prince Consort Road). Coal would be supplied via the junction with GWR at Paddington. It was calculated that 500 hp (373 kW) generating capacity was all that would be required.

If their underground generating station was impractical, the alternative plan was to buy power from the Chelsea Electricity Supply Company, which distributed electricity in the area. It was believed that this company would have sufficient capacity to supply the subway.

The line would be open from 5.30 a.m. until midnight, with a 4-minute service operating until 8.00 a.m.; thereafter a two-minute service would run until midnight. Extra trains would be put on for extraordinary traffic, "Soirees, Conversaziones, and Meetings, at the South Kensington Museum, the Natural History Museum, and the Imperial Institute."

In a perhaps rather desperate move to appease their opponents the promoters suggested allowing the MDR or various public bodies (including the LCC, the Royal Commissioners of the Exhibition of 1851, and the Commissioners of Woods) to undertake the construction of the line. However, it all came to nought. By the middle of March it was reported that the Bill had been dropped, the promoters having withdrawn it.

1892 – A Crucial Year

It was unsurprising that only a handful of tube railway schemes were considered by Parliament in 1891; the C&SLR had opened right at the end of 1890, at about the time that 1891 Bills had to be deposited. Those Bills that were deposited for the 1891 session fell into two categories: resubmissions of earlier plans (CLR), and speculative new plans (C&SLR, SK&PS, N&SLS).

Given that the C&SLR opened at the very end of 1890, the earliest opportunity for speculators to submit schemes for new railways would be the 1892 session of Parliament. This gave them some time to ascertain the advantages and disadvantages of the first tube railway. As such, 1892 promised to be a busy session. Four completely new tube railways were proposed, and in order to ensure a consistent approach a motion was passed by the House of Commons on 1 March for the creation of a Joint Select Committee that would consider all of the tube railway Bills.

The Committees

Five members of the Committee were to come from each House. The House of Lords provided Lords Lauderdale, Strafford, Barrington, Thring, and Kelvin; and, from the House of Commons, T. H. Bolton, J. S. Gathorne-Hardy, Mr Story-Maskelyne, Mr Whitmore, and Mr Stansfeld (Chairman). The list of Bills for them to consider comprised: the Baker Street & Waterloo Railway; the Great Northern & City Railway; the Hampstead, St Pancras & Charing Cross Railway; the Waterloo & City Railway; as well as the CLR extension to Liverpool Street, and a new plan to reach Islington from the C&SLR (discussed in the next section). All four of the new railways ended up being constructed, and little needs to be said about them here, as other authors have already written much about all of them.

The terms of reference, as set out by the House of Commons, were as follows:

> "That a joint committee of Lords and Commons be appointed to consider the best method of dealing with the electric and cable railway schemes proposed to be sanctioned within the limits of the metropolis by bills introduced, or to be introduced in the present session, and to report their opinion as to whether underground railways worked by electricity or cable traction are calculated to afford sufficient accommodation for the present and probable future traffic; as to whether any, and which, of the schemes propose satisfactory lines of route; as to the terms and conditions under which the subsoil should be appropriated; whether any, and, if any, what, schemes should not be proceeded with during the present session; that a message be sent to the Lords to communicate this resolution, and desire their concurrence."

The City Corporation, which is the local authority for the City of London, referred all of the Bills affecting the City to its Local Government and Taxation Committee. This raised a number of key points for its engineer to answer in conjunction with each railway, including the effect of the railways on the streets, their depth and width, and their utility. The Committee's final report of 5 May made the following recommendations:

- Tube railways should be at least 10 feet (3.1 m) below the surface.
- Tube tunnels should be of a uniform size, and should be able to take main line trains.
- A uniform gauge should be employed (and given the previous point, this should presumably be standard gauge).
- Whilst a central underground station at the Mansion House (i.e., Bank station) had advantages, the area might become very congested, and the Bank of England and Mansion House may need to be underpinned.
- Freeholders should not be paid for wayleaves, only for any actual damage caused by construction or operation of the railway.
- All of the Bills should be referred to a joint committee or special select committee for consideration.

Finally, the City Corporation decided that, in order to ensure that it could pass comment on all of the schemes, it would lodge petitions against all of them.

The LCC also considered the future of underground railways, and they proposed that in future the Council should present petitions against all tube railways. This would enable them to secure the insertion of clauses forbidding the companies from bringing forward the front of their buildings beyond the general line of frontage of buildings in the streets,[55] and also to protect the Council's sewers, bridges, and other property.

Before examining any of the individual Bills, the parliamentary Joint Select Committee first took a look at the principles of tube railways in an attempt to define some standards. To this end they took evidence from a number of engineers, including Greathead, who was joint engineer to all of the railways being considered. The process started four days after the report from the City Corporation.

One of the areas for debate was around tunnel sizes. The C&SLR had opened with tunnels just 10 ft 2 ins and 10 ft 6 ins in diameter. From the outset it was realized that these were too restrictive, and Greathead recommended the adoption of 12-feet (3.7 m) diameter tunnels on all future tube railways.

Tunnel Diameters

The diameter of tube tunnels is the factor that governs their cost most closely. The cross-sectional area of the tunnel increases as the square of the diameter; thus, the volume of earth excavated will correspondingly increase. The 11 ft 6 in diameter tunnels of the CLR, although only one foot in diameter larger than the main C&SLR tunnels, would involve the excavation of 20% more earth. The additional 6 inches diameter suggested by Greathead would increase this to 31%.

At the extreme of London's tube railways, the Great Northern & City Railway (see below) with its 16-ft diameter tunnels required 133% more excavation than the C&SLR, and 78% more than Greathead's 12-ft tunnels.

Of course, it is not just the cost of the tunnelling that increases. The additional soil must be transported and disposed of; although fortunately the cost of the tunnel lining only increases in direct proportion to the diameter. The longer-term costs will also be larger, as the ventilation equipment will need to be increased in scale to move a greater volume of air through the tunnels.

Evidence in favour of electric lines was supplied by W. H. Preece, electrician for the General Post Office; Alexander Siemens; Greathead; and Charles Scotter, General Manager of the LSWR.

The Committee issued its report on 23 May. In summary, their findings were as follows:

- The GN&CR Bill should proceed through Parliament normally, as it was a relief line for the GNR.
- All of the other railways were acceptable, with no reason to postpone any of the Bills. They should all be considered together, in the normal way, by a Select Committee for Private Bills.
- Electricity was preferred, but cable haulage is "of recognized utility", especially in the case of lines with steep gradients.

- Instead of having to purchase the entire freehold of any property under which its railway passed, a company should be able to purchase 'wayleaves' – effectively permission to tunnel under the property. Under streets, as long as they are at "sufficient" depth (which was not defined) then the wayleave should be free.
- The companies should be under an obligation to provide an adequate number of cheap and convenient trains (the workmen's trains provision).
- The minimum tunnel diameter should be 11 ft 6 ins (3.5 m). This was a compromise between the existing lines and Greathead's views.

The Baker Street & Waterloo Railway

The Baker Street & Waterloo Railway proposed a tube railway between the two points named in its title. According to the opening ceremony brochure, the route was designed to get businessmen from Westminster to the cricket at Lord's in as short a time as possible so that they could see the last hour's play. Whatever the true reasons, it was quickly realized that this would provide a useful link across London, following as it did Euston Road, Portland Place, Regent Street, and Haymarket.

In evidence against the BS&WR, John Wolfe Barry stated that the 12-ft diameter tunnels should be increased in size so that they could accommodate full-size rolling stock. This was not entirely surprising, as he was engineer to the MDR and MR. The latter company also claimed in their opposition that the line was "an omnibus service which could not possibly be made to pay". Further opposition came from the SER, who were contemplating an extension north from their Charing Cross terminus to connect with the northern railways (i.e., Midland, LNWR, etc.), and so the BS&WR would be an inconvenience, as well as providing competition.

The opposition evidently did not persuade the Committee; however, with the delays following the Committee the Bill was not passed until 28 March 1893. A station was not permitted between Baker Street and Oxford Circus because of objections by the landowners, who were the Crown and Portland estates, but otherwise the line was approved as submitted. Stations were to be provided at **Baker Street**, **Oxford Circus**, **Piccadilly Circus**, **Trafalgar Square**,[56] **Embankment**, and **Waterloo**.

It proved impossible to raise the capital, and the only activity that occurred was the submission of a further Bill in 1896 seeking to increase the permitted capital, and extend the time allowed for the construction, as well as prolonging the line from Baker Street to the Great Central Railway terminus being constructed at **Marylebone**. This was approved and Royal Assent was granted on 7 August 1896.

Plans that were supplied by the BS&WR to the MR showing cross-sections of the tunnels are very detailed, and show the internal details of a tube railway tunnel well. In that regard they can be considered fairly typical of most of the early tube lines.

The running tunnels would consist of rings of segments 1 ft 8 ins (51 cm) long. Six segments, each just under 60° of arc, made up 98% of the ring; the final 7° located centrally at the top of the tunnel, was the key segment, inserted last. This locked the ring into place against the forces of the London clay. The segments were of cast iron ⅞ inches (2.3 cm) thick, with 4-inch (10.2 cm) deep flanges. Each of the six main segments included a hole 1⅜ inches (3.5 cm) in diameter, through which grout would be pumped, to fill any voids between the tunnel and the surrounding ground. The internal diameter of the tunnel was to be 12 feet (3.66 m); with the flanges on both sides, plus the thickness of the segments, this meant the tunnelling of a space 12 ft 9¾ ins (3.9 m) in diameter. Station tunnels would be similar, but larger. Twelve segments, plus the key, would make up each ring, and rings would only be 1½ feet (46 cm) long. They would therefore be similar in size to the running tunnel rings. However, they would weigh almost twice as much because the thickness of the cast iron was increased to 1½ inches (3.8 cm). Two grout holes would be made in each segment, probably because the risk of subsidence over a station tunnel was greater, so more precise grouting would be required.

The Waterloo & City Railway

Associated with the BS&WR was the Waterloo & City Railway (W&CR), by virtue of having three directors in common (two of whom were also directors of the London & South Western Railway, owners of the main line to Waterloo). This was (and remains) the shortest tube railway in London, at just 1½ miles (2.4 km) long, with only two stations at **Waterloo** and **City** (renamed Bank on 28 October 1940). To the south of the Thames the railway would follow Stamford Street; to the north, Queen Victoria Street. The river would be crossed just upstream of Blackfriars Bridge.

The intent was to allow passengers arriving at Waterloo an easy way to get to the City, the only alternatives being horse-drawn cabs or omnibuses. Waterloo was rather distant from the City, being on the south bank of the Thames, and since its opening in 1848 a number of plans had been made to project the railway towards the City. None of these had proved successful as they were above the surface, and therefore expensive to construct because of the extensive property purchase and demolition required.

The W&CR was supported by the LSWR, which enabled a guaranteed 3% dividend to be promised on the capital of £540,000. It was not surprising that following its Royal Assent on 8 March 1893, the W&CR was the first of the 1892 schemes to raise the money needed, and the first to open for business, on 8 August 1898.

As a postscript to the W&CR story, it should be mentioned that the railway was taken over by the LSWR on 1 January 1907, and remained independent of all of the other tube railways until 1 April 1994, when it was transferred to London Underground. Occasional proposals to extend it were made: a connection to Moorgate was promoted in 1913 and is covered in a later chapter. In 1934 the London Passenger Transport Board proposed an eastwards extension from the City terminus to Shoreditch via Liverpool Street, but this is beyond the scope of this book.

The Royal Exchange & Waterloo Railway

It was surprising to see another above-ground line along a similar route to the W&CR being promoted in the same year. The Royal Exchange & Waterloo Railway would have involved a massive viaduct linking the tracks south of Waterloo to a station opposite the Royal Exchange, including a new bridge over the Thames. The line would also connect with the LB&SCR tracks east of London Bridge. Fortunately for property-owners in south London and the City this line was never built, being withdrawn by its promoters in January.

The Mystery of Camden Town

The plans of the Hampstead, St Pancras & Charing Cross Railway are confusing with regard to Camden Town. The original 1892 plans show a station near to the site of Mornington Crescent, and nothing at the site of today's station; however, Mornington Crescent station was clearly added to the line in the CCE&HR Act of 1904. A plan of the line in 1899 shows a station called **Seymour Street** near to Mornington Crescent. Three years later the station is called **Camden Road**, and it has moved northwards. Only with the act of 1904 do we find both stations on the map. It is likely, therefore, that only one station was originally intended to serve the area, and in the years whilst the capital was secured, the exact location was revised several times.

Another north-south tube railway was proposed by the Hampstead, St Pancras & Charing Cross Railway. In the north, the terminus was sited in at the junction of High Street and **Heath Street**. Heading in a south-easterly direction below Haverstock Hill, on a very steep 1 in 24 downhill gradient with stations at **Belsize** and **Chalk Farm**, the line continued through **Camden Town** and south along the Hampstead Road. To the north of the station at **Euston Road**[57] a branch curved east to **Euston**, following the line of Drummond Street[58] and Chapel Street. A passenger subway would link the tube and main line stations. East of Seymour Street the tunnels were placed one above the other, due to the narrowness of the streets. It then ran under St Pancras, to **King's Cross**. The latter station would have been below the Hotel Curve, a single-track line linking the MR to the main line. A footbridge was to be constructed over St Pancras Road, linking the two main line stations and helping passengers to access the tube railway.

The Joint Committee subsequently rejected this final section east of Chalton Street (effectively beyond Euston) because of the concerns of the Midland Railway. They had constructed their massive gothic-style hotel in front of the station some twenty years previously, and did not want it damaged by tunnels underneath.

The main route south of Euston Road station continued below **Tottenham Court Road**, passing **Oxford Street**[59] at St Giles Circus, and into Charing Cross Road (opened in 1887). At the south end it curved east under King William Street (now William IV Street) to a station at the junction with **Agar Street**. A subway leading west under the Strand led up to the forecourt of the SER station at Charing Cross. The running tunnels continued beyond Agar Street to the junction with Exeter Street.

The northern section of the line would involve some steep gradients and both cable haulage and electricity were being considered as options for operating the trains. In the latter case the generating station was to be opposite Chalk Farm station on the North London Railway.[60] This station had a large coal depôt, so the electricity would be cheap to produce. However, much of the debate centred on the cable-hauled plan, because this was seen as being most effective on the steep gradients, as well as cheaper than electricity. Indeed, it was doubted that electric traction would be able to operate trains all of the way to Hampstead. In evidence to the Joint Select Committee cable was the preferred option, with the cable moving at a speed of 16 m.p.h. (26 km/h). Cable was still being discussed as the means of traction in March 1893.[61]

In 1892 the promoters asked the LCC to contribute half the cost of acquiring and demolishing Bozier's Court, which was still extant following the indecision over the CLR proposal to clear it. The LCC again considered the matter, and the £48,000 that would be their half of the cost, and declined, on the advice of their Improvements Committee. The CCE&HR eventually cleared the buildings at their own expense.

The Joint Committee took until 31 March 1893 to approve the plan. On 6 May it was reported that the Bill had not complied with a Standing Order; fortunately, the Standing Order Committee decided to dispense with the Order, permitting the Bill to progress to the House of Lords. Their approval was given, and Royal Assent was received on 24 August 1893. The company had changed its name by this time to the Charing Cross, Euston & Hampstead Railway. Finance was again not forthcoming, and so the remainder of the 1890s was taken up with applying for extensions of time (granted in 1897,[62] 1898, and 1900), and modifications to the route, which are described in a later section.

The Great Northern & City Railway

Alexander Siemens (22 January 1847 – 16 February 1928)
Born in Hanover, Siemens studied in Germany before coming to England in 1867, to work at the workshops of his family's business, called Siemens Brothers, in Woolwich. The next year he was in Persia, assisting in the construction of the Indo-European telegraph line. He then continued the same project in the Black Sea during 1869.

The intervention of the Franco-Prussian War of 1870–71 saw him as a Private in an infantry regiment fighting for Prussia. For this he was awarded the Iron Cross. After the war he returned to England. In 1878 he revoked his citizenship so that he could become a naturalized British subject.

Upon his return from Europe he became a pupil of William Siemens, and took over the Electric Light Department of the Siemens Company in 1879.

In 1894 and 1904 he was President of the Institute of Electrical Engineers, and in 1910–11 he was President of the Institute of Civil Engineers.

He built Westover Hall in Milford-on-Sea in 1897, which 'was acknowledged to be the most luxurious residence along the South Coast of England'.

The final plan for 1892 was that of the Great Northern & City Railway. This was unusual in that its running tunnels were to have a diameter of 16 feet (4.88 m), permitting the passage of main line rolling stock from the GNR. The original proposal from the engineers, Francis Fox and Greathead, was for a conventional-size tube railway, but the GNR Board wanted to operate their own existing trains on the line, hauled by what were termed "electric tractors". Greathead agreed that the increased tunnel diameter was feasible, and the electrical engineer Alexander Siemens concurred that sufficiently powerful electric locomotives could be constructed. The line would therefore allow GNR trains direct access to the City, avoiding the bottleneck north of their station at King's Cross, and providing a more direct route for many of their passengers.

The GN&CR would also be able to run its own trains back and forth along the line to supplement those of the GNR.

The line was 2⅔ miles (4.25 km) long, and started just south of the existing GNR station at **Finsbury Park**, with its up line diverging from the GNR Canonbury spur[63] at Seven Sisters Road and descending into a shallow cutting. Further south, just north of Drayton Park, the down line would have connected. **Drayton Park** was sited in the open air, to the north of the road of the same name, and west of the Canonbury spur. The cutting would have deepened, and would be followed closely by the start of the tube tunnels at Ronalds Road. The tunnels would then proceed south under Highbury Fields, and from Highbury Corner would follow beneath the Canonbury Road to a station at **Essex Road**. The line would then follow the New North Road to **Old Street**, where a joint station with the C&SLR would be made. Finally, the southern terminus was to be at **Moorgate**. The tunnels were unusual for another reason than their diameter: only the upper half was to be made of cast iron, the lower half being constructed of brick. This was for reasons of both economy and noise reduction. The tunnels were actually constructed using the cast iron upper segments and concrete lower segments; these latter pieces were subsequently removed and replaced with the brickwork.

The gradient was very shallow south of Essex Road, with a maximum of 1 in 100. North of that point it increased in places to 1 in 66 in tunnel, and 1 in 52 for the open-air ascent to the GNR. The line was level at all stations – including a section beneath Highbury Corner, which later became the site for Highbury & Islington station.

Although the GN&CR was the first of the 1892 railways to be approved by Parliament, with Royal Assent being received on 28 June 1892, it was not so quick to raise the finance. Its connection with the GNR proved scant help, as the main line company was starting to lose interest in the scheme. Nevertheless, they signed an agreement with the GN&CR in 1894, in which the following key provisions were made:[64]

- The GNR was to pay for a separate station at Moorgate;
- The GN&CR was responsible for Drayton Park station and its facilities;
- The GNR was to construct the line between Finsbury Park and Drayton Park;
- The GNR would be responsible for bringing its trains to Drayton Park station, at which point the GN&CR would take over and deliver them to Moorgate;
- The GNR would run 50 trains per day over the line, with powers to increase this to 100;
- The GN&CR was to have free use of GNR land where needed for its construction, and would construct its own station at Finsbury Park;
- The GNR would pay the GN&CR a proportion of the fares, with the total annual amount being not less than £20,000.
- This latter amount was soon amended to £25,000, after the tube company claimed that it would be unable to raise sufficient capital otherwise. The maximum number of GNR trains was reduced to 70.

After three years of inactivity, an Act extending the construction time was passed on 6 July 1895 – without this they risked losing the Parliamentary powers before any work had been done. The scheme was taken over by a construction company, S. Pearson & Son Ltd. They presumably hoped that the GNR would eventually pay them for the line, once it was built. They were not to be so lucky, as shall be shown later.

The C&SLR Grows Further

After the failure of the planned separate railway from King William Street to Islington, the C&SLR took a long hard look at their awkward City terminus and realized that a difficult decision needed to be made. They would not be able to extend northwards unless the section between the terminus and the north bank of the Thames, with its sharp curves and steep gradients, was removed from the line. The line could not be extended eastwards from King William Street, even to enlarge the station, as the company was not allowed to tunnel any closer to the Monument. The station could not be widened without serious risk of causing subsidence in the streets above, and so at the company's half-yearly meeting on 2 February a motion was carried to put forward an extension Bill.

The Bill, which was considered in the 1892 session of Parliament, was for a line that would separate from their existing railway between Elephant & Castle and Borough. This would pass through a station at **London Bridge** (with a subway under Denman Street to the main line station), and then under the Thames in a new pair of tunnels downstream of the actual bridge. A station at **Bank** would lie 19 ft 8 ins (6.0 m) deeper than the original terminus, and would be beneath the northern section of King William Street. Both stations would remain open for traffic.

A glance at the Underground map will show that this does not describe the situation as built by the C&SLR, as Borough station is still in existence. The new section actually diverges north of Borough, and the original line to King William Street was closed as soon as the new line was opened. The plans submitted with the Bill showed the line diverging north of Borough, as constructed. However, they also show a new subway to be constructed from the east end of the original platforms at King William Street, under Arthur Street East and Fish Street Hill, to the MDR station at Monument. This clearly indicates the intention to keep the original terminus open.

Continuing north from Bank, beneath Prince's Street to **Moorgate**, the rest of the line would be identical to that originally proposed in the previous year, with stations at **Old Street**, **City Road**,[65] and **Angel**. A new power station was to be constructed at this northern terminus, operating in addition to the existing Stockwell facility. This would be on land bounded by Torrens Street, Duncan Street, Duncan Terrace, and City Road. In total, the line was to cost £706,633.

The Bill was given Royal Assent on 24 August 1893 after due consideration by the Joint Select Committee, and consolidation with another C&SLR Bill to prolong the time allowed to construct the Clapham Common extension. The Lambeth Vestry had opposed this latter Bill, but since they did not send a representative to support their petition the Committee ruled in favour of the railway. Work had not yet started on this extension, apparently because the company felt that until the King William Street bottleneck was removed they would not be able to cope with additional passengers.

The powers for the Clapham extension were used in 1893 to construct siding tunnels along the route south of Stockwell, connected to the southbound running line at the station. Two years later a further Bill authorized another extension of time for the Clapham extension, as well as the construction of a further siding at Stockwell to the south of the main line. A further Bill of 1896 allowed them to use additional lands in Borough High Street for the construction of the junction for the new branch to Angel.

More Plans in 1893

The Edgware Road & Victoria Railway

The Edgware Road & Victoria Railway (ER&VR) was to run from near Brondesbury station in a straight line south-east to Victoria, following the pattern of the streets above. The 4 mile 3 furlong 6 chain (7.16 km) line was to be worked by electricity or cable, and constructed as a tube railway with 11 ft 6 ins diameter running tunnels.

The depôt would be at the north end of the line, bounded to the east by Willesden Lane, and to the north by the LNWR through Brondesbury. A single-track tunnel branching from the main line at Palmerston Road would be used for access, following the path of Dyne Road and climbing at 1 in 20 to reach the surface.

The first station, **Brondesbury**, would be near to the depôt, and would provide interchange with the North London Railway, with its buildings to the south of those of the main line. **Kilburn** station would be opposite Belsize Road, and close to the Kilburn & Maida Vale station of the LNWR.[66] The next station south would be opposite **Hall Road**; this would be followed by **Praed Street**, near to the MR Edgware Road station. The surface buildings would be on the west side of Edgware Road, between Praed Street and Market Street.

At the southern end of the Edgware Road, **Marble Arch** station would provide interchange with the CLR through a platform-level subway. The buildings would be on the north-east corner of the junction. The line would shift west slightly to run under Hyde Park, to avoid complaints from the property owners along Park Lane. **Hyde Park Corner** station would be below the western side of the traffic junction and would be entirely underground, similar to the Bank CLR station. Two staircases to the street would be made; one for entrance and one for exit. These would be sited on the island in the middle of the junction, causing the Committee concern about volume of people crossing the road.[67] The lifts were to be entirely below ground. At platform level there would be a concourse between the station tunnels, forcing them to be approximately 35 feet (10.7 m) apart.

The railway would continue following the line of Grosvenor Place and Grosvenor Gardens to its southernmost station at **Victoria**, where the platform tunnels would be below the main line station forecourt. Beyond here the running tunnels would continue to a point 50 yards short of the junction of Vauxhall Bridge Road with Gillingham Street. The steepest gradient on the main route of the railway would be 1 in 100.

Power was to be supplied from a generating station on the north bank of the Paddington basin, on a site bounded to the north by Harrow Road. The Catholic Apostolic Church that occupied the site would need to be demolished, as it was firmly within the limits of deviation. This site would allow a good supply of water, and easy access to a large coal supply. A subway under Harrow Road would allow the cables to link with the railway near to Praed Street station.

Access to the stations would be via stairs, or hydraulic or other lifts. The maximum diameter of the station tunnels would be 25 feet (7.6 m), with 12-feet wide platforms, situated between the running lines.

Each train on the line would carry 150 passengers, and they would run at 2-minute intervals. Locomotives would pull the carriages, just as with the C&SLR. The increase in tunnel size would allow for larger carriages than on the latter line, although the ER&VR promoters described the rolling stock as being otherwise very similar.

The cost of constructing the railway was calculated to be £921,428. With the additional costs for the power station and electrical equipment the promoters looked to raise capital of £1.2 million, with additional borrowing powers for £400,000. The fares were set at 2d per mile for 1st class passengers and 1d per mile for those travelling 2nd class. Workmen's tickets would be available before 7 a.m. and after 6 p.m.

Workmen's Fares

These were generally issued by all railway companies, and entitled workmen to travel at certain times or on certain trains at low cost. The trains would usually run very early in the morning, arriving at the London terminus by 8 a.m., if not earlier. Typically return tickets would be sold for the price of a normal single, and sometimes they needed to be purchased a week in advance. Workmen's tickets had been instituted as the main line railways constructed their London termini. Housing had to be demolished in order to create space for the stations, goods yards, and running lines; in order to keep cost to a minimum, cheap workers housing (often slums) were cleared. The authorities insisted that since the workers would often be forced to move further away from London (along the railway lines), that the railway companies offered affordable fares.

The House of Commons Select Committee considered the railway between 21 and 24 March 1893. There were many petitions against the line from property owners along the line of the railway; the company had chosen a route that passed along some of the wealthier streets in the capital, and it was hardly surprising that the owners of such valuable property would be concerned, given the damage caused by the C&SLR tunnels. Arguments were also made that traffic from the Kilburn area consisted mostly of City workers, and therefore a railway to Marble Arch and Hyde Park Corner would not be used. These petitioners considered that the line would not be able to make a good return on the invested capital. Another concern was about the ventilation of the line. Witnesses were called who claimed that the atmosphere on the C&SLR was even worse than that of the steam-operated MR and MDR, and that people would not want to use such a railway. The promoters claimed that the trains would act like pistons in their tunnels, forcing the air to circulate.

After the summing up from both sides, the Committee stated that the preamble of the Bill was not proved. The basic problem for the railway was that the only tube railway in operation was the C&SLR. This railway had made a number of mistakes in the design (not surprisingly, given that it was the first): the tunnel size; the steep gradients into King William Street; the subsidence of buildings above the brick-built station tunnels. These led to a number of prejudices against tube railways, and until another line demonstrated that they could be settled, it was always going to be difficult to get another tube railway Bill sanctioned. This was obviously a chicken and egg situation.

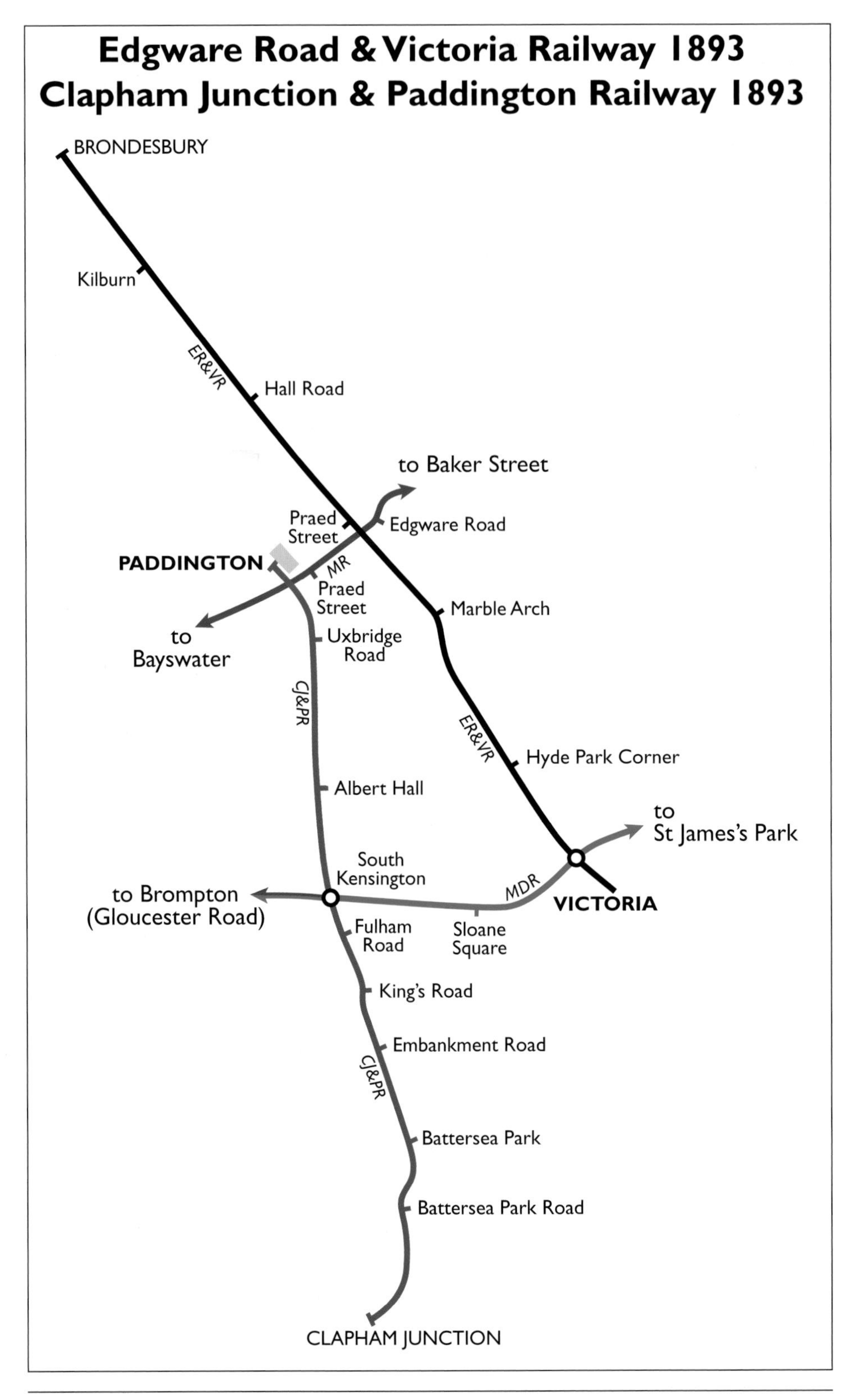
Edgware Road & Victoria Railway 1893
Clapham Junction & Paddington Railway 1893
BRONDESBURY
Kilburn
ER&VR
Hall Road
to Baker Street
Praed Street
Edgware Road
PADDINGTON
MR
Praed Street
Marble Arch
to Bayswater
Uxbridge Road
CJ&PR
ER&VR
Hyde Park Corner
Albert Hall
to St James's Park
South Kensington
MDR
to Brompton (Gloucester Road)
VICTORIA
Fulham Road
Sloane Square
King's Road
Embankment Road
CJ&PR
Battersea Park
Battersea Park Road
CLAPHAM JUNCTION

The Clapham Junction & Paddington Railway

Another railway linking north and south London was proposed in the same year. The Clapham Junction & Paddington Railway (CJ&PR) was further south and west than the ER&VR, and took a similar route to that of the SK&PS from two years earlier.

The railway would start at Eastbourne Terrace, alongside **Paddington**, and the first intermediate station on the line would be on the **Uxbridge Road**. This would be sited at the north end of the Serpentine, and just to the west of where Lancaster Gate station is to be found today. The tunnels would pass due south under Hyde Park to Kensington Road, where a station would be just east of the **Albert Hall**. The costs of the railway included £9,368 to construct a foot subway from the north side of the Albert Hall to the north end of Exhibition Road.

The line would follow this latter thoroughfare to **South Kensington**, for interchange with the MR and MDR. A short distance south would be **Fulham Road** station, followed by **King's Road** station. At the north side of the Thames the seventh station would be located on **Embankment Road**, which today is called the Chelsea Embankment. Across the Thames a station would be sited on the west side of **Battersea Park**, under Albert Bridge Road. The line would then follow the course of Cambridge Road and Battersea Bridge Road to reach the penultimate station at **Battersea Park Road**. Finally, the line would curve to the west under the main line tracks into **Clapham Junction**. The length was given as 4 miles 1 furlong 1.5 chains (6.67 km); the line would be in twin cast-iron tubes. These were expected to be driven in compressed air, and would be 11 ft 6 ins in diameter.

The line was promoted by Baron Sudeley, the Hon. E. S. Churchill, and D. F. Carmichael. The engineers were listed as being Greathead, Henry Ward, and Charles Webber. The inclusion of Webber is further support for the route being similar to the SK&PS, which he had unsuccessfully promoted two years earlier.

The depôt and power station were planned for the south end of the line, on a triangle of land bounded by Falcon Lane to the west, and railways to the north-east and south-east. Trains would be composed of single carriages, which could be coupled together if the demand rose. They would run at the extremely close interval of one per minute. The promoters believed that frequency of trains was more important than the carrying capacity of each train. They estimated that the railway would carry some 11 million passengers each year.

The money for the line was to be raised through the sale of £1,050,000 of shares; an extra £350,000 could also be borrowed. Fares were to be the same as for the ER&VR; of note in the records was the fact that workmen's fares of 1d in morning and evening were to be charged.

Several main line railway companies supported the CJ&PR:

- The GWR, who had their main line terminal at Paddington as well as rights through Clapham Junction to Victoria;
- The LB&SCR, who also operated from Victoria through Clapham Junction; and
- The LSWR, whose trains passed through Clapham Junction on their way to and from Waterloo.

The Duke of Edinburgh supported the scheme because it would provide better access to the Albert Hall and institutions at South Kensington. Local residents wanted the line as well – the promoters produced a petition with 6,000 signatures in favour of the railway (signed by residents of Paddington, Kensington, Battersea and Clapham). However, the MR argued that the new railway would destroy their profitability, cutting off as it did their western circuit via Notting Hill Gate. The MDR shared this view.

An unusual objection was based on concerns as to the effect of electricity on the scientific instruments in the Science and Art Department at Kensington, along Exhibition Road. The institutions gathered mainly on the western side of the road were renowned for their scientific work, and the unknown quantity of an electrically-operated railway could jeopardize this. Even the renowned Lord Kelvin spoke out against the railway.

And so it was that on 20 March the Committee decided that the preamble of the Bill was not proved. *The Railway News* reported five days later that the promoters were considering applying for permission to have this reconsidered, and the Bill recommitted to Parliament. After discussing this possibility with the Committee Chairman, they decided to wait until they could come to an arrangement with the scientific institutions. One of the possible solutions was to substitute cable haulage for electric traction.

However, the railway proposal disappeared after this point. Twelve years later, whilst giving evidence to the Royal Commission on London Traffic, Webber discussed the line, and finished the story with the opposition from the institutions.

The MP for Bethnal Green, Mr Pickersgill, set out a motion before the House of Commons that if passed would affect the Bills of the C&SLR, CJ&PR, ER&VR, CCE&HR, and W&CR. He asked for clauses to be added to all of the Bills that would allow the LCC to purchase the railways after a set period of time. Naturally the promoters of the Bills were unimpressed, and argued against the motion in the press.

Pickersgill argued that the tramways were subject to similar clauses, as set out in the 1870 Tramway Act. He acknowledged that it could have an injurious effect on private enterprise, and prevent people from promoting tube railways; however, he thought that by setting the time period carefully the promoters should still have an incentive to construct new railways. The LCC had been pushing for such legislation for some time, but it was noted that the 1892 Select Committee had completely ignored the issue.

Opponents of the motion argued that changes of this magnitude should be put forward in a separate public Bill (i.e., one promoted by the Government). This motion was, they stated, "a mode of evading the Standing Orders of the House".

Ultimately, as with all matters in Parliament, it came down to a vote. The motion was defeated by 242 votes to 129.

The London, Walthamstow and Epping Forest Railway

One of the most long-running plans for tube railways in the 1890s was concerned with connecting the City to the villages north-east of London, which were starting to become suburbs. The plans were first created in 1891, under the title of the London, Tottenham and Epping Forest Railway, and were for a railway from Whitecross Street, in the City, to Waltham Abbey, via Tottenham and Walthamstow. Running powers over the line were to be granted to the GER, who owned the main line railways in the area through which the new railway would pass. However, the £100,000 deposit required for Parliament could not be found, and on 16 January 1892 it was reported that the promoters had decided not to proceed with the Bill. The scheme remained stalled for a number of years, and by the time the deposit money was arranged, the name had changed to the London, Walthamstow and Epping Forest Railway (LW&EFR).

The LW&EFR was promoted in the 1894 session of Parliament as a tube railway running from South Place, just off Moorgate, to High Beach,[68] north of Chingford. Its promoters were Reuben Button, James Higham, Abraham Surrey Andrews, and Charles Cleverly Paine. These men had a personal interest in promoting the line: Andrews was a resident of Walthamstow, and Button and Paine resided at Stamford Hill, also on the route of the railway. During the 1890s there was often severe overcrowding on the two Great Eastern Railway (GER) branches that served the area, with the workmen's trains that ran before 7 a.m. particularly well loaded. Indeed, such was the problem that the LW&EFR Bill was supported by the GER and Midland Railway since otherwise they would have been compelled to build their own lines to relieve congestion. Higham had a history of promoting transport schemes. After unsuccessfully promoting an omnibus service, in 1864 he promoted a railway to Walthamstow alongside the Bill from the GER for a similar line. The Walthamstow, Clapton & City Railway was a failure, and the GER line was authorized.[69]

The engineers for the line were James Greathead and William Beswick Myers. The LW&EFR was to have a number of connections with main line railways, and it was seen as desirable that these railways should be able to operate their trains over the new line. The running tunnels were therefore to be of 16 feet (4.9 m) diameter. The Bill did not determine the means of locomotion on the railway. The original intention was to use oil-fired locomotives, but electricity was being considered.

From its southern terminus, situated between Liverpool Street and Moorgate stations on the Metropolitan Railway, it was to run almost due north beneath Wilson Street, Paul Street, Pitfield Street,[70] and De Beauvoir Road. The running tunnels were to be superimposed from the terminus to a point under De Beauvoir Road just north of the Regent's Canal, with just 5 feet (1.5 m) between them. This was to "economize on space": in other words, to avoid having to pay for easements below private property either side of the road. The tunnels would be constructed from steel segments, rather than the more usual cast iron.

The line would then curve to the east beneath Stamford Road. For just over one-quarter of a mile (500 m) it again headed north, below Kingsland High Street, before veering to the east again below Shacklewell Lane. At the north end of Shacklewell Lane it would continue diagonally in a north-easterly direction crossing under roads and properties to Northwold Road, near the junction with Geldeston Road. Just north of Northwold Road the line would pass into open cutting, with overbridges to allow Geldeston Road, Upper Clapton Road, and Springfield to cross. Rising to the surface, and then onto an embankment it would pass over Spring Lane on a bridge, which would be situated near to the road junction with Big Hill.

It would cross the GER Chingford and Cambridge lines just to the south of their crossing on the Walthamstow Marshes and continue parallel to Lea Bridge Road until it crossed the Tottenham & Forest Gate Railway, whereupon it would curve northwards to a point to the east of Hoe Street station in Walthamstow. From here it would continue north, parallel to the aforementioned GER lines and roughly equidistant between them. When it was due west of the westernmost extremity of Epping Forest (The Hawk Wood) it would swing north-east to its High Beach terminus at the junction of Avey Lane and Pinnergreen Lane (now called Pynest Green Lane).

The railway was to have three short branches that gave connection to the main line railways. Two were to branch on the Walthamstow Marshes, and would provide a west-facing connection to the Tottenham & Hampstead Junction Railway at South Tottenham station, and a north-west-facing connection with the GER just to the north of Copper Mill Junction. The third connection was to the Chingford branch of the GER at Hoe Street, where the link was to connect the east end of the existing station to the LW&EFR in a north-facing junction.

Over 12 acres of land on the Walthamstow Marshes were to be taken for a depôt, causing a strong objection from the Local Board.

The railway was to have a capital cost of £2.1 million, to be raised by the issuing of £10 shares. It also had the power to raise a further £700,000 through borrowing. The GER, Midland Railway, Fenchurch St & Southend Railway, and Tottenham & Forest Gate Railways made conditional agreements to subscribe to LW&EFR capital. The original sticking point — finding the Parliamentary deposit — was resolved when a group of bankers agreed to put up the sum, which had now risen to £150,000.

The Great Eastern, North London, Midland, and Tottenham & Forest Gate Railways presented petitions against the line. This was a standard procedure to protect their own interests by getting protective clauses inserted into the Bill, rather than actually wanting the Bill to fail. The LCC and the Hackney Board of Works were concerned about the effect of the tunnelling, and so presented their own petitions. Another key concern of the LCC with regard to all railway Bills was the provision of cheap tickets for workmen.

Finally there were the petitions of the East London Waterworks Company and of private landowners who would be affected by the construction and/or operation of the railway. To resolve the opposition of the GER an agreement was signed, allowing them running rights over the LW&EFR for passenger and goods trains. This agreement became the Third Schedule to the Bill. Other agreements with private landowners formed the Fourth, Fifth, and Sixth Schedules.

The Bill was considered by the Select Committee on Railway Bills, chaired by Sir John Kennaway. The main issue that came before the Committee was that of fares. A clerical error in the drafting of the Bill had led to a fare of 1d for a journey of any length being declared. The promoters had intended 1d to be the cheapest fare on a sliding scale, rising to 4d for the longest journeys. Obviously the LCC had been very happy with the original, erroneous fares, and were rather put out by the company attempting to change them. When the LCC insisted on lower fares for workmen the promoters withdrew the Bill, claiming that they would not be able to raise the capital on those terms. Realizing that it did not want to see the scheme fail, the LCC negotiated a compromise that would see the introduction of the cheap fares delayed by at least five years after operations began.

Fares were eventually fixed at 1d for single journeys of up to 4 miles, 2d up to seven miles, 3d up to ten miles, and 4d over ten miles. Return fares were to be double the single fare.

Greathead and Myers gave evidence to the Committee, and explained that, if required, electric locomotives could be used to take trains through the tube tunnel section. This was also proposed for the Great Northern & City Railway, which had been approved two years previously, and was intended to have 16-ft tunnels. The electric locomotives would be substituted for steam at a point (probably a station) just before the tunnel section commenced.

George Turner, General Manager of the Midland Railway, proposed using the railway for an unusual horseshoe-shaped service. Trains would run from Moorgate, over the City Widened Lines parallel to the Metropolitan Railway, to Kentish Town. They would then curve east onto the Tottenham & Hampstead Junction Railway to South Tottenham, before curving south onto the LW&EFR for the journey to South Place, Finsbury.

The Committee approved the preamble for the Bill on 2 May, before beginning consideration of the protective clauses. It was returned to the House of Lords at the end of July, where it was briefly considered and approved by a Committee presided over by Lord Kensington.

Less than one month later, on 25 August 1894, Royal Assent for the London, Walthamstow and Epping Forest Railway was given.

The financial situation appeared to be poor for the railway; the returns that were filed at Companies House for 1894 merely show the authority to raise £700,000 as a mortgage, with no other transactions.[71]

Another Bill was promoted in 1895, seeking to modify the authorized railway. A

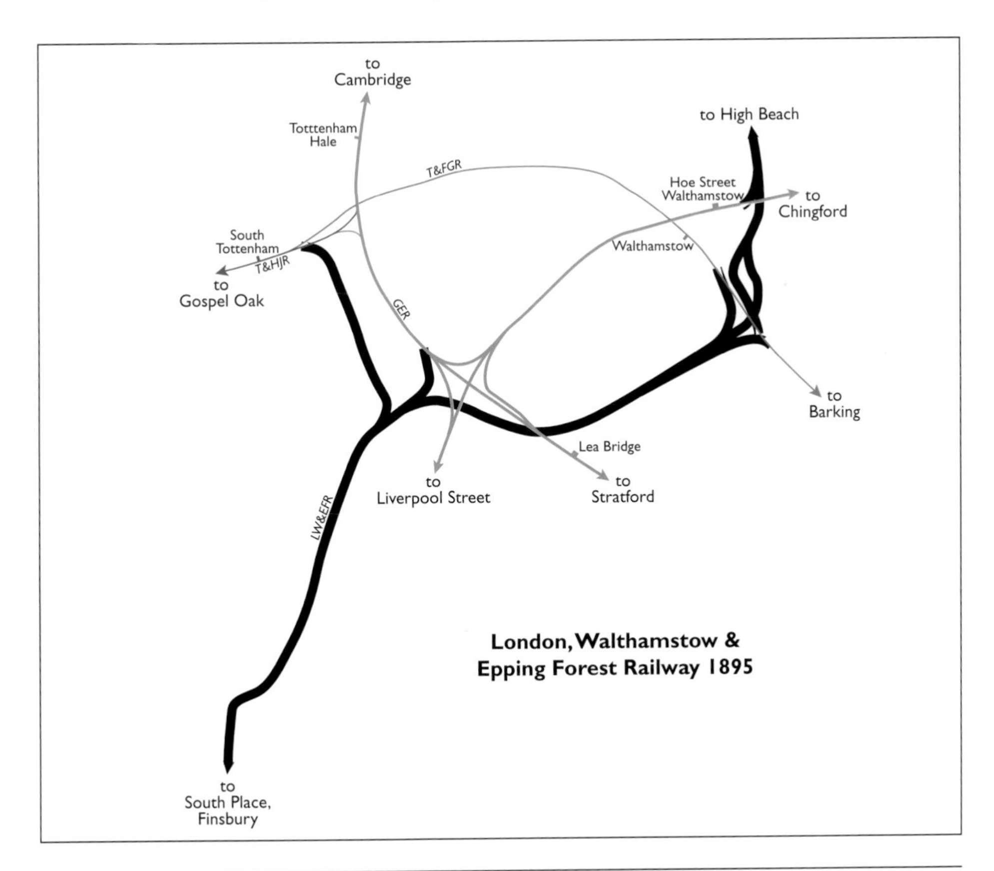

London, Walthamstow & Epping Forest Railway 1895

number of alterations were made in the Leyton area, including the addition of new spurs to the Tottenham & Forest Gate Railway. This would have provided a complex series of junctions allowing trains to be run to and from both railways in almost any direction. Royal Assent was received on 6 July.

The financial situation had still not improved the following year. Presumably in an attempt to reduce the costs, by eliminating the need to purchase rolling stock, an agreement was signed with the Midland Railway in March. The Midland was joint owner (with the GER) of the Tottenham & Hampstead Joint Railway, which was to have a connection to the LW&EFR at South Tottenham. The LW&EFR undertook to construct the railways between South Place, Finsbury, and South Tottenham in accordance with the Acts of the previous years. In return, the Midland Railway would operate between 25 and 50 trains each way per day (except for Sundays, Good Friday, Christmas Day, and Bank and Public holidays). The LW&EFR would be paid all receipts for passengers carried over their line, less 25% operating expenses. They would be responsible for staffing the stations and maintaining the line.

Three months later the promoters, through the intermediary of their solicitors, invited the LCC Chairman or Vice-Chairman to be a director of the LW&EFR, given the interest that the Council had in the benefits that the railway will bring. This was probably to give greater credibility to the company, in a further attempt to attract investors. However, the LCC thought that this would be contrary to practice, and so the invitation was not accepted.

A statement appended to the Companies House file dated 14 December certifies that the mortgage powers were never exercised.[72]

The District Gets Involved

A £1½ million plan to relieve congestion on the MDR was revealed in late 1896. The company proposed to construct a new railway parallel to, and below, its existing line between Gloucester Road and Mansion House. West of Gloucester Road the line would rise on a gradient of 1 in 42 beneath the Cromwell Road (not under the existing line) to meet and join the cut-and-cover railway. A single intermediate station would be constructed at **Charing Cross**, 63 feet (19.2 m) below the existing MDR, with access via hydraulic lifts. The tunnels would be to the east of the SER bridge to prevent interference with the bridge piles. Similar passenger facilities would be provided at **Mansion House**, located 71 feet (21.7 m) below. The provision of only two stations would also allow a much faster service to operate between the City and the west of London. Services would be operated to and from all of the western branches of the MDR.

Two intermediate shafts, each 9 feet (2.7 m) in diameter would be constructed, firstly to assist with the tunnelling, and secondly to house fans for the ventilation of the railway once it was operational.

The 12 ft 6 ins (3.81 m) diameter tunnels would cost around £1 million to construct; the remaining money was for the other equipment and rolling stock required. This would comprise ten electric locomotives and eighty carriages. Trains would be changed over from steam to electric locomotives either at Earl's Court station, or in the covered way beneath Cromwell Road. Rack railway brakes would be fitted to each carriage to prevent a runaway if the air brakes failed.

The engineer, Sir Benjamin Baker, proposed that the generating station be situated in the triangle of land between the railway tracks west of Gloucester Road, although he noted that the MDR might have other plans. Another five to ten acres of land would be required for the depôt.

Backed as it was by the MDR the plan had a smooth ride through Parliament, and was given Royal Assent on 6 August 1897.

The Brompton & Piccadilly Circus Railway

The Brompton & Piccadilly Circus Railway (B&PCR) was planned to connect South Kensington and Piccadilly Circus. From a western terminus just north of the existing **South Kensington** station, it would follow the **Brompton Road** and join **Knightsbridge** at the junction with Sloane Street. Heading east via stations at **Hyde Park Corner**, **Down Street** and **Dover Street**,[73] it would have its western terminus at Air Street, to the west of **Piccadilly Circus**. The depôt would be located at the south-east end of Yeoman's Row in Brompton, and would be reached via a short branch diverging from the main line at Cottage Place. Electricity was to be produced at the generating station at Lots Road in Chelsea. Unlike most of the other proposals, this site was distant from the railway, and the cable would have to be laid beneath the streets of Chelsea. The plans showed it running along Lots Road, Cheyne Walk, Chelsea Embankment, Church Street, King's Road, Arthur Street, Britten Street, Sydney Street, Cale Street, Leader Street, Keppel Street, Fulham Road, Alexander Square, South Street, Thurloe Square, and connecting to the end of the B&PCR at Alfred Place West.

Capital of £600,000 was sought for the scheme, and borrowing of up to £200,000 was permitted. After depositing their Bill for the 1897 session of Parliament, the company soon found that it had a useful ally in the MDR, and a rival to defeat: the City & West End Railway.

The City & West End Railway

In 1896 a tube railway proposal emerged seeking to construct an electrically operated line from Hammersmith to Cannon Street, in the City of London. This was the City & West End Railway (C&WER).[74] It was promoted by a group connected with the CLR (which was by now well under construction), and was partly in competition with the B&PCR. The engineer was Benjamin Baker.

The C&WER commenced with a large loop from the junction of Bridge Road and Black's Road in Hammersmith, curving back on itself and centred around King Street. The terminus at **Hammersmith** was to be just east of the junction of Broadway and Shepherd's Bush Road. The line continued east along Hammersmith Road, with a station sited to the west of the West London Railway station at **Addison Road**.[75] **Earl's Court Road** station was to be at the junction of that road with Hammersmith Road, although this station was a later addition to the line.

Further along Kensington High Street was to be a station at **Kensington Church**, east of the Metropolitan station of High Street Kensington. The C&WER station was to be sited on the east side of the junction with Kensington Church Street, and would have been on two levels. At this point, due to the width of the road, the tubes would have been superimposed, lying 73 feet (22.3 m) and 91 feet (27.8 m) below the surface.

Continuing along Kensington Road and Kensington Gore, the tunnels were gradually to move around to lie side-by-side by the time they reached Hyde Park Gate. The next station was to be immediately north of the **Albert Hall**. To the east of this the line moved north to run below New Ride (now called South Carriage Drive). This was to be followed by **Knightsbridge** station. Originally to be sited at the junction of Knightsbridge and Brompton Road, on the apex of the site, between the two main roads and Knightsbridge Green, this was subsequently amended to be at the junction of New Ride and Edinburgh Gate. At **Hyde Park Corner** the station would have been situated immediately to the west of St George's Hospital.[76] Again, this siting was revised eastward, positioning it north of the Wellington Arch.

The line would then pass along Piccadilly, but actually placed beneath Green Park (keeping it further from the expensive buildings on the north side of the road), with the station at **St James's** sited immediately to the east of Arlington Street. At **Piccadilly Circus** the line would pass below the proposed Baker Street & Waterloo Railway, and the station building was to be on the west side of Haymarket, at the junction with Coventry Street. Passing along beneath the latter road to Leicester Square, the railway would curve southwards to the next station at King William Street (now William IV Street), giving interchange with **Charing Cross**. Further east, after passing below the Strand, was to be a station on the south side of that road where **Wellington Street** intersected it. The line was to pass to the south of the two churches in the Strand, and at the extreme east end of the Strand would be a station on the south side, opposite the Royal Courts of Justice and **Bell Yard**.

Just prior to Ludgate Circus would be a station on the north side of Fleet Street, called **Ludgate Hill** to match the nearby main line station (although it is sometimes shown as **Ludgate Circus**). To the east of the Circus the line would make a slight southwards loop into Carter Lane, to keep as far from St Paul's Cathedral as possible. The terminus for the line was to be beneath **Cannon Street**, on the triangle of land between Queen Street, Queen Victoria Street, and Cannon Street. The line would continue beneath Cannon Street, before curving north up St Swithin's Lane, west into King William Street, and then south-west into Queen Victoria Street, forming a loop.

The power station and depôt for the railway were to be located in Fulham, between the Thames and the Fulham Palace Road. A connection to the main railway was to be constructed beneath the latter road and Queen Street, although this was not for passenger use.

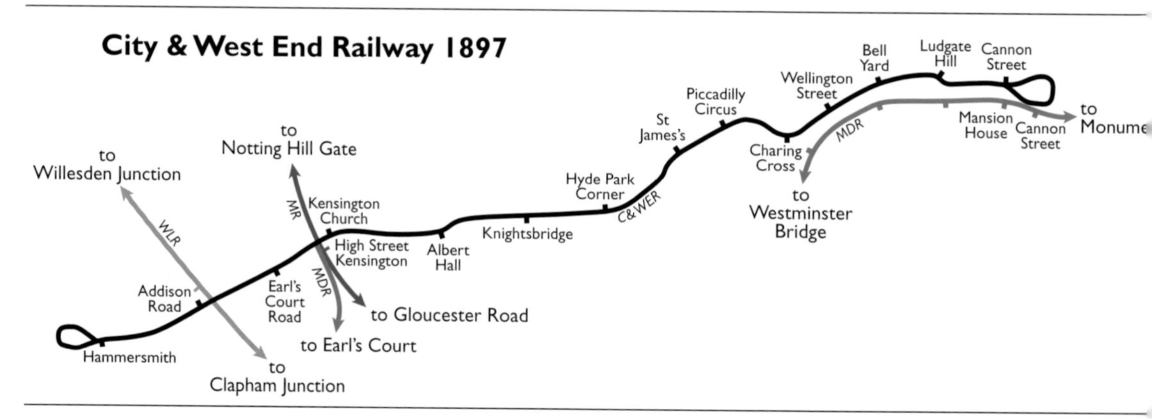

The railway was to be constructed as twin cast-iron tubes situated in the London clay. They were to have a maximum diameter of 11 ft 6 ins (3.5 m). The station tunnels would be 23 feet (7 m) in diameter. The trains would be corridor coaches (i.e., with seats either side of a central aisle) with platforms at each end from which passengers could board and alight. Carriages would be 45 feet long (13.7 m) with 48 seats. They would operate as seven-carriage trains, accommodating 336 passengers, and running every 2 or 2½ minutes during the day.

The promoters looked to raise £3,150,000 as capital for the line. For this, they were to issue 315,000 shares of £10 each. Receipts for the line, assuming the same fares and passenger numbers as for the parallel Metropolitan District Railway (MDR), were estimated at £202,421 per annum. With projected running costs of £152,000 (based on figures from the Central London Railway – not yet in operation), plus interest and dividend payments of £199,500, this would leave the railway company almost £150,000 in the red.

Unsurprisingly, given the route, the MDR submitted a petition against the C&WER. The petition noted that it ran between the same points as the MDR, but at a deeper level, making it less practical. In almost the next breath, the MDR then noted that the deep-level line that they proposed would serve the public better. The MDR looked upon the B&PCR scheme with more favour, and devoted its energies to stopping the C&WER. Its Counsel before the House of Commons Committee considering the Bills emphasized the poor financial outlook for the line, noting that the little potential traffic that they could foresee would be better served by both lines of the MDR, the B&PCR, and buses. They rounded off by claiming that the current promoters should not be given the line because "they are a syndicate and their financial methods disqualify them".

The C&WER had collected figures for traffic along the route of the railway to demonstrate the need for the line. Strangely, they were collected for the company by the Metropolitan Police, apparently free of charge: the policemen involved attended Parliament to give evidence. This followed the police performing the same actions for the promoters of the LCR in 1889, and the CLR in 1890.

The residents of Hammersmith and Fulham were naturally concerned about the well-being of their property, as well as the value, and submitted their own petition. This also showed concern as to potential damage to neighbouring cellars, and interference with proposed utility subways below the streets. An interesting corollary to this concerns the Albert Hall. Whilst giving his evidence in favour of the line, Baker claimed that the Albert Hall authorities were anxious to have a station in the basement of the hall. He could not see how this could be done without causing the public a great deal of inconvenience, and hence the station site was just to the west.

The LCC petition wanted protection for its sewers and subways, the setting back of buildings from the building line to allow for future street widening, clauses to give it the right of approval for the stations and cheap workmen's fares. Their proposal for these fares was 1d single, and 1½d return.

With regard to the workmen's fares, the Parliamentary Agent for the LCC, together with their Chief Engineer, Sir Alexander Binnie, met the C&WER representatives on several occasions. Together they managed to resolve the clauses that the LCC wished to be included. Fares for workmen's trains were to be 1d single and 2d return.

On 8 April 1897 the Commons Committee rejected the C&WER Bill, and the Bill for the B&PCR was passed, leading to Royal Assent on 6 August, the same day as the deep-level MDR scheme. The MDR's support had been very useful to the B&PCR, as well as removing the threat to the existing line. Alfred Powell, the General Manager of the MDR, argued a better case, noting that the deep level line removed any need for the C&WER, and it would operate a faster service. He also suggested that the C&WER should have waited until the CLR had opened.

To conclude the story of the C&WER, a letter was sent from the company to the Chief Commissioner of the Metropolitan Police after the rejection of the Bill, asking for permission to pay a half-guinea to each of the five policemen who had given evidence for each day that they had attended.[77]

Final Schemes of the 1890s

The City & Brixton Railway

We now turn to the last five tube railways promoted in the 1890s. The City & Brixton Railway (C&BR), examined by Parliament in 1898, was unusual in that it proposed taking over the soon-to-be-abandoned tunnels of the C&SLR. For the latter's extension to Moorgate and Islington, junctions were to be made where the new tunnels joined the old. These were sited beneath Borough High Street at the junction with Tabard Street for the up (or northbound) line, and about 100 metres further north, outside Halfmoon Yard, for the down line.

The C&BR proposed joining their tunnels to the abandoned sections where the High Street met Talbot Yard, some 500 metres further north. This would allow interconnection to remain with the C&SLR without interference with the regular traffic.

On the original line from **Bank** (as King William Street was shown),[78] a new station at **London Bridge** would be created on the original section of C&SLR, just north of the junction with the new tunnels. This would allow for the interchange that was originally considered in the planning of the C&SLR, and would be achieved by widening the existing tunnels under Borough High Street between the junction with Southwark Street and the SER bridge.

The new tunnels of the C&BR would diverge from those of the C&SLR and immediately separate from each other, with the southbound tunnel below that of the C&SLR, and the northbound tunnel above. This configuration was retained until south of Borough C&SLR station – but no C&BR station was to be provided here. The line would then diverge from that of the C&SLR, curving east to **St George's Cross**, by which point the tunnels would have just 10 feet (3.1 m) of vertical separation. The surface building would be sited on the north-west side of St George's Circus (the other name for this location), between Blackfriars and Waterloo Roads.

It would then have followed the **Lambeth Road**, with a station at the south-east corner of the junction with Kennington Road, in the grounds of the Bethlehem Royal Hospital (now the Imperial War Museum). Following the latter road it would run, via a station at **Kennington Cross** (at the junction with Kennington Lane), to **Oval**, where it would meet the C&SLR again. A subway was to be constructed at low level beneath Kennington Park and Brixton Roads to allow passenger interchange between the two tube railways there. This would be accessed via a flight of stairs up from the

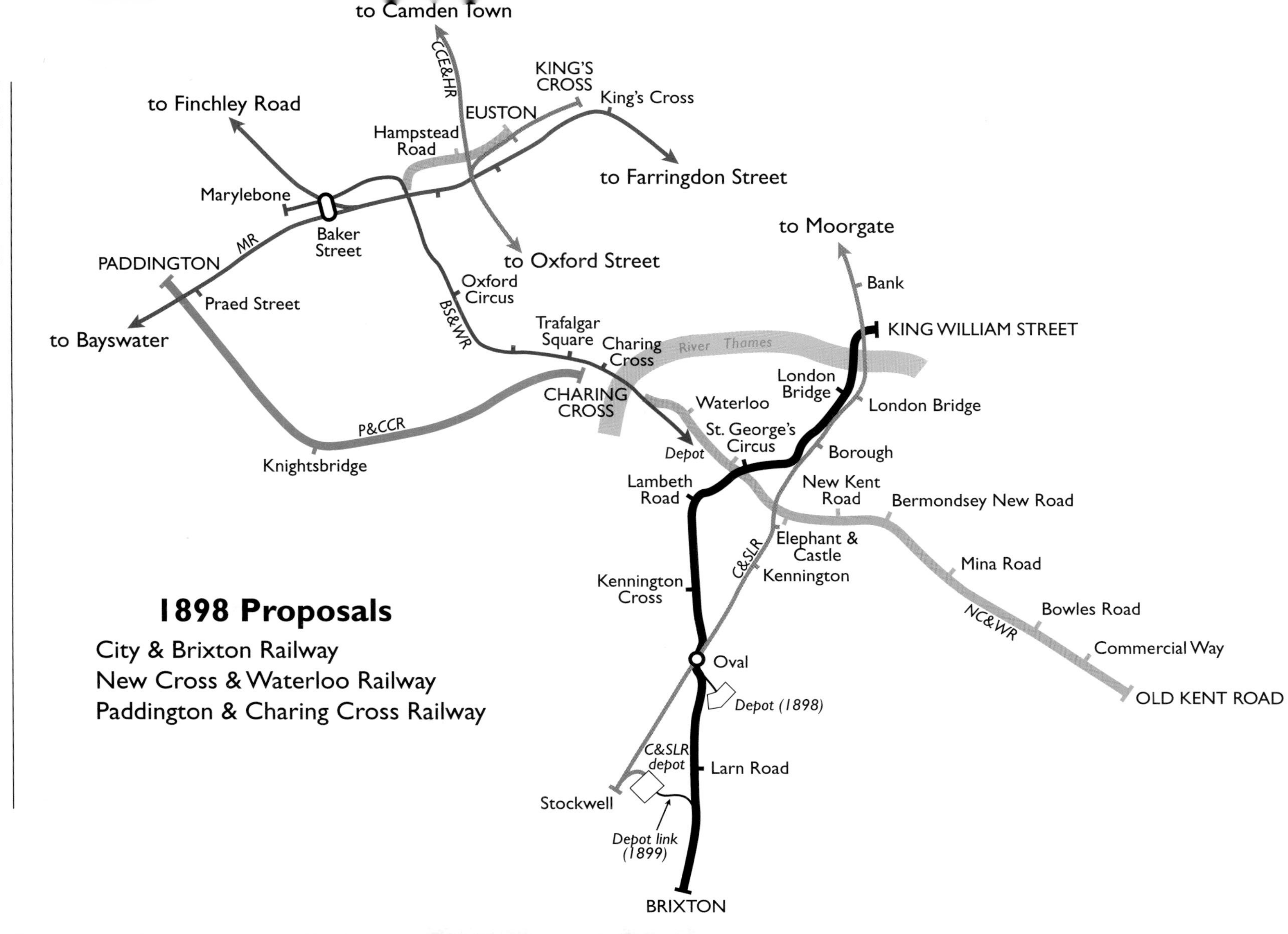
to Camden Town
CCE&HR
KING'S CROSS
King's Cross
to Finchley Road
EUSTON
Hampstead Road
to Farringdon Street
Marylebone
Baker Street
MR
PADDINGTON
to Oxford Street
to Moorgate
Bank
Oxford Circus
Praed Street
to Bayswater
BS&WR
KING WILLIAM STREET
Trafalgar Square
Charing Cross
River Thames
London Bridge
CHARING CROSS
Waterloo
London Bridge
P&CCR
St. George's Circus
Depot
Borough
Knightsbridge
Lambeth Road
New Kent Road
Bermondsey New Road
Elephant & Castle
C&SLR
Kennington
Mina Road
Kennington Cross
Bowles Road
NC&WR
1898 Proposals
City & Brixton Railway
New Cross & Waterloo Railway
Paddington & Charing Cross Railway
Commercial Way
Oval
Depot (1898)
OLD KENT ROAD
C&SLR depot
Larn Road
Stockwell
Depot link (1899)
BRIXTON

C&SLR platforms 49 feet (15 m) below the street, and would run due east up a shallow incline. A flight of stairs then descended to the north end of the C&BR platforms located 41 feet (12.5 m) under the end of Brixton Road and adjacent to Kennington Park. Proceeding south under Brixton Road, there would be one intermediate station at **Lorn Road**, prior to the terminus at **Brixton**. The terminal station would have entrances on the east side of the road, to the north and south of the two elevated main line tracks there, and the running tunnels would actually terminate below the junction of Brixton Hill and Effra Road.

The depôt was to be located on both sides of Camberwell New Road, to the east of the Brixton Road, and extending as far south as Cranmer Road. Access to the depôt would be via an inclined tunnel, which curved north to join the main running tunnels.

The line appeared to have a number of factors in its favour: its engineers were the renowned Benjamin Baker, David Hay, and Basil Mott; it had a pre-built city terminus, which the C&SLR had agreed to sell; and it was connected with the first and only working tube railway, not least by having two directors in common. However, there were some notable problems for it to deal with. Firstly, the King William Street terminus was being abandoned because of the difficulties of operating it. With its steep, sharply-curved approach tunnels it was a serious bottleneck for the C&SLR. Unless the tunnels were widened, it would restrict the C&BR to the same diminutive train sizes as its predecessor, a size that most engineers had already decided was too small. Secondly, the line would effectively duplicate much of the C&SLR. Whilst there was overcrowding on the C&SLR, was this really the best way to tackle the problem?

Capital of £1.2 million was required for the line, with an additional £400,000 of borrowing powers. The construction estimate was £818,040, of which £786,415 was for the new tunnelling, £24,750 was for creating the station tunnels at London Bridge, and the remaining £6,900 was to construct the subway at Oval.

The plans of the C&BR rapidly changed. The C&SLR decided not to sell King William Street and the approach tunnels, but instead to lease them to the C&BR for £4,000 per annum until the new railway was completed. It would then lease the entire new section of C&BR and operate the trains, pay all costs, and keep all revenue. In return, the C&BR would be paid rent of £20,000 in the first year, £21,000 the second year, and so on until the sixth year; thereafter the annual lease would be £25,000. The lease was to run for 999 years. All of this was detailed in the second schedule to the C&BR Bill, dated 16 March 1898.

The following year, more changes were made by another C&BR Act. A new 553-yard (506 m) long single tunnel was to be made, curving north and then west from the C&BR below Ingleton Road (immediately south of the station at Lorn Road) to the C&SLR depôt at Stockwell.[79] An access tunnel with an incline of 1 in 6 would rise to the south end of the depôt, adjacent to the carriage shed. It seems likely, although no definite statement can be found, that the depôt site at Camberwell was to be abandoned, helping to reduce the costs of the railway. Electrical power to the line would come from the C&SLR generating station, sited at Stockwell depôt.

The lease was also changed, and would charge the C&SLR the sum of £25,600 per annum for the same 999-year period. Whilst the removal of the depôt site would have reduced the costs of constructing the line, it still proved impossible to raise the necessary capital, and the scheme remained dormant, like so many others.

The Great Northern & Strand Railway

The Great Northern & Strand Railway was born from the desire of the Great Northern Railway to reduce the congestion at their King's Cross terminal. They reasoned that an underground railway, taking suburban passengers from Wood Green to Holborn, would help to ease the main line traffic. They had previously supported the Great Northern & City Railway (*q.v.*), but delays to the start of construction led to a falling out between the two sides, and instead the GNR transferred its tacit support to the GN&SR. This was independent of the main line company, but proposed to follow its route between Wood Green and King's Cross, before cutting south to terminate at Stanhope Street, north of the Strand. The entire route would be in tunnel, except for a connection with the GNR at Wood Green.

On the northern section, stations would be sited at the same locations as those on the main line: **Wood Green**, **Hornsey**, **Harringay**, and **Finsbury Park**. At the last location the line moved out to the east of the existing tracks, with the station tunnels below Station Road (now Station Place). The next stations south were to be at **Holloway** (for interchange with the now-closed Holloway & Caledonian Road station) and **York Road**. A descent at 1 in 60 would lead into the station at **King's Cross**, under the east side of the main line station of the same name.

Unusually for a tube railway the line would cut across the street pattern as it continued south. It would follow along Marchmont Street to **Russell Square** station, then curve slightly to reach Southampton Row. At the south end of this street would be a station at **Holborn**. The final section of the line ran beneath the maze of slum streets to terminate on the corner of Stanhope and Holles Streets with a station called **Strand**.

When the London County Council decided to clear the slums between Holborn and the Strand by creating new showpiece streets, the GN&SR promoters revised the southern part of their route, instead terminating at the junction of Kingsway and Aldwych, the two main streets that were to be created. Protection was given to the LCC's new roads by a clause that was added to the Bill. This prevented the railway being constructed between Holborn and Strand until Kingsway was constructed, and LCC consent would also be required.

Royal Assent was granted for the GN&SR on 1 August 1899; as with so many other tube railway schemes, raising the finance proved to be very difficult, and construction was delayed until the 1900s, by which time its plans would have altered significantly.

The New Cross & Waterloo Railway

The NC&WR was intended as an extension of the BS&WR, on which construction had still not yet started. It was to be a short tube railway of around 3.1 miles (5.1 km), extending the BS&WR at the south and providing a new branch in the north.

The BS&WR tunnels were to terminate just south-east of the main line station at Waterloo. The NC&WR intercepted them in a junction north of the station where they crossed under Belvedere Road. The platforms at **Waterloo** on the new route were to be under Waterloo Road at the junction with Sandell Street. A surface station was to be built at this location as well. The line would continue to **St George's Circus**, with the station on the corner between Lambeth Road and Westminster Bridge Road. Continuing in the same direction London Road would be followed to **Elephant and Castle**. The station here would connect with both the C&SLR station (being sited between it and the actual Elephant & Castle Inn) and the LC&DR station. The running tunnels would pass beneath those of the C&SLR.

Curving eastwards the line would follow the route of the **New Kent Road**, the station buildings being sited half way along its length at Munton Road. At the junction with the Old Kent Road and **Bermondsey New Road** the station would be located in the apex between the Old and New Kent Roads. The line would then pass along under the Old Kent Road to **Mina Road**, which was also one of two sites for the railway's electricity generating station. However, the more likely site was adjacent to the next station, at **Bowles Road**, on the north side of the Surrey Canal, and the south-west side of the Old Kent Road, where plentiful water would be available from the canal.

The penultimate station on the southern part of the railway would be at **Commercial Road** (now Commercial Way), with the buildings on the north-east side of the road. The line would continue a short distance south-east to its terminus at **Old Kent Road**, adjacent to the LB&SCR station.

Returning to Waterloo station, the BS&WR tunnels planned under the main line station would be retained for access to the depôt at the south end of the line, located to the north of Lower Marsh. Another connection to the depôt was proposed by the NC&WR, leading southwards to join the main route in the vicinity of Morley Street.

The northern part of the line diverged from the BS&WR under the Marylebone Road, and immediately curved eastwards under Regent's Park. At the eastern edge of the Park it adopted the route of Longford and Drummond Streets, with a station provided at the junction of the latter with the **Hampstead Road**. It continued eastwards beneath the Euston branch of the CCE&HR to terminate in platforms on the western side of Seymour Street (now Eversholt Street), for interchange with **Euston** main line station.[80]

The tunnels were to be on average 60 feet (18.3 m) below the surface. It can be assumed that the means of locomotion would be the same as the BS&WR, and from the information deposited with Parliament this was taken as being electricity.

The promoters were given as James Heath MP, Robert Read, and Thomas Soden, with R. M. Parkinson listed as the engineer. The capital for the 3 miles 3 furlongs 2 chains (5 km) of 12-ft diameter tube railway was set at £975,000; borrowing powers of £325,000 were given. Two classes of accommodation were to be provided on the trains, with 1st class fares being 2d per mile (or part), and half this for 2nd class. Agreements were to be made with the LSWR, the BS&WR, and the W&CR, presumably to facilitate passenger interchange and through running (with the BS&WR) at Waterloo.

The line impressed *The Railway News*, which described it as being "of considerable importance . . . it should secure a large portion of the traffic now falling to the tramway company whose lines run along the Old Kent Road to Waterloo".[81]

Although the promoters contacted property owners who would be affected by the line, it was not listed in the summary of 1898 Railway Bills published in *The Railway News*. Although deposited with Parliament it made no headway at all in the 1898 session, and became another London tube railway 'has-been'.

The Paddington & Charing Cross Railway

The Paddington & Charing Cross Railway appeared very briefly at the beginning of 1898. It commenced on the south-west side of Paddington station, taking in a large block of land from the edge of the main line station to Charles Mews (now Eastbourne Mews), and extending from Craven Road in the south to Bishops Road (today's Bishops Bridge Road) in the north. It is likely that a surface depôt would have been constructed here, with a track connection to the GWR. The station on the P&CCR at **Paddington** was to have been in the vicinity of Charles Street (now Chilworth Street), with a subway sloping from the platforms to connect with the existing subway that crossed under the main line station platforms.

A tunnel at a gradient of 1 in 8 would connect the surface site to the running tunnels north of the station. It seems unlikely, therefore, that a running connection for passenger trains was to be operated.

South of the station the tunnels would pass beneath Spring Street and Sussex Square to reach Hyde Park. This would be crossed in a south-easterly direction to the intermediate station at **Knightsbridge**. A subway would link the platforms with the station, which was to be sited on the corner between Knightsbridge and Brompton Road.

Continuing east to Hyde Park Corner the line would carry straight on under Green Park to Cleveland Row and Pall Mall, before curving south-east under Trafalgar Square to arrive at **Charing Cross** station, with the platforms underneath Craven Street, on the south-west side of the main line station. The total length was 3 miles 7.75 chains (a fraction under 5 km).

The railway was to be either cable-hauled or electrically-powered. The tunnels were to be 16 feet (4.9 m) in diameter, allowing for the passage of main-line rolling stock, and adding considerably to the costs of construction, which was estimated at £1,225,734. The proposed capital was £1.5 million, plus additional borrowing powers of £500,000. A report in *The Railway News* also stated that agreements were to be entered into with the GWR and SER.

In January 1898 when the Bill was considered for the very first time by Parliament, the promoters failed to appear. As such, without support, the scheme was declared "dead" on 21 January.

The North West London Railway

Passing in a straight line across London, the North West London Railway (NWLR) was to connect Marble Arch with Cricklewood. Promoted in 1899, its engineers were Benjamin Baker, Sir Douglas Fox, and Francis Fox. Most of its route (apart from the north end) was identical with that of the Edgware Road & Victoria Railway from six years earlier. The costs were 25% higher though, with capital of £1.5 million, plus borrowing of £500,000 being sought.

(Charles) Douglas Fox (14 May 1840 – 13 November 1921)

Fox was born in Smethwick, one of the sons of Sir Charles Fox. Sir Charles was also a railway engineer, whose firm worked on the London to Birmingham Railway, erected the Crystal Palace, and helped to design the Waterloo & Whitehall Railway, a tube railway proposal of 1865 that was only partially built.

Douglas Fox studied at King's College, London, where he later became a fellow. In 1863 he married Mary Wright, with whom he had one son and four daughters.

He was knighted in 1886.

He was President of the Institute of Civil Engineers, a member of the Institutes of Mechanical Engineers and Electrical Engineers, and an honorary member of the American Institutions of Civil and Mechanical Engineers.

His first experience with electric traction was gained on the Liverpool Overhead Railway, which opened to the public on 6 March 1893. He was the engineer for the superbly constructed Great Central Railway, which included the Catesby and Marylebone Tunnels. He was also engineer to the CCE&HR, and the GN&CR.

Fox had given evidence against the CLR on behalf of property owners, including the Royal Exchange, the Mercer's Hall, and Bow Church, and so had experience of both sides of the tunnelling arguments.

He was a director of the Electric Construction Company from its beginnings in May 1889, a company that manufactured equipment for a number of tramways and railways. This included the re-equipping of the C&SLR power station with new electrical equipment in 1900, when it was extended from its original city terminus to a new station at Moorgate.

Outside his engineering interests, he was also a Justice of the Peace, and deputy director of the Improved Industrial Dwellings Company, founded by Sir Sydney Waterlow for improving the housing of the working classes.

At **Marble Arch** the line was to start 103 feet (31.4 m) beneath the Edgware Road. A 6¾-chain (136 m) subway at low level was to connect the southern end of the NWLR platforms to the CLR platforms. It would pass beneath the CLR, and a flight of stairs would connect to a passage between the two CLR platforms. The next station at **Harrow Road** would have access at the junction between Praed Street and Edgware Road, and also further north at the corner of Harrow Road. Interchange with the MR station at Edgware Road was considered at this station.

Further north a station would be on the western corner of the junction of **Maida Vale** and Sutherland Avenue. Another station, called **Kilburn**, would be sited opposite Belsize Road, with interchange to Kilburn & Maida Vale LNWR station across the road.[82]

Interchange with the North London Railway would be afforded at **Brondesbury**, where station access would be arranged both sides of the main line station. The northern access would also facilitate connections with the MR at Kilburn station, although this access would be effected via the street.

An almost continuous gradient of 1 in 100 uphill as the line passed north had nearly halved the depth to just 53 feet (16.2 m). However, the tunnels would get deeper again as the surface gradient increased over Shoot Up Hill, with the next station, opposite Minster Road, at a depth of 82 feet (25.0 m), provisionally called **West End**. The hill rapidly levelled off, bringing the tunnels to just 38 feet (11.6 m) below the road at the final station on the line, called **Cricklewood.**[83]

The line continued north for a short distance before narrowing to a single tunnel. This rose towards the surface, curving west, to the main depôt site for the railway, located immediately to the south of the Midland Railway Dudden Hill line. Sidings and car sheds would probably have been located at this site; some records also mention a generating station.

Another depôt site was immediately north of the MR at Kilburn, bordered by the railway to the south, Mapesbury Road to the west, Dartmouth Road to the north, and Exeter Road to the east. A single line tunnel would rise from a junction with the line under the latter road on a 1 in 17 gradient. Records indicate that a generating station would be located on this site. Willesden Urban District Council, whilst not objecting generally to the Bill, were against the use of the Dartmouth Road site and the Exeter Road tunnel.

The LCC wanted Edgware Road to be widened near to the stations, and they sought to add a clause that would force the railway to set back the line of the buildings wherever they purchased them for stations. This would, they claimed, help alleviate congestion near to the new premises.

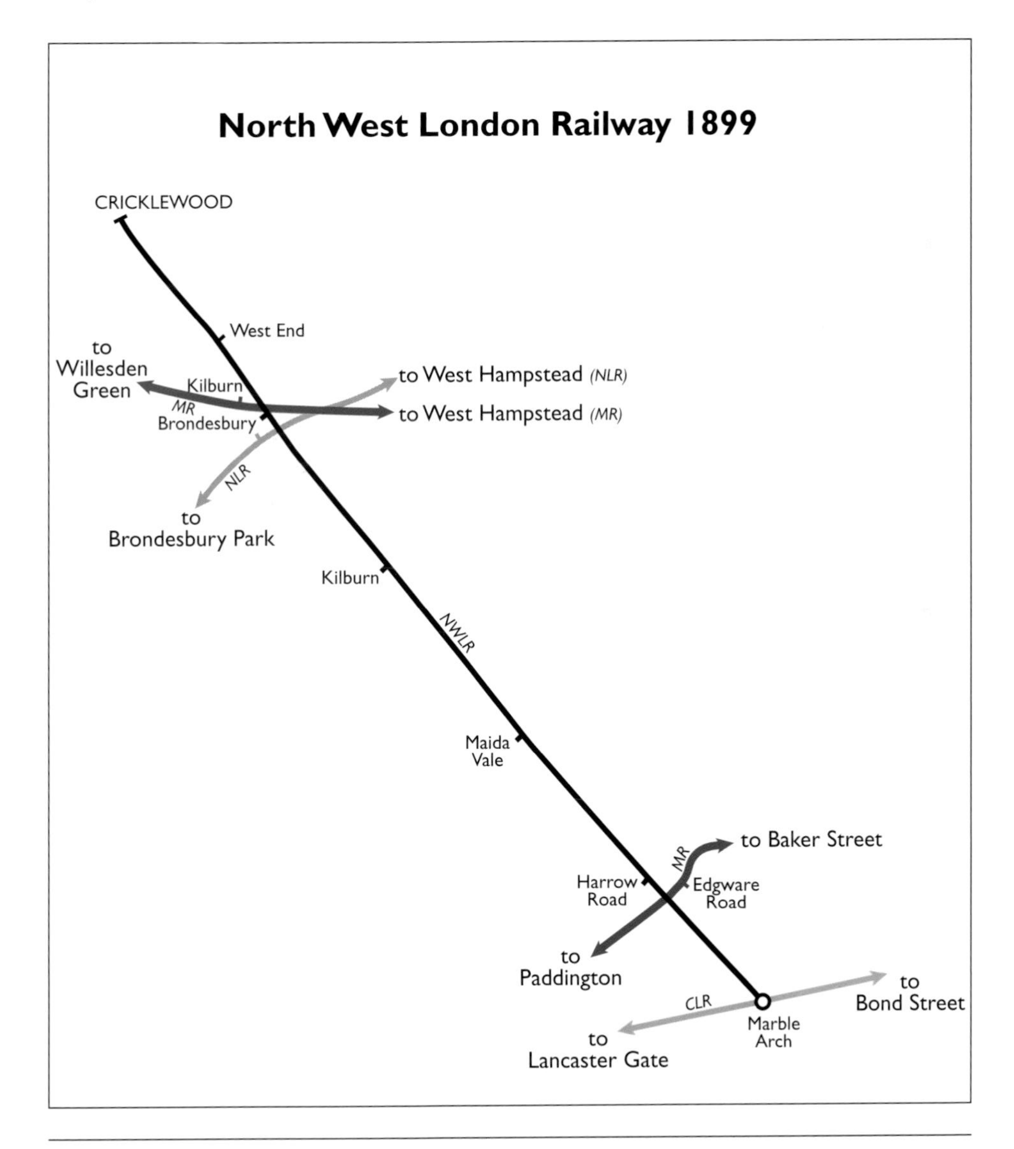

The running tunnels were to be slightly larger than had previously been suggested for tube railways (excepting the GN&CR), being 12 ft 6 ins (3.8 m) in diameter. Stations would have a maximum diameter of 30 feet (9.1 m).

It was estimated that 3 million passengers would be carried per year. Each train would carry 350 people, and large lifts at each station would have a total capacity of 250. The journey time end to end would be roughly 20 minutes.

Regular fares on the railway were to be 3d per mile 1st class, 2d per mile 2nd class, and 1d per mile 3rd class. Workmen's fares on the railway were to be 2½d return, and 1½d single. The LCC wanted them to be lower, but the Committee permitted the company's proposal after Sir Henry Oakley, Chairman of the CLR, gave support. The promoters explained carefully that if the tickets were any cheaper then they would not be able to make the line pay. However, the Committee did allow the workmen's tickets to be valid until 8.00 a.m., half an hour later than the promoters had planned. This was the only matter contested by the promoters, and the line was granted Royal Assent on 9 August after a remarkably smooth passage through Parliament.

Tubes for Other Towns

London was not the only place in Britain for which tube railways were proposed. Following unsuccessful Bills in 1887 and 1888, the Glasgow Subway was finally approved by Parliament in 1890, and opened in 1896.[84]

A syndicate was formed in 1896 for building a tube railway in Manchester. Two years later, the Brighton Underground railway was promoted. It was to be 5 furlongs 7.25 chains (1.15 km) long, and was to connect from the LB&SCR station to King's Road, with openings under the parade communicating directly with the beach. The capital was to be £120,000, with borrowing of £40,000. Very early on in the Parliamentary session the Bill was withdrawn by its promoters, and disappeared.

Tube railways for Manchester were proposed again in 1902 and 1903, but neither Bill was successful. The proposal for 1902 was interesting in that the line was to be circular, like the Glasgow Subway, with a length of 2 miles 45 chains (4.1 km).

Of course, the passing of a Bill does not necessarily mean that the construction of the railway will follow shortly, and the NWLR was no exception. The 19th century was not an easy time for raising money. The only proven tube railway was the C&SLR, which was not providing a spectacular return for its investors, and many people preferred to wait for the CLR to open before they would contemplate putting up any capital. The second South African (Boer) War, which started in late 1899, unsettled the money markets, and was stated to be the principal cause of the railway being postponed.[85]

The Cricklewood, Kilburn & Victoria Railway

It appears that the promoters of the NWLR were not alone in seeking to build a railway along the Edgware Road alignment. The Cricklewood, Kilburn and Victoria Railway Construction Syndicate Ltd was incorporated on 5 August 1898 for the purposes of building a similar railway, but continuing south to Victoria. They were evidently too late, as on 13 November 1899 the company solicitors wrote to the Companies Registration Office, informing them that the company did not intend to carry on business. They did not know when it had suspended operations "as it has never commenced to carry out the object for which it was formed". The reason for the decision was that "other parties promoted and carried a Bill though Parliament last session for the purpose of making a railway over a portion of the line contemplated by the Company" – in other words the NWLR promoters had stolen their thunder.[86] The company was dissolved on 12 April 1901.

Changes to Earlier Plans

A number of the railways authorized earlier in the 1890s but yet to start construction (or even raise the necessary finances) submitted amendments between 1897 and 1900. Sometimes these were minor changes to improve a small part of the scheme; other Bills were for major alterations to the route of the railway.

The Great Northern & City Railway

In 1897, the GN&CR was requesting a further extension of time in order to raise the capital and start construction. Relations with the GNR were, by now, very strained, and hence it was no surprise when the main line company petitioned against the extension of time on the grounds that the GN&CR were financially weak, and there was little prospect of the line being built. They stated that Finsbury Park was in urgent need of rearrangement, but this could not proceed until they knew what was going to happen with the underground railway.

The officers of the GNR finally contacted the GN&CR and offered not to object to the Bill if the 1894 agreement between the two companies guaranteeing numbers of trains, minimum revenue, etc., was cancelled. An appropriate clause was added to the Bill, and it received the Royal Assent on 6 August 1897.

The London, Walthamstow & Epping Forest Railway is Abandoned – Almost

The promoters of the LW&EFR put forward two Bills in 1897: one for an extension of time, and the other for the complete abandoning of the scheme. The provisions for workmen's fares imposed by the LCC had reduced the attractiveness of the railway, and it was still struggling to raise the necessary capital.

By the end of January 1897 the promoters decided to withdraw the extension of time Bill, and concentrate on the abandonment Bill. This proceeded through Parliament well, without requiring amendment. It had passed all of the House of Commons stages, and had received two readings in the House of Lords, when it was suddenly withdrawn – this was almost certainly because the railway proposal had been taken over by a new promoter.

The Central London Railway

The station at Davies Street (renamed **Bond Street** before opening) was causing problems for the promoters of the CLR. Getting the required land was proving troublesome, and so they introduced a Bill in 1897 for resiting the station slightly. Negotiations with the nearby landowners continued, and the situation was eventually resolved as originally intended. The Bill was therefore withdrawn in early June.

The Baker Street & Waterloo Railway

Construction work had actually started on the BS&WR in June 1898. Staging had been erected in the Thames near to the Hungerford Bridge, and the tunnels were being excavated both north and south. At the same time, they were looking to make three route changes in the Bill for the 1899 session of Parliament, which would collectively add 2 miles 29 chains (3.8 km) to its length. The smallest was at the south end, abandoning the last section of line running south-east under Waterloo station, and instead curving it to the south to terminate under Addington Street.

At the other end of the railway the route was extended beyond the station at Marylebone to run beneath Great James Street[87] and Bell Street to a station at **Edgware Road,** 52 ft 6 ins (16 m) below Corlett Street. The line then curved to the south to run below the Paddington Basin of the Grand Junction Canal. The BS&WR's **Paddington** station would be located 27 ft 3 ins (8.3 m) under the canal itself. From here the running tunnels would curve north-west between the side of the main line station and the canal, before merging into a single tunnel, passing beneath the main branch of the canal, and swinging north-east. This tunnel would rise to the surface on the north side of Blomfield Road, where a depôt would be located. A pedestrian subway would run from the tube station to the end of an existing subway beneath the western platforms of the main line station. A new power station would also be provided at Paddington.

The third, and arguably most interesting, part of the Bill was for a branch from Regent's Park to Euston looking similar to that proposed by the New Cross & Waterloo Railway in the previous year. The branch was to diverge just north of the former station, and curve in a wide loop under the Park to exit near to **Cumberland Gate** on the east side. A station would be sited just inside the Park, to the west of the Outer Circle, with the platform tunnels at split level 70 feet and 81 ft 3 ins deep (21.4 and 24.8 m). Continuing west the line would run beneath Cumberland Street, Cumberland Market, and Edward Street, as well as the proposed Charing Cross, Euston & Hampstead Railway tunnels, with **Euston** station tunnels beneath Cardington Street to the west of the main line station, 46½ feet (14.2 m) deep. Overrun tunnels allowing trains to be reversed or stabled would continue east as far as Seymour Street.[88]

A new subway would be constructed at Trafalgar Square, linking the south-east corner of the main island in the Square with the corner of Charing Cross and Northumberland Avenue, and then south-west to the far side of Charing Cross (near to where Admiralty Arch was subsequently built). Stairs would connect this subway to street level, as well as to the BS&WR booking hall.

The MR, who saw their route along the north side of the Inner Circle threatened, provided fierce opposition to the Bill, and as a result of this the northern extensions were rejected by Parliament. The remaining part of the Bill (for the Trafalgar Square subway and the deviation at Waterloo) received Royal Assent on 1 August.

In 1900 the BS&WR returned with a less extensive Bill. This was for two modest extensions, one at each end of the line. At the north end, they again proposed an extension to Bishop's Road, at **Paddington**. A long passenger subway below Eastbourne Terrace would connect to the main-line station. This was less than ideal, but would allow the line to be extended further west: Royal Oak and Willesden were mooted as a possible route.

At the south, the line was to be extended from Waterloo to **Elephant & Castle**, with a low-level passenger subway connecting to the C&SLR platforms. A spur from the main line at Lambeth would lead to a site that had been purchased adjacent to St George's Circus, which was to be used for the depôt and power station.

Although the MR put up more strong opposition to the plans, the BS&WR emerged as the victor this year, Royal Assent being granted on 6 August.

The Brompton & Piccadilly Circus Railway

Towards the end of 1898 the authorized but financially impoverished B&PCR was purchased by the MDR, and most of the board was replaced by MDR men. An eastward extension to Long Acre was proposed in their Bill of 1899. From the original terminus at Air Street, Piccadilly, the line would run south under **Piccadilly Circus**, with the station buildings on the site of today's Trocadero Centre. Passing east under Coventry Street and **Cranbourn Street**,[89] the platforms would be located beneath the latter road to the east of Charing Cross Road. The tunnels would end below the junction of Cranbourn Street, Long Acre, and St Martin's Lane.

At the western end of the original railway two short tunnels were added below Thurloe Square, curving in an S-shape to link the B&PCR to the authorized deep level line of the MDR below South Kensington station. A subway from Alfred Place West (the B&PCR station) to the southerly platform of South Kensington MDR station was also added to improve the interchange for passengers.

After due consideration by Parliament the Long Acre extension was rejected, but the connection with the MDR was accepted, as well as a number of additional measures allowing the MDR to inject up to £200,000 of capital into the B&PCR. An increase in capital of £533,000 was permitted to pay for the MDR link, as well as for the construction of the MDR deep level line between South Kensington and Earl's Court, which powers were transferred in the same Bill. Royal Assent was received on 9 August 1899. In the following year the railway promoted a Bill for an extension of time. This was subsequently withdrawn, and promoted instead via the MDR's Bill of 1900. The latter Bill also contained provisions for making agreements with the MR and B&PCR for electrification.

The Charing Cross, Euston & Hampstead Railway

The south end of the CCE&HR was altered by their Act of 1898. Instead of terminating outside the Garrick Theatre in Charing Cross Road, the route was extended south. Curving around the north and west sides of the church of St Martin-in-the-Fields, it terminated at 23 Craven Street. This would allow a new station to be added giving passengers the ability to transfer to and from the South East Railway at **Charing Cross**. Parliamentary approval was given on 24 July 1898; this Act also extended the time permitted for the construction of the line (as had an Act of 3 June 1897).

A large change was made to the CCE&HR in their 1899 Bill. The short branch to Euston and St Pancras was diverted north up Eversholt Street, rejoining the route authorized in 1893 at Mornington Crescent (although the station of that name was not added to the plans until 1904). The line towards St Pancras was dropped, as was the original section of main line under the Hampstead Road between Euston Road and Mornington Crescent.

A new branch was added between Camden Town and **Kentish Town**, following the Kentish Town Road, with an intermediate station at **Castle Road**.[90] Beyond the terminus it rose to the surface up a gradient of 1 in 9.5, curving to the east. Sidings and a power station would be located to the south of the main line at Kentish Town.

On 9 August 1899 Royal Assent was received; this did not affect the impecunious state of the company, and construction was still a distant dream. Their 1900 Act of 25 May proved this; it was for an extension of the time permitted to build the line.

The City & South London Railway

The additional sidings constructed by the C&SLR at Stockwell were evidently useful, as a Bill of 1898 added siding tunnels 7.5 chains (150 m) long to the south of Clapham Common station, beneath Clapham Common South Side. These would replace the earlier sidings, which were being extended as the main line to Clapham.

The 1898 Bill also extended the time allowed for the construction of the Islington extension, which was opened as far as Moorgate on 25 February 1900. This was the only section of the C&SLR constructed in 11 ft 6 ins (3.5 m) diameter running tunnels, allegedly to improve ventilation; all subsequent work (including the line to Angel, opened on 17 November 1902) used their traditional diameter of 10 ft 6 ins (3.2 m).[91]

The station at Angel was the subject of the 1900 Bill for the C&SLR. This Bill, which became an Act on 25 May, overrode the 1893 Act and allowed them to make the station tunnel at Angel up to 30 feet (9.2 m) in diameter (previously the maximum had been 23 feet). This allowed Angel to have a single tunnel containing an island platform, similar to those already made at Euston, Clapham Road, and Clapham Common.

Work is started on the Great Northern & City Railway

In 1898, Pearsons finally started construction of the GN&CR. More capital had been subscribed: not enough for completion, but enough to make them believe that they could succeed with the line. Unfortunately, the GNR switched its support to the Great Northern & Strand Railway at the same time that a new GN&CR Bill was being promoted for two main works. The first of these was concerned with extending the railway to the GNR station at Finsbury Park. The line was originally intended to diverge from the GNR tracks south of the station; with this Bill, Pearsons were intending to get their own station. The second piece of work was to deviate the Canonbury spur of the GNR, freeing up a large block of land on which the GN&CR wanted to construct a generating station and depôt.

The Bill sought to raise £400,000 for the works, of which the usual three-quarters would be as shares. Despite having all opposition neutralized the promoters withdrew it from Parliament on 23 June. With relations with the GNR breaking down, the changes proposed in this Bill were undoubtedly too much for the main line company.

An editorial in *The Railway Times* berated the GNR for not supporting the GN&CR in the same way that the LSWR supported the W&CR. The GNR needed additional traffic facilities, especially to the City, and a guaranteed return on GN&CR stock would mean that the capital could be easily raised.[92]

Litigation in late 1900 annulled the 1894 agreement on guaranteed traffic, and led to the GNR agreeing in 1902 to construct a tube terminus below Finsbury Park, to be leased to the GN&CR, into which it ran when it opened on 14 February 1904.

Arnold Frank Hills
(12 March 1857 – 7 March 1927)

After an education at Harrow School and University College, Oxford, at which he showed a great interest in sporting achievement, Hills almost immediately joined the board of the Thames Iron Works, Shipbuilding and Engineering Company, based in Blackwall, east London. The company was suffering from increased competition from similar works in the north of England, whose costs were lower. During the 1890s he achieved a revival of the Thames Iron Works, constructing a number of large warships, as well as a single electrical locomotive for the C&SLR in 1898. However, the competition was too great, and after the construction of the battleship *Thunderer* in 1910, the works closed due to lack of business.

Hills was a philanthropic man, and spent much of his spare time helping to improve the lives of his workers by arranging lectures, concerts and clubs for them to attend, at the cost of the company. One of the clubs included the original football team for the works in 1895, which later became West Ham United (after splitting from the iron works in 1900). Hills remained associated with the club until 1904.

He was a vegetarian and believer in total abstinence, and worked himself very hard. Overwork led to him becoming completely paralysed in 1906, and having to be carried around his works in a chair.

In 1897, Arnold Frank Hills, Chairman of the Thames Iron Works Company, replaced the promoters of the LW&EFR, and it is highly likely that his first action was to withdraw the abandonment Bill that was on the crux of receiving Royal Assent. Negotiations with the LCC over the workmen's trains provision made him believe that the railway had a future.[93] Hills promoted the LW&EFR Act of 1898, which sought to extend the time permitted to purchase land and construct the railway. The powers of the 1894 Act were extended by three years, and those of the 1895 Act two years, giving a final expiry in 1902. Royal Assent was granted on 1 July 1898.

Strangely, the year 1898 also saw the promotion of the LW&EFR (Abandonment) Bill. This was read once in the House of Lords, referred to the Examiners, and then discharged.

Another LW&EFR Act, which obtained Royal Assent on 9 September 1899, abandoned the original junction with the GER Cambridge line. This was replaced with a new link to the GER that connected south of Clapton Junction, and would allow trains to run to the LW&EFR from either the Cambridge or Chingford lines. The diagram below can be compared with that for 1895. The new line would join the LW&EFR main route at a point 56 feet (17.1 m) below the surface, and curve beneath Mount Pleasant and Bakers Hill, before emerging on the surface and joining the GER.

The GER agreed to run a minimum of 60 trains between the station at Finsbury and either their line or the T&HJR per working day. The 1896 agreement with the Midland Railway was also reconfirmed in this Act.

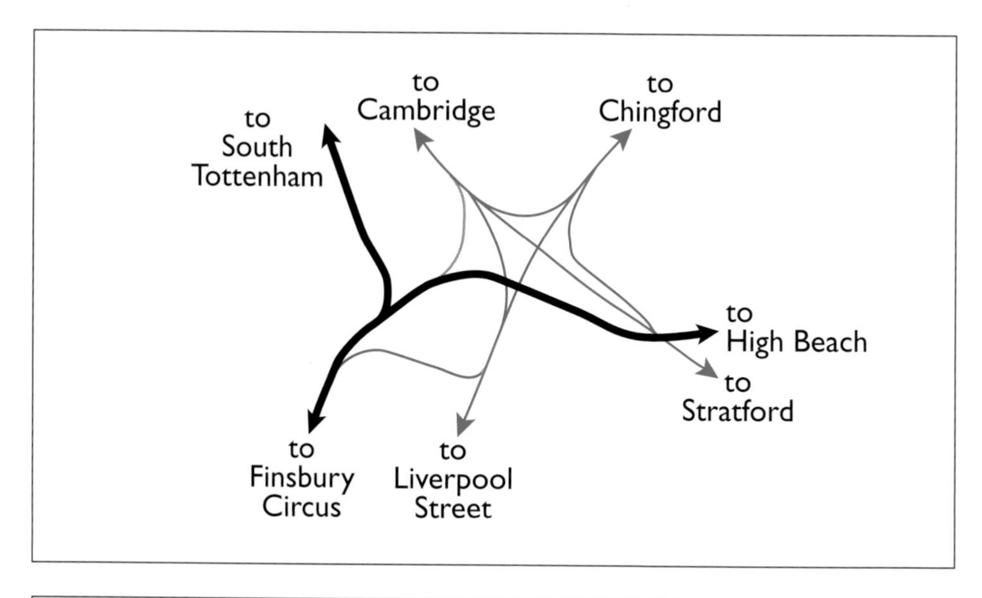

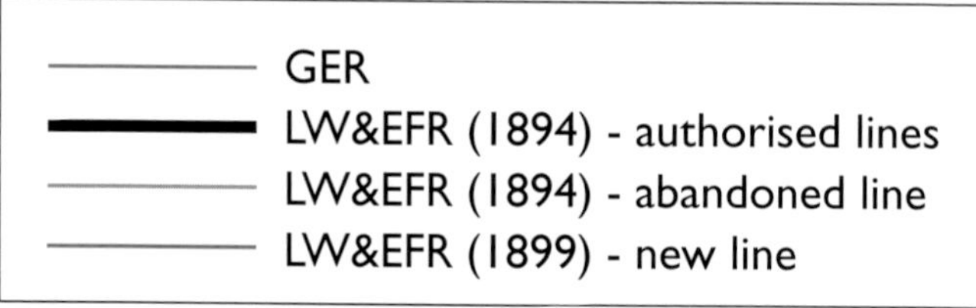

The 1899 changes to the London, Walthamstow & Epping Forest Railway

At the end of 1899, in another ploy to raise the necessary finance, the promoters asked the Corporation of the City of London to guarantee a 3% return on the capital of the company up to £500,000, for ten years. They noted the great benefit that the line would bring to the City. However, the Corporation members were, understandably, unhappy with the suggestion, one calling it "an insult to their common intelligence",[94] and decided to ignore the proposal.

By 1900, the LW&EFR was still no further advanced. It continued the fight against new schemes that threatened it, submitting a petition against the East London Water Bill. This Bill was part of the preparatory work for the construction of the Lea Valley reservoirs, and proposed diverting the River Lea into a new channel to the east. This channel would have conflicted with the route of the LW&EFR.

The East London Waterworks Company signed an agreement with the railway, in which they guaranteed the furthest east that the diversionary channel would run, and the railway agreed to be diverted slightly eastwards. The water company also permitted the purchase of a small parcel of land by the railway in order to allow the movement of the line.

The proposed reservoirs would take a large amount of land that the railway was probably hoping would be used for housing by its future passengers. To the east lay Epping Forest, which was also blocked to speculative builders. These factors further reduced the attractiveness of the railway.

The Bill for 1900 sought to raise a further £680,000 of capital from the public (since the Corporation of London refused to help). A short section of line through Walthamstow that was authorized to be in a cutting was now proposed to be in a short section of tunnel. However, the Bill and the railway did not succeed. On 25 May 1900 the House of Commons agreed to a resolution from the Standing Orders Committee, which proposed the introduction of an abandonment Bill for the line.[95] This new Bill replaced the original LW&EFR Bill for the year.

Six years after it was originally granted the Royal Assent, the LW&EFR had finally given up. The struggle to raise the necessary finances had proved too much, and in October 1900 the LW&EFR Bill was not proceeded with, and dropped by Parliament. It was considered in the press beforehand that the railway "might even now be saved if the Board of Trade would allow four-fifths of the deposit to be withdrawn"[96] – although the £120,000 that this would bring would not help get the works underway. However, the abandonment Bill was passed by Parliament, and gained Royal Assent on 6 August 1900, putting an end to the story of the LW&EFR. A tube railway would not reach Walthamstow until 68 years later, when the Victoria Line opened.

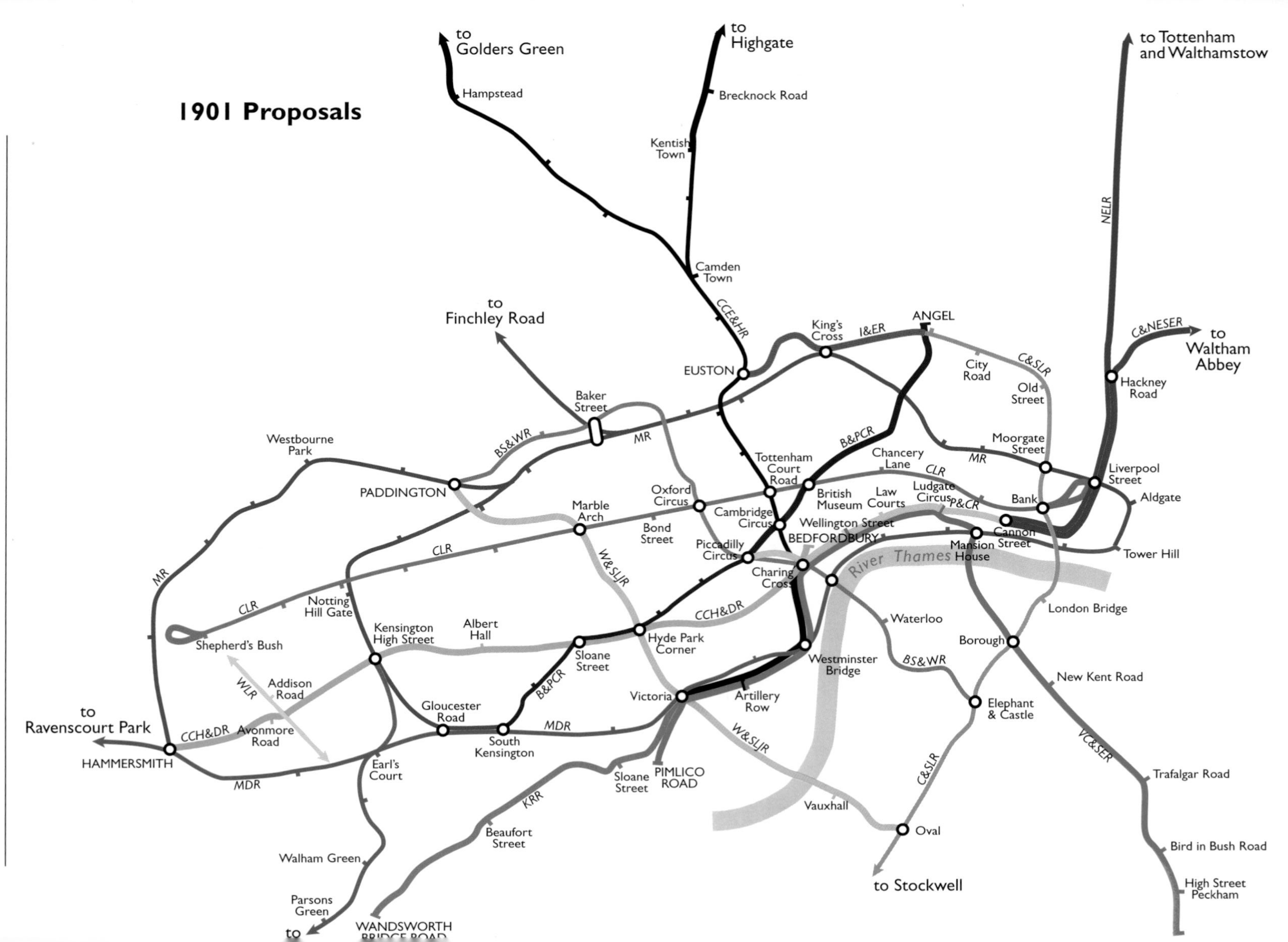
1901 Proposals
to Golders Green
Hampstead
to Highgate
Brecknock Road
Kentish Town
Camden Town
CCE&HR
to Tottenham and Walthamstow
NELR
C&NESER
to Waltham Abbey
Hackney Road
to Finchley Road
EUSTON
King's Cross
I&ER
ANGEL
City Road
C&SLR
Old Street
Baker Street
BS&WR
MR
Westbourne Park
B&PCR
Moorgate Street
Tottenham Court Road
Chancery Lane
CLR
Liverpool Street
Aldgate
PADDINGTON
Oxford Circus
British Museum
Law Courts
Ludgate Circus
P&CR
Bank
Marble Arch
Cambridge Circus
Wellington Street
Cannon Street
Bond Street
BEDFORDBURY
Mansion House
Tower Hill
Piccadilly Circus
River Thames
W&SLJR
Charing Cross
Notting Hill Gate
Waterloo
London Bridge
CCH&DR
Kensington High Street
Albert Hall
Shepherd's Bush
Sloane Street
Hyde Park Corner
Borough
Westminster Bridge
New Kent Road
WLR
Addison Road
Victoria
Artillery Row
Elephant & Castle
Gloucester Road
to Ravenscourt Park
Avonmore Road
South Kensington
MDR
HAMMERSMITH
Earl's Court
Sloane Street
PIMLICO ROAD
VC&SER
Trafalgar Road
KRR
Vauxhall
Oval
Beaufort Street
Bird in Bush Road
Walham Green
to Stockwell
High Street Peckham
Parsons Green
to
WANDSWORTH

The 1901 Proposals

The early years of the twentieth century saw a reprise of the 'Railway Mania' that had originally occurred in Britain in the late 1840s. The success of the Central London Railway (CLR), which had opened to the public on 30 July 1900, spurred many speculators to submit Bills to Parliament proposing tube railways connecting various parts of the capital. By the close of 1900 twelve such schemes had been submitted.

The CLR had opened earlier in the year, and within a short period began to worry the residents of property along its route. The heavy, unsprung locomotives that were used to haul the trains were causing vibration that could be felt on the surface – not a good thing in the light of the many new schemes that were being deposited. A Committee was appointed to investigate, headed by Lord Rayleigh; this produced its final report in 1902, and resulted in the CLR replacing its rolling stock with multiple-unit trains. These had the motors fitted to the carriages, as with current Underground trains.

An attempted revival of the City & West End Railway in 1900 was dropped due to the concerns about vibration, and the Bill was never deposited with Parliament; from the limited evidence available it would have been very similar to the 1897 proposal.[97] However, the other schemes were not so easily deterred.

New plans, as opposed to changes to existing or authorized schemes, are highlighted in bold in the table overleaf.

The City & Brixton Railway sought an extension of time to construct their line. They were still unable to raise the capital, and needed more time to keep the powers granted in their Act for the construction of the line. The Brompton & Piccadilly Circus, Central London, Charing Cross, Euston & Hampstead, and Islington & Euston Bills were all for extensions of previously authorized railways. The other seven schemes were new railways for 1901.

The Bills received their first readings before the House of Lords on 25 February 1901. To ensure that a consistent approach was taken when considering the proposals the Earl of Morley (Chairman of Committees) moved a resolution in the House of Lords on 4 March declaring that a Joint Select Committee should be appointed by the government. The motion was agreed, and three days later the House of Commons agreed a similar motion. Balfour confirmed in answer to a question that all of the current tube railway Bills would be referred to the Committee.

Railway Name	From	To	Via
Brompton & Piccadilly Circus	Piccadilly Circus	Angel	Shaftesbury Avenue, Theobalds Road, and Rosebery Avenue
	Brompton Road	Chelsea	Fulham Road
Central London	*Terminal loop at Shepherd's Bush, and extension to Liverpool Street with terminal loop*		
Charing Cross, Euston & Hampstead No. 1	Hampstead	Golders Green	
Charing Cross, Euston & Hampstead No. 2	Kentish Town	Highgate	Archway Road
	North of Charing Cross	Victoria	Whitehall
Charing Cross, Hammersmith & District	**Hammersmith**	**Charing Cross**	**Kensington and the Mall**
City & Brixton	*Extension of time*		
City & South London	*Pedestrian subway at Angel*		
City & North East Suburban Electric	**Monument**	**Waltham Abbey**	**Hackney Road and Walthamstow**
Islington & Euston	**Angel**	**Euston**	**King's Cross**
King's Road	**Victoria**	**Eel Brook Common**	**King's Road**
North East London	**Cannon Street**	**Tottenham and Walthamstow**	**Liverpool Street and Kingsland Road**
Piccadilly & City	**Piccadilly Circus**	**Cannon Street**	**Strand**
Victoria, City & Southern Electric	**Victoria**	**Peckham**	**City and Southwark**
West & South London Junction	**Paddington**	**Kennington**	**Marble Arch and Victoria**

With this large number of Bills to consider, the standard approach of debating each in both Houses would take a large amount of time, if each were to be considered in a similar manner. The standard method for dealing with this situation in Parliament is to appoint a Committee to consider the matter and report back. To this end, Sir John Dickson-Poynder, MP,[98] asked Gerald Balfour,[99] President of the Board of Trade (BoT), if he had considered arrangements for the Committee stage of the tube Bills. Balfour confirmed that Bills receiving a second reading before the Lords would be sent to a Private Bill Committee. Because of their close interest, the London County Council and the Corporation of London would probably be given a *locus standi*.

> *Locus standi*
> A *locus standi* is a right to appear and be heard in court. In the context of Parliamentary Bills, it is an automatic right to present a case, usually in opposition to a Bill. Being the statutory authorities for London, the LCC and the Corporation of London generally had *locus standi* with respect to all of the tube railway Bills.

The Chairman of the Ways and Means, J. W. Lowther, who proposed the original Commons motion, had discussed the matter with Morley and Balfour, and together they decided that this was the best way to consider the Bills. With good foresight he anticipated that none of the Bills would be able to proceed in the 1901 session of Parliament, but thought that the Committee

> might lay down broad principles which, in future sessions, would enable promoters to bring forward bills dealing with such railways.[100]

Before the Committee was appointed, Sir Francis Powell[101] asked if the First Commissioner of Works had considered the potential risk to the Albert Hall and Albert Memorial that was posed by the tube railways proposed to run along Kensington Gore. The Commissioner, Akers Douglas,[102] confirmed that he was in discussion with the relevant promoters, and that precautions would be insisted upon.

On 22 March the Lords appointed their five Committee members who were to be Lord Windsor (the Chairman), the Earl of Lauderdale, the Earl of Rosse, Viscount Knutsford, and Lord Herries. Just over a month later on 23 April the Commons appointed their five: Dickson-Poynder, Sir William Arrol, Thomas Ashton, Mr Cawley, and Sir Michael Foster. Their remit was to report:

1. Whether the proposed routes were best for London, and if not, how should they be altered;
2. How to protect property along the line of the routes;
3. Any special terms and conditions that should be imposed upon the construction and working of the railways; and
4. Which schemes should proceed.

There was to be no consideration of the issues of vibration until Lord Rayleigh's Committee investigating the vibration problems on the CLR had made its report. Nor was the Committee to consider the financial and engineering aspects of the railways, as they would still be subject to the normal scrutiny process once their work was done.

One Bill was withdrawn from examination by the Committee. The C&BR Bill, being for a simple extension of time, was considered in the normal way by Parliament, and was given Royal Assent on 17 August. It should be noted that no work had yet started on this line, and the company had explained in February that the condition of the money markets had prevented them from raising any capital. The C&SLR had, by this time, changed its mind again, and was negotiating to sell the King William Street branch in its entirety to the City & Brixton company, rather than leasing the tunnels.

The Committee sat between 2 May and 2 July 1901,[103] and took a large amount of evidence from people connected with the tube railways. The promoters of the railways employed barristers to represent their cases, and to disparage the proposals that rivalled their own schemes. The barristers were originally asked to decide upon the order that the Bills would be presented, but being unable to agree, the Committee proceeded in alphabetical order.

Extended Railways

The Central London Railway

The CLR had opened its line from Shepherd's Bush to Bank in the previous year, and had an immediate success on its hands. However, it was by no means perfect, and one of the main problems was the rolling stock. Electric locomotives pulled the carriages through the tunnels, and at the termini needed to be uncoupled and transferred to the other end. Even with the best efforts of the railway staff this procedure could not be accomplished in less than 2½ minutes, restricting the service to a maximum of 24 trains per hour.

The answer was thought to be reversing loops at each end of the line. The Chairman of the CLR told the Committee that with the loops they could run a train every two minutes. After the passengers had all left the train, it would proceed into the loop tunnel and be turned around ready for the return journey. As such, the CLR Bill for 1901 proposed the construction of loops at Shepherd's Bush and Liverpool Street. The western loop would have been entirely beneath Shepherd's Bush Green. Trains would have run around it in an anti-clockwise direction because of the layout of the tunnels already in place. At the eastern end three options were provided in the Bill: the loop could either have been below the main line station, or running beneath Threadneedle Street, Old Broad Street, Liverpool Street, Bishopsgate, and back to Threadneedle Street. The third option was for a simple reversing siding for the line, presumably in addition to the existing pair of sidings built on the route of the Liverpool Street extension.

Capital of £800,000 was needed for the loops (of which £200,000 was to come from borrowing). The company estimated the loop at Shepherd's Bush to cost between £50,000 and £60,000, whilst that in the City, with its more expensive wayleaves, would be £400,000. The narrow streets and tight junctions between Bank and Liverpool Street would mean that the tunnels would pass under a lot of expensive property.

A second CLR Bill was also deposited, for the provision of additional lifts at Shepherd's Bush station, which was getting overcrowded. This Bill also sought to raise additional capital of £200,000. This Bill was uncontentious and unopposed.

The Charing Cross, Euston & Hampstead Railway

In September 1900 the CCE&HR was purchased by Charles Tyson Yerkes, an American financier who had taken an interest in London's fledgling urban railways (and who is discussed in more detail later). He saw the potential for extending the railway into rural areas so that it could develop the traffic, rather than just linking established sites of population, and as such, two Bills were deposited by the CCE&HR for the 1901 session. The first extended the line northwards to **Golder's Green**, then a small hamlet (and spelled with an apostrophe). This would allow the railway to reach the surface and establish car sheds, a depôt, and a power station on a site adjacent to the Finchley Road. It would also allow the gradients to be eased under Hampstead, although the stations would be considerably deeper; this would allow electricity to be used throughout the line. The promoters were considering an intermediate station near to Jack Straw's Castle on Hampstead Heath, although the only station that they would confirm in 1901 was sited at Holly Hill (just across the road from the site of Hampstead station today).

The second Bill was for two extensions, to Highgate and Victoria. The Highgate extension prolonged the Kentish Town branch that had been added in 1899. The depôt at that location was dropped, and the railway was to proceed 2 miles 1 furlong 3.5 chains (3.5 km) northwards to terminate at the junction of Archway and Bishops Roads, with stations at **Brecknock Road**, **Archway Tavern**,[104] **Archway Road** (between Cromwell Avenue and Causton Road) and Highgate. The latter station would have interchange with the GNR station at the same point, and would have been situated on the western side of the junction between Archway Road and Southwood Lane. Gradients would have been steep: between Kentish Town and Archway Tavern they were 1 in 80, and this doubled to 1 in 40 for the remaining mile to **Highgate**.

At the southern end of the original railway the line would continue due south from the Garrick Theatre, via a station at **Charing Cross**, at a lower level than the BS&WR platforms, and into Whitehall. At Parliament Square the station would probably have had interchange with the nearby MDR station at **Westminster**.

The line would curve westwards into Victoria Street and via an intermediate station at **Artillery Row** to **Victoria**, where it would terminate beneath the yard in front of the station. This extension would have added 12 furlongs (2.4 km) to the CCE&HR at a cost of £866,960.

The City & South London Railway

The C&SLR was not promoting an extension in 1901, at least, not under its own name. The Bill that it did promote in its name was for an increase in the capital for the company (through the sale of more shares), an extension of time for building the northern extension, and the construction of a pedestrian subway from their station at Angel. This would run from the station, sited in Torrens Street, a distance of 110 yards (101 m), to the Royal Agricultural Hall in Upper Street.[105] They estimated that this would cost £300,000 to construct.

There was comment in the press around the middle of 1901 about the finances of the C&SLR, and the subway was seen as an expensive irrelevance. The dividend paid by C&SLR shares had fallen over the previous years, from 2⅛% in 1898, to 1⅞% in 1899, and 1¼% in 1900. *The Tramway and Railway World*, on 29 June 1901, considered that the construction and then abandonment of the section to King William Street showed an extravagant use of capital expenditure, estimating that around £250,000 of capital had been wasted. Other new costs included subways, for example linking the station at Elephant & Castle to the BS&WR, authorized in their 1900 Act.

In February *The Railway Magazine* called the Angel subway a "useless projection", given that the Royal Agricultural Hall only opened intermittently, and in view of the MDR's similar "white elephant" at South Kensington.[106] They did not favour the extension to Euston either, and suggested extending to Alexandra Palace, via the Pentonville, Caledonian, Holloway, Seven Sisters, and Hornsey Roads, and then via Crouch End.

By late spring the company was having problems with its Bill, and it was decided to sacrifice the Angel subway to allow the extension of time and increase in capital. This had the desired effect, and the remaining parts of the Bill received Royal Assent on 2 July.

The Islington & Euston Railway

The I&ER was a subterfuge on the part of the C&SLR, in that it was pretending to be an independent railway. It was not very subtle, given that its first named promoter was Charles Mott, Chairman of the C&SLR. The reason for the different name was that the directors of the C&SLR considered that they might have difficulty raising the capital given the poor dividend being paid by the existing railway at the time.

It was intended to extend the line for 1 mile 5 furlongs (2.6 km) from Angel to Drummond Street, **Euston**, via a station between **King's Cross** and St Pancras. Between the two stations the line would form a large loop around the north side of St Pancras and its Somers Town goods depôt to avoid tunnelling beneath any part of those large structures.

Subways would link the tube stations to the main line stations at Euston and King's Cross; St Pancras would probably have a similar connection. A deep level subway would link the platforms to those proposed by the GN&SR at King's Cross.

Capital of £420,000 was sought, and the extension was estimated to cost £387,653 to construct. The tunnels would have been 11 ft 6 ins (3.5 m) in diameter, and would have included a walkway for allowing passengers egress in the event of an electrical breakdown.

The Bill was not heard by the Committee in 1901, and was carried over to the next session.

The Brompton & Piccadilly Circus Railway

The last mention of the B&PCR was when it received Royal Assent for its Act of 1899, which added a junction with the MDR's authorized deep level route. However, nothing was done towards constructing the line until the MDR was itself taken over in March 1901 by Yerkes, who now owned three underground railways: the CCE&HR, the MDR, and the B&PCR.

Before the Joint Select Committee the engineer for the B&PCR, Sir James Szlumper, detailed the extension from Piccadilly Circus to Holborn, running beneath Shaftesbury Avenue. An intermediate station would provide interchange with the authorized CCE&HR, presumably at **Cambridge Circus** where those two lines would cross. The terminal station would be at, and named for, **Museum Street**, and would provide interchange to the CLR at its British Museum station.[107] The further extension to Islington was not being proceeded with, until the Vibration Committee had reported.

Balfour Browne, Counsel for the Piccadilly & City Railway, argued that the B&PCR route was inferior for passengers travelling to the City, as they would be forced to change onto the CLR, whereas the P&CR (described below) was a through route. Szlumper disagreed, and argued that a route to north London was of more importance; he objected to the proposal from the promoters of the P&CR that their line should be connected to the B&PCR at Piccadilly Circus, breaking the proposed through route to Museum Street. Lord Windsor pointed out that the Committee was not deciding upon such matters, only the suitability of the routes.

The extension along the Fulham Road to Chelsea was not even discussed by the Committee, presumably being far less contentious than the line to Angel.

New Railways

The Victoria, City & Southern Electric Railway

The Victoria, City & Southern Electric Railway was to connect Victoria to the City, and then southwards through Southwark to Peckham. Its promoters were Robert Jewell, R. H. Spence Browne, and Robert Roby Jewell. The capital for the 7 mile 28 chains (11.8 km) railway was set at £3.3 million; plus borrowing of £1.1 million.

The intention was to construct a tube railway with 12 ft diameter tunnels from south-west of Victoria station, adjacent to the Ebury Bridge and **Pimlico Road**. At the north end of the main line station, and across Victoria Street from the MDR station would lie their **Victoria** station. Heading east along Victoria Street, the first station would be at **Artillery Row**. The station building would be further south, almost opposite Howick Place, and a long subway at low level would connect the lower lift landings with the platforms. The station at **Westminster**, sited between Parliament Street and Canon Row would in all likelihood have had interchange with the MDR. Here the line would curve northwards under Parliament Street and Whitehall to **Charing Cross** station, on the south-west side of the main line station.

Now curving eastwards again, the line would follow the Strand to its next station at **Wellington Street**. This would be followed by **Chancery Lane** station, located opposite the Royal Courts of Justice on the south side of the Strand. At the eastern end of Fleet Street the station at **Ludgate Circus** would be on the north-west side of the road junction. Unusually the line continued straight on, under Ludgate Hill, and curved around St Paul's Cathedral, ignoring all of the concerns and protests raised in the past about tube railways passing so close. The final station would be at **Mansion House**, with the surface buildings on a site bounded by Cannon Street to the north, Bow Lane to the west, Great St Thomas Apostle Street to the south, and Queen Street to the east. It seems likely that MDR interchange would be provided. Between Charing Cross and Mansion House stations the line would be on two levels, allowing it to curve sinuously around the churches of St Mary-le-Strand and St Clement Danes, and St Paul's Cathedral and remain as far from their foundations as possible. This section of the line would also be rather deep, with platforms at depths of up to 119 ft (36.3 m).

This railway was to have its depôt at the Grosvenor Canal, beyond the station at Pimlico Road. Both running tunnels would continue to the surface at a gradient of 1 in 5; a power station would be provided at this depôt, using canal water.

A second and entirely separate railway would head south from **Mansion House** station (with platforms at right-angles to, and at a slightly higher level than those on the previously-described section), under the Thames, and follow Southwark Bridge and Marshalsea Roads to an interchange with the C&SLR at **Borough**. Crossing this other tube railway at near right-angles, the VC&SER would follow Great Dover Street to the junction with the Old Kent Road and the **New Kent Road**, the station being sited in the acute angle between the latter two roads. Taking a south-easterly course the railway would then follow the Old Kent Road as far as its junction with **Trafalgar Road**, at which point it would curve southwards with the station on the inside corner. The next station would be at the north end of Peckham Hill Street, opposite **Bird in Bush Road**. A large surface site east of the canal was to be purchased for a generating station – presumably the plentiful supply of water from the canal made this a logical choice.

The penultimate station was to have been in **Peckham High Street**, opposite the end of Hill Street. The line would then have continued due south to **Peckham Rye**. A very large surface site was proposed here, on a triangle bounded by Rye Lane, Copeland Road, and Atwell Road. The location for the station was not identified, but given that the platforms extended to the southern tip of the site it is likely that it would have been opposite Peckham Rye station. A depôt would have been on the rest of the land, with a single tunnel branching from the main line north of the station and rising at 1 in 5 to the surface.

The promoters may have decided that with over seven miles of railway to operate it would be easier to split it into two. Problems on one section (for example, a broken-down train) would have no impact on the service of the other. With separate generating stations even electrical malfunctions could remain isolated on one section.

On 22 January one of the Parliamentary Examiners noted that there was no appearance from the promoters, and so the Bill was marked as "dead". This would have come as a relief to property owners in Fleet Street, who in January were reported in *The Railway News* as forming a committee to protect their interests from this and the Piccadilly & City Railway scheme.

The King's Road Railway

The name of this railway described its route, which extended for a distance of 2 miles 6 furlongs 2.72 chains (4.5 km), in 12-ft diameter running tunnels. It basically followed the King's Road south-west from the main line station at **Victoria**. It would start to the north of the main line station near to Victoria Square and under Buckingham Palace Road, and then curve west below Pimlico Road. The first intermediate station would be at **Sloane Street** (at the junction with Manor Street), and then the line would curve north-west slightly in a loop to join the route of the King's Road.

Beaufort Street was to be the next station, with the southern terminus at **Wandsworth Bridge Road**, adjacent to Eel Brook Common. The power station was to be near to the south end of the railway, at Lots Road and adjacent to the Thames; it would have been immediately to the north of the power station being constructed by the Metropolitan District Electric Traction Company (described in the next chapter).

The promoters believed that there was a strong case for a railway along this route: the population of Fulham had trebled in the previous year. Already there was an omnibus every minute along the King's Road, and they estimated that over 1,000 people per hour travelled on them. Both first and second class accommodation was to be offered on the trains, and passengers would be carried for a flat fare.

The West & South London Junction Railway

Running in a north-west – south-east diagonal, the West & South London Junction Railway (W&SLJR) sought to connect Paddington to the C&SLR at Kennington Oval. The line was to pass beneath Marble Arch, Park Lane, Hyde Park Corner, Victoria, Vauxhall and the Oval, running in 12-ft diameter tunnels.

Starting at the western end of Bishop's Road Bridge, to the north-west of **Paddington**, the line proceeded under Eastbourne Terrace and Spring Street. It would then cut under property as it curved east until it reached the line of Chester Place, Hyde Park Square, and Upper Berkeley Street West (now Connaught Street).

At Edgware Road it would curve south-east to **Marble Arch**, and then under Park Lane (altered in May 1901 to the eastern edge of Hyde Park) as far as **Hyde Park Corner**. The station was to have been on the south side of Knightsbridge, at Nos. 8 and 9. This site was Crown property, and the Office of Woods agreed to terms in June. Grosvenor Place would be followed to **Victoria**; the main line station would be skirted to the north, and then the route would resume its south-easterly course under Vauxhall Bridge Road to the Thames. Passing under the river just downstream of the bridge, the line would continue past **Vauxhall**, into Harleyford Road, and curve around the Oval to the south before terminating in Camberwell New Road. The southern terminus would be at **Oval**.

Both the KRR and the W&SLJR had the same promoters: F. & D. Sheridan, and a syndicate called the Electric Railways Company Ltd. This syndicate will be examined in the next chapter. The capital for the railway was given as £2,250,000; borrowing on mortgage was £750,000. This included an easement payment to the Crown of £7,477 12s 6d. The scheme nearly fell at the first hurdle; on 21 January it was successfully opposed for failing to comply with Standing Orders. The promoters had not given the required notice to the lessees and occupiers of Nos. 2, 3, and 4 Grosvenor Place, whose cellars and vaults were over the line of route. It was also claimed that the deposited plans were inaccurate. In April the promoters agreed to include clauses in the Bill that would protect the cellars and the subsoil under these cellars and vaults. This satisfied the Lords, and so the Standing Orders were dispensed with, allowing the Bill to proceed.

Some of the only remaining records pertaining to the W&SLJR are from the various London waterworks companies. The Grand Junction, Southwark and Vauxhall, and Lambeth companies all had fears for their pipes being damaged by electrolysis, and were to submit petitions. The Parliamentary agent for the railway wrote to all three companies informing them of protective clauses in the Bill, and persuaded them all to withdraw their petitions. He informed them that if they were still unhappy then they could resubmit their petitions before the Bill was debated by the House of Lords.

The Charing Cross, Hammersmith & District Railway[108]

The eastern terminal station of the CCH&DR was recorded as **Bedfordbury**, a small street to the north-east of Trafalgar Square. It is likely (but not documented) that an entrance would have been provided on this street; however, the main entrance would have been located at the junction of Agar Street and the Strand.

Charing Cross station would be the next station to the west, sited just south of Trafalgar Square. Continuing west under the Mall, and towards Buckingham Palace, the line would divert slightly to the north under Green Park to a station at **Hyde Park Corner**. Further stations would be at **Sloane Street**, and then **Albert Hall**, before **Kensington High Street** was reached, where interchange with the MR and MDR would be achieved via a subway to their station.

Further west, after passing beneath the West London Railway south of their Addison Road station, less convenient interchange with that line would be afforded through a station at **Avonmore Road**. The western terminus for the line would be at **Hammersmith Broadway**. Power would come from a generating station to be erected in Queen Street, south of this station.

The London & Provincial Electric Construction Company Ltd originally promoted the railway, with the engineer being Charles Scott Meik. Opposing the line was the MDR, whose Chairman, James Forbes, claimed that the line would have no source of profit except by abstraction from his company.

As with the W&SLJR, the Grand Junction Waterworks Company raised a petition on the grounds of electrolysis. This was similarly withdrawn after discussion with the company's Parliamentary agent.[109]

The Piccadilly & City Railway

In its original form the P&CR proposed an underground tube railway connecting the B&PCR from its terminus at **Piccadilly Circus** to the North East London Railway (NELR – see below) at Cannon Street. From its end-on junction with the B&PCR situated beneath Piccadilly where that road meets Air Street the railway was to follow the line of Coventry Street, passing 24 feet (7.3 m) above the BS&WR. It would then curve south and then east to beneath the Strand, on a 1 in 47 downhill gradient, with a station at **Charing Cross**, situated on the site of the Lowther Arcade, to the east of Adelaide Street. This site is today occupied by the offices of Coutts and Co., the famous bankers. This station would have been around 26 feet (7.9 m) below the rail level of the CCE&HR.

The railway would continue eastward along the Strand, with the tunnels moving to a position with one above the other to the next station at **Wellington Street**, where that road meets the Strand, with the station on the south-eastern corner of the junction. The churches of St Mary-le-Strand and St Clement Danes were carefully avoided by the railway curving to the north of them, being completely under property on the north side of the Strand at one point. The station at **Law Courts** was to be at the junction of the Strand, Fleet Street, and Bell Yard, on the south side of Fleet Street occupying the entire site of Thanet Place. This latter road disappeared some time prior to 1914,[110] but was roughly south of the Temple Bar in the centre of Fleet Street. This station was to have a subway into the Royal Courts of Justice at the request of the Benchers of the Temple.

The line would follow Fleet Street to **Ludgate Circus**. A station here would give interchange with the main line station, and pedestrian subways would be provided beneath the streets. From here it would curve slightly to the south and progress along Carter Lane[111] and Cannon Street just to the south-east of St Paul's Cathedral, with a terminus at **Cannon Street** main line station.[112] Immediately prior to the terminus the tunnels would roll back to the same level as each other, with the twin tunnels of the station being parallel.

As mentioned previously, the promoters for the B&PCR strenuously objected to the P&CR connecting to their existing line at Piccadilly Circus, as it would prevent their own extension towards Islington. Instead, they proposed an interchange station, at which passengers could transfer between the railways. When pressed, their Counsel admitted that there were no engineering reasons preventing a through connection being provided, thus revealing their arguments to be rather disingenuous.

The idea for the railway originally came from the Siemens Brothers electrical company, but the driving force rapidly became a man called Clinton Edward Dawkins, senior partner at the merchant bank of J. S. Morgan. He was promoting the railway with John Pierpont Morgan, the American son of the bank's founder, and Arnold Hills, Alexander Siemens, and George von Chauvin; the latter two were both partners in the Siemens company, in which Morgan also had a financial interest. J. Pierpont Morgan's son Jack, also a financier, had suggested to his father that the bank should take a one-quarter interest in the P&CR as well as the North East London Railway (about which see below) on 14 December 1900. Confirmation was swiftly received from the senior Morgan, and so began the Morgan interest in London's underground railways. The capital for the line was set at £1.5 million, with an additional £500,000 available as a mortgage if required.

Clinton Edward Dawkins (1859 – 2 December 1905)

The son of an official in the Foreign Office, Dawkins was educated at Cheltenham College, and then read Moderations and Greats at Balliol College.

He joined the Indian Office in 1884, and two years later became the Private Secretary to Lord Cross, the Secretary of State. In 1889 he became the Private Secretary to the Chancellor of the Exchequer.

He then moved from government and made his first foray into the railway business. On 20 March 1890 he became the Peruvian representative of the Peruvian Corporation Ltd, which was founded to cancel Peruvian external debt, and finance railway construction.

Around five years later he returned to the corridors of power, and become Under Secretary of State for Finance in Egypt. From here he progressed in 1899 to be Finance Minister for India, during which time he helped to introduce a new currency system.

In England he was a Director of the Electric Traction Construction and Equipment Company Ltd.

Morgan searched for over a year for someone to head his London office. In April 1899 the post was offered to Dawkins, with a one-year delay to allow him to complete his role in India, and so in April 1900 he joined the London offices of J. S. Morgan. He was a senior partner, and spent six months of 1901 studying public transport in the USA. He was knighted in 1902.

After a long period of ill health, punctuated by heart attacks, he died in 1905 at the young age of 46. To quote Kynaston, "Clinton Dawkins possessed neither the physical endurance nor the business capacity [of Edgar Speyer]. By early 1904 at the latest, and probably much earlier, old Pierpont Morgan was convinced that he had made a profound mistake in appointing him as resident senior in London."

The Bill received its second reading before the Lords on 1 March, prior to it being considered by the Committee.

Before the Committee,[113] Balfour Browne for the P&CR stated that he felt that the B&PCR was a block line (i.e., one with no real purpose other than to obstruct the railways of another company). This was a statement he was to repeat over the coming years. Their proposed extension beyond Piccadilly Circus would cause the P&CR

difficulties in forming a satisfactory connection, as was originally proposed. Francis Fox, giving engineering evidence in favour of the line, stated that either an interchange station would have to be built at Piccadilly Circus, with no running connection between the railways, or a junction would need to be formed. The junction was preferable, and would be constructed as a flying junction (i.e., one in which crossing routes pass at different levels) so that there was no requirement for crossovers. Such a junction might conflict with the LCC sewer, and so added to the complexity arising from the extension of the B&PCR, since the latter railway would have to pass beneath the P&CR at a gradient of 1 in 44.

The Grand Junction Waterworks were also to petition against the P&CR on the grounds of electrolysis of their pipes. The promoters offered to add a clause to the Bill compelling them to use an insulated return (i.e., not to return the current via the running rails), and to pay full compensation in the event of any damage caused by electrolysis.

When the turn of the opposition came, Sir James Szlumper (engineer for the B&PCR) opposed the P&CR. He felt that the Metropolitan District Railway (MDR) already serviced the entire area it was planned to serve. With regard to the junction, he commented that not everyone arriving at Piccadilly Circus wanted to go to the City, and that some wished to travel towards the British Museum and Chancery Lane.

James Staats Forbes, the Chairman of the MDR, supported Szlumper's views, and stated of the P&CR that "if this Committee had the power tomorrow to pass the Bill it never could raise a shilling".[114]

One oddity that may have arisen had the two railways been joined is that of their tunnel sizes. The P&CR proposed tunnels of 13 feet (4 m) diameter; the B&PCR planned theirs to be 11 ft 6 ins (3.5 m). It was suggested by Fox that the B&PCR trains, being smaller, could operate throughout the combined railway, whereas the larger P&CR trains would be confined to their section east of Piccadilly Circus. Whether this unusual solution would have been acceptable to Parliament and the Board of Trade is uncertain.

Were the B&PCR to block the connection then the P&CR had a backup plan – connect to the Charing Cross, Hammersmith & District Railway at Charing Cross. A short length of additional railway beneath the Strand was all that would be required. It would leave a short appendix of a line between Charing Cross and Piccadilly. Rather than proposing to abandon this, it was merely noted that it would be "inconvenient" to work it. The plan was to run it as a shuttle, with no through trains from the P&CR 'main line'; this would be rather like the Holborn – Aldwych shuttle that operated for many years on the Piccadilly Line. Charing Cross would be constructed as an interchange station for the shuttle.

The North East London Railway

On 3 October 1900 Douglas Fox wrote to the Board of the Great Eastern Railway:

> I have been approached by several influential people who are desirous of reviving in some form or other a North Eastern Underground Railway from the neighbourhood of Liverpool Street to serve Clapton and Walthamstow.
>
> I understand that your Company feel the necessity for additional accommodation.

Would it be at all agreeable to you if an independent Combination were formed to carry out a Line, which, whilst serving the locality, might be valuable to you for through traffic. If so, I should be glad to have an opportunity of talking the matter over with you in more detail.

It has been suggested that such a line should run under your Company's property as far as Clapton. I would suggest as a precedent, the arrangement made by the Great Northern Company with an independent Company for the "Wood Green and Strand" Railway.[115]

Although the GER Board declined to be involved, the scheme was placed before the same Joint Select Committee as the P&CR in 1901. It was for another tube railway that commenced at Cannon Street, where it had a proposed end-on connection to the P&CR as well as a connection to the authorized deep-level District railway. It would be necessary for the line to descend at 1 in 40 to a level beneath the Waterloo & City Railway to join the deep-level MDR.

From Cannon Street it would run to Tottenham, via Liverpool Street and follow the course of Bishopsgate, Shoreditch High Street, Kingsland Road, Stoke Newington Road, Stamford Hill, and High Road (today these form the A10). It was to terminate beneath the garden of a house called Fairleigh Dene, in Broad Lane (which was noted as being occupied by one William Vernon), 50 yards (46 m) from the milestone in the High Road.

It had a branch that diverged at Stoke Newington, below the junction of Stamford Hill and Cazenove Road, and ran east with a station at Upper Clapton Road to surface on the Walthamstow Marshes. It would rise onto an embankment, with a connection to the GER Old Cambridge line swinging off to the north. The line would cross the GER on a seven-arch viaduct, and the River Lea on a 150-ft long metal span bridge with adjacent brick arches, each of 50-ft span.[116]

Another viaduct over the GER line to Stratford would be crossed before the line descended into a cutting to pass beneath the Lea Bridge Road just over one-quarter mile north-east of Lea Bridge station. It would then have curved gently north, remaining in a cutting 20–25 feet (6.1–7.6 m) deep, with stations sited in wider cuttings between Manor and Vicarage Roads, Bromley and Leyton Roads, Grove and Lea Bridge Roads, and Maynard Road and Shernhall Street. The Chingford branch of the GER would be passed under just west of Wood Street station, and the line was to terminate in north Walthamstow, on the east side of the Chingford Road, in an area called Chapel End.

Two power stations were planned for the line. The first was to be erected on the Hackney Marshes, adjacent to the GER. The second was to be on the northern edge of the Regent's Canal, between the Kingsland Road and Kingsland Basin. Additional land was to be taken on the Walthamstow and Leyton Marshes (estimated at 6 acres, but up to 30 acres was permitted) and at Knotts Green, presumably for depôts. Provision was also made for land at Tottenham, just beyond the proposed terminus, on the block bounded by High Road, Broad Lane, Talbot Road and Tottenham Green. This was to be used, if required, for sidings, and would have been an open yard below street level.

Trains were proposed to run every 2½ minutes along the railway south of the junction. The branches would probably be served by alternate trains, and shunting necks would be provided at the termini, rather than loops. Upon questioning, the engineer, Sir Douglas Fox, stated that he did not want the branch to diverge any further south as it would get poorer traffic levels.

Charles F. Jenkin, the assistant works manager at Siemens Brothers, explained how the railway would operate at 500 or 600 volts DC using multiple-unit rolling stock. An insulated return would be used for the line to prevent electrical interference with other railways. If a short circuit occurred on both positive and negative supplies simultaneously then circuit breakers would automatically remove the current.

The NELR was promoted by the same five men who promoted the P&CR, and was once again backed by the finance of J. S. Morgan. Arnold Hills, promoter of the London, Walthamstow & Epping Forest Railway in the late 1890s, had considered his options following the failure of the latter railway, and had decided that the NELR was the best alternative.

The finance for the NELR was to be raised by the issue of 450,000 shares of £10 each; once the capital had been raised the company would then be permitted to borrow an additional £1.5 million as a mortgage. Fox put the estimated cost of the railway with great precision at £3,562,029.

The Great Eastern Tube

The map published with the Committee Report showed the GER tube railway plans. These were proposed to run from Queen Street in Romford to Liverpool Street, round a loop and then out to Waltham Abbey. This would prevent a dead-end occurring at Liverpool Street, with the need to reverse trains – instead they could keep on going.

On 4 July 1900 the GER engineer, John Wilson, had been asked to consult with Benjamin Baker about these tubes. They were to be 54 feet (16.5 m) below rail level at Liverpool Street, and would have conflicted with both the NELR and the C&NESER. The engineer for the latter noted that if the GER were to construct their tube railway below their main line then no clash would occur. No plans had been deposited in 1901, since the ideas were insufficiently developed. Certainly there is no record of the GER Board having discussed the proposals.

Like the P&CR, the Bill for the NELR received its second reading before the Lords on 1 March. When the Joint Select Committee considered the Bill, objections to the new railway were predictably received from other railway companies. The GER, in the form of its Chairman, Sir Henry Oakley, was concerned that in placing the NELR under Bishopsgate this would preclude them from constructing their own tube railway in this position. They were also concerned with potential damage to their existing lines, and interference with their railway by the use of electricity, the construction works and the operations. However, the petitions had only been submitted to protect their position, as they generally supported the concept of a tube railway to the north-east of London, as it would bring in more traffic to Liverpool Street. They did not want both the NELR and C&NESER constructed through – one was thought to be quite sufficient.

The North London Railway and the Metropolitan Railway objected in separate petitions because they saw the NELR as unnecessary competition. They also gave similar reasons to the GER with regard to damage and interference. The MR believed that tube railways should not be extended into the central district of London as through routes, but instead should be radial lines bringing commuters from the suburbs down to main stations, such as those on its own railway.

The Central London Railway, which had opened the previous year, was promoting a loop from its Bank terminus up to Liverpool Street, and then back through the City to Bank and Hammersmith along a similar line to that of the P&CR and the NELR. It

The proposed tube railways of the GER, the C&NESER, and the NELR in 1901

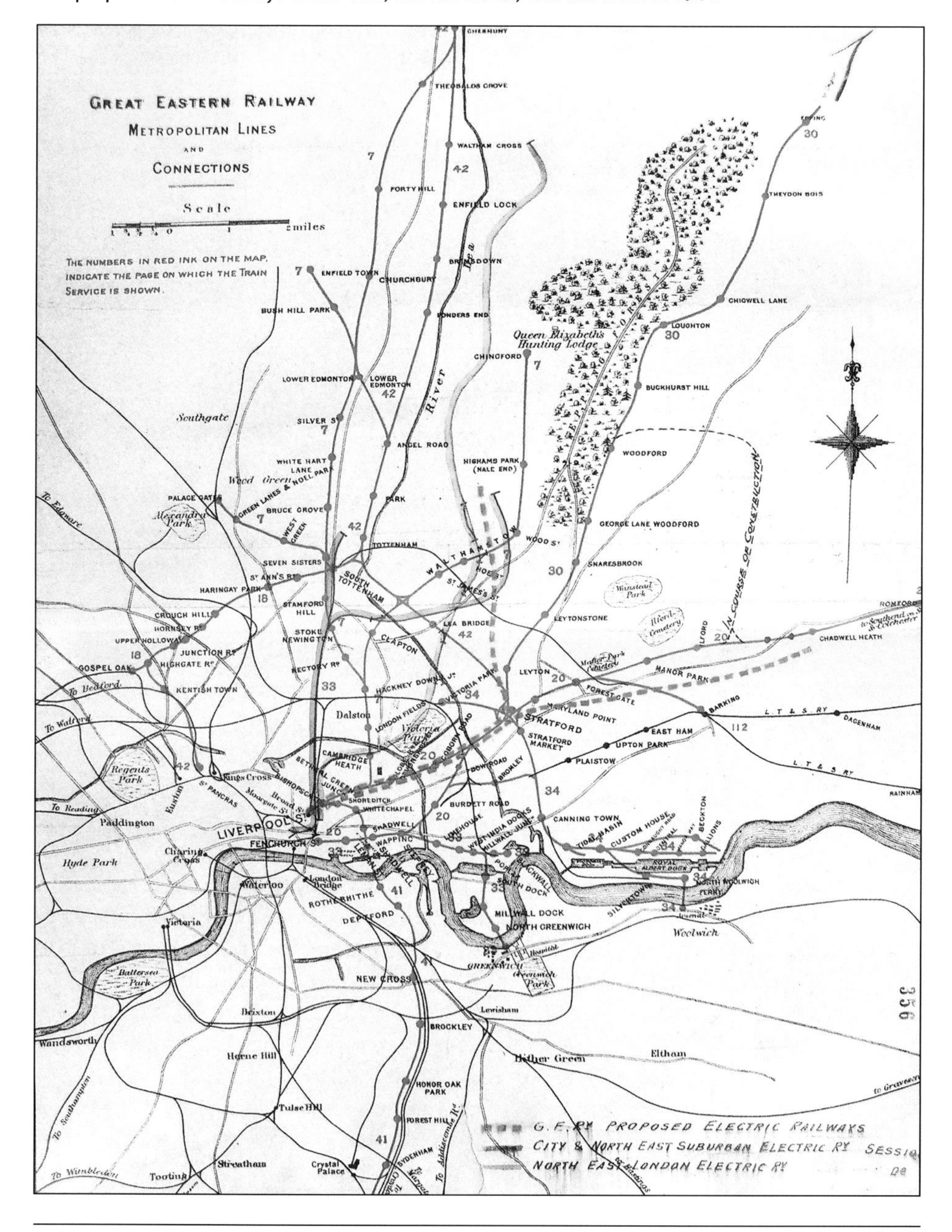

objected because it believed that both schemes would not be approved, and it wanted its scheme to succeed. Fox noted to the Committee that there were no engineering reasons why both schemes should not be constructed though.

Tottenham Urban District Council had held local meetings to discuss the NELR, to which they had originally objected owing to the lack of workmen's fares. A meeting of 7 May agreed that the Council would submit a petition opposing the railway for this reason. When the Committee's report was published a clause was inserted into the Bill for the provision of such fares.

The Managing Director of Tottenham Hotspur football club, Charles Roberts, supported the proposed line at the Select Committee, on the grounds that the competing main line railway (the GER) could not supply enough trains on match days. Winning the FA Cup that year meant that Tottenham Hotspur expected even larger crowds in future at their White Hart Lane ground; however, the Committee was not impressed with the evidence, coming as it did from a mere football club.

The London County Council felt that the money proposed for the Walthamstow branch would be better spent on extending the Tottenham branch northwards. This would allow it to serve the new housing estates planned by the LCC. The Chief Engineer of the LCC, Sir Alexander Binnie, went further and suggested that the Tottenham branch be extended north and then east, and join the end of the C&NESER to form a large loop.

The last two petitions were from the Skinners Company and the Merchant Taylors, two of the long-established City guilds with extensive property holdings. They were both concerned with the potential damage to their buildings.

Additional clauses were inserted into the Bill to protect the interests of: Walthamstow and Leyton Marshes; Middlesex County Council; the Tottenham & Forest Gate Railway; the City & South London Railway; the Regent's Canal and Dock Company; the Lea Conservancy Board; the Havering & Dagenham, Ripple, Barking, East Ham, Leyton and Walthamstow Commissioners of Sewers; the Society of Friends; Wisbey and Co; the Skinners Company; the New River Company; the Gas, Light & Coke Company, and the Waterloo and City Railway.

The Committee allowed the NELR to continue to the normal committee stage, but observed that it would prefer the line to be extended north from Tottenham so that it would serve the new London County Council estates planned for the Wood Green area. It also recommended that the Walthamstow branch should be dropped if another railway – the City & North East Suburban Electric – were to be built.

The City & North East Suburban Electric Railway

In November 1900 plans were deposited with various authorities for the City & North East Suburban Electric Railway (C&NESER). This was another railway considered in 1901 by the Joint Select Committee, and was to be a long-distance commuter railway running from the heart of the City, at the junction of Cornhill, Leadenhall Street, Gracechurch Street, and Bishopsgate. It was to extend over fourteen miles north to Farm Hill Road in Waltham Cross, running along Bishopsgate and Shoreditch High Street (similar to the NELR) before swinging to the east beneath the Hackney Road. It would have skirted the northern edge of Victoria Park whilst curving to the north, before rising to the surface. Hackney Marshes would be crossed on an embankment.

The line would then descend into a combination of cuttings and covered ways as it passed through the increasingly built-up district of Walthamstow. Lea Bridge Road was to be passed just to the south-west of where the Gospel Oak to Barking line crosses the same road. The Chingford branch of the GER would be passed to the east of Hoe Street station (now Walthamstow Central) and the line would then continue roughly northwards along the line of Hoe Street. A loop line almost 800 m long would be constructed north of Hoe Street station; this allowed each line of the railway to run beneath separate, but parallel streets,[117] presumably because the railway could not easily be accommodated beneath just one. A station on Forest Road, half way along this section, would have a platform on each line.

To the north of the loop the line would rise onto a slight embankment, following the line of Chingford Road, Old Church Road, and Sewardstone Road (today these form the A112) to Waltham Cross.

Connections would be made with other railways where these were crossed:

Connection to	Location
GER (Old Cambridge line)	Lea Bridge (described as Low Leyton in the Bill, but shown as Lea Bridge on plans)
Tottenham & Forest Gate Railway	Near Lea Bridge Road, and the former Lea Bridge station
GER (Chingford branch)	Hoe Street

In addition, a 370-yard (340 m) long spur would be made on the Hackney Marshes to the River Lea, allowing barges to transfer goods to the railway; this line would curve tightly back on itself on a 1½-chain (30 m) radius curve so that it was facing south-west.

Although the original intention, as described above, was for the railway to be in tunnel from its terminus in the City to the southern end of Hackney Marshes, an amendment was submitted on 23 May 1901. This continued the line in tunnels and cuttings across the marshes, and connected to the cuttings and covered ways of Walthamstow without rising above the surface. The link to the GER Old Cambridge line was removed.

Electricity was to be supplied from a power station to be constructed on the Hackney Marshes, to the west of the existing GER sidings at Temple Mills. The amendment plans show the power station being moved slightly to the east, so that it was directly adjacent to the sidings. A second railway, better described as a siding, connected the power station to the GER, but with no connection to the C&NESER main route. A 5-minute service would be operated along the line.

The railway was promoted by Sir James Kenneth Douglas Mackenzie, Baronet of Tarbat, William Henry Tugwell, Nathaniel Fortescue,[118] Edward Thomas Read, and Gerald Ward Martin. No more is recorded about them in the company documents, and the railway had a new promoter when it next appeared before Parliament.

In his evidence to the Committee,[119] the engineer, Richard Hassard,[120] claimed that the scheme was identical to that of the 1894 LW&EFR proposals. A quick glance at the maps shows that this is not the case – there are substantial differences throughout the length of the route.

In order to save costs he suggested that the railway could share tunnels with the NELR where the two lines ran parallel, between Monument and Hackney Road. This gave rise to concern from the NELR, who thought that this would block their 2½-minute service. Fox, for the NELR, said that there would be no problems with superimposing the lines; indeed, this is what happened between Moorgate and Old Street with the City & South London Railway and Great Northern & City Railway (for which Fox was also engineer).

At Liverpool Street the line would not pass beneath the GER station; it was noted, however, that its tracks would be 55 feet (16.8 m) below the level of the rails in the main line station and 80 feet (24.4 m) below street level.

Support for this proposal came from a local landowner and MP, T. C. Warner, who saw the potential for erecting many houses for workers upon his land at Higham.

The Joint Select Committee noted that it would prefer a more easterly route at the City end of the line to serve Whitechapel, but otherwise allowed the Bill to proceed in the 1902 session.

Further Evidence

The MR appeared to be opposing every tube railway Bill. Their representative before the Committee was, according to *The Tramway and Railway World*,

> disclaiming any attitude of general hostility to tubular railways, but claiming for the company that they should be allowed to keep the traffic they had secured by the facilities they offered, and which they were prepared to increase to meet public demands.[121]

The LCC gave a mass of evidence not relating to any one scheme. Binnie advocated fast, frequent services, and so objected to junctions on tube railways, which he felt would be a source of delays. Interchange stations should be provided where lines met with public subways. The local authority should control the subways.

He also believed that it would be many years before the authorized deep-level line of the MDR would be constructed, and this led on to another point. For how long should an authorized line on which construction has not even started be allowed to object to competing railways? Similarly, for how long should extensions of time for such lines be authorized? The necessity of following the roads should be removed, and deep tunnels under private property permitted, upon payment of an easement. His views were also in agreement with those of the City Corporation, the local authority for the City of London.

The Parliamentary agent for the LCC, Mr H. L. Cripps, objected to all of the railways, promoted as they were by rival companies. He wanted to see one management operating a system of railways with a consistent fare structure (including cheap fares for workmen). He also wanted the Metropolitan Railway to plan a deep-level line akin to that of the District. This would allow the original railways to act as a pure Inner Circle, with the suburban traffic diverted to the deeper lines. Consistent fares and trains for workmen should be arranged as well, as all of the Bills had differences in this respect.

The Chief Inspecting Officer of Railways for the Board of Trade, Colonel H. Yorke, was invited to give more general advice as to the construction and operation of tube railways. Since the BoT was the government body that would supervise the construction and operation of railways this was a useful step.

Yorke's comments covered a number of points, and were based on the experiences of the C&SLR, the W&CR, and the CLR. He felt that junctions should be in the open, and that the value of loops would be reduced with multiple-unit stock, since this could easily be reversed without having to turn or shunt. Long routes were of dubious value, he continued, because of the potential for problems; a broken-down train would cause disruption along the length of the railway, and hence a greater number of shorter lines would be preferable. On the subject of fares he considered that a uniform fare on each system would support economy and simplicity. All-night services, whilst perhaps beneficial for some users, would probably not be possible because of the need to examine the line and make repairs each night.

The Recommendations of the Committee

The Committee issued its report on 26 July. The report was highly detailed, and made a number of recommendations with regard to the eleven individual schemes that were placed before it, and London tube railways in general. The most notable of these were:

- that the railways should be constructed on sound economic principles;
- that the lines should connect well-recognized centres of traffic to each other, or to districts from where large numbers of people have to be carried to or from their work;
- that shallow subway lines were being developed in Europe and the USA, and the BoT should hold an inquiry into their use in London;
- that interchange stations between underground railways were desirable, but converging junctions between the running lines were not (since they lead to scheduling difficulties);
- extensions of time for railways already authorized, but not completed (or even started) should be carefully considered, to prevent block lines from being created;
- the LCC (and presumably others) had difficulty opposing extension of time Bills where they had not opposed the original Bill – this should be changed;
- shuttle services from one end of a line to another, possibly with loops at the end that do not preclude the extension of the line, are preferred to circular routes;
- that wayleaves under private property should be purchasable, repeating the recommendation made in 1892 by the Joint Select Committee, but still not fully enshrined in law, and
- that there should only be one line constructed between Hammersmith and the City.

Their recommendations specific to individual schemes were as follows:

Scheme	Recommendation
Brompton & Piccadilly Circus	Reject, but an extension to Angel with extension interchange to the C&SLR (under construction) would be favourably received.
Central London loops	Drop eastern (City) loop. Western loop may not be required if experiments with multiple-unit trains are successful.
Charing Cross, Euston & Hampstead (two Bills)	One of the two northern branches should be operated as a shuttle, with an interchange station at the junction.
Charing Cross, Hampstead & District	Should be connected end-on with the P&CR to form a through route between Hammersmith and the City. The connection should be at Piccadilly Circus, or failing that, Charing Cross.
City & North East Suburban Electric	Should be moved further east between Victoria Park and the City, so providing a link with Whitechapel and avoiding duplication with the NELR.
Islington & Euston	Approved.
King's Road	An interchange station at Victoria should be provided, and an extension to Putney Bridge would be desirable.
Piccadilly & City, North East London	Joining with NELR may make the line too long – consideration to be given to operating west and east sections separately, with interchange in the City (perhaps Cannon Street). Walthamstow branch should be dropped if C&NESER is approved.
West & South London Junction	Perhaps should abandon the section from Paddington to Marble Arch, and instead connect to the NWLR at the latter.

The appendix to the report included some statistics. The Bills that had been submitted in 1901 proposed a total of 51.6 miles (83.0 km) of railways, of which around 33 miles (53 km) were above ground (principally in the LW&EFR and Regent's Canal & Dock Railway Bills,[122] powers for both of which were described as "abandoned or practically inoperative"). The total cost of all of the schemes was £23,678,000.

The Committee also had some points to make about the control of planning for London's railways.

> The question of underground railways in London and the suburbs and of their working is so complicated, and of such importance, from a financial as well as a traffic point of view, that the Committee are disposed to agree with the views of the Corporation of London,

and the London County Council, that in some way there should be a more direct control and supervision of all projects for such underground railways. Whether this should be effected by the supervision of some public department as the Board of Trade, or by some body like the Light Railways Commission, or by a Joint Committee of members of both Houses of Parliament, appointed at the beginning of each session, to consider all projects affecting the relief and distribution of traffic in or near London, is a question which appears to them to deserve serious consideration.

Overall, the report was favourably received by the press and commentators, with the Editor of *The Tramway and Railway World* noting that

> It is pleasant to find that they have included in their recommendations so many points which everyone concerned in the matter has been urging for a long time.[123]

D. N. Dunlop, writing later in the year in *The Railway Magazine*, commented that the recommendations

> show that Parliament intends to consider the interests of the community at large rather than that of the projected companies.[124]

By the time that the Committee had reported, it was too late for any of the Bills to proceed — as predicted by *Transport*, which back in May

> doubted whether he [Yerkes] will be very happy when he finds how things stand just now ... the Charing Cross, Euston & Hampstead Bill is still hung up in the joint committee, and the chances of it, or any of the other "tube" Bills getting through this session are becoming increasingly remote.[125]

On 2 August the Earl of Morley proposed, and gained agreement, that they should be suspended until the 1902 session of Parliament. This is an action normally only undertaken when Parliament is dissolved for a General Election, but it is permitted by precedent when the actions of Parliament have caused a Bill to be delayed through no fault of its own – in this case, because of the time taken by the Joint Select Committee. All of the deposits made to Parliament were returned, and the agents for the Bills had to notify the Private Bill Office of their intention to proceed in the next session. Those proceeding were to redeposit their unchanged Bills by the standard time for the 1902 session, signing to confirm that their Bill was identical to that of 1901. The petitioners against the Bills were also left in the same situation, in that if they had not already been heard then they would be in the next session.

The intervening time gave the promoters an opportunity to make modifications to their routes, by the submission of new Bills.

The LCC continued to consider the issues of underground railways throughout 1901. They favoured construction of shallow subway railways along streets, such as that they proposed from the Embankment to Southampton Row, at a cost of £282,000. A visit to Boston convinced them that far more traffic could pass through such a system as a subway rather than a tube railway.

Financing the Tubes

It was one thing to draw up plans for a tube railway and deposit them with Parliament. Getting them approved and sanctioned was proving to be difficult, although the success of the CLR was proving to be a great encouragement. The real problem, as has been shown by the Victorian schemes, was paying for them.

All of the promoters sought to raise the money by allowing the public to purchase shares in their railways. Once a certain (usually large) proportion of the shares had been purchased, additional funds could be obtained by borrowing on a mortgage.

During the 1890s the cost of money was very low – interest rates were for the most part less than 4%, and a rate of 2% prevailed for most of 1895 and 1896. They peaked at 6% in December 1899, for a couple of months, before returning to 3–4% for the next four years. The problem was that investors were cautious, and railways, particularly in London, were not seen as a good investment.

Cut-and-cover railways were also expensive to build: the MDR remained in an impecunious state for most of its existence. It was under construction when the Overend Gurney crisis broke, preventing it from raising all its authorized capital, and causing its contractors to collapse. The Ordinary shares last paid a dividend in 1882, of a measly ⅜%; the preference shares did slightly better, as would be expected, but only by occasionally taking money from the reserve fund.

The C&SLR fared similarly. By 1897, its dividend had climbed to just 2%. It is therefore hardly surprising that the public were not rushing in droves to invest their money in the tubes. The W&CR was only constructed in the 1890s because of the 3% return on the investment guaranteed by its backers, the LSWR. The unfortunate GN&CR was constructed at the expense of its contractor after the withdrawal of support from the GNR.

This experience undoubtedly caused the CLR problems, which resulted in around three-quarters of the shares being purchased by a syndicate of the promoters and some foreign investors. The syndicate was created by The Exploration Company Ltd, a Rothschild-backed mining finance company. Many of the remaining shares were used to pay the contractors, who happened also to be owned by the promoters. The better route of the CLR, combined with its more generously-sized trains, made it an instant success, and its first dividend was 2½%. This then increased to 4% in the following year, a level that was maintained for the next five years.

Of the other plans that Parliament authorized in the 1890s, most had spent their time applying for extensions of time to given them a better chance of raising the capital. The only one that had started construction was the BS&WR, and that was in a very precarious state.

As with the CLR, a mining finance company came to the rescue. The London & Globe Finance Corporation (L&GFC) signed a contract with the BS&WR in November 1897, which led to the directors of the railway company being replaced by those of L&GFC. The latter company also took over as the main contractor for the line; the actual construction was then subcontracted to an east London company. The finance company would receive £1,766,000 of BS&WR shares in return for the work. This may seem a slightly strange acquisition for a mining company, but in 1900 the then-Chairman, Lord Dufferin, explained that the BS&WR had been acquired as a way of diversifying their interests.

Whitaker Wright (1845 – 26 January 1904)

Born in Cheshire, Wright emigrated to the USA in 1866. He entered the mining industry, first as a prospector, and then as a consultant, and was a millionaire by the age of 31. During a financial crisis he lost his fortune, and in 1889 he returned to Britain. He set himself up as a company promoter, and created companies that invested in the shares of mining companies, particularly in Western Australia, where gold was being mined. The public flocked to own shares in his companies, and he quickly recouped a healthy profit. One of the characteristics of his companies was the presence on their boards of titled individuals who took very little part in the activities of the companies, but served to reassure the public about the respectable nature of the business.

One of the mining companies was Lake View Consuls, which had been promoted by Wright in 1896. It had purchased mining leases in the Lake View and Boulder East Gold Mining Company, and initially performed very well. From a starting price of £1, its shares rose to a high of £28, and £1,318,000 in dividends was paid out by the end of 1899. In 1897 he merged these companies to form the London & Globe Finance Corporation which had £2 million of capital. Wright owned about one-third of the shares in this new corporation.

In late 1899 the Lake View Consuls fell by 50%, causing a heavy loss. Wright initially concealed this by transferring Lake View purchase contracts to Standard Exploration, a sister company of the L&GFC. Further losses in Lake View in 1900 could not be concealed – the shares dropped 20% on 18 December alone. The *Financial Times* initially advised investors to hold steady, and not sell their shares, but a week later they took a different view, reporting on the imminent collapse. Desperate attempts to restructure the company, with Wright retaining control, also failed, in part because of the number of other failures that were occurring on the London Stock Exchange.

It then emerged that Wright had sold most of his shares previously, and invested in property. This revelation, together with the loss of many people's investments caused Wright to flee to Paris, and then to New York. He was extradited and convicted of defrauding investors of £5 million. The prosecution alleged that the value of the company's assets had been grossly exaggerated, and that the contract transfer was another attempt to defraud investors.

The L&GFC was controlled by Whitaker Wright, who had spent over thirty years in the USA after emigrating as a young man. He had gained and lost a fortune, and returned to Britain in 1889. During the mid-1890s he regained a fortune by getting the public to put their money into his investment corporations, which specialized in mining companies. The L&GFC was created in 1897 by combining these investment companies.

However, all was not as it seemed with the L&GFC. In 1899 a large loss in one of the mining companies was concealed by various financial manœuvrings within Whitaker's companies. The following year, additional losses caused the whole edifice to crumble. The launch of new companies, and a public subscription for BS&WR shares all attempted to stave off disaster. By the end of 1900 the BS&WR was up for sale, and on 28 December the company finally collapsed. An American syndicate headed by Albert Johnson was considering purchasing the railway for £500,000, but the deal was never made.

Wright fled first to France, and then to the USA, in an attempt to avoid his investors, many of whom had been ruined. He was extradited and stood trial at the Royal Courts of Justice in London, after successfully arguing that it was a civil matter. Following a guilty verdict, and sentencing to seven years imprisonment, he continued to protest his innocence. He then took matters into his own hands by committing suicide; he was seen to brush his mouth with his handkerchief, according to one report,[126] and swallowed a capsule of potassium cyanide. A phial containing more capsules was found on his body, as well as a cocked and loaded revolver.

Not surprisingly, the work on the line slowed almost to a standstill. The subcontractors continued to be paid by the railway company, which raised funds by issuing calls on their shares.

Whitaker Wright, by Harry Furniss (National Portrait Gallery, London)

Charles Tyson Yerkes (25 June 1837 – 29 December 1905)

The Yerkes family arrived from Wales in Pennsylvania in 1682, and adopted the Quaker faith. Charles Yerkes was brought up in Philadelphia, and attended a Quaker school. His father was president of one of the city's banks.

Charles started work at the age of 17, as an apprentice clerk in a grain commission broker's office. Here his aptitude for finance first showed, with his employers so pleased with his first year's work that he was awarded $50 (apprentices normally went unpaid).

At the age of 22 he opened his own brokerage office, and three years later purchased a banking house. This proved to be a successful venture for him for a number of years, until unfortunately the bond market collapsed following a major fire in Chicago in 1871. Yerkes found himself unable to make one of his monthly payments to the City of Philadelphia. Refusing to give the City preference over any of his other creditors, he declared himself bankrupt. As a result of this he served seven months in prison for "technical embezzlement", before appealing and being pardoned by the governor. He then worked to rebuild both his fortune and his reputation, and began to speculate in railway stocks. Once his finances were in better health his creditors were repaid in full, with 6% interest.

He continued to deal in stocks, working in Philadelphia, before switching to the North Dakota property market in 1880. In the autumn of 1881 he moved to Chicago, following divorce and remarriage. Here he really started his involvement with railway and tramway finance, purchasing municipal franchises that brought monopoly powers. By various complex schemes he sold vast amounts of stock in his tramways, which were always popular because of the high dividends. These were paid by the sale of more stock. It was not a method that could last but, so long as he could sell before the other investors, he made handsome profits. He described his business method as "Buy old junk, fix it up a little, and unload it upon other fellows".

The tactics and techniques used by Yerkes were often dubious. He was not above employing bribery and blackmail in order to get the City's lawmakers to give his companies franchises, and rivals were often bought out and either joined with his syndicate, or disbanded. He would keep a low profile, getting friends and family to own stock so that he was not seen as the majority shareholder. This technique was used in 1894 when he bought the Lake Street Elevated Railroad, partly to defend another one of his companies from a competitor.

During the mid-1890s he was responsible for the construction of the Chicago Loop, one of the most famous parts of Chicago's public transport system today. Even though property owners objected, he would acquire rights to build and transfer them back and forth between his companies to ensure that the scheme was decidedly to his advantage. The loop and associated lines had to be completed by January 1897 under the terms of the franchise agreed with the City. An overly optimistic construction plan, combined with financial problems meant that three extensions of time had to be granted, moving the completion date to the end of 1899. Even this proved to be too tight, and corners had to be cut. Trains started to run on 30 December 1899, with some temporary works in place. The company decided to run one train each day until the line was complete, but the Public Works Commissioner declared parts of the line unsafe; Yerkes ordered the trains to run regardless. The next day the motorman of the first train was arrested. An officer of the railway company was on board and took the controls. Fifty policemen lined up across the track in an attempt to stop him, but he sped up and they scattered for their lives. Timbers were then placed across the Loop tracks, and the train finally halted. A five-month extension was granted in order to complete the Loop safely. The elevated railways became very popular, and the trains were crowded. A city councilman requested that more cars were added to the trains to reduce this crowding, but Yerkes famously replied, "Nonsense! The straphangers pay the dividends!"

In 1899 he sold $100 million worth of stock; four years later it was worth only $15 million. He sold out after legislation to extend his franchises failed, even though he had paid bribes of $1 million to the city aldermen; protesters against the legislation had paraded with guns, sticks, and nooses in the streets of Chicago.

He purchased controlling interests in the CCEHR, B&PCR, GN&SR, and BS&WR tube railways in London, together with the MDR and formed the UERL as the owning company, of which he was Chairman. This was arranged with help and financial assistance from Edgar Speyer, of Speyer Bros. When asked in an interview the secret of his success, he said:

"To the fact that I have studied the subject thoroughly in every detail; surrounded myself with intelligent, hard-working men, who were willing to work as I, which means that they worked from seven in the morning till as late as necessary at night. From the moment I took up my life-work I never strayed from the project, but concentrated every nerve and brain power upon the end I had in view. Whenever I benefited greatly by an enterprise, I made it a rule to present the faithful half-dozen employees in immediate touch with me with a few hundred shares, with the advice to hold onto them. It is a pleasant as well as a profitable thing to reward fidelity."[127]

Like Morgan, Yerkes had a strong philanthropic streak, and one of the largest beneficiaries was the University of Chicago. They were given the world's most powerful telescope, at Lake Geneva, Wisconsin, for which Yerkes footed the entire bill for the observatory, in return for it bearing his name. He had only agreed originally to pay for the telescope, but was outsmarted by the University's new professor of astronomy, George Hale. When Yerkes appeared to be shying away from paying, Hale leaked to the press an account of Yerkes's generosity. Yerkes could see no way out of the trap that had been laid; denying the story would lead to public humiliation; in December 1892 he agreed to pay up. To this day the telescope's 40-inch (102 cm) diameter glass lens is the largest of any in the world; all subsequent instruments use curved mirrors to reduce their weight.

Yerkes was a great art collector, intending that his massive collection should form a museum after his death. However, he left a number of large debts, including one of £160,000 to the UERL, and his artwork and New York mansion were auctioned to raise sufficient funds. His second wife, Mary, survived him, and continued to dispute aspects of his will until her death in 1911.

Yerkes was said in his obituary[128] to be a most agreeable man to deal with. He was a non-smoking teetotaller, and also avoided tea – a legacy of his Quaker upbringing. At meetings his voice was calm and placid, whilst giving the impression of great power and energy. Although he often looked grave (as all published photographs demonstrate), he had a "singularly agreeable smile". It was noted in the same article that although some of his dealings in the USA were allegedly disreputable, he had been the "soul of honour" in his British transactions. Whilst his observatory and telescope was his claim to fame in America, he would be remembered on the other side of the Atlantic for his "gift of cheap, rapid communication in the most congested city in the world."

Charles Tyson Yerkes

The B&PCR was still busy planning, but without any finance construction was as far off as ever. The MDR was certainly in no state to provide any helping injection of capital, although in October 1901 it did agree to transfer the powers for the section of their deep level line to the B&CPR. It seemed as though a new approach was needed in order to get things moving.

Mention has already been made of the man who was starting to revive the tube railway scene in London — Charles Yerkes. He had creatively financed the tramways and elevated railways in Chicago for a number of years, but was beginning to find that his methods of alleged bribery and devious accounting were bringing too much attention from legislators. Although he was a multimillionaire, he could not rest from business, and so turned his eyes to London. The first investment he made was the £100,000 take-over of the Charing Cross, Euston & Hampstead Railway. All attempts by the original promoters to raise the capital had proved unsuccessful until Robert Perks, a railway solicitor, brought the line to the attention of Yerkes.

Perks was also a large shareholder in the MDR, and invited Yerkes to invest in that company and help it achieve its goal of electrification. Yerkes, together with his American syndicates, purchased enough MDR stock to gain control by March 1901. Three months later the news was officially announced, and in July the Metropolitan District Electric Traction Company (MDETC) was incorporated. This company raised the £1 million required for the electrification scheme, and was controlled by Yerkes, the Managing Director.

The B&PCR, which was always in the pocket of the MDR, was transferred to Yerkes (in the form of the MDETC) by agreement of the B&PCR Board at a meeting on 12 September 1901. Plans were afoot to increase the size of the line, and after much negotiation the Great Northern & Strand Railway was taken over by the B&PCR in the same month. Finally, Yerkes then began to look to the quiescent BS&WR. The directors of that company agreed a sale in February 1902, with the final agreement coming less than a month later. The purchase price was set at £360,000 plus interest.

Yerkes had now spent a considerable sum of money on his tube railways, and needed far more to construct them – more that even he wished to provide. Accordingly, in March he contacted Speyer Bros, a finance house specializing in railway finance. Edgar Speyer, the senior partner in London, examined the scheme and agreed to help. A new company, the Underground Electric Railways Company of London Ltd. (UERL) was formed with £5 million of capital, to be raised as half a million £10 shares. Fewer than one-third of the shares were purchased by British investors – a wise move, given the financial history of Yerkes. The UERL was primarily controlled by Yerkes, Speyer Bros, Speyer and Co. of New York, and the Old Colony Trust Company of Boston, Massachusetts. Yerkes was the Chairman; this was both obvious and logical, given that he remained very much in touch with his railways.

The UERL took over the MDETC with effect from 8 June, winding up the latter company and paying its shareholders in a mixture of cash and shares. As well as controlling the tube railways, the MDR, and being responsible for the electrification of the latter, it was also responsible for the construction of a large power station in west London. This power station would supply electricity to all of the UERL railways (including the District, once electrification was completed).

Edgar Speyer (7 September 1862 – 16 February 1932)

Edgar Speyer was born into a Jewish family in Germany, and educated at the Realgymnasium in Frankfurt-am-Main. In 1884 he became a partner in his family's banking houses of Speyer Bros., London; Speyer & Co., New York; and L. Speyer-Ellissen, Frankfurt. He was the resident partner at the latter for three years, before moving to London. In 1892 he became a naturalized British citizen.

Following the help he provided in financing the MDETC and UERL, he joined the board of the latter in 1903. Following the death of Yerkes he became Chairman of both companies in 1906, and remained so until 1915.

In July 1906 he was made Baronet, and three years later joined the Privy Council. Politically he was a Liberal. He was very interested in music and the arts, and was one of the founders of the Whitechapel Art Gallery. Strauss and Debussy conducted concerts at his home in Grosvenor Street. His American wife, Leonora, was a professional violinist and won the Pulitzer prize for poetry in 1927.

During the First World War Sir George Makgill called his patriotism into question, and in response he offered to resign as Baronet and from the Privy Council. The King would hear none of it, giving him great support. This did not eliminate the whispers, however, and in 1915 he joined his brother in New York. As a result of new legislation in 1921 he was struck off the Privy Council, and his naturalization was revoked together with that of his family.

Until his death in Berlin he remained a director of Speyer-Ellissen in New York.

John Pierpont Morgan (17 April 1837 – 31 March 1913)

Morgan was born in Hartford, Connecticut, and was the son of the financier Junius Spencer Morgan, partner in the finance house J. S. Morgan, which was originally founded by the famous philanthropist George Peabody. Together with his cousin he established the firm of J. P. Morgan & Company in 1862. This lasted only a short time before he joined his father's bank as its US agent, trading under the name of Dabney, Morgan & Company, and began to earn itself a reputation as "a firm of high repute that dealt largely in railroad stocks"[129]. These stocks were not merely confined to the USA; the firm was "very popular with railroad men and railroad contractors" in London as well. It was at Dabney, Morgan & Co that Morgan won his first railroad victory, in gaining control of the Albany & Susquehanna Railroad.

Morgan moved out from under the shadow of his father by joining the merchant bank of Drexel & Company in 1872, as partner. The bank thus became Drexel, Morgan & Co, and was renamed J. P. Morgan 23 years later. As well as this, he was also active in the firm of J. S. Morgan, (which later become Morgan, Grenfell & Co.) in London, and Morgan, Harjes & Co. in Paris.

Morgan developed an immense amount of financial control both inside and outside the USA, and on several occasions managed to prevent major financial collapses on Wall Street. He created vast industrial combines, firstly with a railroad empire that spanned the United States. Most notably he created the United States Steel Corporation, formed in 1901 by buying out Andrew Carnegie's steel company, and joining it with other steel industry companies that he had previously merged. This was the world's first billion-dollar corporation. In the same year he attempted to dominate the Atlantic shipping business by forming the International Mercantile Marine Company.

Morgan married twice; his first wife tragically died four months after the wedding in 1861. His second marriage was longer-lived, providing him with two daughters and a son.

He listed his recreations in Who's Who as "dog fancier and yachtsman"; all of his four yachts were called Corsair. In addition he was a great collector of art, and after his death some of his collection was bequeathed to the New York Metropolitan Museum of Art. The private library that he constructed beside his house on Madison Avenue opened as a public institution in 1924.

John Pierpont Morgan

It is probably easier to draw parallels to Morgan with Speyer than it is with Yerkes. Both were successful financiers in companies that were primarily founded by their forebears. Certainly they would have seen each other as their business rival.

However, Morgan had much in common with Yerkes too. Both had become multi-millionaires through their control of American railroads. Both were supremely ambitious, and ruthless with it. And from around 1900, both had begun to turn their eyes and fortunes to the markets in Britain.

Morgan was born into a banking family. His father, Junius, was a partner in the Peabody merchant bank, and took over the company after its founder died, renaming it J. S. Morgan & Company. From an early age the younger Morgan had shown financial astuteness, and by the age of 27 he had an annual income of over $50,000. In 1869 he moved into the railroad business, taking an interest in the Albany & Susquehanna Railroad. From this his empire grew, and expanded into other areas of industry.

For most of his life Morgan split his time between the USA and Europe, and England in particular. J. S. Morgan had offices at 22 Old Broad Street in London, and lived at 13 Prince's Gate.

He loved technical innovation: his New York office and home were two of the first buildings in that city to be equipped with electric lighting. This led to him becoming a major backer of Thomas Edison, who founded the General Electric Company in the USA.

The Syndicates

Back in Britain, a few people realized that the tubes could be an opportunity to make a lot of money. They decided that the best way to do this was to create syndicates to promote the Bills through Parliament, and then sell the approved railway on at a profit. Alternatively, the fledgling railway company could purchase itself from the syndicate from the capital that it raised. Either way, the syndicate was in a far better position to make money than the railway company.

The prime movers behind the syndicates were a solicitor by the name of Fordyce Sheridan, and Hermann Gwinner, director of the National Mutual Life Assurance Society. Together with a small group, they created a number of companies to act as syndicates that could promote some of the tubes. Other men included Sir Owen Randal Slacke, CB (Chairman of the Kent Consolidated Coal Fields); Lieutenant-General Sir Richard Sankey, KCB; the Rt Hon. Lord Teynham; John MacAlister;[130] and George Riley (who owned a Lambeth engineering company).

J. P. Morgan in 1902 (Library of Congress)

Scheme	Syndicate	Promoters
Charing Cross, Hammersmith & District Railway	London & Provincial Electric Construction Co. (1901) The Charing Cross Syndicate Ltd (1902)	Richard Stafford Charles Gwinner Allan John Lawson George Dennis Martin Henry William St Quintin
City & Crystal Palace Railway	City & Crystal Palace Electric Railway Syndicate Ltd	Gwinner Riley Jamieson Ritchie
City, Wandsworth & Wimbledon Railway	Unknown	Gwinner Thomas Arrowsmith Meates Riley Ernest Schenk
King's Road Railway	Electric Railways Company Ltd	MacAlister Sankey Sheridan Slacke MacAlister Teynham
Victoria, Kennington & Greenwich Railway	Electric Railways Company Ltd	Jocelyn Braydon Harding Cox Gwinner Frederick Horner MacAlister Sankey Sheridan Slacke
West & South London Junction Railway	Electric Railways Company Ltd	Gwinner MacAlister Sheridan Slacke Sankey Teynham Wilson

Not one of these schemes was successful. The Select Committees that examined the Bills took a close look at the finances, and these were all rejected or withdrawn following consideration of the financial evidence.

The accompanying diagram shows the tangle of links between the individuals, syndicates, and railways that were promoted between 1901 and 1903.

Whilst creating a briefing for their Counsel as part of their opposition to the King's Road Railway, the LB&SCR carried out some very interesting investigative work. They discovered that the W&SLJR was promoted by the Electric Railways Company Ltd

(ERC), which was to pay William Shawe £50,000 for helping to promote the Bill. They believed that Shawe was a "dummy", and was actually a clerk of "the notorious Mr Fordyce Sheridan", who was "well known in connection with a blackmailing case".[131] This was very carefully worded, as at the trial in question Sheridan was only convicted of libel, the charges relating to blackmail having been dropped by the prosecution.[132] The intent was to imply the dubious nature of the financing behind the new railways.

The web of syndicates in 1901 and 1902

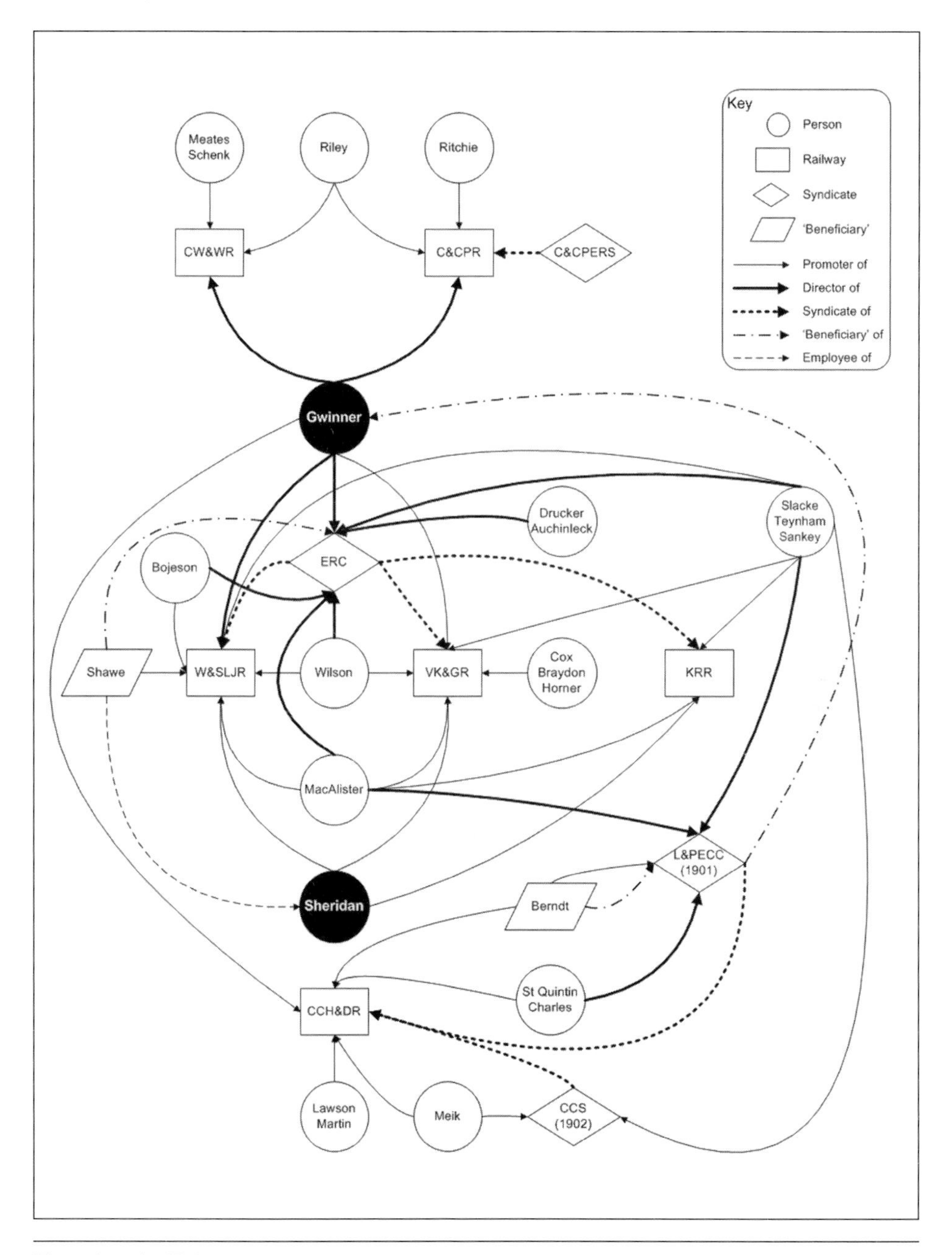

The Memorandum of Association for the Electric Railways Company states that it was formed to carry into effect an agreement between William Shawe and Mr Sigurd Svend Bojeson (who, it was noted, did not have residence in Britain, and only listed The First Avenue Hotel, Holborn as his address). Other directors of the ERC were Lieutenant-Colonel W. H. Auchinleck, (who was not a director of any of the railway companies), and Adolph Drucker, a former MP "who is wanted in the bankruptcy Court, but declines to attend".

The capital of the Electric Railways Company was £75,000, of which £47,323 had been raised by early 1902. A document listing the ownership of the shares showed that Shawe owned 34,423 of the shares, by far the majority, and unusually was listed as having no occupation. Gwinner, by comparison, was listed as 'Gentleman' – he owned 252 shares. More details came to light in *The Railway News*. The W&SLJR was the idea of Sheridan, who was friends with, and sometimes in debt to, Bojeson. They began to promote the line together, with Shawe acting as nominee. The ERC was set up to raise the money to pay for the promotion, including the Parliamentary deposit. However, in January 1901 the promoters could not find the £95,000 deposit for the W&SLJR, and Sankey had to borrow money from one bank that Sheridan then used as a deposit at another bank to raise the £95,000 as a mortgage.

The following January they then invited the public to subscribe to 10,000 preference shares, but applications for only 1,241 shares were received, leaving a shortfall for the 1902 Parliamentary expenses. Money was found from a variety of sources, and the deposit was made. As explained in the next chapter, the failure of one of their Bills led to the withdrawal of another. At the subsequent General Meeting the shareholders rejected the company accounts, leading ultimately to a winding-up order being made. The Official Receiver for the ERC stated that the troubles stemmed from the directors embarking on a costly undertaking with insufficient funds. He also noted that the directors had performed a great deal of work for the company, without ever having been paid.

The London & Provincial Electric Construction Co Ltd also had Slacke, Sankey, Teynham, McAllister, Charles, and St Quintin as directors, and, under the terms of an agreement dated 15 February 1901, would pay Louis Berndt £50,250 for his assistance. The first £5,250 was to be in cash, with the remainder in fully paid up shares in the company. A subsequent agreement, of 20 November, allowed the full amount to be paid in shares. Berndt was also entitled to appoint one director of the company.

The capital of the London & Provincial Electric Construction Company was also £75,000, and just £1,475 had been raised by the end of 1901. Louis Berndt had 12,865 shares allocated to him, but had not paid for these. A further £2,700 was raised on loan during 1902 and 1903 – one of the lenders being a certain Hermann Gwinner. However, in June 1903, less than a month after the final loan, the company agreed to be wound up. This was confirmed at an Extraordinary General Meeting in July. The final dissolution took place in 1912.

The L&PECC was replaced by the Charing Cross Syndicate in promoting the CCH&DR in 1902. This appeared to be a more realistic attempt to promote the railway, in that it counted the company engineers (Meik and Middleton), as well as the electrical manufacturers of Willans & Robinson Ltd as subscribers. However, Slacke, Sankey, and Teynham were still involved.

It was believed that the syndicates were attempting to obtain Bills that could then be sold at a heavy profit. In effect, the syndicate would raise money from the public buying shares. The total capital for the syndicates was very low in comparison to the other railways. As soon as a syndicate obtained an Act, the agreement in its Memorandum of Association would come into force. The prospectus for the City & Crystal Palace Railway stated clearly that

> Upon the Bill becoming an Act it is intended that the Company incorporated by the Act shall take over the interest of the Syndicate on terms to be agreed upon, and to at once proceed with the construction of the Railway.[133]

In other words, the new railway company, incorporated by the Act, would need to raise the full sum via another public subscription of shares. From this money, it would need to buy out the syndicate, who would walk away with a large percentage of their original capital. The railway company would shoulder the risk of construction and operation, as well as having paid a large sum to the syndicate up front.

The Scam

As we shall see in the next chapter, the City & Brixton Railway was proving unsuccessful in raising its finance, and so it put forward an abandonment Bill. This led to an intriguing new proposal: The City & Surrey Electric Railway (C&SER). This company was incorporated in May 1902, with eight shareholders, one of whom included the civil engineer S. G. Fraser, who was involved with the LUER and the C&NESER. The others included a steel manufacturer, a railway contractor, and two solicitors. Each subscribed to one £10 share from the total allocation of 15,000. The rest were allotted in consideration of the National Electric Traction Company. This had been incorporated four years earlier as the Drake & Gorham Electric Power and Traction Company Ltd, with £250,000 of capital (although only £7 had been subscribed). By the end of 1898 it was involved with five light railways in the UK.

At an Extraordinary General Meeting on 15 February 1900 the company name was changed to the National Electric Traction Company Ltd (NETC). Very little appeared to happen for the next two years. On 14 July 1902 the C&SER issued a prospectus,[134] described by the C&SLR as "not very understandable" – an understatement. The latter company was not particularly happy at the C&BR being hijacked by this newcomer, especially when the details for the new scheme were examined.

The prospectus offered shareholders dividends during the construction of the line, 5% interest, and a bonus of 17½%. It overwhelmed the reader with statistics ("One thousand millions sterling are invested in British Railway Shares", "Nearly 40,000,000 [passengers] were carried in one year by one City Tube alone", etc.), and placed the names of the engineers Sir Benjamin Baker, David Hay, and Basil Mott at the top of the advertisement. This was rather disingenuous: they were actually the engineers for the C&BR, which the C&SER wanted to take over.

This railway was to take over the now-disused station at King William Street, and run trains south through Kennington and Camberwell to Brixton (using the C&BR powers), whereupon the line would rise to the surface. It would then continue through Tooting, Streatham, and Norwood to Croydon, and then beyond to Warlingham (in Surrey) and Westerham (in Kent), with a branch to Caterham and Reigate. The lines

CITY & SURREY ELECTRIC RAILWAY.

In the new **CITY** and **SURREY** project an inexpensive Light Electric Railway will join and continue this system when the Railway comes to the surface after leaving Brixton. It is intended to then connect up with other Electric Railways. **Over One Hundred Miles** of these Light Railways, suitable for extensions, **are fully authorised** in Surrey and Kent.

The City and Surrey Syndicate now being formed is the preliminary step to dealing with these Acts of Parliament and other Powers **already granted** and to acquiring the sole use of the mile of City railway approach with the Freehold Terminus already built. During the last four years nearly one hundred thousand pounds have been expended in successful applications to Parliament, payment of deposits, &c., in this matter.

Owing to another route being taken by the new Islington Electric Railway, the whole of the City approach works, fully equipped and passed by the Board of Trade, are available to the Syndicate.

The City and Surrey Syndicate thus derives the full benefit of a very large expenditure already made, and Acts of Parliament granted, with the prospect of becoming owner of the most important railway route from London into Surrey and Kent.

THE CITY & SURREY ELECTRIC RAILWAY COMPANY, LIMITED,

66, Victoria-street, Westminster, S.W.

on the surface were to be constructed as light railways, and in a previous advertisement in the *Financial Times* of 7 July (shown above), the company noted that over one hundred miles of these light railways were already authorized. This same advertisement depicted a C&SLR-style locomotive pulling carriages around a very sharp curve (perhaps away from King William Street). The tunnel also contains, rather strangely, a belt-driven dynamo, which certainly would not have fitted into the diminutive tunnels!

Further claims of the C&SER were rather ironic, given the problems that the C&SLR had experienced with the station at King William Street, which had forced them to abandon the terminus because of the difficulty of expanding it and extending. The new company quoted a tube railway contractor as saying that the line would be so popular that their main difficulty would be handling the traffic without extending the terminus. They promptly noted that "extensions will no doubt become necessary".

A five-minute train service was proposed, and given that the route was "lined with the residences of the wealthier classes of City men", premium fares would be charged. Express trains would be used for the long distance traffic, a claim that raised many questions about the practicality of the scheme. Certainly the "express" trains would not be very fast on the approaches to the City terminus, and *The Railway News* described the plan as "preposterous".

On 23 July 1902 *The Times* published a letter from Benjamin Baker, engineer to both the C&SLR and the C&BR. Baker denied any connection with the C&SER, which had not actually identified its engineer. In a front-page editorial, the periodical *Transport* asked who was responsible for "this barefaced production". An article taking up three columns inside described the company as " a most impudent attempt to obtain money from the public".[135] This publication was also scathing about the conduct of many newspapers that had been paid to print the C&SER advertisement but simultaneously warned the public against investing in the scheme – *The Times*, the *Daily Mail*, and *The Economist* all came in for criticism on this score. It went on to quote from the *Statist*, which had analyzed the prospectus and described it as "too silly to deal with". This latter journal had investigated the syndicates behind the plans, and determined that the most important had just £157 to its name. They continued by asking "how any men with a modicum of brain matter can lend their names to the front-page adornment of such as prospectus." As we have seen, the engineers listed on the cover had nothing to do with the scheme, and were not happy at the association.

A letter published by the NETC to accompany the prospectus claimed that the route was fully authorized – of course, this was disingenuous, as it was referring to the City & Brixton line. *Transport* concluded that the whole thing was "about the most impertinent and barefaced attempt which has ever been made to obtain money from the public."

On 2 August, the *Financial Times* published a notification of a private meeting of C&SER shareholders. This was, in the view of the *FT*, to cover "its immediate winding up and the return of the money inveigled out of the public's pockets by the National Electric Traction Company, the latest alias of Mr Harry J. Lawson". This meeting, held on 8 August, voted to merge the two companies — but no mention was made of returning any money.

An intriguing letter was published in *The Railway Times* on 13 September 1902. The correspondents wrote concerning the meeting, at which they had been invited to join the board of the NETC. They sought more information about both companies, but that which they received did not justify them joining the board. The NETC had been informed of their decision, but since no list of subscribers for the C&SER could be found, the letter was by way of informing them via the press. Things became clearer when it was discovered that the whole C&SER scheme was a confidence trick, designed to swindle people into buying shares in the National Electric Traction Company. It was not the first time Lawson had tried this tactic, but it indirectly led to his conviction for fraud in 1904.

Henry John Lawson (23 February 1852 – 12 July 1925)

Lawson was a colourful character with a history in road transport. His first foray involved patenting a safety bicycle, followed by a gas-propelled tricycle. In 1896 he purchased the Daimler motor car patents, and formed the British Motor Syndicate. His strategy was simple: form a new, heavily over-capitalized company, issue an attractive prospectus that promised spectacular returns on the investment, pay the dividends for a couple of years, and then liquidate. Much of his skill was learnt from another notorious company promoter, Ernest Hooley.

Lawson specialized in getting the nobility to join the boards of his companies, in return for a fee.[136] Of course, he would be paid a sizeable licensing fee, as the companies were usually formed to exploit his patents. He was, by all accounts, very persuasive, and a born showman.

He was reputed to have made £500,000 from a deal involving the Dunlop Tyre Company in the mid 1890s, before moving into cars. He was partly responsible for the repeal of the "Red Flag" Act, limiting motor cars to a speed of 4 m.p.h. (6 km/h), and organized the first motor show, and the first London to Brighton run.[137]

He even had an early connection with public transport in London: in 1898 he registered the London Steam Omnibus Company Ltd, which intended to run a bus service using 28-seat steam buses. A year later, and without having actually operated a bus, the company was renamed the Motor Traction Company Ltd, and began operating a service using two of the first petrol-engined buses in London. His final bus service ran in 1904.

By 1901, he was encountering difficulties. His patents were costing more and more to protect, and they were being challenged in court. His companies began to fail. It all ended in 1904, when he was accused of fraudulently obtaining public money through his Electric Tramways Trust Ltd (which owned shares in the NETC).[138] He was found guilty, and sentenced to one year's hard labour. He continued to believe in his innocence, and may have avoided conviction had he chosen to employ a barrister. His colleague, Hooley, had done so, and was acquitted of the charges.

In 1915 he started a business which took £200,000 of capital and liquidated in just eight months, Lawson having to retreat from an onslaught of missiles thrown by angry shareholders at a meeting.

Despite the fortune that he made in his lifetime, at his death in Harrow he had just £99 to his name.

Henry Lawson

The 1902 Committees

Bills From 1901, with Some Additions

The recommendation from the 1901 committee concerning the desirability of a route from Hammersmith to the City of London led to four bills proposing such railways being submitted for the 1902 session of Parliament. Both the B&PCR and the CLR dropped their 1901 Bills for more extensive replacements, whilst some of the other proposals had additional 1902 Bills to modify their original schemes. The key schemes being considered were (with the new schemes and changes for 1902 in bold):

Railway Name	From	To	Via
Baker Street & Waterloo	***Extension of time***		
Brompton & Piccadilly Circus (extension)	**Piccadilly Circus**	**Charing Cross (junction with deep-level MDR)**	
	Piccadilly Circus	**Holborn (junction with GN&SR)**	**Leicester Square**
	South Kensington	**Parsons Green**	**Fulham Road**
	Abandonment of authorized section from Cottage Place to depôt at Yeoman's Row in Kensington		
Central London (extension)	**Shepherd's Bush**	**Bank**	**Hammersmith, Hyde Park Corner and Ludgate Hill (forming a large loop)**
Charing Cross, Hampstead & Euston No. 1	Hampstead	Golders Green	
Charing Cross, Hampstead & Euston No. 2	Kentish Town	Highgate	Archway Road
	North of Charing Cross	Victoria	Whitehall
Charing Cross, Euston & Hampstead No. 3	**Charing Cross**	**Embankment**	
Charing Cross, Hammersmith & District No. 1	Hammersmith	Strand	Kensington and The Mall
Charing Cross, Hammersmith & District No. 2	**Hyde Park Corner**	**Strand**	**Piccadilly Circus and Leicester Square**
	Hammersmith	**Castelnau**	
City & Brixton	***Abandonment of the entire railway***		

City & Brixton	***Abandonment of the section between Lambeth Road and Brixton***[139]		
City & Crystal Palace	Cannon Street	Crystal Palace	Peckham Rye
City & North East Suburban Electric No. 1	Cannon Street	Waltham Cross	Hackney Road and Walthamstow
City & North East Suburban Electric No. 2	**Cannon Street**	**Hackney**	**Whitechapel**
	Abandonment of section from Cannon Street to Hackney via Shoreditch		
City & Old Kent Road	**King William St**	**Bricklayers Arms**	
City, Wandsworth & Wimbledon Electric	**Cannon Street**	**Wimbledon**	**Clapham Junction**
East London, City & Peckham	**Plaistow**	**Peckham Rye**	**Gracechurch Street**
Edgware & Hampstead	**Edgware**	**Hampstead**	**Hendon**
Great Northern	**Finsbury Park**	**GN&SR**	
Great Northern No. 2	**Finsbury Park**	**Drayton Park**	
Great Northern & City	**Moorgate**	**Lothbury**	
Great Northern & Strand	**Strand**	**Temple**	
	Also a deviation at Finsbury Park, and abandonment of the line north thereof		
Islington & Euston	Euston	Angel, Islington	King's Cross
King's Road No. 1	Victoria	Eel Brook Common	King's Road, Chelsea and Eel Brook Common
King's Road No. 2	**Eel Brook Common**	**Putney**	**Parsons Green**
London United Electric	Hammersmith	Charing Cross	Hyde Park Corner
	Marble Arch	Clapham Junction	Sloane Square
North East London No. 1	Cannon Street	Tottenham	Monument, Hackney, and Kingsland Road
North East London No. 2	**Cannon Street**	**Ludgate Circus**	**Upper Thames Street**
	Tottenham	**Southgate**	**Palmer's Green**
North West London	***Extension of time and increase in tunnel size***		
Piccadilly & City No. 1	Piccadilly Circus	Cannon Street	Strand
Piccadilly & City No. 2	**Piccadilly Circus**	**Hammersmith**	**Piccadilly and Kensington**
	Abandonment of section from Ludgate Circus to Cannon Street		
Victoria, Kennington & Greenwich	**Victoria**	**Greenwich**	**Kennington**
West and South London Junction	Paddington	Kennington Oval	Marble Arch, Victoria, and Vauxhall

The MDR sought to increase the permitted time for its deep-level line as part of a wide-ranging Bill, which also included powers for the MDETC to supply electricity to the Yerkes tubes. The MR had a Bill which too concerned electrification: it wanted to electrify the Hammersmith & City Railway, and the East London Railway.

All of the Bills listed above were read before the House of Lords in late January and early February. On 10 February Lord Glenesk put forward a motion for the reappointment of the 1901 Joint Select Committee to examine all of the tube railway Bills, thus preventing haphazard development. The Earl of Morley opposed the motion, and detailed the current position of the tube railway Bills. Nine had survived the break since 1901, and 22 new Bills had been added.[140] Of these new Bills, four were withdrawn by the end of January; two were for extensions of time; one was for an abandonment; and twelve for line extensions and modifications, leaving only three completely new railways. These were the London United Electric Railway (LUER), the Edgware & Hampstead, and the City & Crystal Palace (although it could be argued that the CLR loop, being longer than the original line, comprised a new railway).

From the total of 27 Bills to be considered, if the double Bills are discounted (e.g., the P&CR was promoting the 1901 Bill, and had introduced a No. 2 Bill for 1902), as well as the extensions of time, abandonment, and the very small line extensions, only 13 schemes remain. The 1901 Joint Select Committee had considered all of these the year before, with the exception of the four new proposals. All that re-appointing the Committee would achieve would be the delay of all schemes for another year.

Glenesk suggested that the Committee should be given the power to pass the Bills. This did not find favour, and Morley's counter-suggestion was the appointment of at least two Committees to speed the proceedings. He was acutely aware of the cost, both to Parliament and to the promoters, of dragging the legislative process out further than strictly necessary.

Morley was supported by Viscount Knutsford and Earl Spencer, and so Lord Glenesk withdrew his motion. Spencer warned, though, that multiple Committees would need to work in a uniform manner in order to reach a sensible conclusion.

Two Select Committees of the House of Lords were created. One chaired by Lord Windsor was convened for the purpose of debating tube railways along an east-west axis; a similar committee to consider north-south railways was chaired by Lord Ribblesdale.

Views from the Authorities

Before considering the Bills before his Committee, Lord Windsor invited Colonel H. Yorke from the Board of Trade to give some general views about tube railways, as he had given to the Committee of the previous year.

The key points that Yorke made were, in summary:

- Confluent junctions in tubes should be avoided;
- Woodwork should not be present near to any electrical part of the rolling stock, unless protection was provided by use of a non-flammable material;
- Wooden sleepers should not be creosoted, but protected by some other "mineral solution". Even if only scorched, creosote released noxious vapours. He suggested that metal sleepers could be used if the electrical problems could be overcome, and that they would eliminate the vibration problem;

- Wood should not be used for sub-surface stations and platforms;
- No gap should exist between the trains and the platforms;
- Space should be allowed in the tunnels either side of the trains to allow passengers to pass in case of an emergency. This might mean increasing the proposed size of some of the tunnels to a minimum of 12 feet (3.7 m) – Yorke's personal preference was a minimum of 13 ft 6 ins;
- Rigid conductors were preferable to flexible cables;
- Ventilation matters should not be ignored, and larger tunnels would assist;
- Lighting must be provided in the tunnels between stations;
- The BoT should have greater powers of inspection for electric railways as opposed to "ordinary railways";
- A clause should be inserted into all Bills for electric railways, giving the BoT powers to approve the designs for track, tunnels, platforms, stairs, lifts, passageways, rolling stock, lighting and ventilation, and compelling the companies to construct only their railways and trains in accordance with the approved plans.

The Treasury was also involved. Since the Crown was a major landowner in London, including the major parks, and many of the railways were to pass beneath the parks, a number of easements were arranged. The Office of Woods arranged for the Crown Surveyor to assess each scheme for an appropriate sum. The following table details all of the easements that were agreed with promoters.[141]

Railway	Location	Easement
CLR 1902	Albert Hall – Hyde Park Corner Hyde Park Corner – Ritz Hotel	£10,395
CCH&DR 1901	Alexandra Gate – Hyde Park Corner Hyde Park Corner – The Mall Under The Mall	£5,850 £2,525 £3,575
CCH&DR 1902	Albert Memorial – Hyde Park Corner Hyde Park Corner – The Mall Under The Mall	£16,167 10s
C&NESER 1901	Victoria Park	£7,314
C&NESER 1902	Victoria Park	£7,215
LUER 1902	Queens Gate – Hyde Park Corner Marble Arch – Knightsbridge Road	£7,830 £5,467
W&SLJR 1901	Marble Arch – Hyde Park Corner	£5,775
W&SLJR 1902	Marble Arch – Hyde Park Corner	£5,500

The LCC Tramway Subway

One other Bill was put forward by the LCC, and relates to the tube railway story. This was for the construction of a tramway subway under the new road it was constructing between Holborn and the Strand. Studies made by the LCC in 1899 and 1901 concluded that shallow subways were preferable to deep-level tubes, and as a tramway operator it made sense for the LCC to use the subways for trams. The construction of Kingsway was an ideal opportunity to prove the utility of the subways without disrupting traffic along an existing street.

Accordingly the LCC (Subways and Tramways) Act 1902 authorized the subway from Theobalds Road to the Embankment, at a cost of £282,000.[142] A steep entrance ramp at a gradient of 1 in 10 was constructed in the centre of Southampton Row. South of the tunnel portal, twin 14 ft 6 ins (4.4 m) cast-iron tubes carried the trams to the south side of Holborn (and under the Fleet sewer), whereupon the tunnel was constructed as a double track tunnel 20-ft (6.1 m) wide. The roof was made of steel troughing that supported the roadway above.

Separate cast-iron tubes were again used beneath the Strand, and the tramway exited onto the Embankment through the north-western abutment wall of Waterloo Bridge. The headroom only allowed single-deck tramcars to be used, and rather than an overhead wire they collected their current from a conduit situated between the running rails (as was the usual practice for the LCC trams).

Two stations were provided: one at Holborn, to the south of the street of that name, and the other at Aldwych, where that road meets Kingsway. A third station at Wellington Street was never completed. Steps connected the underground island platforms to the streets above.

Unfortunately for the LCC the subway was not profitable, as the single-deck cars could not be made to pay. In 1929 work was undertaken to enlarge it so that regular double-deck tramcars could operate. The subway remained in service until 1952, when trams finally left London's streets. In 1964 the southern end reopened as the Strand underpass for light motor traffic.

Rails to Nowhere

Several of the schemes that were eagerly announced to the press at the end of 1901 did not even make it off the blocks. For various reasons they failed to get before the Committee, and therefore even less information about them is forthcoming.

Withdrawn Bills

Four proposals were to prove very short-lived. Three were deposited with Parliament, but abandoned by the end of January 1902, and the other was never even deposited.

The City & Old Kent Road Railway (C&OKRR) proposed a short line connecting **King William Street** and **Bricklayer's Arms**. This latter station had been opened as a passenger terminus by the Croydon & South Eastern Railway in 1844, but had proved a dismal failure. It was too far from the City and the West End, and by 1852 all regular passenger traffic had ceased. However, the station took on a new lease of life as a goods station.

The promoters of the C&OKRR must have seen their line as something akin to the W&CR, linking a south bank terminus remote from the City to that place by a short underground line. They had also noted the possible abandonment of the C&BR, and proposed that the western end of their line would connect with the abandoned C&SLR tunnels to King William Street, providing them with a ready-made, if somewhat awkward, City terminus. No intermediate stations have been recorded, but the most likely location would be at Borough.

The Bill was never deposited with Parliament after the initial announcement by the promoters. The nature of the line, linking a badly-designed City terminus to a station with no regular passengers was not encouraging from the outset, and one can only wonder at what led the promoters even to consider it.

The City, Wandsworth & Wimbledon Railway (CW&WR) was promoted by Herman Gwinner, in conjunction with one of his syndicates. Commencing to the west of **Cannon Street**, it would run south under the river, and follow Southwark Bridge Road past **Southwark Street** before turning to the west, to **St George's Circus**, where the station would be sited to the east at Lancaster Street. It would then continue along Lambeth Road, with a further station at **Kennington Road**, and turn south to follow Lambeth Walk and Tyers Street, running parallel to the main lines from Waterloo. It would proceed south-west through **Vauxhall** (with the station at the north side of Kennington Road, adjacent to Goding Street) to follow the line of the Wandsworth Road. Further stations would be provided at **Miles Street**, **Wandsworth Road** (for interchange with the LC&DR main line out of Victoria), and **Queen's Road** before **Clapham Junction** was reached, on the south side of the main line station.

The line would pass west via a station at **St Anne's Road** into Wandsworth, where it would then curve to the south towards Wimbledon. The station at **Wandsworth** would have its platform tunnels beneath the River Wandle, just south of the centre of the town.

The line would follow beneath Buckhold Road and Merton Road before heading to the west under land that was, at the time, not built up, before reaching the line of Clonmore Street. The railway would copy this route as far as Lavenham Road, ascending all the way until it entered daylight to the south of the latter road. A cutting would take it south to the LSWR and MDR line at **Southfields** station; it would enter twin tube tunnels just north of this point. The generating station for the railway would be sited between the west side of the cutting and the LSWR line.

The tunnels would then follow the route of Vineyard Hill Road, Lake Road, and Woodside, before curving south-east into Wimbledon Hill Road. The terminus would be at **Wimbledon** station, providing further interchange with the LSWR and the MDR, 9 miles 27 chains (15.0 km) from Cannon Street.

The cost of constructing the line in tunnels of 13 feet (4 m) diameter tunnels was estimated at £3,341,293, which makes the capital of £6 million rather surprising. Could it be that the syndicate, again containing Gwinner, was over-capitalizing in order to boost their profits? If so, it was not a particularly clever scheme for making money. The railway press noted that the line was, in different parts, in competition with the C&SLR, the LSWR between Vauxhall and Wandsworth, and the MDR from Wandsworth to Wimbledon. *The Railway News* thought that it was a rather pointless line for this reason and its official abandonment on 1 February confirmed their view.

A scheme to link Plaistow, in East London, with the southern suburb of Peckham

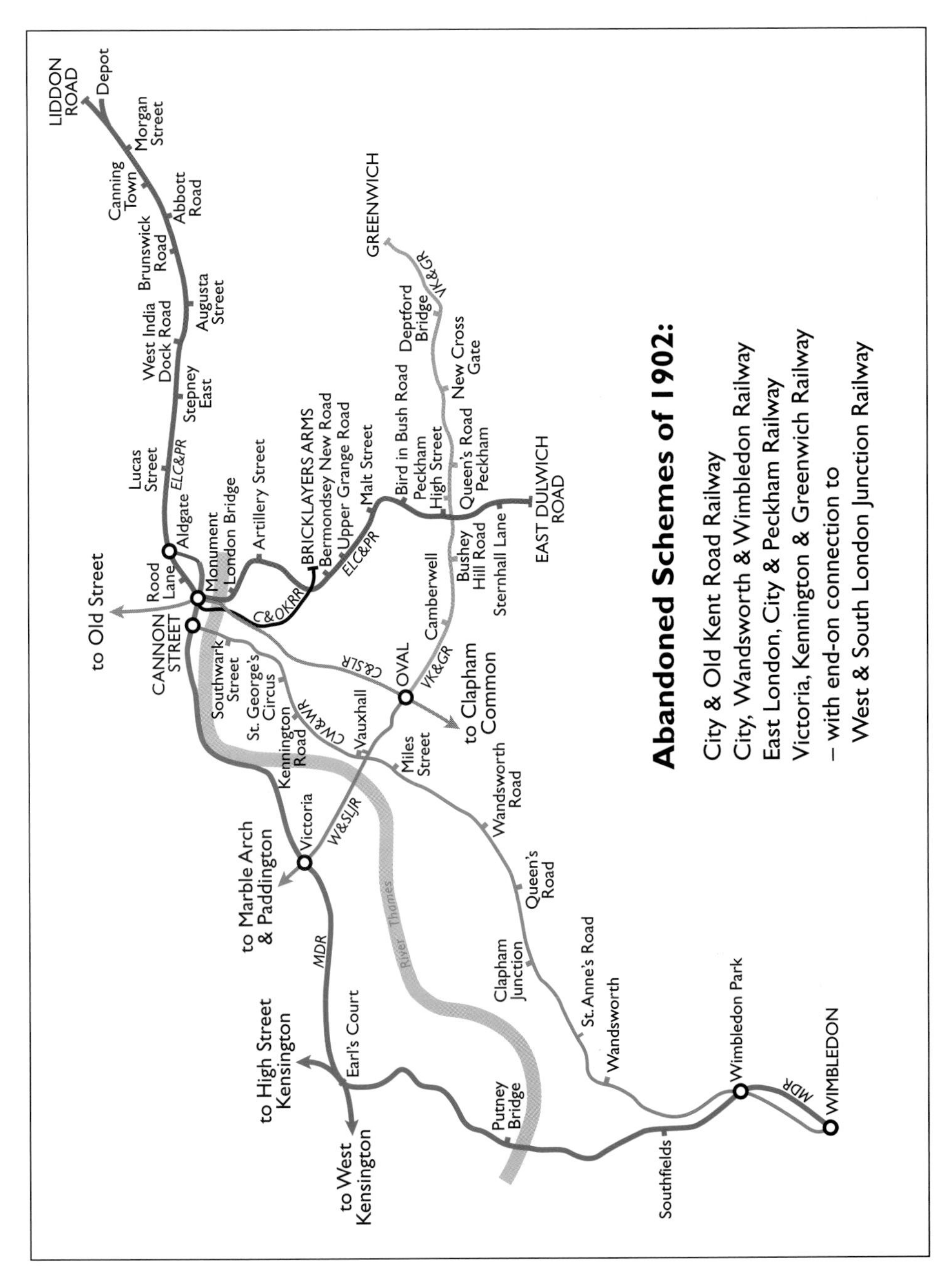

was described under the name of the East London, City & Peckham Railway. The route was to be 9 miles 70 chains (15.9 km) long, and started in the south adjacent to Peckham Rye Common, with a station at **East Dulwich Road**. It headed north under Peckham Rye, cutting the corner at **Sternhall Lane**, and surprisingly providing no station for interchange at Peckham Rye main line station. From Rye Lane, it would cross **Peckham High Street** and continue north below Hill Street (under which the platforms would lie).

Curving to the right the line would follow Peckham Park Road, with a station at the junction with **Bird in Bush Road**. At Old Kent Road it would swing left, and enter a station at **Malt Street**. The second station on the Old Kent Road would be at **Upper Grange Road** (now Dunton Road); the third at the junction with **Bermondsey New Road** (now Tower Bridge Road). The railway would curve north-east under this road. Beyond Grange Road the railway would follow the line of the new road that was about to be constructed by the LCC as the southern approach to Tower Bridge.

Just north of the tracks into London Bridge station there would be a station at **Artillery Street** (now Druid Street). The line would then bear east under Tooley Street, with a station north of **London Bridge** main line station. Swinging to the north, and crossing the Thames just downstream of the actual bridge, the first station in the City would be under Fish Street Hill, probably providing interchange with the MDR at **Monument**. Further City stations would be at the junction of **Rood Lane** and Fenchurch Street, and at **Aldgate**, opposite the MR station, and perhaps with direct interchange for passengers.

Upon leaving the City the line took a straight course due east, following Commercial Road. Stations would be provided at **Lucas Street**, **Stepney East** main line station,[143] and **West India Dock Road**. It would then continue beneath East India Dock Road via **Augusta Street** (the south end of which is now Annabel Close), **Brunswick Road**, and **Abbott Road** before reaching **Canning Town** station on the GER. Here the line would curve to the north-east under Barking Road. The penultimate station would be at **Morgan Street**, with the terminus of the line at **Liddon Road**.

The railway would have two generating stations. The southern one would be in Peckham, between the line of the railway under Hill Street, and the Surrey Canal. That to the east would be on the River Lea in Poplar. A subway 4 feet under Abbott Road would be provided to link the generating station to Abbott Road station. The main depôt for the line was in the east. A branch would diverge from the main line under Barking Road, near the junction with Adine Road. This would head east, rising to the surface at a site east of Prince Regent Lane and south of the Northern Outfall Sewer.

Capital was to be £3.6 million, and costs were said to be £3,480,126. As with the CW&WR, the proposal was withdrawn from Parliament in the early part of 1902.

The final scheme that came to nothing was the 4 miles 57 chains (7.6 km) Victoria, Kennington & Greenwich Railway (VK&GR), which was promoted in conjunction with the W&SLJR. An end-on running connection would have been provided between the two railways immediately east of Oval station.

The promoters proposed a line from Victoria, eastwards under the Thames to Kennington following the line of Vauxhall Bridge Road and the Oval, which section would be constructed by the W&SLJR. The VK&GR section would then start near to Foxley Road in Camberwell, and would then continue by following the line of Camberwell New Road, past Camberwell Green, and along Peckham Road, Peckham High Street, Queen's Road, and New Cross Road into Deptford. It would then turn north-east along Greenwich High Road to terminate at King William Street, in Greenwich. For much of their length the 12-feet-diameter tunnels would be at different depths, allowing them to overlap slightly and not pass under private property. They would only be on the same level at the extremities, and for a short section under Queen's Road.

The stations for the line would have been at **Camberwell** (west of the Green, near to

Camberwell Station Road), **Bushey Hill Road**, **Peckham High Street**, **Queen's Road Peckham** (west of the main line station, between Montpelier and Asylum Roads), **New Cross** (the western station, renamed New Cross Gate on 9 July 1923; no interchange was provided with the eastern New Cross station), **Deptford Bridge**, and **Greenwich**.

The generating station for the line was to be at the western end, on the north side of Camberwell New Road immediately east of Oval station. Capital was set at £3 million, with additional borrowing powers for £1 million; the construction costs were estimated to be £2,275,917. Again, the parliamentary deposit was not made, and the scheme was officially abandoned by the promoters by the middle of February.

The Ribblesdale Committee

The Committee chaired by Lord Ribblesdale considered eleven of the remaining Bills. The other peers on the Committee included the Earl of Clanwilliam, and Lord Aberdare.

Charing Cross, Euston & Hampstead Railway, and the Edgware & Hampstead Railway

The CCE&HR had three Bills that would extend their line from each of its three ends. However, the Standing Order Committee decided that the extensions from Charing Cross Road to Victoria, and from Archway Tavern to Highgate, did not comply with Parliamentary Standing Orders, and struck them out. What remained were extensions from Kentish Town to Archway Tavern, from Hampstead to Golder's Green, and from Charing Cross to the MDR of the same name, including a subway connection to Charing Cross main line station. The original line at Hampstead was deviated slightly by the 1902 Bill, and an extension of time was again sought for the previously authorized works.

The main opposition to the Bills came from some of the residents of Hampstead, who felt that the Heath would be ruinously injured by the tunnels being cut far below it. *The Times* took up their cause, and in an article on Christmas day 1900, made the bizarre claim that the railway would drain the water from the soil, and shake the trees at the surface, in places over 200 feet (61 m) above the tunnels. These views came directly from the petitions of the Hampstead Heath Protection Society, which noted that

> The proposed railway is laid out directly under an avenue of fine timber trees, and your petitioners fear that the vibration which the use of the railway would occasion, and the withdrawal and disturbance of water which would result from its construction, will have an injurious effect on this avenue and on the surface of the Heath elsewhere.[144]

When this was presented to the Committee, the Counsel for the CCE&HR was quite exasperated:

> Just see what an absurd thing! Disturbance of the water when we are 240 feet down in the London clay – about the most impervious thing you can possibly find; almost more impervious than granite rock! And the vibration on this railway is to shake down the timber trees! Could anything be more ludicrous than to waste the time of the Committee in discussing such things presented by such a body![145]

He pointed out that the railway would bring people to visit the Heath, not ruin it. The Edgware & Hampstead Railway sought to construct a line between those two places. The terminus at Hampstead had obviously been suggested prior to the CCE&HR No. 1 Bill; as it stood, the two Bills would construct two railways between Hampstead and Golder's Green, with a junction at the former station. Naturally, the very thought of this enraged the Hampstead Heath protesters even more.

This situation did not make sense, and Yerkes made an agreement with the E&HR Board. This curtailed their line at Golders Green, at an end-on junction with the CCE&HR.[146] The Lords approved all four Bills as modified on 16 July 1902. After a further enquiry in the Commons as to possible damage to the Heath, the Bills proceeded to receive Royal Assent on 18 November. Those of the CCE&HR were consolidated into one single Act.

The Great Northern & Strand Railway

The GN&SR was, prior to the Yerkes take-over, to have run from Wood Green to the Strand, but as part of the purchase agreement with the Great Northern Railway, Yerkes had to give up the right to construct the line from just south of Finsbury Park. The GNR would construct and rent a tube station at that site to the GN&SR, as proposed in their Bill for 1902; this would be to the west of the main line station, so as not to interfere with the Great Northern & City station under Finsbury Park. The GN&SR Bill deleted the original Railway No. 1, between Wood Green and Finsbury Park, and deviated the line into Finsbury Park to connect to the tunnels that the GNR would build. A plan for the tunnels to continue to the north of the station and merge into a single siding tunnel was never built.

At the south end of the line the company sought powers to extend around the east side of Aldwych and south along Norfolk Street to the **Temple** station on the MDR. This was an obvious and convenient point of interchange for the line; unfortunately, opposition from the Earl of Norfolk, who owned the land under which the extension would lie, and others caused it to be removed from the Bill.

The final provision was for the company to be merged with the B&PCR (details later). The Bill, as amended, was given Royal Assent on 8 August.

The Islington & Euston Railway

The C&SLR was not so fortunate with its Islington & Euston Railway Bill. Strong opposition was given by the MR, who objected to the competition that would be posed between King's Cross and Moorgate Street. In contrast, managers from the LNWR (Euston), Midland Railway (St Pancras), GNR (King's Cross), and LB&SCR (London Bridge) supported the scheme, noting the poor connections between the northern termini and London Bridge station. The Metropolitan argued that passengers arriving at the main line stations would be encumbered with luggage, which would not fit into the small C&SLR trains; this was refuted by the LB&SCR and LNWR.

Mr Abraham C. Ellis, General Manager of the MR appeared before the Committee to state, rather presumptuously, that the people of Islington did not want to go to Euston, and vice-versa. There was not sufficient traffic between Islington and Euston to justify the line, and that the forthcoming electrification of the MR and MDR would provide "an infinitely better service than these tube railways could do."[147] Any extension of the C&SLR should go north or north-west. It transpired that Ellis was concerned that the line might be extended from Euston to join the BS&WR at Baker

Street, providing direct competition along most of the north side of the Inner Circle. Overall, he felt that the CCE&HR would provide a better service for people wanting to get to south London from Euston.

The arguments of the MR must have carried weight with the Lords Committee, as they decided that the preamble of the Bill was not proved, and thus rejected it.

The City & Brixton Railway

Still the money for the C&BR was not forthcoming, and finally a Bill to abandon the plans was announced on 15 November 1901. Four days later a second announcement confused the railway press, by stating that the C&BR Bill would abandon the portion of the line south of Lambeth Road. *The Tramway and Railway World* noted that the two announcements would "give the promoters the alternative either of bringing in a bill for the total abandonment, or one for the partial abandonment, of the project". Clearly the promoters were hedging their bets. *The Railway News* reported on 13 February that the C&SLR had asked the C&BR to truncate their line as described because of concerns of overcrowding. Interchange between the two lines would be at London Bridge, and in the morning peak would be from the C&BR to the C&SLR, as the latter line extended north of the City. However, the C&SLR trains were already full by this point, and the company could not see any point in encouraging traffic from Brixton to overload their system further. The same report also elaborated the agreement between the companies: the C&SLR was to work both lines. The first £10,500 of earnings from the C&BR would go to that company. The C&SLR would keep the next £10,500, and thereafter the C&SLR would keep three-quarters of the earnings.

The Bill for complete abandonment of the line was itself abandoned early in the Parliamentary session. The other Bill was progressing slowly, and was reported in July 1902 as heading for Royal Assent. However, by the end of the month the C&SLR noted that the Bill was held up because of confusion caused by a possible take-over of the C&BR by a company called the City & Surrey Electric Railway, which has been discussed in the previous chapter. On 29 July it was reported that the C&BR Bill had been withdrawn by its promoters.

The Great Northern & City Railway

The GNR had two Bills concerned with tube railways before the Committee. The first, as we have seen, was for the GN&SR at Finsbury Park. The second was to provide the same facilities for the GN&CR, together with twin tunnels leading south to their Drayton Park station, which was signed on 22 July. Their agreement with the GN&CR was for the station and tunnels to be leased to the latter for a 999-year term, following construction by the GNR. This included the provision of lifts for passenger access to and from the subterranean platforms. An agreement of 29 January between the two companies restricted the tube company to its subterranean terminus for all time, with no extension to the north.

The GN&CR had a Bill of their own, for a 270-yard (247 m) extension south from Moorgate to **Lothbury**. This would bring them closer to the heart of the City, something that the MP for North Islington strongly supported, stating that the gap between the city and Moorgate would act as a deterrent otherwise. The station at Lothbury would be entirely underground, with staircases to each corner of the road junction. Five lift shafts would be sunk, each containing a 70-person lift car. Had a full-length train ever used the extension, it would have been arriving at Lothbury before it had fully departed Moorgate, since the running tunnel between the two stations was to be shorter than the platform tunnels.

The engineer, Sir Douglas Fox, explained that the station could be connected to that of the C&SLR and CLR at Bank if the Committee so desired. This would be via a passenger subway of about 150 yards (137 m), which would cost around £7,000 or £8,000 to construct.

It was explained that the line could not be brought any further south because the C&SLR tunnels were placed one above the other in Prince's Street, due to the narrowness of that road. The GN&CR, being above the C&SLR at Moorgate, would have great difficulty placing its two large tunnels above one another, and above the C&SLR, and this would have a major risk of causing subsidence to nearby buildings, including the Bank of England.

A new station was also to be constructed between Essex Road and Drayton Park, at **Highbury**, with the surface buildings on Holloway Road. Fox explained that all of the tunnels along the length of the line were complete, and would have to be opened out to make the new station.

The final part of the Bill was for the construction of a power station at Poole Street, on the banks of the Regent's Canal; this eventually supplied electricity for just ten years, before the power supply was switched to the MR substation at Moorgate.

The MR opposed the Bill, noting that the extension would pass just 36 feet (11 m) below their line at Moorgate. They explained that all other railways passing below their line had left sufficient room for them to construct a deep-level line (akin to that of the MDR) should they so desire in future.

Although the Bill was given Royal Assent on 8 August, and construction subsequently commenced, the impecunious state of the GN&CR meant that the extension was never finished. The tunnelling shield still remains at the end of the southbound running tunnel at Moorgate.

The City & Crystal Palace Railway

The Ribblesdale Committee considered the C&CPR between 6 and 9 May 1902. Of the three men who promoted it, Hermann Gwinner and George Riley had been involved with the unsuccessful City, Wandsworth & Wimbledon Railway.

Their plan was for a tube railway from Cannon Street to the Penge entrance of the Crystal Palace, a distance of 7 miles 16 chains (11.6 km). At the southern end it was to rise to the surface to allow easier interchange with the tramways. Its northern section, between Cannon Street and Peckham, was virtually identical in route to the Victoria, City and Southern Electric railway that had been abandoned in the previous year.

The City terminus for the line would be 100 feet (30.5 m) beneath Queen Street, where the promoters considered a possible junction with the C&NESER. This station would be called **Cannon Street**. The tunnels would then pass south under the river parallel to Southwark Bridge, with their crowns some 37 feet (11.3 m) below the river bed. Staging in the river would be used to sink shafts from which the northern part of the line would be constructed.

The line would potentially have a passenger interchange with the C&SLR at

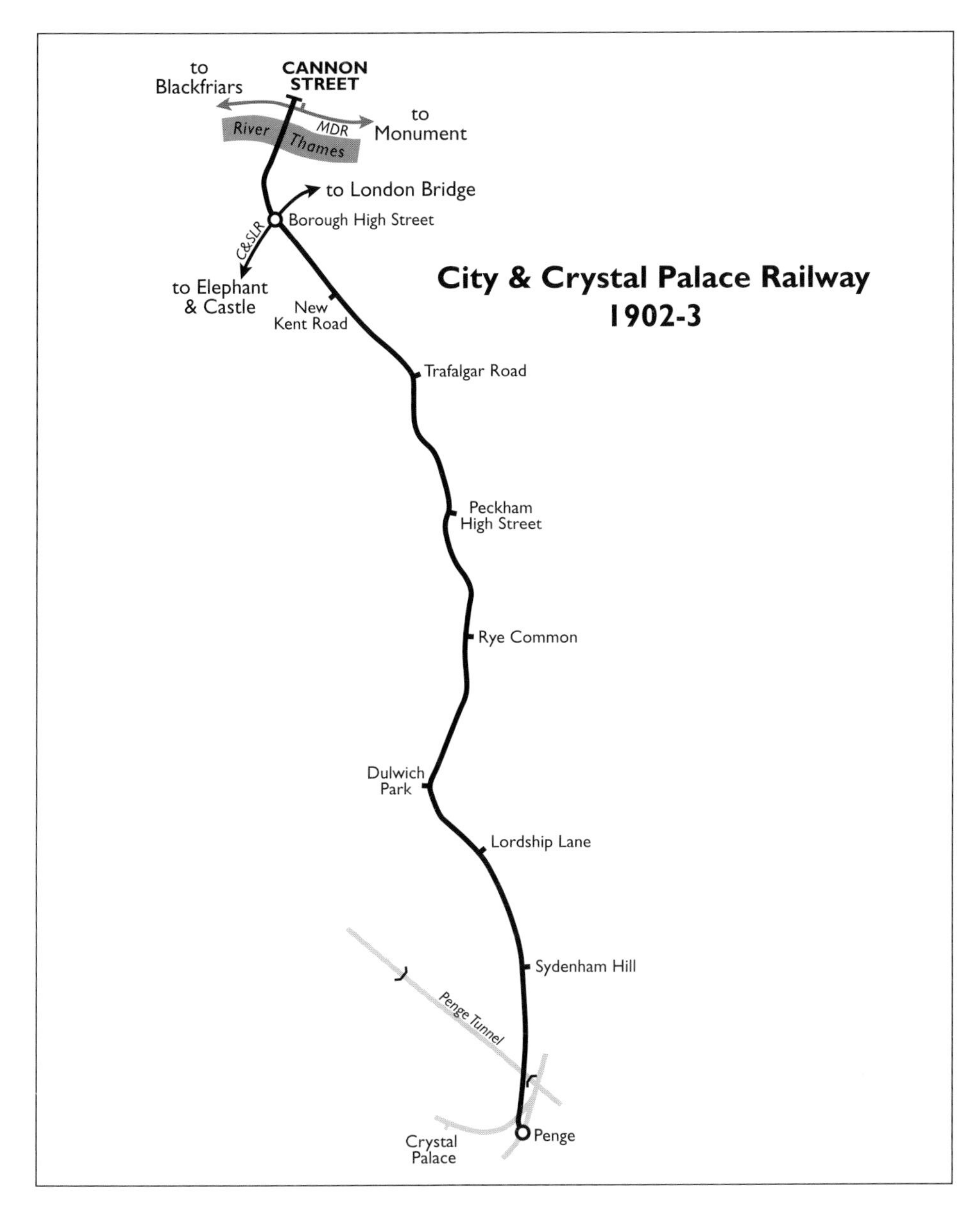

Borough High Street. It would continue south-east under Great Dover Street to a station at the junction with **New Kent Road**, whereupon it would take up the route of the Old Kent Road. At **Trafalgar Road** (now Trafalgar Avenue), it would curve southward towards its next station at **Peckham High Street**. Passengers wishing to change for the station at Peckham Rye would need to walk south to that station, as there would have been no direct connection. Continuing south below Rye Lane, the next station would have been at **Rye Common**, probably in the vicinity of East Dulwich Road. A clause in the Bill forbade any works on the Common itself, either permanent or temporary. The same clause stated that the tunnels had to be a minimum of 40 feet (12.2 m) below the surface of the Common.

Beyond this point the line would curve to the right following the course of Barry Road to **Dulwich Park** and **Lordship Lane** stations. This latter station would benefit the estate of Dulwich College, who supported the railway. The exact location is not stated, but it is likely to be in the vicinity of the main line station of the same name, since closed, which was sited just west of the modern road Lapse Wood Walk.

Leaving the streets behind, the line would pass over 200 feet (60 m) under **Sydenham Hill**, with the station to the south on the road of that name. It would cross under Penge tunnel on the SECR and finally curve east under Crystal Palace Park and emerge at the surface to terminate near **Penge** station,[148] opposite the entrance gates of the Crystal Palace. This station would be in an open cutting, which was to allow the large crowds of people attending events at the Palace to be managed far more easily than if they had to descend to an underground platform in lifts. The cutting would have been between Crystal Palace Park Road and Lawrie Park Road. It would have been laid out to allow for a future extension to Croydon, some 3¼ miles (5¼ km) distant.

The depôt and power station for the railway were to be at Hill Street, just north of Peckham High Street, and on the east side of the Peckham branch of the Surrey Canal. This would allow easy access to coal and water for the generating station. A spur from the main tunnels would lead to the surface for access. Bonar Road, adjacent to the site, would be stopped up, thus forming a cul-de-sac.

The canal company were not at all happy about this, claiming that the railway company was proposing to trespass upon their towpath and bank. They were also unhappy about the railway passing under the canal, noting that they did not have any lock gates to seal the section off in the event of the railway breaching the canal through subsidence. The railway showed that the tunnel crowns would be 42 feet (12.8 m) below the canal bed, and the chances of their damaging the canal were minimal.

The tunnels for the line were to be made from cast iron tubes with an internal diameter of 13 feet. Only half of the line would lie in London clay; the rest would be tunnelled though the Woolwich and Reading beds, layers of sand and gravel that underlie the clay. These beds are waterlogged, which means that tube railways have to be constructed using compressed air to hold back the water, slowing down work and adding to the costs. The LCC engineer was very concerned about this, noting that the "danger to sewers and buildings will be considerable".

The stations were on average 0.8 miles (1.3 km) apart, which was further than on the CLR. This would increase the average speed on the line to around 16–18 m.p.h. (26–29 km/h). Gradients were to be easy, with the steepest being 1 in 60. The track was to be identical to that on the W&CR, which was not surprising given that they had the same engineers, William Galbraith and Harley Hugh Dalrymple-Hay. Bullhead rail was to be fixed into cast iron chairs mounted on longitudinal sleepers. This was to prevent the vibration that was currently plaguing the CLR.

The heavy locomotives used by the CLR served as a warning; the C&CPR intended to use multiple-unit rolling stock, with sprung motors to reduce the axle load to 2 tons. All of these measures would keep vibration to a minimum.

When the plans were deposited at the end of 1901, a sum of £5 million was intended to be raised, of which £3.75 million was to be through the sale of shares. By the time the Select Committee considered the line, the promoters had reduced the figure to £4.6 million, with £3.45 million from shares. The cost of the railway construction was unchanged at £2,964,041. The railway was being promoted by the City & Crystal Palace Electric Railway Syndicate Ltd. Concern was raised as to the contracts that this group had in place. No prospectus had been issued, and just £6,866 had been privately subscribed towards the promotion costs. However, the Committee was shown a properly printed, and yet apparently draft prospectus, which raised a few eyebrows. Upon questioning it was found that the engineer Galbraith had never even met the promoters, and was engaged purely to plan the line; Dalrymple-Hay had met them once. Neither knew anything about them. Galbraith was certainly not pleased to discover that his name was on the draft prospectus, as this made him one of those responsible for its content.

The LCC, who favoured the concept and route of the railway, raised concerns about the finances. In particular they felt that something was not quite right about paying £70,000 in interest during the construction of the railway. A detailed study of the costs for the line showed an apparent £250,000 extra in the finances, beyond the budgets for contingencies and expenses. Counsel for the C&CPR disputed this, claiming that the figure was £48,860 and was for contingencies. The London, Brighton & South Coast Railway, who opposed the scheme, made the excess £600,000. They also noted[149] that as their line was responsible for the success of the Crystal Palace, and had supported it financially, it was unfair to have this competition. They claimed that if the C&CPR were to be sanctioned then the Palace would suffer, as they would not be able to support it financially to the same extent. They also reiterated the points about the unsuitable soil conditions, and the dubious financial affairs of the company and its syndicate. Finally, they pointed out that their line would be quicker, based on the average speeds of the CLR. The C&CPR disputed this, claiming that they would connect the City to Crystal Palace in 20 minutes, compared to the minimum of 25 shown in the main line company's timetable.

The British Electric Traction Company, who were prepared to help finance the line to a sum of £10,000, had an interest in the tramways at the Crystal Palace end of the line. Their Managing Director stated in evidence that he saw no problem with the finances; it transpired that he too was unaware of the details of the promoters. He believed that there might be excess capital of £100,000 in the scheme.

Before the Committee, the Chairman of the Crystal Palace Company, Ernest Schenk, explained that the line should pay a 4% return on the investment, assuming that it carried 40 million passengers per year. His company was prepared to invest £1 million in the railway, although no documents backing this could be produced. The Committee was highly sceptical of this claim, and posed a number of questions about another of his projects. Schenk had asked for an extension of time to raise the finance for the Isle of Man tramways, but refused to explain why this was required. His only comment was that there was no problem with his ability to raise capital.[150]

One of the promoters, Riley, came before the Committee and explained that when the Bill became an Act the railway company would take over the interest of the Syndicate, leaving the latter with a profit. However, he was the only promoter to appear; there were difficulties in getting either of the other promoters to attend and give evidence. In the circumstances, it is therefore not at all surprising that on 9 May the Committee decided not to proceed any further with the Bill, without even hearing the evidence from the opposition.

Other Bills

Other minor tube railway Bills were deposited for the BS&WR and NWLR. The latter company wanted an extension of time for the completion of their railway, and to increase the diameter of their tunnels from 12 ft 6 ins to 13 feet. It was explained that their directors had always intended to wait until the CLR had opened before commencing their line. Their Counsel declared that the promoters were now ready to start work, just as soon as the finance could be arranged. There was nothing contentious about the Bill, and the preamble was agreed on 13 May. A little debate with the LCC occurred; the Council was concerned about authorized Bills that had not started construction indefinitely applying for extensions of time, and thus blocking other possible schemes. The promoters offered to add a clause to their Bill extinguishing their powers unless substantial progress had been made two years after the passing of the Bill.

The BS&WR also sought an extension of time, needed because of the delays in financing and construction that had occurred to date. Again, the Bill was uncontroversial and the preamble was approved the day after the NWLR Bill was passed.

The Windsor Committee

The Windsor Committee sat from 16 April until 5 June 1902, and listened to the cases for and against each scheme. The Lords who sat on the Committee were, in addition to Lord Windsor, the Earl of Lauderdale, Lord Knutsford, Lord Zouche of Haryngworth and the Marquis of Bath. Lords Windsor and Knutsford and the Earl of Lauderdale had sat on the 1901 Committee, a fact that did not go unnoticed by the MDR. Given that the Morgan proposals had received tacit approval in 1901, unlike the B&PCR plans, they were bound to suspect an element of bias against them. Later in the year, at their half-yearly general meeting, the MDR Chairman Robert Perks commented that

> it did seem to us unfortunate—to use a very mild expression—that three of these noble Lords who had already committed themselves on this important issue should have thought it to be their duty to sit in judgement on our operations.[151]

Each railway was represented by its promoters and engineers, as well as a Counsel. Cross-examination by the Lords and by representatives of other railways (both existing and proposed) was performed. Many schemes opposed the plans of each other, but a few had begun to reach agreements.

The Charing Cross, Hammersmith & District Railway

In 1902, the plans for the CCH&DR were amended to connect to the P&CR at **Agar Street**, off the Strand with an end-on running connection and station. This would comply with the suggestion of the 1901 Joint Select Committee. However, this was a minor addition. In the west, the line was extended south from Hammersmith, under the Thames, to **Lonsdale Road** in Barnes (at the junction with Bridge Road). The power station and depôt would be adjacent to the railway on the south side of the river. A short railway would rise to the surface from the tunnels to assist in the disposal of spoil from the tunnels. Barges would be used to carry away as much as possible. This line would then be used for depôt access once the railway was operational.

The most radical change was the addition of an extra line through the West End. This would branch from the end of the main line at Agar Street (where the P&CR would potentially continue the main route), and curve round under King William Street (now William IV Street) and Leicester Square to a station at **Coventry Street**. The line would then pass beneath Piccadilly Circus, into Piccadilly, and back to Hyde Park Corner with an intermediate station at **Walsingham House** (the same location as today's Green Park station). At **Hyde Park Corner** separate platforms would be made for this line to the east of the platforms on the main route. There would be no running connection to the other route, but passengers would be able to interchange between the trains by walking along a low-level subway 40–50 feet long (12–15 m). A similar arrangement would exist at Agar Street, with platforms on both the main line (under the Strand) and the Piccadilly branch (under King William Street). Passengers would pass between the platforms via a passageway, since trains would not run from the Piccadilly line to the main route; the running connection at this point would only be for rolling stock transfer. This would comply with the suggestion from the previous year's Joint Select Committee that junctions should be avoided on running lines. A shuttle service would operate the length of this line.

Hyde Park Corner station would be entirely below the surface, with access via stairwells in front of St George's Hospital (on the south-west corner of the junction) and in front of the Park gates.

Changes to the original route included the dropping of a station at Down Street, and the routeing of the line along Kensington Gore under Hyde Park, placing it equidistantly between the Albert Memorial and the Royal Albert Hall. Concerns had been raised previously about its proximity to the latter building.

The running tunnels were increased in size to 13 ft 6 ins (4.1 m) diameter; the minimum at stations would be 21 feet (6.4 m). Reginald Middleton, engineer to the line, advocated using brick tunnels throughout, as being cheaper, reducing vibration, and lasting longer compared with cast iron. It would also, he claimed, be easier to construct cross-passages between the tunnels. The ballast was to be finer than on railways hitherto constructed, and would probably be gravel; he mentioned that sand might be even better for absorbing vibration. The rails would be of 90 lb/yd (44.7 kg/m) flat-bottomed rail, mounted on longitudinal sleepers laid in the ballast, and joined by extra-long fishplates. All of these measures were aimed at reducing vibration.

Unusually, electric lifts were specified for the stations (most lifts at the time were hydraulic). Multiple-unit trains were to be used. Unfortunately, consideration of the Bill ceased before any further details of them could be provided.

The power station was to generate 5000 V for distribution to three or four sub-stations along the route of the line. There it would be reduced and fed to a single central conductor rail, with the current returning via the running rails. The promoters noted that if their line was connected directly to the P&CR, as had been suggested the previous year, additional collector shoes could be fitted to their trains to allow them to work over the P&CR track with its two conductor rails.

Other questions raised during the Committee phase concerned the rationale behind two separate lines between Hyde Park Corner and Agar Street. The promoters explained that they desired to get passengers to Charing Cross from the west as quickly as possible; indeed, they reckoned that their line would achieve this in 17 minutes, compared to 24 by MDR, principally by having no intermediate stations between Hyde Park Corner and Charing Cross. However, the Piccadilly route was also desirable for traffic purposes. It was kept as a shuttle, rather than being the main line, because the additional stations would slow trains from the west. They also noted that they could connect to the CLR proposal at Charing Cross, and were rather surprised to learn that the CLR scheme was a self-contained loop that would not be enhanced by a junction with a parallel railway! The promoters stated that the new proposals for 1902 linking Hammersmith and Charing Cross (by the P&CR, the CLR, and the LUER) were "jumping their claim", as they had proposed this route the previous year.

In opposition to the CCH&DR Bill, the P&CR noted that their route served the Piccadilly district better as it was on their main line. The London United Electric Railway, promoted by the owners of the London United Tramways, noted that their trams brought passengers to the Barnes side of Hammersmith Bridge, and that this was therefore their traffic by right.

The GWR opposed the Bill because of concern about damage to the West London Railway, of which they were joint owner. They also voiced concern about electrical interference with the signalling equipment emanating from the tube line. Together with the MR they were joint owners of the Hammersmith & City Railway, which linked Paddington with Hammersmith. Another petition was submitted by the two companies, who objected because they believed that the CCH&DR was "wholly uncalled for and unnecessary ... the construction of these railways cannot be justified whether with regard to the demands for railway accommodation or the probability of a remunerative return on the expenditure of capital involved".[152] Essentially they objected to the competition.

The LCC, as usual, brought up the subject of workmen's fares. The company had not specified a single fare, and the last train on which workmen's tickets were to be permitted in the morning was 7.30 a.m. – the LCC wanted this to be 8 a.m. The Council also brought up a concern that had been raised by the Navy League: that of potential damage to Nelson's Column. However, the LCC could not oppose the Bill on these grounds, as the Column was the responsibility of the Office of Works.

A lot of the discussion was about the origin of the capital and equipment. The promoters felt that the American-financed tubes would source their equipment from America – as the CLR had done. Counsel for the Yerkes-owned B&PCR refuted this in their case, stating that all of their contracts were being placed in England.

Additional promoters were named in 1902 as Willans & Robinson Ltd and Armstrong Whitworth & Company Ltd, both of whom were manufacturers of engines, as well as the Glasgow-based iron works Merry & Cunningham. The railway was owned by The Charing Cross Syndicate Ltd, a small company set up by the promoters with £10,000 capital. An agreement of 11 April 1902 between the railway and Willans & Robinson, in which the latter agreed to supply capital, in return for executing much of the construction work was cited. Mark Robinson, Chairman & MD of Willans & Robinson was questioned, and admitted that he was a member of the Charing Cross Syndicate. He also claimed that the London & Provincial Electric Construction Co had ceased all interest in the CCH&DR. However, as shown in the previous chapter, some of their directors were part of the new syndicate in 1902.

The capital for the railway was increased by £1.2 million to £3.3 million, and borrowing powers were raised by £400,000 to £1.1 million. Construction costs were estimated at £459,000 per mile. The Committee raised concerns as to the large difference between cost and capital; these questions were not answered well by the promoters. It was shown that the line was perhaps over-capitalized by as much as £1.25 million. The LCC noted in their minutes that the cost per mile was "unduly large when compared with the scheme of the CLR Company".

On 13 May the Charing Cross, Hammersmith & District Railway became the first scheme to be completely rejected by the Windsor Committee.

The King's Road Railway

The King's Road Railway (KRR) had, in their No. 2 Bill, proposed a 1 mile 3 furlongs 0.76 chains (2.2 km) extension of their line. It would continue beneath the New King's Road at Eel Brook Common, curving slightly southward to pass immediately west of **Putney Bridge** MDR station. On the north bank of the Thames it would cross under Vestry Wharf, and on the south Brewhouse Lane. Passing under property, it would terminate at the junction of Montserrat Road and Putney High Street, just north of **Putney** station, on the south side of the river. This was in accordance with the suggestion of the 1901 Select Committee.

They also proposed a pair of subways, one connecting the KRR station in Buckingham Palace Road with Wilton Street, to the east of the main line station. The other was to link in to the existing subway between the main line and MDR stations.

The power supply for the line was also being reconsidered, and the new Bill would allow the KRR to enter into agreements with the W&SLJR, the MDR (whose new power station was being constructed adjacent to the proposed site for the KRR power station), the MR, and the LSWR.

The line was supported by all of the borough councils through whose areas it would pass, with the exception of Westminster. However, the opposition to the Bill was strong.

The MDR objected, as would be expected for a railway that competed between Putney Bridge and Victoria. The LB&SCR, part owners of Victoria station, lodged a petition against the KRR. They had concerns about potential damage to Victoria station and the Grosvenor Hotel, which was being renovated by them at the time, and was located immediately adjacent to the site for the KRR station. They noted that the station was built on very marshy ground, a legacy of it being a filled-in canal basin; this would make the ground more susceptible to subsidence when tunnelling occurred. The subway connection also incurred their wrath, with them stating that the existing subway could barely cope with the traffic. They did not want lots of people crowding into their station forecourt to use someone else's railway. They pointed out that the CCE&HR had proposed a similar connecting subway the previous year (when their No. 2 Bill included an extension to Victoria), but they had agreed not to connect to the existing subway. Finally, the financial state of the KRR company might make it impossible to pay compensation to them in the event of any damage occurring.

The LCC was very concerned about the apparent over-capitalization of the company. In part this was because the 1901 and 1902 Bills were being promoted separately. On 22 April the promoters wrote to the LCC noting that the Bills would now be promoted together, by one company, and that this would allow the total capital to be reduced from £2.5 million to £2 million.

The primary concern of the Committee was also around the backing and finance for the railway. It emerged that the Electric Railways Company was a syndicate with a strong interest in the KRR and W&SLJR. Much questioning about this syndicate and its finances ensued, and MacAlister, one of the promoters, appeared to give evidence. He did not do himself or the Bill any favours by declining to give any information about his financial situation, including whether he would be prepared to subscribe to the capital. He also denied trying to sell the Bill shortly beforehand. On 27 May Lord Windsor asked if they had heard all of the financial evidence; when this was confirmed, Committee decided that on the basis of this, the preamble was not proved.

The West & South London Junction Railway

The W&SLJR was substantially unchanged from the previous year. The plans show that the promoters sought to make modest changes to the route at Hyde Park Corner. These were to move the line further from St George's Hospital, on the west side of the junction. This would have the effect of placing a short portion of the line under the gardens of Buckingham Palace, on the opposite side of the junction. The station tunnels would be 70 feet (21.4 m) beneath the main junction, with the access passage at their extreme northern end, running west under Knightsbridge to the station building. However, whilst moving the line away from the hospital was perfectly acceptable to the Office of Woods, tunnelling beneath His Majesty's gardens was completely forbidden.

Further amendments were made in February 1902, when it was suggested that the pedestrian access to the station should be from stairs in the street at the junction, connecting to a circular subway and the booking hall, similar to that constructed by the CLR at Bank. The proposal was still for the line to cut under Buckingham Palace gardens, and the promoters resolved to fight the Office of Woods on this point, as they were under pressure to stay away from property, including the hospital, on the west side of Hyde Park Corner and Grosvenor Place. Unfortunately a gap exists in the records at this point, and the next record is of a Heads of Agreement document being signed between the railway and the Office of Woods on 10 April.

Ultimately it was all in vain. The scheme was never even considered by the Committee, as it was withdrawn by the promoters in consequence of the KRR Bill being rejected. On 2 June the Lords noted that it "would not be proceeded with, upon application by the promoters". It was agreed later in the week that the promoters should meet the expenses of the petitioners against the Bill.

The Central London Railway

In 1901 the CLR had put forward a modest Bill for terminal loops at each end of their railway. In 1902, their idea of a loop had taken on a whole new meaning. They withdrew their 1901 Bill, and replaced it with a proposal to convert their entire line from Shepherd's Bush to the Bank, along the line of the Bayswater Road and Oxford Street, into a very large elongated loop. This, they hoped, would eliminate the concern expressed the previous year at the construction of a terminal loop in the city.

The existing siding tunnels at Bank extended beneath Threadneedle Street as far as Old Broad Street. These would be continued up the latter street, beneath the Dutch church at Austin Friars, Great Winchester Street, and Blomfield Street, to **Liverpool Street** station, which would be sited beneath Liverpool Street itself. To the east of this

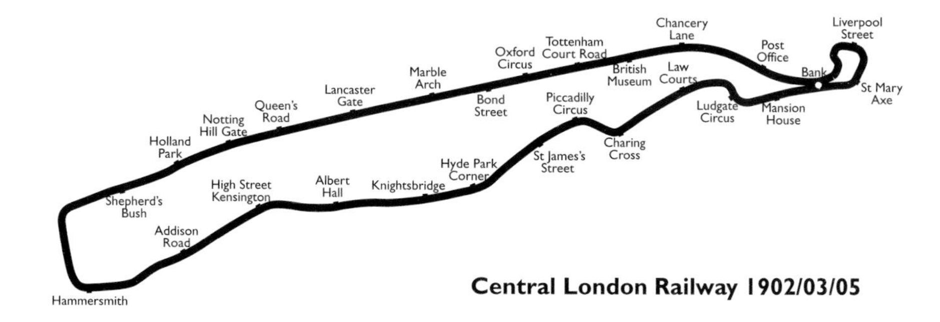

station it would then curve sharply into **St Mary Axe**, where the station would be at the south end, and into Leadenhall Street and Cornhill, before returning to **Bank**. This would have a different set of platforms, sited 47 feet (14.3 m) beneath the original pair, and 14 ft 8 ins (4.5 m) beneath the C&SLR. Strangely, separate lifts and even separate booking halls were planned for the new station. Throughout the City loop the running tunnels would be at separate levels to thread more easily through the narrow streets. Almost all of the curves would be of a tight 5 chain (101 m) radius. The engineer, Sir Benjamin Baker, described the City section not as a loop, but as "a corkscrew; it does not return into itself."[153]

The line would then continue through to **Mansion House** (also shown as **Cannon Street** on some plans), with buildings on the corner of Garlick Hill. The promoters hoped to construct an interchange station with the MDR and its proposed deep level line at this station. Westwards the line would continue into Queen Victoria Street. At the far end it would turn north into New Bridge Street, with **Ludgate Circus** platforms below, where passengers would be able to change for the SE&CR.

Curving west again into Fleet Street the railway would then follow a similar line to Hammersmith as many of the others Bills proposed. This would run via stations at **Law Courts** (at Norfolk Street, and with interchange to the GN&SR) and **Charing Cross**, under Leicester Square, and **Piccadilly Circus** (for interchange with the BS&WR) into Piccadilly. The line of Piccadilly would be followed by the railway with an intermediate station at **St James's Street** before **Hyde Park Corner** was reached. Surface buildings would be provided to the west of St George's Hospital.

The line then continued directly across the junction and into **Knightsbridge**, where the station would be sited at the junction with Sloane Street. Following the south edge of Hyde Park the next station would be at **Albert Hall**, just to the west of that building. Interchange with the MR and MDR would be possible at **High Street Kensington**, and with the West London Railway at **Addison Road**. The last new station would be at **Hammersmith**, on the corner of Brook Green Road (today called Shepherd's Bush Road). Interchange with the MDR would be effected at this station. Beyond Hammersmith the line was to turn north up Hammersmith Grove and rejoin the original CLR to the west of Shepherd's Bush station. One running tunnel would pass along the south side of Shepherd's Bush Green and connect to the dead-end tunnel at the station; the other would loop under the Green to join the depôt access tunnel at Caxton Road. A third tunnel would lead from the depôt, under Wood Lane, and join the new line in a west-facing junction at Bamborough Gardens. This would give maximum flexibility for trains to enter service in both directions.

Between Leicester Square and Norfolk Street, and from Norfolk Street to Upper Thames Street, the tunnels would be at different levels. Law Courts station would be all at the same level. The running tunnels would diverge to pass either side of St Clement Danes.

The existing power station adjacent to the depôt at Wood Lane needed expanding to provide sufficient electricity for the extended railway. The depôt site was to be expanded northwards to accommodate this, as well as providing additional sidings for trains. Had this been built the north edge of the depôt would today be north of White City station.

The 2d flat fare pioneered by the CLR from their opening would continue on the extended route, as would the 2d workmen's return before 7.00 a.m. Four electric lifts would be provided at each station.

Construction costs were estimated at £2.11 million, with land purchases a further £873,000. Electrical equipment, including trains, would add £798,000. The disposal of the excavated spoil for most of the line would be via two single tunnels constructed between the line and the Thames, beneath Norfolk Street and St Paul's Wharf. These would have piers built at their ends in the river, allowing barges to carry away the spoil.

Much of the debate focused on the large, heavy buildings in the City, and whether the tunnelling in the streets directly outside their walls would damage them. Particular concern was shown for the banks, many of which had underground vaults and strong rooms. The slightest shift in the foundations could jam their heavy security doors, rendering them useless. Another building of concern was the church in Austin Friars, under which the railway would directly pass at a depth of 47 feet (14.3 m). The company agreed to take special precautions at this point.

Support for the scheme was provided by officials from the LNWR, the GWR, the C&SLR, the GER, and the SE&CR, as well as the LCC and the Corporation of London. As was usual for tube railway schemes, the MR expressed strenuous opposition, pointing out their planned electrification, and claiming that there was no way that the line could be profitable. Lord Zouche questioned the wisdom of having the line duplicating the authorized B&PCR between Piccadilly Circus and Sloane Street.

Douglas Fox, engineer for the P&CR, in his evidence opposing the plan, thought that the concept of a closed circuit railway under the centre of London was most objectionable, both to the public, and from an engineering perspective.

The main section of the plan, the loop to the west of Bank, was rejected by the Committee on 16 May. Without this, the CLR abandoned the loop east of Bank and left the Bill to pass with a few minor improvement works permitted to the existing line. The CLR felt that, having been the pioneers for an east-west railway in London, it was most unfair that they should not be allowed to construct the Hammersmith to Piccadilly line.

The Brompton & Piccadilly Circus Railway

The suspended 1901 B&PCR Bill was withdrawn,[154] and replaced by a Bill that sought authorization for three new extensions. These were to join it to the Great Northern & Strand Railway (GN&SR) at Holborn, the MDR deep-level line at Charing Cross, and to extend it from South Kensington to Fulham. The sections from Holborn to Strand and from South Kensington to Fulham would be operated as self-contained shuttle services, with passengers having to interchange to the B&PCR main line.[155] The promoters noted that the deep-level MDR between South Kensington and Charing Cross would also operate as a shuttle if this Bill was passed, with the B&PCR taking over the through route to Mansion House.

The Fulham line would diverge from the main line at Ovington Gardens, immediately to the east of Brompton Road station, and follow the Fulham Road to the MDR station at Walham Green.[156] Additional platforms on the branch would be provided at **Brompton Road**. Into this short section of line would be fitted six intermediate stations, at **College Street**, **Neville Street**, **Drayton Gardens**, **Redcliffe Gardens**, **Stamford Bridge**, and **Maxwell Road**. The stations at Neville Street, Drayton Gardens, and Stamford Bridge would have their buildings on the north side of Fulham Road; all of the other stations would be on the south side. The sections accompanying the plans for the line do not have stations shown at either Redcliffe Gardens or Maxwell Road, even though land for the buildings is marked. These may have been provisional stations that were confirmed in early 1902, after deposition of the plans but before they were clearly identified before the Select Committee.

At **Walham Green** the line would curve in from the east, under the MDR, and join the route of this railway on the north side of the line at Eel Brook Gardens. It would then run parallel to the MDR, and on the surface to its terminus at **Parsons Green**, giving a total of eight stations in just under 2½ miles (3.9 km). The only junction with the MDR tracks would be to the south of the terminus.

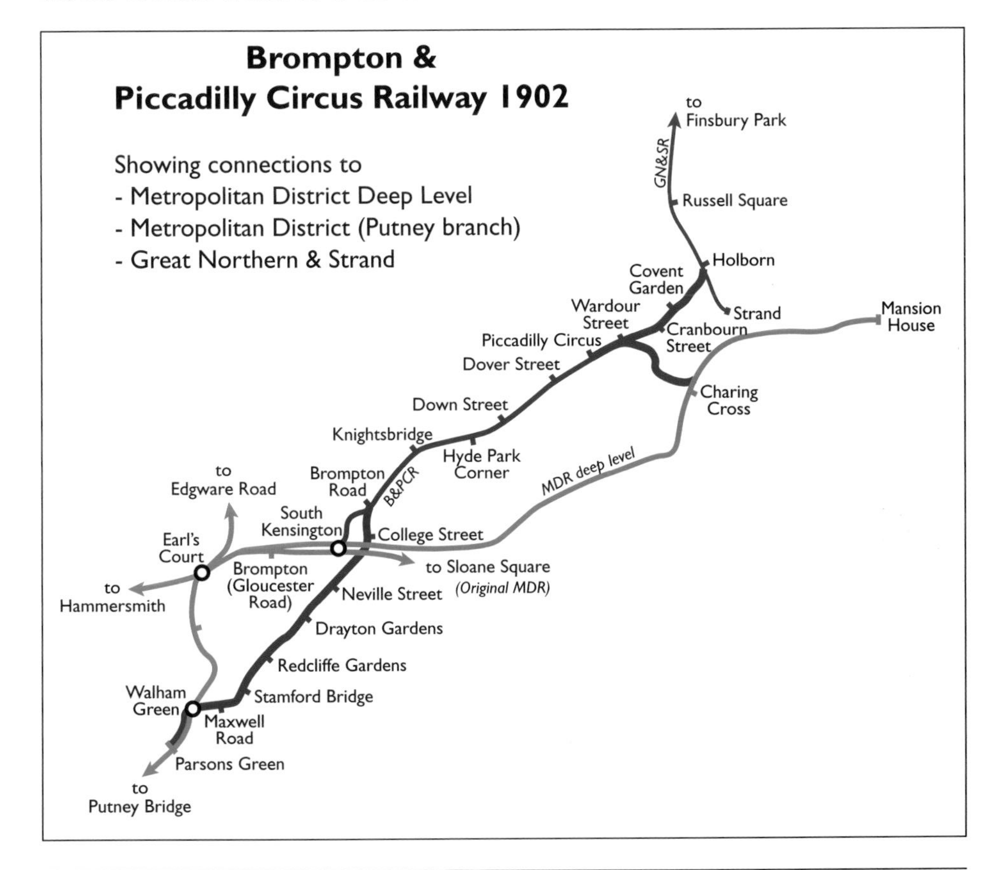

East of Piccadilly Circus the twin tunnels were to separate vertically (i.e., they would be at different depths below the surface). This would allow the line to Charing Cross to have separate platforms, and would enable cross-platform interchange to be provided with the Holborn route. These platforms would be at a new station at **Wardour Street**, a very short distance from Piccadilly Circus. However, it must be remembered that the original B&PCR platforms at the latter location were to be west of the actual Circus, since the tunnels were to terminate at Air Street. After passing under Coventry Street and Leicester Square, the next station would be constructed at **Cranbourn Street**, on the eastern side of the Charing Cross Road. Another short distance on would be **Covent Garden**, sited half-way along Long Acre. Finally the extension would progress under Great Queen Street and curve northwards to join the GN&SR south of Holborn station, and just north of Parker Street. It is not clear from the plans how the junction would be laid out; it would not be as finally constructed, as we shall see later.

The route to Charing Cross would diverge just east of **Wardour Street**. It would continue diagonally across Leicester Square and under Green Street. Curving east under Charing Cross Road it would loop to the north of the church of St Martin-in-the-Fields, and southwards into Adelaide Street. Continuing to the west of Charing Cross SER station under Craven Street and Brewers Lane, (and about 21 feet (6.4 m) below the proposed CCE&HR) it would reach Northumberland Avenue. At the junction with the Embankment it would curve sharply to the left to parallel the MDR deep-level line, with which it would form a junction to the east of **Charing Cross**. For most of its length it would have the tunnels one above the other, making it easier to weave them under the narrow streets and thereby minimizing the potential cost of easements.

In October 1901 the B&PCR suggested to the MDR that the B&PCR should construct the section of MDR deep level line between Earl's Court and South Kensington. The MDR Board were amenable, and a heads of agreement document was drawn up. This facility would allow the two companies to transfer trains at the Earl's Court junction. In effect, it extended the B&PCR to Earl's Court and gave the tube railway a surface connection at that point.

The MDR Board placed its seal onto the agreement on 24 April; it was also agreed that the MDR would supply electricity to the tube line from the MDETC power station. The agreement was enshrined in the Act when it was eventually passed.

As part of their 1902 Bills, the B&PCR and GN&SR agreed that if both Bills were successful then the latter would be absorbed into the B&PCR, the whole route then becoming known as the Great Northern, Piccadilly & Brompton Railway (GNP&BR).

Section 31 of the Bill contained provisions that were to come into effect if the P&CR Bill were passed. The B&PCR was not to deviate vertically by more than 10 feet (3.1 m) along streets shared with the P&CR. There was to be no interference with P&CR. Finally, any disputes between the companies were to go to arbitration.

In a similar manner, section 32 contained provisions for the eventuality of the LUER Bill being passed. The main condition was for the vertical deviation at Sloane Street, which was not permitted to be more than 3 feet (92 cm) downwards, since the LUER would have two levels of tunnel at this point.

In the event, only the extension from Piccadilly Circus to Holborn to provide a link to the Great Northern & Strand, the take-over of the latter railway, and the change of name to the Great Northern, Piccadilly & Brompton Railway were approved by the Committee. The line from South Kensington to Parsons Green met stiff opposition from the Fulham Road hospitals.[157] They argued that the vibrations from the railway would disturb their patients, and place them at risk. Three doctors gave evidence against the line, describing the need for absolute quiet in the hospital during operations. The hospital architect also opposed the scheme, particularly because of the risk to a water tower near to the route of the tunnels. They also noted that the MDR provided an alternative route, making the new line unnecessary.

Engineering concerns, namely a sharp curve of 3½-chain radius (70 m) and a steep gradient of 1 in 40, caused rejection on 16 May of the proposed link from Piccadilly Circus to the MDR deep level line at Charing Cross. Yorke had objected strenuously to the line, and stated that if approved he would be forced to impose a speed restriction as low as 12 m.p.h. (19 km/h) through it. Sir Douglas Fox had noted that the link would introduce four levels of tube railway at Piccadilly Circus: the Baker Street & Waterloo (at the top); the B&PCR 'main line'; the B&PCR Charing Cross link; and the P&CR at the bottom. He intimated that this would not be a good situation, playing on the fears of the Committee members about the risks of subsidence from too much tunnelling in one place.

The Morgan Tubes

The Piccadilly & City and North East London Railways were all still financed by the merchant bank J. S. Morgan. Morgan had financial interests in the American firm General Electric, as well as its British subsidiary British Thomson-Houston, and the Siemens electrical business, all of which were involved with the electrification of railways. In April 1902 Morgan was approached by the C&NESER, and agreed to add this railway to his collection of tube railways. The three Morgan tubes were henceforth promoted as a combined system over which through fares could be booked. This was a key selling point because in 1902 transferring from one railway to another very often meant buying another ticket at the point of interchange.

The Piccadilly & City Railway

The P&CR was a more extensive proposal in 1902. Negotiations with the B&PCR had failed to reach agreement for a connection. One of the key problems concerned the size of the running tunnels; the P&CR proposed tunnels some 2 feet (60 cm) larger in diameter than the B&PCR, which was unwilling to enlarge. The latter railway had itself received approval for an extension along Shaftesbury Avenue to Bloomsbury Square.

Following the recommendation of the 1901 Joint Select Committee a second Bill was being promoted. The Piccadilly & City Railway (No. 2) Bill lowered the planned route between Charing Cross and Piccadilly Circus, taking it below the BS&WR and B&PCR. It also extended the railway to Hammersmith along Piccadilly, past Hyde Park Corner and along the same line through Kensington as the LUER except that it was not to be beneath Hyde Park, but under the road. The stations would have been in the same locations, plus the P&CR proposed an additional station at the junction of Kensington High Street and Earl's Court Road, which was to be named after the latter road, with platforms 46 ft 6 ins (14.2 m) below street level.

To the east the line had been cut back to Ludgate Hill, where it was to meet an extended NELR, as described in the next section.

A depôt was to be provided at Hammersmith, on the south-east side of Bridge Street, with the power station between it and the River Thames. A single-track spur line would lead from the main line at Hammersmith to the depôt, rising on a steep 1 in 34 gradient to reach the surface. Power stations were to be constructed in Hammersmith and Lambeth, the latter requiring cables across the Thames, which would be carried across Waterloo Bridge in a shallow subway.

The North East London Railway

In late 1901 Clinton Dawkins held discussions with the CLR and with the MDR to see if an agreement could be reached in which they would not object to the Morgan railways. These talks failed, primarily because the CLR would not withdraw their proposed loops at each end of their existing railway, and the MDR would not countenance any other company offering a competing service between Hammersmith and the City.

Large changes were made to the ends of the proposed NELR between 1901 and 1902. In the City it was extended to terminate at Ludgate Hill (with an end-on junction to the other Morgan tube, the P&CR). This also involved a large deviation to the south to avoid St Paul's Cathedral following objections to the original P&CR route by the cathedral authorities.[158] This deviation swung the railway south to Upper Thames Street to run to the south of the MDR and Waterloo & City Railway (W&CR) before rejoining Cannon Street to the west of the main line station, and would add £660,000 to the cost.

In the north the connection to the GER near to Clapton station was removed from this Bill. At the recommendation of the 1901 Committee the line was extended, through the new London County Council estates that were being constructed at Tottenham, to terminate at Chase Side in Southgate, and the final 190 m of the original line at Tottenham were deleted. This new part of the line would have been almost entirely above ground, with the tunnel portals being located at The Avenue in Tottenham. Both this addition, as well as the St Paul's Cathedral deviation, were put forward in the North East London Railway (No. 2) Bill. The power station for the line was to be located on the Regent's Canal, for easy access to coal and water.

Some 32 acres of land for sidings, workshops, and employee housing were required at Palmer's Green; a large, rectangular plot of land was proposed, with its western edge along the boundary between Edmonton and Southgate. This was to avoid provoking further opposition from Southgate District Council, who were already against the new railway company. The names of the promoters were changed as well. Arnold Hills was removed, and Dawkins and Morgan were moved to the front of the list. The Honourable Egremont John Mills was added to replace Hills.

The CLR, which had presented a petition against the PC&NELR, suggested that the NELR portion could be retained north-west of Liverpool Street, where passenger interchange could be arranged with its proposed loop line. This would benefit passengers by allowing them the choice of routes via Oxford Street or Piccadilly. Sir Douglas Fox countered that this would be outweighed by the inconvenience of having to change trains, and boarding already-loaded CLR trains.

The London United Electric Railway

A Bill was placed before Parliament on 18 November 1901 by the owners of the London United Tramways (LUT). The LUT were branching out into railways because of continued opposition from the Kensington and Westminster Councils to the extension of their tramways from west London. This opposition dated from the first successful introduction of horse trams into London in 1870, at which point the local vestries (the forerunners of the councils, and owners of the streets), refused to sanction the new mode of transport though the areas over which they had control. This was reinforced in 1872 when Parliament prohibited the construction of tramways in central London, following extensive lobbying by the vestries. The LCC continued this opposition, and sought to acquire many of the independent tramway operators. Those it could not acquire it would prevent from entering the centre of London. Indeed, in his evidence to Parliament on 22 April 1902 George White, Chairman of the LUT, categorically stated that the LCC had blocked every attempt to extend tramways into the centre of London.

The LUT realized that a tube railway was the ideal solution. It could allow its passengers from west London to be transported into the centre without rebooking onto the MDR or Hammersmith & City Railway (which connected with the City via Paddington and King's Cross).

James Clifton Robinson (1 January 1849 – 6 November 1910)

Robinson had a life-long interest in tramways, which started at the age of 12, when he began work with the tramway pioneer George Train. He worked in the USA twice, from 1866 to 1871 and from the late 1880s to 1891, during which he constructed a pioneer system of cable and electric tramways in Los Angeles.

Whilst working in Cork, Ireland, between 1873 and 1875 he met and married his wife, Mary Martin. They had one son, also called Clifton.

During the mid-1880s he was general manager of the Patent Cable Tramways Corporation.

Upon his return to Britain from the USA in 1891 he became Managing Director and Engineer of Imperial Tramways, Director and Engineer of Bristol Electric Tramways, and Managing Director and Engineer of the London United Tramways, over which he started London's first electrically-powered tramway service on 4 April 1901, in west London. To quote his last entry from *Who's Who*: "In 1902 concerned in promotion of great Tube Railway system in London. In 1906 designed and carried into successful operation system of through booking between electric tramways and underground railways in London." After the LUT was absorbed by the UERL in 1902, Robinson was made a Director of the latter company, as well as of the MDR.

He was an Associate of the Institute of Civil Engineers, and a Member of the Institute of Electrical Engineers.

Robinson was knighted for services to transport in 1905. He died suddenly whilst in New York, five years later, and is buried in Kensal Green Cemetery.

However, a tube railway also posed a threat. The CLR, already with its terminus at Shepherd's Bush, was looking to extend this in a loop via Hammersmith, as previously mentioned. James Clifton Robinson (General Manager of the LUT) had a meeting with his counterpart at the CLR, which "proved unsatisfactory".[159] Robinson discussed the matter with White and convinced him that they needed to promote their own underground line. Back in 1884, when he was general manager of the Patent Cable Tramways Corporation, Robinson had given evidence to Parliamentary committees in favour of the City of London & Southwark Subway, subsequently renamed the City & South London Railway. This was to be a cable-hauled line, until the liquidation of Robinson's company caused the adoption of electric traction.[160]

The LUT's plan was for two separate underground railways. One was to run between Clapham Junction and Marble Arch, and the other between Hammersmith and Charing Cross, with terminal loops at each end. There was to be no running connection between the two lines, but a passenger interchange station would be provided at Knightsbridge.

The Hammersmith loop was to run north-west from Kensington High Street to Shepherd's Bush Green, then south to Hammersmith before returning east to Kensington. It then followed the High Street to the southern edge of Hyde Park and along to Hyde Park Corner. The line continued east along Constitution Hill (but below Green Park) and The Mall to the Duke of York's column. The Charing Cross terminal loop ran from this point through Trafalgar Square to the junction of the Strand and Duncannon Street, curved south-east beneath Charing Cross station to the junction of Northumberland Avenue and Whitehall Place, and then partially under the latter street to rejoin the main line.

A small spur line was originally proposed from Hammersmith, passing 32 feet (9.8 m) beneath the bed of the Thames, to Lonsdale Road in Castelnau, where it would rise to the surface. This would have met a tramway proposed by the LUT in their 1901 Bill, but which had been struck out by Parliament. The spur was dropped during the Committee hearings as it was agreed with the LCC that they could build a new tramway across Hammersmith Bridge, and it was felt that this would be serving the same catchment area. The cost of the spur could therefore be saved.

The depôt for the line was to be in Hammersmith, sited between the Thames and Fulham Palace Road, and to the north of Crab Tree Lane. Trains would gain access via a tube line that would loop round from the end of the main line at Hammersmith. This line was to be about 40 feet (12.2 m) below the surface until its final approach to the depôt, whereupon it would rise to the surface. A power station for the north-south line was to be at Chelsea Bridge; for the east-west line two were to be provided, located on the depôt site in Hammersmith, and at Hanover Square.

The promoters of the line were listed as Robinson, White, Samuel White (George's brother), and Edward Everard. Robinson was recorded as being the engineer for the line, and subsequently gave much of the technical evidence.

Finance for the line was set at £4.5 million, issued as 450,000 shares of £10 each, with an additional £1.5 million that could be raised on a mortgage once the shares had been fully subscribed. An estimate of 9 February 1902 placed the cost of the line at £5,413,250, of which the majority was £3,510,000 for the construction of the tunnels, and £520,000 was for the electrical equipment, including the power stations.

A technicality arising out of the dates that the Bills were issued meant that the LUT formed the LUER as a separate company. On 26 February an Extraordinary General meeting of the LUT approved the LUER Bill, and resolved to seal petitions against the P&CR and the CLR Bills.

The City & North East Suburban Electric Railway

In addition to their suspended Bill from 1901, a new Bill was added for the 1902 session of Parliament. This was known as the City & North East Suburban Electric Railway (No. 2) Bill. It made a number of alterations to the railway proposed in the previous year.

Following the recommendations of the Joint Select Committee the southern end of the route was moved to the east, so as not to take the same line as the NELR. Two separate routes were suggested that would lead from the terminus at Cannon Street station, via Aldgate, to rejoin the original line of route in Walthamstow, and again terminating in Waltham Cross. One of these routes was to be sited beneath the existing MDR line between Cannon Street and Whitechapel, and to this end the C&NESER promoters had asked the MDR for permission for these works. They informed the MDR that they would be allowed to run their trains over the C&NESER between Cannon Street and Whitechapel, a statement that the District must have found highly presumptuous. However, the MDR did not reject the proposition outright, and even worked with the C&NESER to plan the junctions between the two railways.

The Chairman of the District, Robert Perks, entertained these discussions from November 1901, and even offered financial support of £5,000. Yerkes, upon being told of the request, refused permission, believing that only the District should be allowed to construct additional lines beneath its existing one. The C&NESER solicitor, Walter Webb, wrote to Perks on 22 April 1902 protesting the change of heart, and also, more significantly, noted that the refusal of the MDR to assist them had driven them to ask Morgan for help. By 1 May Morgan had loaned the company £1,500 for Parliamentary expenses, and had been promised options on two-thirds of the shares.

It is therefore likely, although not confirmed by the evidence available, that there was never any intention by the C&NESER to construct both routes between Monument and Aldgate, but instead that they were alternatives. The preferred route was beneath the District; if that company ruled this out the alternative routeing could be adopted. Both routes are described in the next chapter.

The Formation of the London Suburban Railway

The P&CR was reaching an agreement with the NELR by the time the Windsor Committee began to hear its case. The Bills of the two companies were consolidated before the Committee in April, and henceforth the company was known as the Piccadilly, City and North East London Railway (PC&NELR). Clinton Dawkins explained to the Committee that amalgamation with the Charing Cross, Hammersmith and District Railway had been pursued, as recommended by the 1901 Committee, but that the negotiations had failed. The PC&NELR felt that the proposals of the CCH&DR were inferior to their own, particularly in regard to the route and the financial backing.

Discussions with the CLR had gone nowhere as well, and resulted in what was described as a friendly understanding that "nothing was left but to fight".

Following the amalgamation of the P&CR and the NELR, the next successful agreement was with the separately-promoted LUER, which had a parallel route between Hammersmith and Hyde Park Corner. Following an approach by Dawkins to George White, Morgan had acquired a half-share in the LUER line from Hammersmith to Hyde Park Corner. On 18 April Browne announced that the companies had "practically amalgamated", and the agreement was accepted by the Windsor Committee on 29 May 1902;[161] this bound the companies together forever. It prevented needless competition between the P&CR and the LUER, and allowed both companies to progress their schemes together. The LUT Board heard that an

> understanding had been arrived at with the promoters of the P&C group of Bills for joining hands in endeavouring to obtain authorisation of lines which could subsequently form through routes and be worked as a combined undertaking, and incident thereto it was proposed that the Company should issue through tickets from Tramway to Tube and vice-versa. An agreement had been prepared to embody this principle and it was resolved that any Directors be authorised to affix the seal to same.[162]

The LUER retained the right to promote the Bill for their section of the route, and only they would promote the north-south line. The combined scheme was now to be known as the London Suburban Railway (LSR). White described the proposed board of the combine as having eight to ten directors, i.e., two or three from each of the component railways. D. N. Dunlop of *The Railway Magazine* quoted Robinson, describing the combined railways:

> A scheme which not only meets in the most emphatic way the recommendations of the Joint Committee [of 1901], but offers the only true solution of the burning question of the hour – the relief of overcrowded London.[163]

Dunlop went on to consider that, whilst the scheme was impressive, and probably had better financial backing than the Yerkes tubes, Yerkes had more experience and a more complete set of railways around London. The Committee had a "knotty problem" to resolve.

The westernmost portion of the route would be that of the LUER, including their large terminal loop at Hammersmith. To the east of Hyde Park Corner the route of the P&CR and NELR would be used. This necessitated the abandonment of the proposed LUER Charing Cross loop. Terminal loops in the City had been frowned upon by the 1901 Committee for taking up a large area and so possibly blocking other schemes.

Fox (through his firm, Sir Douglas Fox and Partners) was to be joint engineer for the LSR with S. G. Fraser, engineer to the LUER. Fox was a veteran of many tunnelling schemes, most relevantly the GN&CR and the Mersey Tunnel. One potential difficulty was the difference in tunnel sizes; the LUER proposed tunnels of 12 feet (3.66 m) diameter, whilst the P&CR had recommended a diameter of 13 ft 6 ins (4.15 m). On questioning Sir Douglas agreed that the LUER were amenable to increasing their diameter to match the larger measurement. The B&PCR objected in their petition to the larger tunnels on safety grounds, but could produce no convincing justification for this statement.[164]

It was also restated that the merchant bank of J. S. Morgan was financially supporting the complete package of lines. The capital was probably to come from England, unless it was cheaper to raise it in America. The capital cost of the PC&NELR was £11,380,000, of which the P&CR and NELR promoters (i.e., J. S. Morgan) were to control five-eighths of the undertaking, with the LUER to have the remaining three-eighths. Morgan were to raise the capital and have sole control of the section between Palmer's Green and Charing Cross, whilst capital and control were to be split equally between the latter station and Hammersmith. The Marble Arch to Clapham Junction line was to be financed and controlled entirely by the LUER.[165] This division was to cause a major dispute later on.

The final part of this large railway scheme was put into place when the C&NESER approached Morgan and was brought into the combine; this explains its amenability to moving the southern end of its route away from the line of the NELR. Another result of this was that on 25 April the PC&NELR announced that the branch to Walthamstow was to be dropped, in accordance with the recommendation of the 1901 Committee, as this would partially duplicate the C&NESER.[166]

Together with the C&NESER, Morgan was now promoting four railway schemes stretching across London from Shepherd's Bush and Hammersmith in the west, to Southgate and Waltham Abbey in the north-east, with a length of 38 miles (61 km).

The company intended to source as much of the equipment as possible for the railways from British manufacturers. Those mentioned included Siemens (who were London-based), the British Thomson-Houston Company (of Rugby), and the Manchester firm of British Westinghouse. As previously noted, Morgan had financial interests in the former two companies, and had involved them in the plans for the railway right from the beginning in 1901.

Throughout April and May 1902 the Committee considered petitions against the scheme, brought by a variety of competing railway companies, as well as affected land-holders and businesses. Where necessary, clauses were added to the relevant Acts in order to meet the demands of the petitioners or the Committee.

To protect property owners along the length of all proposed tubes, a "Special Compensation Clause" was added to all Bills. This clause would provide compensation, payable by the railway to "the owner, lessee, or occupier of any land, house or building which shall be injuriously affected by reason of the working of the railway".

This compensation could be claimed within two years of the opening of the railway.

Similar objections to those raised in 1901 were received from the competing main line railways. Both the GER and GNR, who had most to lose from competing with the north-eastern branches of the LSR, derided the estimates of traffic prepared by the LSR. Indeed, at a GER meeting in August, the Chairman of that company, Lord Claud Hamilton, noted that in order to return a 3½% dividend on its ordinary shares, the NELR would need to carry over 63 million passengers per year, equating to 190,000 people every day of the week. In 1902 the GER and GNR were carrying just over 83,000 passengers per day on average from the same area. Hamilton concluded that tube schemes were financially unsound.[167]

The GER sought to prove that an electric tube railway was unnecessary, and that steam locomotives on surface lines could provide the same speed and acceleration. This combined with the larger carriages would obviate the need for the tube. James Holden, the locomotive superintendent of the GER, provided the Committee with details of a new tank locomotive being designed for just this purpose. With 10 driving wheels, it was to accelerate to 30 m.p.h. in 30 seconds, 50% faster than other steam locomotives, and also faster than an electric train. It would pull 320-ton trains containing three times as many passengers as an LSR train. However, Holden had to concede that the frequency of such trains would not be as great as on a tubular electric railway due to the constraints of the track layout at the entrance of Liverpool Street station.[168]

The Great Northern Railway, in the form of William Grinling, chief traffic manager, argued that the north-east of London was already well served by the GNR main line into King's Cross. The GNR also had connections with the Great Northern & City tube railway under construction from Finsbury Park to Moorgate (and seeking powers to extend southward to Lothbury), and the authorized Great Northern & Strand Railway, linking Finsbury Park with the Strand. Furthermore, the traffic levels in the area did not warrant an additional railway, and the fares proposed were far too low.

The LCC had considered all of the tube railway schemes. They did not object to, but drew attention to the finances of, the C&NESER and the NELR. They objected completely to the P&CR and the LUER, as well as the B&PCR, CCE&HR, CCH&DR, and City & Brixton Railway.[169] Their main objection was to the embankment across the Walthamstow Marshes, and they encouraged the company to consider a continuation of the tube tunnels at this point. The company regretted that due to the nature of the soil, it being water-filled gravel, this would not be possible.

The Corporation of London, which supported the circular proposal of the CLR, decided that it would give support to the NELR, but only if it ran no further west than Cannon Street.[170]

Balfour Browne (Counsel for the LSR) claimed that the rival B&PCR was not intended to be constructed; it was instead a block line introduced by the Metropolitan District Railway to thwart the City & West End Railway, a scheme of 1897. In 1902 he now considered both this and the proposed CLR extension to be block lines. The works being carried out by the B&PCR were nothing more than "a little bit of hoarding" and "a man and a boy".[171] As if to disprove this point, the B&PCR Board authorized construction to start at their meeting on 10 April; by 8 May Szlumper was reporting that the sinking of two shafts at Knightsbridge had commenced. One had reached a depth of 40 feet; the other was half that depth.

The MDR complained in their petition that they might not have built their railway had they realized that they would be exposed to competition. Their Chairman noted that the Yerkes schemes would provide a set of railways from Hammersmith to the City via Westminster (both the MDR and the deep-level line) and Piccadilly (the B&PCR, with its connection to the deep-level District), as well as the GN&SR serving stations to Finsbury Park. The CCE&HR would connect the locations in its name to the B&PCR via interchange at Leicester Square, and the BS&WR would provide a service from south of the river to Edgware Road. An all night service would run on the deep-level District and B&PCR (the logistics of this were not, apparently, considered). The view of the MDR was that there was no need for the LSR.

They were busy improving their facilities for the public, including assisting the B&PCR and electrifying their lines,[172] and felt that this would be "adequate to the requirements of the public". They also noted that the City & West End Railway of

1897, along a very similar route, had been rejected at the same time that the B&PCR was approved, and no circumstances had changed in the meantime; therefore this scheme should be rejected as well.

The petition of the MR gave similar arguments about electrification. They also voiced concerns about the construction below the Metropolitan and Metropolitan District Joint line between Mansion House and Monument. Most intriguingly, and in a slightly paranoid vein, they also noted that the finances included 15% for contingencies, and thought that this should be investigated:

> It is either for the purpose of financing the undertaking in an extravagant manner never heretofore sanctioned when disclosed to Parliament or for other purposes and operations prejudicial to your Petitioners' interests [i.e., those of the MR].

They also alleged that the PC&NELR was "badly designed", and feared that it would cause interference with their signalling apparatus due to the electrical working of the line. There was no provision for ventilation, sidings, or other terminal works, nor for lifts and other accesses.

The Waterloo & City Railway had, as a result of its petition, a clause[173] added to the C&NESER Act preventing the tunnels of the latter railway from approaching within 4 feet (1.2 m) of its own tunnels.

The City & South London Railway had a similar section added to the Act, which prohibited the PC&NELR from venturing closer than 4 feet (1.2 m) above, or 5 feet (1.5 m) below their existing tunnels.

Objections on the quite understandable grounds of competition between Piccadilly Circus and Charing Cross caused the Charing Cross, Euston & Hampstead Railway to submit their petition against the P&CR section of the line. A report by their engineer, which has not been located, gave grounds for opposing this line, as well as the LUER and CCH&DR. It was felt that the NELR would not be approved if the P&CR Bill failed, as the two were so inextricably linked.[174]

The Lambeth Waterworks, who were objecting to the north/south line of the LUER, raised concerns about potential electrolysis. Nature had published an article in 1900, shortly after an address on the subject by the President of the Institute of Electrical Engineers. It calculated that for the CLR, if 1% of the return current utilized gas or water pipes, some quarter ton of iron would be leached from the pipes in the vicinity of their substation each year! This seems an alarmingly large amount, but whatever the actual figure is, such electrolysis is the reason that the London Underground, to this day, uses two current rails.

The East London Waterworks had objected to both the NELR and C&NESER, believing that both would affect their water supply pipes through construction, operation, and also through electrolysis and fusion caused by the electrical working. To allay their fears, and those of their colleagues from Lambeth, reassurance was supplied that the electrical circuits would be fully insulated to prevent this occurrence, and promising compensation if it did.

However, the local councils in the north-east now supported the Bill. Middlesex County Council expressed concern that good interchange with the proposed tramways in the area would be provided, and Fox ensured that the bridges over main roads would be constructed with a width sufficient to accommodate the trams. So long as the railway used the electricity from its generating station for only its railway, Edmonton Urban District Council was content, as they were considering entering into power supply.

The LUER scheme was backed by Hammersmith Council, who liked the fact that the LUT had extensively widened Hammersmith Broadway, which had involved the purchase of some expensive property. The Borough Surveyor, Hugh Mair, stated that the alternative scheme of the CLR was objectionable because of its circular route. Upon questioning by Counsel for the CLR, the local MP, William Bull, who also served on the Council, denied being paid by the LUER to support their plans.

Religious objections were expressed by Richard Day, the surveyor to the Diocese of London and Canterbury. The proximity of the line to the church of St Martin-in-the-Fields, at Trafalgar Square, troubled him and reminded him of the damage caused to Christ Church in Newgate Street by the construction of the CLR. St Martin has deep foundations in poor soil, and any draining of water from the soil could cause cracking of the Wren-designed church. Similar concerns were given for St Clement Danes, in the Strand, which is constructed on a series of arches standing on 12 pillars. The railway was to pass just 70 feet to the north, where it would be 50 feet below the surface. Balfour Browne, for the PC&NELR, argued that St Mary Woolnoth, beneath which the C&SLR had constructed their Bank station, was completely undamaged ("they did not break a window"), in spite of the works, which were far greater than those planned beside St Martin or St Clement Danes. He blamed the damage at Christ Church on the sinking of three shafts for a station beside the church. Lord Robert Cecil, Counsel for the Ecclesiastical Commissioners for England, noted the presence of a station in the vicinity of St Clement Danes (presumably Temple, on the MDR). Browne countered that this was some 400 feet away, and this was not a similar situation.

The Duke of Westminster recommended the approval of the Bill on 26 May following the insertion of clauses designed to protect his property in the West End.

On the same day the Windsor Committee approved the Bills of the PC&NELR, but with some amendments. On 12 May the Committee had deleted the northern tip of the NELR section, from Palmer's Green to Southgate, which would have impinged upon one half acre of Southgate cricket pitch. This was due, explained Lord Cecil and Charles Steele, to concern about the damage to the pitch, which had been donated to the community by the famous Walker cricketing family. The Walkers were a brewing family, and had lived in the area for over a century and owned the Arnos Grove Estate. The prospect of a cricket pitch being ruined by an upstart railway was more than could be tolerated. The plans of the railway deposited with Parliament do not show the cricket pitch, and a previous author suggests that the American financiers "probably did not understand the power of the affection for Walker's cricket".[175]

Fox offered to divert the line to the north, which would reduce the amount of land taken. The area would be made up with extra land elsewhere on the pitch, and the railway company also offered to relay the pitch if necessary. Unfortunately due to the presence of Southgate Cemetery to the west it was not possible to avoid the pitch altogether, and so the final section of the line was deleted by the Committee.

Four days later the loop section between Addison Road and Hammersmith via Shepherd's Bush was removed and with it the flying junction, of which the Committee had expressed some disquiet. Their concerns were based upon the operation of a junction with a 2½-minute service of trains travelling in alternate directions.

After the approval of the Bills the Committee continued with much debate concerning vibration and property damage following the problems found by the CLR.

On 3 June the Committee continued to discuss the finer points of station siting. The main issue was the station at Aldwych. One of the LCC's major improvement schemes for London involved the clearance of the slums between High Holborn and the Strand, and the construction of a wide new thoroughfare connecting these two streets. At its southern end, it was to terminate at a new crescent-shaped street, with a set of prestigious office buildings located on the island between the crescent and the Strand. The construction of this area was completed in 1905, with the new road being called Kingsway, and the crescent-shaped road Aldwych.[176]

The PC&NELR were intending to purchase compulsorily the eastern portion of the new crescent-shaped block between Aldwych and the Strand for their station. The plans accompanying their Bill for 1902 show a triangular block of land, looking rather odd because it is superimposed onto the old street pattern, with no sign of Aldwych. The block would have taken all of the eastern part of the site between Aldwych and the Strand, including what is now Melbourne Place.

Access to the station was to be provided from both new streets adjoining the block. The LCC was intending to erect "one of the finest blocks of buildings in London", according to their surveyor, Mr Andrew Young. This was to help pay for the cost of the slum clearance scheme. A model was produced of the western block, which was to harmonize with both the central and eastern block, although design work had not been completed for them.

Mr Moon, Counsel for the railway, proposed that the station could merely occupy the ground floor of the block, allowing the LCC design to be used and the upper floors to be let as offices. He suggested that the railway should be treated in the same way as any other potential customer looking to take part of the building. Young stated that they would not be wanted as a customer. The proposal did not find favour, as other prospective tenants would object to the railway bringing all classes of people into the centre of their block! The LCC was particularly concerned with the prospect of newspaper boys, who apparently congregated at railway stations.[177]

Moon noted that the LCC had permission to construct their own tramway subway beneath the new Kingsway. This was to have a station at Aldwych, and so how did it differ from the railway proposal? Young prevaricated, and claimed that this was not the same thing at all. The LCC-preferred option was for the station to be sited below the Strand, probably at the eastern junction with the Aldwych, with pavement entrances. The railway was not amenable, because the road was under the jurisdiction of the Corporation of Westminster, with whom the railway had agreed not to construct stations under roads, and so this would require a change to the agreement.

The next suggestion from Young was to construct the station to the north of Aldwych, on the eastern arm, where a site was available beside Carr's restaurant (roughly the position of Aldwych Post Office today). The site would be cheaper than buying part of the crescent, and the saving would offset the additional costs of longer subways to the platforms (which were still to be sited below the Strand).

The following day the LCC offered the PC&NELR this site free of charge, so keen were they to get the railway to drop their purchase order on the crescent. This finally appeared to gain grudging acceptance from the railway company.

Another concern of the LCC was that, since the PC&NELR and LUER were still nominally separate railways, a passenger travelling from Hammersmith to the City could be charged two full fares, one by each company. To counter this, the companies agreed to confirm their alliance in the final Act.

Concern over the drying up of wells and springs was discussed the next day, 4 June. The appropriately-named William Wells, surveyor to the Phillimore Estate in Notting Hill, felt that the tubes of the railway would drain away the water from the gravelly soils of Campden Hill, finishing their water supplies and perhaps causing subsidence. This had occurred before, when the Metropolitan Railway had constructed its line from Paddington to South Kensington; expensive underpinning of houses was required, and the wells in Hornton Street dried up.

The owners of the Adelphi and Vaudeville theatres and the Albert Hall, all of which were passed closely by the line, requested permission to appoint supervisory engineers to protect their interests, at the expense of the railway. Permission was granted for the engineers, but they were to be paid for by the petitioners and not the railway.

The First Schedule to the Bill, specifying the lands of which the subsoil may be used, was soon joined by the Second Schedule (for an agreement of 29 May) joining the PC&NELR and LUER, and providing through bookings and fares.[178]

On 5 June the preamble of the LUER Bill was approved, and hence the complete scheme from Hammersmith to Palmer's Green was permitted to progress before Parliament. However, the C&NESER Bill had been withdrawn on 14 May.[179] There had been continued opposition from the Yerkes factions, but more importantly the Committee had deleted the crucial section from Mansion House to Whitechapel, citing concerns about property disturbance. Mr Page KC, Counsel for the line stated upon questioning that the promoters wished to proceed with the remaining section of line from Whitechapel to Waltham Abbey. They hoped to get approval in the next session of Parliament for an alternative route between Whitechapel and the City. For the PC&NELR Browne noted that whilst Morgan had originally promised to find two-thirds of the capital required for the C&NESER they could no longer consider it a part of their scheme. Friendly relations would probably resume next year if the PC&NELR was sanctioned and the C&NESER promoters arranged an alternative City route.

The next day, Browne stated that without this crucial section the railway was "not sufficient", and that the promoters had decided to withdraw the complete Bill.

The local authorities for the area to have been served by the C&NESER passed resolutions deprecating the withdrawal of the Bill. A deputation from the authorities visited Dawkins on 24 May. Morgan changed their minds, and promised financial support once again, provided that the line was satisfactorily connected to the PC&NELR. Consequently on 26 May Browne again appeared before the Committee and asked for them to discharge the withdrawal. The MR and NLR strongly opposed the application, and the Committee declined the request.

Rejection for Other Bills

As we have seen, the Committee rejected practically all of the east-west schemes except for those promoted by Morgan – many because of the dubious motives and finances of the promoters. It was felt by *The Railway Engineer*[180] that the rejection of all non-American backed schemes was "grossly unfair", and that the merits of these schemes had not been considered at all. However, *The Engineer* said that

> on the whole, the tube railway projects have come out of the Parliamentary Committee mill better than was expected. Out of the 100 miles of projected lines about 40 miles have been sanctioned; not a bad proportion considering how many of those rejected were obviously competitive with existing lines.[181]

The table below summarizes the situation:

Railway Name	**Linking**	**Result**
Brompton & Piccadilly Circus (extension)	Piccadilly Circus – Charing Cross	Rejected on engineering grounds
	Piccadilly Circus – Holborn	Accepted
	Brompton Road – Parsons Green	Rejected
Central London (extension)	Shepherd's Bush – Bank loop	Mostly rejected
Charing Cross, Euston & Hampstead No. 1	Hampstead – Golder's Green	Accepted
Charing Cross, Euston & Hampstead No. 2	Kentish Town – Archway	Accepted
Charing Cross, Euston & Hampstead No. 3	Charing Cross – Embankment	Accepted
Charing Cross, Hammersmith & District (Nos. 1 & 2)	Castelnau – Strand, plus Piccadilly shuttle line	Rejected on financial grounds
City & Brixton	*Partial abandonment*	Ran out of time
City & Crystal Palace	Cannon Street – Crystal Palace	Rejected on financial grounds
City & Old Kent Road	King William St – Bricklayer's Arms	Never deposited
City, Wandsworth & Wimbledon	Cannon Street – Wimbledon	Withdrawn by January
East London, City & Peckham	Plaistow – Peckham Rye	Withdrawn by January
Edgware & Hampstead	Edgware – Hampstead	Accepted; section from Golders Green to Hampstead dropped
Great Northern & City	Moorgate – Lothbury	Accepted
Great Northern	Finsbury Park GN&SR station	Accepted
Great Northern No. 2	Finsbury Park – Drayton Park	Accepted
Great Northern & Strand	Strand – Temple	Rejected
	Abandonment of Wood Green – Finsbury Park	Accepted
	Merger with B&PCR	Accepted
Islington & Euston	Euston – Angel	Rejected
King's Road (Nos. 1 & 2)	Victoria – Putney	Rejected on financial grounds
Victoria, Kennington & Greenwich	Victoria – Greenwich	Withdrawn by January
West & South London Junction	Paddington – Kennington Oval	Withdrawn following rejection of KRR

The Morgan Tubes

In several sessions of the Windsor Committee the route of the combined lines proposed by the Morgan combination was described by Sir Douglas Fox, engineer to the P&CR and NELR, and Mr S. G. Fraser, engineer to the LUER. This was done with many interjections and questions from petitioners against the scheme, and some small modifications to the route were carried out before the Committee.

In May 1902, *The Railway News* published a map of the Morgan tubes. Features to note on this map include:

- The PC&NELR stretching from Chase Side Southgate in the north to Hammersmith Broadway and Shepherd's Bush in the west. The line is depicted as it was originally in Parliament, before the Palmer's Green to Southgate section and the Shepherd's Bush loop were rejected.
- The north-south line of the LUER, from Marble Arch to Clapham Junction, with interchange to the PC&NELR at Sloane Street.[182]
- The C&NESER from Monument to Waltham Abbey.
- Electrical generating stations at Hammersmith and Chelsea.[183]
- The large network of LUT routes that would feed passengers into the line at Hammersmith and Shepherd's Bush.

A Detailed Route Description

The Piccadilly, City & North East London Railway

The Hammersmith loop was to be double track, running under Holland Road, Shepherd's Bush Green, Shepherd's Bush Road, Brook Green Road (now the southern end of Shepherd's Bush Road), and Hammersmith Road, rejoining itself at the junction of Holland Road and Kensington High Street. The junction was to have a fly-under, with the trains from the east to Shepherd's Bush passing under those from Hammersmith heading towards London. This would avoid conflicting train movements and was to be partly in the open. About 100 yards of the line north of Hammersmith would have been in an open cutting. This loop and the Holland Road junction were removed from the Bill on 16 May.

A non-passenger section of railway would run from Hammersmith Broadway curving due south to the power station and depôt at Rainville Road. This line would have an average depth of 40 feet (12.2 m), before it rose to the surface immediately before the depôt.

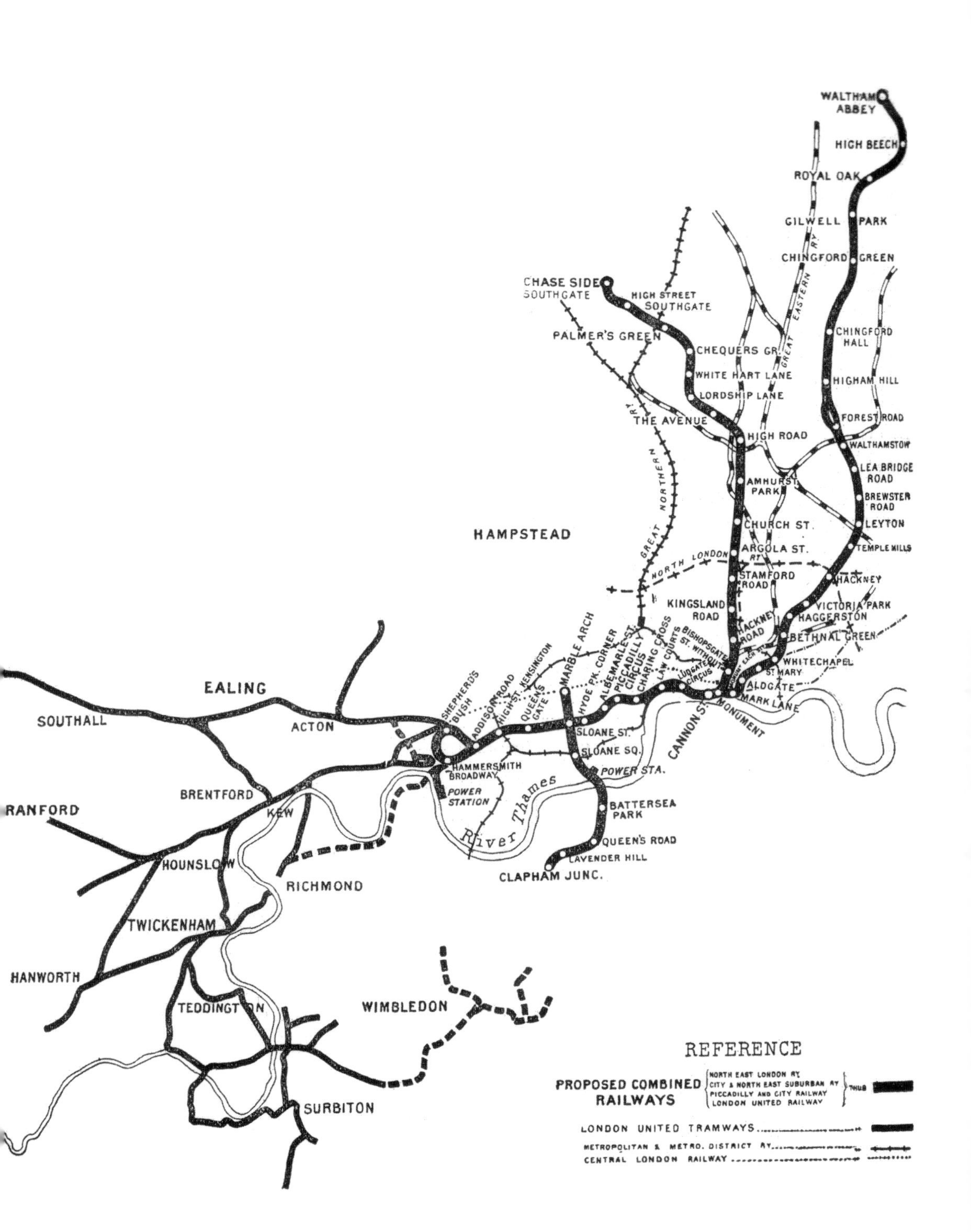

The Railway News map of the Morgan Tubes

Stations were to be provided at **Shepherd's Bush**, **Hammersmith Broadway** (on the north side of the road), and **Addison Road**. These last two stations would provide interchange with the Metropolitan District and Metropolitan Railways, and the West London Railway respectively. In April 1902 Addison Road station was referred to as Warwick Road, but was presumably renamed to match the WLR station.

It then followed the line of Kensington High Street, Kensington Gore, and Knightsbridge to Hyde Park Corner, but was placed beneath Hyde Park to avoid interference with the large houses along the perimeter of the park. This had been agreed with the park authorities, and a price had been fixed (but was not recorded). A station at **High Street Kensington** would provide further interchange with the Metropolitan Railway, with the site opposite the MR station, and to the west of the railway. A larger site is also shown on the north-east corner of the High Street and Church Street. This is the location of the original P&CR station. Due to the width of the street the tunnels and platforms would be arranged with one above the other, to ensure that they stayed below the public street.

A 150-feet (46 m) long subway connection would be provided directly to the Albert Hall from the next station east, provisionally named **Queen's Gate**, and located just to the west of the Hall. The line was then to pass between the Albert Hall and the Albert Memorial (described by Robinson as a "Scylla and Charybdis", when referring to the difficulties of threading a tube railway between them satisfactorily). Although requested, no indemnities could be given to the authorities of the Albert Hall that compensation would be paid in the event of damage being caused – this would have made financing the line impossible.

The next station at **Sloane Street** would provide interchange with the other LUER line between Clapham Junction and Marble Arch. It is likely, although unproven, that a connection between these two lines would have been made near to this station, allowing trains from the north-south line access to the main depôt at Hammersmith. Any such connection would have been for empty stock movements only, and probably would have been single track, bearing in mind the economies that the promoters needed.

The station buildings would have been on the north side of Knightsbridge, opposite Sloane Street, with possibly a smaller entrance to the west at Knightsbridge Green. Between this station and Piccadilly Circus the tunnels would be positioned approximately 20 feet (6 m) below those of the B&PCR.

The station at **Hyde Park Corner** caused concern due to the proximity of St George's Hospital on the south side of Knightsbridge. Plans show the tunnels passing a minimum of 65 feet (19.8 m) from the hospital. Further reassurance was given that the station itself (i.e., the platform tunnels) was to be under Hyde Park, with only a subway below the street to provide an entrance at numbers 8 and 9 St George's Place. This entrance would have been at a very similar location to the original Piccadilly Line building at Hyde Park Corner station. According to the Bill, the main station entrance was not to be east of the Hyde Park gates. The P&CR Bill proposed to construct a pedestrian subway some 12 feet (3.7 m) wide from the north side of Knightsbridge to the south side, then turning east to the Wellington Memorial: whether the combined railway scheme included this subway is not recorded.

Progressing along Piccadilly the next station would have been at **Albemarle Street**, only slightly closer to Piccadilly Circus than the present Green Park station. The plans show sites for this station on both sides of Piccadilly, one on the cornet of Albemarle Street, and the other across the road on the corner of Arlington Street. The level of the tunnels had been lowered at **Piccadilly Circus** station so that they could pass 20 feet (6.1 m) beneath those of the B&PCR. The P&CR had originally proposed a connection to the latter company's tunnels at this point, hence its plans from 1901 had placed the line higher. The PC&NELR tunnels would also cross beneath the Baker Street & Waterloo Railway (BS&WR), which is now the Bakerloo Line. The PC&NELR proposed either a joint station at this point with the BS&WR, or at least interchange between the two companies. A clause inserted into the Bill whilst the Windsor Committee sat stated that the PC&NELR station entrance was to be at the corner of Haymarket and Coventry Street, and that of the B&PCR was to be across Haymarket on a site bounded by the Circus, Haymarket and Jermyn Street. A subway beneath Haymarket was to connect the two premises. No mention was made of a platform-level connection, and as separate (and rival) companies it would not have been in their immediate interests to arrange such a subway. Some form of low-level ticket office would be required,[184] and the costs of running this in addition to the original tunnelling costs would not have been viewed with favour.

The line then curved southwards to a station at **Charing Cross**, where a subway beneath the Strand would provide access to the main line station owned by the South Eastern & Chatham Railway (SECR). A joint station with the approved but unstarted Charing Cross, Euston and Hampstead Railway was to be provided, located at the junction of Strand and Adelaide Street and on the site of the Lowther Arcade. This led to objections from Coutts and Co., the bankers, who had just acquired most of the site between Strand, Adelaide Street and William IV Street for their new offices. Their representative was very keen on understanding how much of the site would be required for the station. Fox estimated the land requirement as being a site 80 by 100 feet (24 x 30 m), part of which was the Coutts site, and part an adjacent site.

Continuing along the Strand the next station on the line was to be provided on the half-moon shaped piece of land that is bounded by the Aldwych and the Strand, with access from both streets. The station was to be directly opposite the end of Kingsway, and in July 1902 was shown on a plan as being called **Law Courts**. Neither this road nor the Aldwych had yet been built, but both were planned as part of a large redevelopment plan for the area that was eventually completed in late 1905. Interchange via a subway with the planned Great Northern & Strand Railway (GN&SR) station at Strand (constructed, and later renamed Aldwych) was proposed, as well as another subway directly to the Law Courts. This station was to replace the 1901 proposal for a similarly-named station at the junction of the Strand, Fleet Street, and Bell Yard. That the proposed station of 1901 had been omitted in the 1902 scheme had not been communicated to the Bank of England, who sent a representative to the Windsor Committee to express concern due to the proximity of their Fleet Street branch. The line was to pass to the north side of St Mary-le-Strand and St Clement Danes, in order to protect the land of the Duke of Norfolk, which lay to the south of the Strand.

Interchange with the London, Chatham and Dover Railway (LC&DR) was at **Ludgate Circus**, where the LC&DR already had their Ludgate Hill station. The P&CR originally wanted to have their station directly below Ludgate Circus, but the

Corporation of London objected for various reasons, including the presence of the Fleet Sewer. Therefore the station was to be sited on the corner of Fleet Street and Bridge Street, with entrances onto Fleet Street and Bride Lane. The LC&DR "refused to entertain" the proposed direct passenger interchange; the P&CR remained hopeful, and it was explained that the tube station could be double-ended. Separate lifts would connect the main line station with the eastern end of the tube platforms, which were directly below the forecourt of the existing station and on an 8-chain curve. If the Corporation of London so desired, a subway would be constructed beneath Fleet Street giving access to the tube station from the north side of the road.

At this point the line transferred to the NELR, and the deviation to avoid St Paul's Cathedral began. From its position just south of Ludgate Circus the line curved to the south beneath the LC&DR viaduct, and the running tunnels were placed one above the other (presumably to minimize the amount of private property under which they ran). Once below the viaduct and facing due south the line curved east so that it ran below Upper Thames Street (and below some property on the way), and above and to the south of the MDR and W&CR.

It would originally have been above the level of the authorized deep-level District Railway, since the NELR had proposed an end-on connection. Since this was no longer the case, Fox stated that they had decided to lower the tunnels by 30 feet, placing them below the deep-level District. The additional costs incurred from the deeper lift shafts at three stations would be compensated by the line being deeper in the London clay, and so compressed air working would not be required.

Tunnelling using Compressed Air

Tunnelling using compressed air was used in weaker soils, such as sands and gravels; the higher air pressure held back the water and unconsolidated soil. It had the disadvantage of requiring the miners to spend time in decompression chambers at the end of their shifts. This was so as to avoid getting the dreaded 'bends', which have caused paralysis and even death.

The use of compressed air required the provision of airlocks to maintain the pressure at the tunnel face. If the air pressure was not carefully controlled then a 'blowout' could occur, in which the air blasts a hole from the tunnel face to the surface. During the construction of the Baker Street & Waterloo Railway, compressed air was used under the Thames. Huge spouts of water occasionally erupted from the surface of the river if the air pressure was raised too high.

Continuing east, Upper Thames Street was followed to Lambeth Hill, at which point the line swung back to the north to pass below Garlick Hill, Queen Street, and College Hill to **Cannon Street**. At this station interchange would be provided to the MDR (at their Mansion House station), the terminus of the C&NESER and the proposed City & Crystal Palace Railway. The PC&NELR station would be above the shunting neck of the deep-level District railway and below the C&NESER. A lift and emergency stairs were noted at this station – we can presume that similar facilities were to be provided at all stations, since escalators were not yet in use on underground railways in London.

From Cannon Street the line was to run beneath the MDR and above the

C&NESER as far as **Monument** station. At Monument there would be interchange with the MDR, the proposed City and Brixton Railway, the C&NESER, and the City & South London Railway. The latter company had moved their station from the cramped confines of the terminus at King William Street to a through station at Bank less than two years previously, as part of their northern extension to Moorgate and then Angel. The PC&NELR platforms would have a 7-chain (141 m) curve, and have been located just below the C&SLR, aligned beneath Gracechurch Street. The station building itself was planned to be sited on the corner of Fenchurch Street.

A sharp turn to the north would have been necessary to follow Gracechurch Street, under which the line would have continued to the main line station of Liverpool Street, although the proposed tube station was shown on the map of July 1902 as **Bishopsgate Street Without**. Due to the narrowness of Bishopsgate the tubes would have been one above the other, with the higher tube some 71 feet below the road surface. The station building was to be located at the corner of Bishopsgate and New Street, opposite the GER terminus. Passengers would be able to transfer to the main line station of the Great Eastern Railway, and the Metropolitan Railway. The MR was unhappy about the 31 ft 6 ins vertical distance between their railway and the PC&NELR, as they wanted sufficient space to insert a station between them should they decide to construct their own deep-level line. Sir Douglas Fox agreed to lower the PC&NELR by three feet to accommodate this request, and to insert a clause in the Bill to this effect.

The Central London Railway (CLR), currently terminating at Bank, had also planned an extension to Liverpool Street, and even received Parliamentary approval in 1892. Problems in negotiations with the GER caused this to be dropped, and the Joint Select Committee and the Windsor Committee rejected further proposals in 1900 and 1902. Had the extension been built, the PC&NELR proposed direct passenger interchange between their stations. It was to be seven years before Parliamentary powers were obtained for the extension, and the CLR did not actually complete it until 1912.

North of Bishopsgate Street Without, the GER was initially concerned about the depth of the line where it passed below its own tracks from Liverpool Street. It wanted to be able to construct an express tube parallel to its line at some unspecified point in the future, and needed to be sure that sufficient space was available above the PC&NELR. It was eventually satisfied with the 30 feet depth provided.

The line as far as Tottenham was substantially unchanged from the 1901 Bill, with stations at **Hackney Road** (at its junction with Shoreditch High Street, Kingsland Road, and Old Street), **Kingsland Road** to the south of the Regent's Canal, **Stamford Road** where that road meets the Kingsland Road, and the junction of **Arcola Street** and Stoke Newington Road. The next station would have been located where Stoke Newington High Street meets **Church Street**, and unusually no interchange would be provided to the GER station at Stoke Newington.

Further north a station was to be located at the road junction of Stamford Hill and **Amhurst Park**, and at the junction of Tottenham Green and High Road, although this station was to be called **Seven Sisters Road** (or **High Road** on earlier plans). No indication is given as to whether interchange would be provided with Seven Sisters GER station (distance between the station sites makes it unlikely) but interchange would be possible with the newly authorized tramways of Middlesex County Council.

After turning to the north-west at Philip Lane, the next station was in the open on the Southgate extension, and would have been at **The Avenue**, near to the current-day intersection with Gloucester Road. This station was just to the north of the tunnel portals, which were sited at Higham Road. Continuing as a surface railway on an embankment about 18 feet (5.5 m) high, the western edge of the LCC Tottenham estate was first to be served by **Lordship Lane** (located at the junction with Westbury Avenue, on the site of Grainger's Farm, and at the south-west corner of the estate). Serving the north-west corner of the estate, where the line ran northwards, would be **White Hart Lane** station (probably between the junctions with Rivulet and Fenton Roads). The railway was obliged to create roads and bridges on the estate as required by the LCC. At this point the line would have entered a short 30-feet (9.1 m) deep cutting to keep it level as it passed through high ground.

The northern LCC Tottenham estate would have one station at **Chequers Green** (near the current junction of Tottenhall Road and Pasteur Gardens, on the site of Eley's Farm). This station would have been sited just to the west of the main sidings and workshops for the railway, which were to cover approximately 32 acres.

The line then left the estate, turned back to the north-west, and passed through **Palmer's Green** with the station on Green Lanes between Hazelwood Lane and Lodge Drive. This station would again provide interchange with the MCC tramways.

The final two stations proposed for the line, but deleted by the Windsor Committee, were to be at **High Street Southgate** and **Chase Side Southgate**. The former station was to be sited at Ash Lodge, which was in 1881 the first seat of Southgate local government. The proposed demolition of this building, today marked with a blue plaque, was another reason for local opposition to the railway. Beyond this penultimate station the line would have skirted the northern edge of Southgate cricket ground, and removed one corner. After skirting the northern edge of the cemetery, the line was to swing north-west to terminate at the junction of Chase Side and Chase Way. The route through Southgate would have been placed into a cutting around 20 feet deep.

Presumably the company had been hoping to develop Southgate into a commuter suburb, in a similar fashion to the growth of Golders Green after the arrival of the CCE&HR in 1907. In 1902, it was "little more than a huddle of cottages, a smithy, a church and a chapel",[185] and so the potential for growth was high.

The London United Electric Railway (North–South Line)

The north-to-south line promoted by the LUER, and part of that company's Bill, was to start beneath Park Street, 20 yards south of its junction with Oxford Street, with **Marble Arch** station. Passenger interchange with the CLR would be provided, and an end-on junction with the proposed North West London Railway was also considered as a possibility. This would allow a direct service between Clapham Junction and Cricklewood.

The line would head southwards, and pass beneath the Serpentine lake in Hyde Park. On the south side of the park a station would be built at the junction of Knightsbridge and **Sloane Street**. Passenger interchange with the PC&NELR main line would be possible (almost certainly without the need to book a new ticket). This station site would have been at the same point as the Knightsbridge station planned (and eventually built) by the B&PCR.

Sloane Street would be followed to a station at **Sloane Square**, where the building would have been on the south side of the square to the east of the railway. Interchange with the MDR would be provided at this station. The railway would the pass beneath Lower Sloane Street and Chelsea Bridge Road to the **Chelsea Embankment**, where a station was proposed. By May this station had been deleted from maps of the line. The power station would have been to the east of the line at this point.

From here the railway would pass 53 feet (16.2 m) beneath the Thames slightly to the east of Chelsea Bridge. It would then adopt the alignment of Queen's Road (now Queenstown Road), and the first station south of the river would be at **Battersea Park**, below Victoria Circus at the south-eastern corner of the park.[186] The next station would have been called **Queen's Road**, and would have been at the junction with Wandsworth and Cedars Roads. The corner site would have been used for the station buildings. The line would have turned westwards at this point.

The penultimate station would have been at the junction of **Lavender Hill**, Latchmere Road, and Elspeth Road, with the building on the north side of the line. A short distance beyond this would have been the terminal station, located slightly to the south-west of the main line station at **Clapham Junction**. The tunnels would continue past the station platforms into a small depôt. This would probably have been built at the surface, on the block bounded by St John's Hill, Varden's Road, Strathblaine Road, and Strath Terrace. It would have been connected to the running tunnels 75 feet (22.9 m) below street level via a tunnel with a gradient of 1 in 5, suggesting that the cars would be raised by cable haulage. This would have been similar to the system employed on the C&SLR at their Stockwell depôt.

The LUER was responsible for constructing the line from Clapham Junction to Marble Arch, as this was not part of the key route of the LSR.

The City & North East Suburban Electric Railway

The line was to commence, possibly with an end-on junction to the deep-level District Railway, beneath Queen Victoria Street. This location is opposite the church of St Nicholas, at **Cannon Street** station, in the City of London. From here it would run east along Cannon Street. At the east of that road the line was shown on the maps as taking two routes. This was probably due to the discussions taking place with the MDR with regard to building beneath their existing railway: the preferred route would pass beneath the MDR, but a substitute was also provided in case (as happened) the negotiations failed. By having two authorized routes the company would not risk a year's delay, and the costs of another Bill, if the controversial section was rejected.

The first route followed beneath the MDR/MR joint line from Cannon Street to an interchange station at **Monument**, and along Eastcheap, Great Tower Street, and Byward Street to **Mark Lane** station (situated just to the west of the current Tower Hill station). Interchange would be provided with the MDR here. This line would then continue below the existing railway as it swung north under Minories and then east again to a point beneath Whitechapel High Street located between Aldgate and Aldgate East stations. As mentioned earlier, this route was rejected by the MDR after negotiations with the C&NESER.

The second route would diverge from the MDR beneath Eastcheap and swing slightly northwards below Mincing Lane, Fenchurch Street, and Aldgate. It would join the route of the other line between the site of Aldgate and Aldgate East stations, under the junction of Whitechapel High Street and Goulston Street. This route was more direct between Monument and Aldgate, but missed out on interchange with the MDR at Mark Lane. On 28 April, Fraser announced that this route, as well as a planned running connection with the MDR somewhere along the section of line between Aldgate and Whitechapel, was to be abandoned. This was most probably due to the cost of acquiring the wayleaves beneath the expensive City property on the northern route, and the opposition from the MDR and nearby property owners to the Whitechapel connection.

A station was to be provided at **Aldgate** on whichever route was chosen. It is likely, although unconfirmed, that interchange with one or both of the existing Metropolitan and District stations would have been provided.

Once below Whitechapel High Street the line continued beneath the MDR, with a station just to the east of Fieldgate Street called **St Mary's**, presumably giving interchange with the now-closed MDR station of the same name.[187] The next station east was to be **Whitechapel**, again with MDR interchange. The station was to be to the east of the MDR station, on the corner of Whitechapel Road and Cambridge Road.

Although not shown in great detail on any of the plans of the time, it is likely that the route would have avoided passing beneath property, and so would have swung north under Cambridge Heath Road to a station at **Bethnal Green**, almost exactly where the Central Line station is sited today. The line then swung north-east, probably below Victoria Park Square and Approach Road. The next station would have been named **Haggerston**, and would have been located at the junction of Approach Road, Sewardstone Road, and Bishop's Road just south of Victoria Park.

The line was to continue along the north-west edge of **Victoria Park**, where the station would have been located a little to the north of Grove Road. At the north end of the park, **Hackney** station was to be at the junction of Wick Road and Cadogan Terrace. It would then continue across the marshes on a 20 feet (6 m) high embankment to **Temple Mills**. A connection to the GER was again suggested, but further east than in 1901, since the new alignment crossed to the south-east of Ruckholt Road. This was to be a connection to a GER siding, rather than the main line, presumably to allow coal trains access to the tube railway's power station.

North of this point the line would have roughly followed the course of High Road Leyton, (with stations at **Leyton** and **Lea Bridge Road**) and Hoe Street to **Hoe Street** station (now Walthamstow Central). About 500 m south of this station the new line in the 1902 Bill followed the proposed alignment from the previous year. Stations between here and the terminus would be at **Forest Road**, **Higham Hill**, **Chingford Hall**, **Chingford Green**, **Gilwell Park**, **Royal Oak**, and **High Beech**, with the terminus at **Waltham Abbey**.[188]

Regrettably it appears that the engineering plans for the line were destroyed during the First World War.[189] However, a number of archives retain the plans that railway promoters were required by law to deposit. Whilst these do not feature details of station layouts or buildings, they include detailed maps showing the route of the lines. When in tunnel, they indicate the location of the platform tunnels, but on the surface just the line of route. Gradient profiles show where the tunnels are superimposed (instead of the more common side-by-side position), and where other railways are crossed.

Tunnels

Prior to the amalgamation with the Piccadilly, City & North East London Railway, the LUER was to adopt running tunnels 12 feet (3.66 m) in diameter, just slightly larger than those used by the CLR. Station tunnels were to be of 30 feet (9.15 m) maximum diameter, and the shafts down to the railway, initially used for construction and eventually used for lift shafts when at stations, were to have a maximum diameter of 40 feet (12.2 m).

The P&CR and NELR were proposing larger running tunnels of 13 ft 6 ins (4.12 m) diameter, and the C&NESER was to have a diameter of 13 ft 3 ins (4.04 m). This was to provide an innovation only introduced to the Underground on the Jubilee Line Extension at the end of the century – a walkway along the side of the tunnel for emergency purposes. In fact, the proposal was to have such a platform along both sides of the tunnel.

The Windsor Committee were dubious about this idea, and worried that in the event of an accident people might be more likely to injure themselves falling from a walkway just 2 feet (60 cm) wide and 2 ft 6 ins (76 cm) above rail level.

More importantly for the operation of the railway, larger tunnels would allow higher speeds to be run on the line, and the large traction motors required for this could be placed below the floor of the carriages, rather than taking up valuable seating space. When the CLR introduced multiple-unit trains in 1903 they lost a large amount of passenger space in each driving motor car because of the equipment compartments behind the driver's cab. The larger tunnels would also improve the ventilation of the railway, which was to be aided by the installation of large electric fans that would be used to force fresh air into the tunnels. Fox was insistent on active ventilation, stating that the movement of the trains was insufficient to keep the air fresh.

As part of the agreement between the LUER and PC&NELR the former company agreed to increase the size of its tunnels to make it compatible.

The tunnels were to be placed not less than 30 feet (9.15 m) below the surface (this was originally 25 feet, but amended before the Committee) and constructed of iron rings, with proper grouting behind. The Bills permitted the replacement of the lower part of the rings with brickwork if the companies so desired. This was probably due to the influence of Fox, who was using this style of tunnel for the construction of the Great Northern & City Railway, for which he was also engineer. This line was constructing even larger tunnels of 16-feet (4.88 m) diameter to accommodate main line rolling stock. Fox claimed that this method of construction reduced the noise level in the tunnel and also the cost of construction of the larger tunnels. In the City of London the spoil was to be removed directly to the river via Broken Wharf, which was to be taken over completely by the railway. A subway would be constructed directly between the wharf and the railway, below Upper Thames Street at this point.

Gradients in the tunnels were, where possible, arranged to assist the acceleration and braking of the trains. This was similar to the CLR, which was arranged with the tracks descending from stations at a 1 in 30 gradient, and arriving up a 1 in 60 gradient.

Tunnel lighting was to be provided, but would not be permanently illuminated. Switches would be provided at all stations to allow the lights to be activated in an emergency.

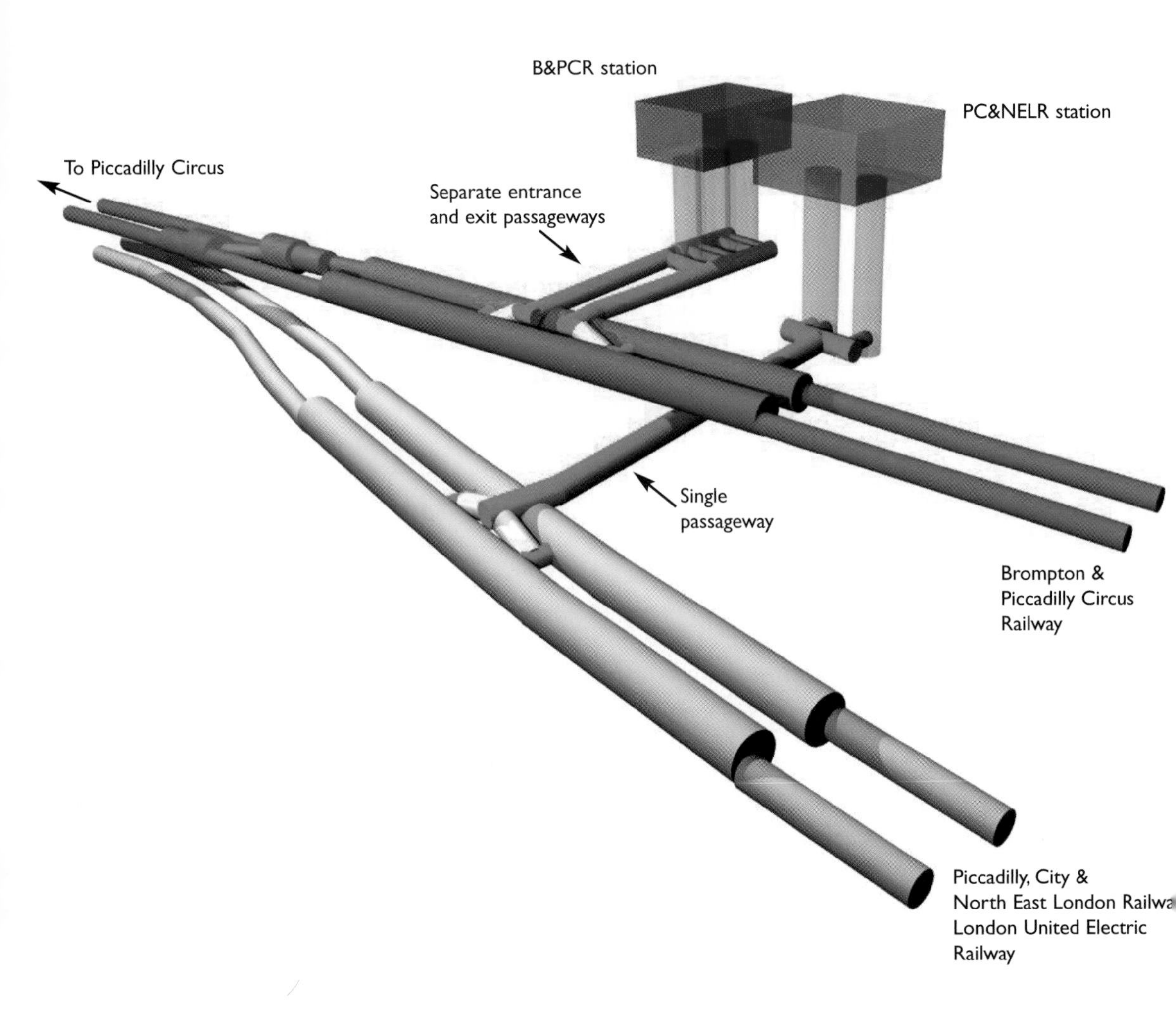

Hyde Park Corner, looking south-east, showing both Yerkes and Morgan stations

Stations

Station tunnels were to have a maximum diameter of 35 feet (10.68 m), although at some of the smaller stations it appears that this would be reduced. For example, Albemarle Street was to have 23 feet (7 m) diameter platform tunnels. Platforms were to be 400 feet (122 m) long, allowing them to accommodate eight-car trains (see below); this would make them some 50 feet (15.3 m) longer than those of the Yerkes tube railways.

A single drawing of the proposed layout at Hyde Park Corner[190] following the amalgamation of the LUER and PC&NELR shows two parallel station platform tunnels accessed by a single subway 220 feet (67 m) long. This subway passed over the southern platform tunnel and connected to two flights of stairs leading down to the platforms. These linked to the platforms near to their centres. Unfortunately no detail is shown for the station building.

It seems likely that other stations would have a similar layout, as similar tube railways of the time tried to standardize their systems. The single subway to the platforms is surprising though; all of the Yerkes-designed stations had two passageways, one for each direction of passenger flow. Whether Hyde Park Corner was thought to have low traffic potential, and therefore could have a simpler layout will never be known.

The *Financial Times* reported that the LUER was considering doing away with lifts, and installing innovative "travelling staircases" in their place, as this would speed up passenger flows.[193]

The 'Travelling Staircase'

A machine for moving passengers from one level to another had been installed at the Seaforth Sands terminus of the Liverpool Overhead Railway in 1901.[191] This was the first installation of a 'travelling staircase' at a British station, and its opening was described in detail in *Transport* on 15 March 1901. It was not like a modern escalator,[192] but rather an inclined conveyor belt. Wooden slats covered with india-rubber were moved upwards by a steel chain; a rubber handrail moved at the same speed. A combing arrangement, as found on modern escalators, was used to prevent items from being caught at the top of the escalator. As the journal noted, "so perfect is this action, that even cotton waste will not catch at this point"!

The machine could transfer 3,500 people per hour from street level to the elevated railway, and was placed alongside a conventional staircase used by those descending from the platform – and perhaps those too scared to use the new-fangled machine.

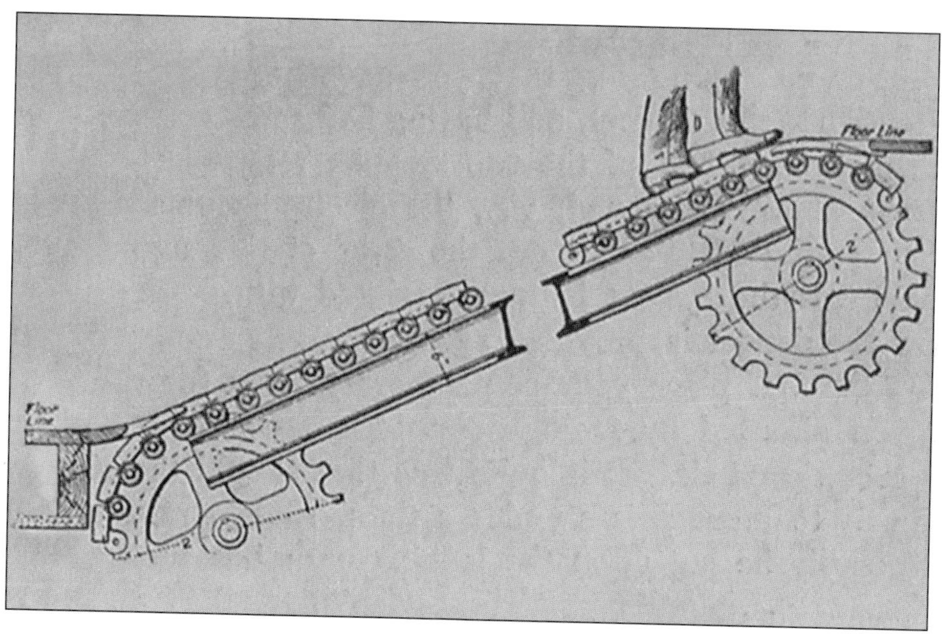

A cutaway diagram of the Seaforth Sands travelling staircase (from *Transport*)

Track

The rails to be used for the line were to be the same as those used on the Waterloo & City Railway, namely 87 lb/yd (43 kg/m) running rails in 30-feet lengths. These were to be fixed to wooden sleepers in a concrete track bed without the use of loose ballast. The sleepers were to be of non-flammable wood, and not creosote-treated. This again followed the pattern of the GN&CR. No sleepers were to be stored in the tunnel.

Between the running rails was to be a footpath, constructed of fireproof materials. Track maintenance staff could use this at night, as well as passengers in case of emergency.

Two conductor rails were to be used, to prevent electrolysis from occurring, which was more likely if the running rails were used for current return. The conductor rails would be positioned one above the other, and beneath the emergency walkway in the tunnels.[194] They would have been additionally protected by angle iron that was to prevent accidental contact. This positioning would make track access easier and safer both for maintenance and also in emergencies. The return current would not affect the running rails; this would help to prevent giving electric shocks to people on the line.

Rolling Stock

The lines of the PC&NELR were to be operated by multiple-unit rolling stock. This was to avoid the problems encountered by the CLR, which had locomotive-hauled trains from its opening. Many complaints of vibration had been received from property owners along the route of the line, and these were traced to the large, unsprung and gearless traction motors in the locomotives. Experiments with multiple-unit stock showed that these reduced the vibration to less than a fifth that of the locomotives. In May 1902, whilst the Windsor Committee was in session, the CLR placed an order for multiple-unit stock to replace its locomotives.

It was for this very reason that Charles F. Jenkin, an electrical engineer employed by Siemens, highlighted to the Committee that the unsprung axle load for the PC&NELR stock would be just 1¾ tons.

Trains would be composed of eight cars[195] (they were also termed coaches), each around 50 feet (15.25 m) long, and would be divided into two halves, each consisting of two motor cars and two trailer cars. Off-peak the trains would be uncoupled to reduce the train lengths, and therefore the number of train-miles operated. The cross-section of the cars was described as similar to those on the CLR, namely 8 ft 6 in (2.6 m) wide, although the possibility of making them 3–4 inches (7–10 cm) wider was considered. An eight-car train would have a capacity of 384 people. No detail of the cars is provided, but it may be assumed that the company envisaged rolling stock similar to that on the CLR, with an end gate on each car to allow passengers to board. One "conductor" per car would be provided, presumably to operate the end gates. The use of the term conductor suggests that they would also be used for revenue collection purposes, which was certainly James Clifton Robinson's preferred approach, being in line with the practice of his tramways.

The total rolling-stock requirement for the PC&NELR and C&NESER was 102 trains, of which 60 would be for the former railway. These would be procured at an estimated cost of £1,208,000, assuming a cost of £1,950 for the motor cars and £795 for the trailers.

It was expected that an average speed (i.e., including time stopped at stations) of 18 m.p.h. (29 km/h) would be attained on the line, and so larger, more powerful motors would be required than used on other tube railways. In order to maximize passenger space in the cars it was envisaged that the motors would be placed below the floor. This was not to occur on the smaller-diameter London Transport railways until the advent of the experimental 1935 Tube Stock. The wheels of the cars were to be larger than those of CLR trains to assist with the higher speeds. By contrast, the Yerkes lines claimed an average speed of 16 m.p.h. (26 km/h), explaining that the passengers would not be able to endure anything higher. Their engineer, James Chapman, stated, "A passenger cannot be handled like a bullet in a gun".

Power Supply

The situation regarding the location of the electrical generating stations for the railways is somewhat confused, principally because of the number of power stations proposed by the different companies at different times. The LUER had originally planned two power stations, one at their Hammersmith depôt site, and the other near to the north-south line at Chelsea Bridge.

The C&NESER proposed to construct their power station to be on the Hackney Marshes, with a plentiful supply of cold water obtainable from the River Lea, and coal provided via sidings on the adjacent GER.

The original P&CR was to have two power stations. Generating Station A (as it is called on the plans) was to be in Lambeth, adjacent to the Thames and immediately to the south-west of Waterloo Bridge. This site today is occupied by the Museum of the Moving Image, part of the South Bank complex. In 1902 it consisted of (from north to south) Canterbury Wharf, Grellier's Stone Wharf, and the Lambeth Lead Works. The latter establishment included a shot tower. These would all be swept away by the power station, which would be connected to the railway at Wellington Street by a cable, which was to be carried across the Thames on Waterloo Bridge. Generating Station B was to be at Hammersmith, between the depôt and the Thames, to the south-east of the Hammersmith Bridge approaches, and on a site close to that proposed by the LUER. The cable was to run above the line, along Bridge Road, connecting to the main railway at Hammersmith. Two power stations were also planned by the NELR, one in Hackney, near to the Regent's Canal, and the other on the Hackney Marshes.

Following the amalgamation of the railway proposals the sites of the P&CR, the NELR, and the LUER were dropped, and a single replacement for them was mooted on the NELR section. This was at Kingsland Road, on the south side of the canal, on the block bounded by Whitmore Road, Kingsland Road, and Canal Road.[196]

In order to provide the intended train service Jenkin estimated that 40,000 kilowatts (KW) of power would be required. This was to be supplied by three power stations, to be located at Hackney (on the NELR section), Hammersmith (on the LUER section), and Hackney Marshes (for the C&NESER). Jenkin did not mention the power station at Battersea Bridge, as the north–south line was the exclusive preserve of the LUER.

All of the power stations would have convenient access to water and coal, both essential for generating the vast amounts of electricity that would be required by the railways. As well as the current for the trains, auxiliary generating equipment would be installed for powering station lighting and lifts.

The Hammersmith power station was to be located on the bank of the Thames to the south of the centre of Hammersmith. The 14-acre site was at the north end of Rainville Road, and would have been connected to the main railway by a short line leading north to the west end of Hammersmith Broadway station. The equipment would have supplied up to 12,000 KW to the system.

At Hackney the site was to the north of the Regent's Canal, adjacent to the Kingsland Road on just over half an acre of land and on the line of the railway between Kingsland Road and Stamford Road stations. It too would have had a capacity of 12,000 KW. The third power station would have been on C&NESER, at Hackney Marshes, with a capacity of 16,000 KW.

On 22 April, the day after this information was given to the Committee, Mr Jenkin continued to be examined. He amended the figures, reducing the total power requirement to 36,000 KW, from two power stations, although he did not identify the superfluous installation. Following this explanation the Electrical Inspector for the Board of Trade, Major Philip Cardew, corroborated the figures as being reasonable for the described railways. The power stations were to cost £920,000.

Three-phase power was to be supplied from the power stations to 22 substations located along the lines. These would each house five 300 KW rotary converters, which transformed the high voltage electricity distributed from the power stations at 10 KV AC, to 500 V DC. This would then be fed to the current rails. Insulated current return was to be used to prevent electrolysis, which would cause advanced corrosion of the metal tunnel rings. One of the converters at each substation would be a spare.

The evidence from maps shows that the location of the generating stations continued to alter with time. By July 1902 the locations are Hammersmith, Battersea Bridge (on the LUER north–south line, to the north of the Thames), and Kingsland Road. The C&NESER had by this time been rejected, and the Hackney Marshes power station with it.

Train Services and Fares

A regular service of trains was to be provided on both lines promoted by the combine. From 7.30 a.m. and 9.30 p.m. a 2½-minute service would be operated on the entire PC&NELR line between Hammersmith and Palmer's Green, and on the section of the C&NESER between Cannon Street and Walthamstow. To the north of the latter station a 5-minute service was planned. The average wait at each station on all of the lines was estimated at 20 seconds.

At the Hammersmith loop it was intended that trains arriving at Addison Road from London would be sent around the loop in alternate directions, giving a 5-minute service in each direction.

Between 5 a.m. and 7.30 a.m., and 9.30 p.m. and 1 a.m. a 5-minute service was to be operated on all sections of both lines. Most surprisingly, a 30-minute service was proposed from 1 a.m. until 5 a.m. Robinson of the LUT was questioned about the need to inspect the track each night and fitting this around a 24-hour service. His optimistic view was that most work (e.g., repairs to a broken rail, signalling, etc.) could be accomplished in the 30-minute period between trains late at night, and that the workmen would be able to stand to the side in the wide tunnels to let trains through if necessary.

A comparison was produced between the PC&NELR and services on competing railways, which showed the convenience and superiority of the proposed route. This was provided as an appendix to the Promoter's Statement in favour of the second reading in the House of Commons (reproduced below).

The table compares the two routeings to the City: from Hammersmith (in the upper section) and from the Palmer's Green area (in the lower section). In both sections the first three columns show services and fares available at the time from competing companies; the final column shows the service and fares on the PC&NELR ('The Proposed Railways'). The table clearly demonstrates the 24-hour service to be operated, and that the proposed fares were the lowest for any route. Between Hammersmith and the City, the PC&NELR was also the shortest and quickest route.

It was calculated that the PC&NELR would have a maximum capacity of 345 million passengers per year, with an estimated usage of 138 million. The C&NESER was estimated to draw 92.5 million passengers, with a maximum capacity of 231 million, and the Clapham Junction to Marble Arch line would have a maximum capacity of 89 million. No estimate of passenger numbers for the latter line was given.

Following the merging of the LUER and the PC&NELR proposals, concern was expressed to the Committee that since three companies were involved perhaps each would charge a separate fare over their section. This was resolved on 4 June 1902 by the insertion of a clause that permitted only one (unified) fare structure across the whole undertaking.

COMPARATIVE SCHEDULES.

TUBE AND TRAIN.

HAMMERSMITH, CHARING CROSS, AND CITY.

	METROPOLITAN DISTRICT RAILWAY.	LONDON AND SOUTH WESTERN RAILWAY.	METROPOLITAN RAILWAY.	THE PROPOSED RAILWAYS.
Route	Hammersmith to City (Mansion House or Cannon Street).	Hammersmith to City (*Viâ* Addison Road) Ludgate Hill.	Hammersmith to City (Moorgate Street).	Hammersmith to City (Monument).
Fares	Ordinary, 3d. & 4d. Workmen's Return, 2½d. & 3d.	Ordinary, 4d. Workmen's, *None issued.*	Ordinary, 3d. Workmen's Return, 3d.	Ordinary, 2d. Workmen's Return, 2d.
Route Miles	6⅝	10¼	7⅞	6⅜
Time Occupied	34 Mins.	45 Mins.	35 Mins.	24 Mins.

Train Service.

Metropolitan District Railway		London and South Western Railway		Metropolitan Railway		The Proposed Railways	
5.0 a.m. to 7.30 a.m.	*5 Trains per Hour.*	7.30 a.m. to 7.30 p.m.	*1 Train per Hour.*	5.0 a.m. to 7.30 a.m.	*6 Trains per Hour.*	5.0 a.m. to 7.30 a.m	*12 Trains per Hour.*
7.30 a.m. to 9.30 p.m.	*6 Trains per Hour.*	7.30 p.m. to 7.30 a.m.	*None.*	7.30 a.m. to 9.30 p.m.	*6 Trains per Hour.*	7.30 a.m. to 9.30 p.m.	*24 Trains per Hour.*
9.30 p.m. to 12.0 p.m.	*5 Trains per Hour.*			9.30 p.m. to 12.0 p m.	*4 Trains per Hour.*	9.30 p.m. to 1.0 a.m.	*12 Trains per Hour.*
12.0 p.m. to 5.0 a.m.	*None.*			12.0 p.m. to 5.0 a.m.	*None.*	1.0 a.m. to 5.0 a.m.	*2 Trains per Hour.*

CITY, TOTTENHAM, AND PALMER'S GREEN.

	GREAT NORTHERN RAILWAY.	GREAT EASTERN RAILWAY.	NORTH LONDON RAILWAY.	THE PROPOSED RAILWAYS.
Route	Palmer's Green to City (Moorgate Street).	Silver Street to City (Liverpool Street).	Highbury to City (Broad Street).	Palmer's Green to City (Cannon Street).
Fares	Ordinary, 7d. Workmen's Return, 2d.	Ordinary, 7d. Workmen's Return, 2d.	Ordinary, 2d. Workmen's Return, 2d.	Ordinary, 2d. Workmen's Return, 2d.
Route Miles	8⅝	7⅞	3⅜	8¾
Time Occupied	36 Mins.	32 Mins.	9 to 13 Mins.	32 Mins.

Train Service.

Great Northern Railway		Great Eastern Railway		North London Railway		The Proposed Railways	
5.0 a.m. to 7.30 a.m.	*2 Trains per Hour.*	4.0 a.m. to 7.30 a.m.	*3 Trains per Hour.*	5.30 a.m. to 7.30 a.m.	*3 Trains per Hour.*	5.0 a.m. to 7.30 a.m.	*12 Trains per Hour.*
7.30 a.m. to 9.30 p.m.	*3 Trains per Hour.*	7.30 a.m. to 9.30 p.m.	*3 Trains per Hour.*	7.30 a.m. to 9.30 p.m.	*7 Trains per Hour.*	7.30 a.m to 9.30 p.m.	*24 Trains per Hour.*
9.30 p.m. to 12.0 p.m.	*2 Trains per Hour.*	9.30 p.m. to 12.0 p.m.	*2 Trains per Hour.*	9.30 p.m. to 12.0 p.m.	*5 Trains per Hour.*	9.30 p.m. to 1.0 a.m.	*12 Trains per Hour.*
12.0 p.m. to 5.0 a.m.	*None.*	12.0 p.m. to 4.0 a.m.	*None.*	12.0 p.m. to 5.30 a.m.	*None.*	1.0 a.m. to 5.0 a.m.	*2 Trains per Hour.*

Robinson, during his cross-examination by the Committee, preferred a scheme whereby fares would be collected by conductors on the trains (or on the trams, if that is where a passenger started the journey). A ticket for the entire journey would be issued and punched, and the passenger would retain it for inspection.

The maximum permissible fares as defined in the Bill were: 3d/mile for 1st class, 2d/mile for 2nd class, and 1d/mile for 3rd class. Workmen's fares were to be provided, at a cost equivalent to the single fare for a return journey. Through fares were to be provided from all destinations served by the tramways of the LUT to any station on the Morgan combine under the agreement of 29 May 1902. This was to encourage use of the railway, and this would speed up passenger flows (since they would not need to buy another ticket when transferring from tram to tube), as well as saving the passengers money. In an appendix to the proceeding of the Windsor Committee the following through fares were suggested:

City to Acton:	3d (for an 8-mile journey)
City to Ealing:	4d (for a 10-mile journey)
City to Richmond:	4d (for a 10-mile journey)
City to Hounslow:	6d (for a 14-mile journey)

The fares originally proposed for the PC&NELR line are shown in the table below. Figures in bold are taken from primary sources;[197] the other figures have been speculated to fill in the gaps.

	Palmer's Green	Seven Sisters Road	Stamford Road	Monument	Cannon Street	Charing Cross	Hyde Park Corner	Sloane Street	High Street Kensington
Hammersmith Broadway	**4**	4	3	**2**	2	**1**	1	1	1
High Street Kensington	4	4	3	2	2	**1**	1	1	
Sloane Street	4	4	2	**1**	1	1	1		
Hyde Park Corner	**3**	3	2	1	1	**1**			
Charing Cross	**3**	**3**	**2**	**1**	1				
Cannon Street	**2**	**2**	**1**	1					
Monument	2	1	1						
Stamford Road	**2**	**1**							
Seven Sisters Road	**1**								

The fares from Clapham Junction on the north-south line were to be 2d to Charing Cross, and 3d to Cannon Street or Marble Arch. Sloane Street to Marble Arch would cost 1d.

The table below shows fares for the C&NESER section.

	Waltham Cross	Chingford	Walthamstow	Victoria Park
Cannon Street	**4**	**3**	**2**	**1**
Victoria Park	**3**	**2**	**1**	
Walthamstow	**2**	**1**		
Chingford	**1**			

On 26 July 1902 the fares for the PC&NELR line were adjusted before the House of Commons. Many were raised by 1d (shown in italics in the table below).

	Palmer's Green	Seven Sisters Road	Stamford Road	Monument	Cannon Street	Charing Cross	Hyde Park Corner	Sloane Street	High Street Kensington
Hammersmith Broadway	***5***	*5*	***4***	***3***	*3*	**2**	**1**	1	1
High Street Kensington	*5*	*5*	*4*	*3*	*3*	*2*	1	1	
Sloane Street	***5***	***5***	***4***	***3***	*2*	1	1		
Hyde Park Corner	***4***	**4**	**3**	***2***	*2*	**1**			
Charing Cross	**3**	**3**	**2**	**1**	**1**				
Cannon Street	**2**	**2**	**1**	1					
Monument	2	1	**1**						
Stamford Road	**2**	**1**							
Seven Sisters Road	**1**								

The fares on the north-south line were also adjusted, but not so much. Fares shown in italics below were reduced by 1d.

	Marble Arch	Sloane Street	Sloane Square	Battersea Park	Queen's Road	Lavender Hill
Clapham Junction	**2**	**2**	**2**	***1***	**1**	**1**
Lavender Hill	**2**	2	2	1	1	
Queen's Road	2	**2**	**1**	**1**		
Battersea Park	**2**	***1***	**1**			
Sloane Square	**2**	1				
Sloane Street	1					

Costs

Almost all of the costs noted in this and other sections come directly from the Parliamentary records. A number of these exists, with varying annotations and alterations made to them at various stages as the Bills progressed through the Committees and through Parliament. The numbers should therefore be seen as indicative, rather than definite statements.

The following table of costs was presented to the Windsor Committee to explain the division of the costs between the various railways in the group. Borrowing was only to be permitted once all of the shares had been issued and were fully paid up.

It is interesting to note the exactitude with which the construction figures are given in comparison to the other estimates. The interest was to be paid out of the capital at 3% for a construction period of two years. The final column gives the total cost and interest of the scheme during the construction phase.

	Shares	Borrowing	Capital	Construction	Equipment	Interest	Total
LUER	3,750,000	1,250,000	5,000,000	3,677,074	730,000	264,420	£4,671,494
NELR	3,750,000	1,250,000	5,000,000	3,405,280	850,000	255,317	£4,510,597
P&CR	1,500,000	500,000	2,000,000	1,444,449	220,000	99,867	£1,764,316
C&NESER	3,000,000	1,000,000	4,000,000	2,532,998	900,000	205,980	£3,638,978
Total	12,000,000	4,000,000	16,000,000	11,059,801	2,700,000	825,584	£14,585,385

The equipment costs were to be split as follows:

Power stations, comprising		920,000
Equipment	720,000	
Land & Buildings	200,000	
Line equipment, comprising		232,000
Cabling	80,000	
Equipment	152,000	
Sub-stations, comprising		340,000
Converters, etc.	135,000	
Transformers, batteries and switches	205,000	
Rolling stock, comprising		1,208,000
Motor cars	858,000	
Trailers	350,000	
Total		2,700,000

Based on the estimated passenger numbers (shown above), the income of the railways was given as £1.5 million annually. The profit from this was predicted to be of the order of £750,000, giving a return on the initial capital of 4.7%.

The Progress of the Bills

The House of Lords

The King's consent to the PC&NELR and LUER Bills to proceed was given on 12 June 1902, and so they were reported from the Select Committee to the House of Lords, with the amendments that had been added by the Committee.

Eleven days later the second reading of the Bill was order of the day, and the Chairman of Committees, the Earl of Morley, moved the third reading. Two clauses had been added at the second reading, and he had had these printed and circulated to the Lords. The first clause was a "complicated one" about damage that the railway might cause when in close proximity to another (with the section between Sloane Street and Piccadilly Circus, parallel to the B&PCR obviously in mind). The second clause was the 'Board of Trade clause', which added that the Board must approve all permanent way, platforms, tunnels, rolling stock, lighting, ventilation, and other equipment before works on the line commenced. This clause was then amended to cover all subsequent works, to prevent the railway introducing sub-standard equipment after work had started. These clauses were approved by the Earl of Camperdown and Lord Windsor. The Bill was passed, and sent to the House of Commons, with the official notification being sent one day later.

The House of Commons

On 24 June the Bills were read for the first time, and passed to the Examiner of Petitions for Private Bills. Here the petitions against the Bills could be properly considered.

In July the MDR and B&PCR petitioned the House of Commons against the second reading of the Bill on a technicality, namely that the original Bills for the railway did not mention the LUER and were therefore in breach of Standing Order 3. This was countered by the promoters statement in favour of dispensing with the Standing Orders, which pointed out that the LUER could not have been named as the Bills originated in 1901, before the LUER was in existence. The statement therefore claimed that the petitions of the MR and MDR were served with "bad grace". The promoters had spent some £60,000 on Parliamentary and other expenses, and lodged £500,000 in Parliamentary Deposits – there was no doubt that the railways would be constructed. They regretted the breach, but stated that in the circumstances it was unavoidable. The Standing Order Examiner, Mr C. W. Campion,[198] felt that the issue was between the Houses of Parliament rather than the promoters, since the agreement had been sanctioned by the Windsor Committee.

Another problem arose with the Standing Orders, when Campion reported both Bills for not having published details of the through bookings and fares between the three railways. The B&PCR again wanted the complaint upheld, as this would lead to the failure of the rival Bills. The Standing Order had not been met because when the Bills were originally submitted the previous November, no amalgamation had taken place. Fortunately, after ¾-hour of private consideration, the Standing Order Committee decided that "the necessary Parliamentary requirements should be dispensed with, and that the combined Bills should proceed to their further stages".[199]

The promoters then published their statement in favour of the second reading. This described the route of the line, the fares, and listed the following points in its favour:

- An extensive set of routes under one management.
- Tramway connections for travel to the suburbs.
- Low fares.
- Through tickets for tram and tube journeys.
- Experience of the promoters and the engineers.
- Well-known directors, who were resident in England.

An additional compensation clause was added to the Bill, which allowed owners of property which had suffered damage to claim against both the PC&NELR and the B&PCR along the shared section of route. An arbitrator would decide which company was responsible. The B&PCR agreed to this.

The MP Claude Hay,[200] addressing concerns relating purely to his own constituency, and without reference to the wider benefits that the schemes might bring, attempted to get all of the tube railway Bills rejected at the second reading before the Commons. He felt that they omitted to provide for the congestion of traffic, and supplied inadequate means of communication within his constituency – rather unfair on those railways that passed nowhere near Shoreditch. A long correspondence between Hay and the various promoters took place within the letters page of *The Times*. *The Railway Times* was glad that only ten fellow MPs supported him, and noted that one constituency should not be able to override the needs of the metropolis.[201]

During the reading other railways continued to petition against the scheme, producing various arguments for its rejection or alteration. In July the B&PCR protested, during the second reading before the House of Commons, that it was unprecedented to permit one railway the right to build, and then after they have raised capital and started construction, to allow another railway to be built below the first for a distance of nearly two miles. This was obviously a reference to the section from Sloane Street to Piccadilly Circus, which would have had eight stations, four on each line. This view was supported by Lord Alwayne Compton, who called the PC&NELR a "pirate company" for competing against a line already sanctioned by Parliament. Robert Perks noted that the MDR had not been allowed to use the Strand route, and that they had had to pay for the use of the Embankment.

The LUER Bill had its second reading on 16 July 1902. Mr Banbury,[202] expressed the same arguments as Perks to the House, and felt that excessive vibration would be caused. He suggested that the Morgan group was, like George Hudson (the 'Railway King' of the 1840s Railway Mania), before its time, and that the electrification of the

District should proceed before considering such schemes. He was countered by John Butcher,[203] who noted that Parliament had never prohibited competing traffic routes before. William Bull[204] claimed that the District had done little to help the public, and threw his weight behind the scheme.

Over thirty years before the formation of the London Passenger Transport Board, John Burns[205] advocated the amalgamation and electrification of the MR, MDR, and CLR, and felt that the American financiers would probably run away, leaving the British investors to shoulder the losses. William Peel[206] thought that this argument was due to anti-American prejudice.

Thomas Ashton,[207] who had served on the Joint Committee for Underground Railways in 1901, wholeheartedly supported what he termed an excellent scheme, and thought that it was the best laid before Parliament. Following a little further debate 250 MPs voted for the LUER Bill, with only 69 against. The PC&NELR Bill then passed as a formality, given that it was now seen as entwined with the fortunes of the LUER.

Dawkins sent a jubilant telegram to Morgan headquarters in New York:

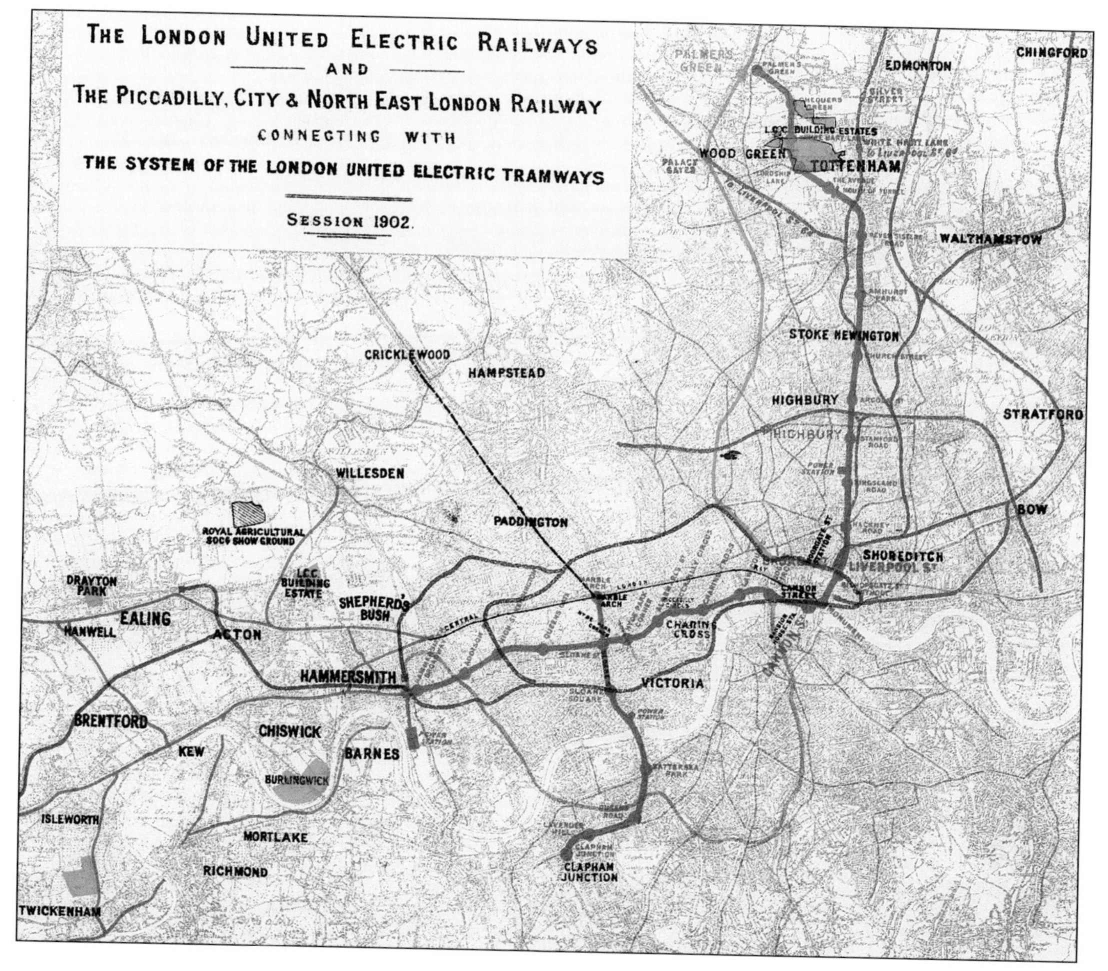

A map of the Morgan Tubes, shown as thick red lines, published in July 1902

> We are emerging with flying colours from a tremendous battle for a Parliamentary bill ... for the construction of a great through route of electric tube through London linking on with the new tramway systems NE & SW. Every kind of prejudice and trick was invoked against us, but after an unusual full dress discussion we got a majority of 181 in the H of Commons for our scheme.

A clause to protect the B&PCR from damage caused by the PC&NELR was added to the Bill, as well as clauses to protect Post Office property at West Strand, other (unspecified) Post Office premises, Middlesex County Council, the Church of St Dunstan in the West, and the Church of St Botolph without Bishopsgate.

Concern about the increasing number of amalgamations between railways in London had led to Balfour Browne appearing before the Lords for the P&CR and NELR on 30 July, and upon questioning denying that this was a prelude to all of the railways combining into the Yerkes group:

> We have absolutely nothing to do with the Yerkes group, and have had no communication with them at all. In fact, we are antagonistic to them. The only reason I have not opposed the B&PCR Bill is because on the little bit where we are running over each other we are not competitive.[208]

Once the Bills had passed their second reading, they were all referred to the General Committee of the House of Commons on Railway and Canal Bills for further and final investigation. The members of this Committee were Sir Lewis McIver[209] (Chairman), G. Whiteley, G. Montagu, and A. Emmott, and they divided the Bills into two groups for consideration. These groups reflected the original Select Committee split into north-south and east-west routes. The first group to be considered was the BS&WR, CCE&HR, GN&CR, and NWLR, and the second took the B&PCR, GN&SR, LUER, and PC&NELR.

At the suggestion of Peel, McIver laid down a Commons Instruction that the combined sets of railways that comprised the PC&NELR were to be constructed in their entirety. To ensure this, security was to be taken from the company.[210]

On 30 July, Browne enquired of the Committee what course they intended to pursue with regard to the LUER and PC&NELR Bills. If the Committee were prepared to meet on 2 August (a Saturday) then they would be able to consider the Bills. McIver disagreed, and thought that there was little chance of them being completed before the Parliamentary recess. A motion put forward by the MP Claude Hay postponed the final reading of the B&PCR Bill, which had been accepted by the Committee. The motion was approved, and McIver adjourned all three Bills, with them to be debated next on 16 October.[211]

"A Breach of Faith"

Having been approved by the Windsor Committee, all seemed to be well for the PC&NELR. Unfortunately a dispute was simmering below the surface between the two groups of promoters – J. S. Morgan and the London United Tramways.

It was mentioned previously that the ownership of the combined railway was split between the two promoters, with five-eighths going to Morgan, and three-eighths to the LUT. The LUT, and their Chairman George White, were unhappy with this, and wanted the split to be equal, even though their original scheme was substantially less than half of the complete line. Their justification for this was that the LUT would bring a very large number of passengers onto the railway from its trams, and also had greater expertise in the construction and operation of transport undertakings.

White had proposed another scheme for equal control to the PC&NELR on 28 July. He suggested that the railways should be run by a committee consisting of six members, three appointed by the LUT and three by Morgan, with an arbitrator to resolve any disputes. The costs of construction were to be split with the LUT responsible for their north-south line, Morgan to pay for the Charing Cross to Palmer's Green section, and the remainder from Charing Cross to Hammersmith to be divided equally.

White had also been unhappy about the addition of the C&NESER to the LSR scheme, believing that it might prevent any of the LSR from being approved by Parliament. The addition had occurred without any consultation with the tramway company.

Morgan were unwilling to alter the arrangements, perhaps understandably since the P&CR and NELR were by far the larger portion of the railway, and on 2 August 1902 their solicitor informed his counterpart at the LUT that the new proposals would not be considered. This did not ease the already uncomfortable relationship between the two companies. White was furious, and decided to sell his shares in the LUT and drop all involvement in the scheme. It is worth quoting his letter in full:

> I have to acknowledge yours [i.e. letter] of the 8th inst. [September], from which I gather there is now a desire that Sir Clinton Dawkins and I should meet to discuss this matter, but you will probably not be surprised that I decline to fall in with the suggestion.
>
> Let me remind you that throughout the whole progress of the Piccadilly and City and London United combined Tube Bills in Parliament your clients, as promoters of the one Bill, have displayed an entire disregard of the relations which should have existed with us as promoters of the other Bill. For example, no sooner had we arranged to join forces than your clients, without any communication with us, saddled our scheme with the North-East Suburban Bill (promoted by other parties) and thus endangered the passage of the combined undertaking, as was evidenced by the fact of the Lords Committees promptly eliminating that portion of the scheme.
>
> Then, in April, when at your request we devoted much time in framing a draft agreement to give effect to our arrangement as we understood it, you scoffed at our idea of our having what we regarded as an essential and proper control in the management of the combined undertaking, and dismissed the matter with a curt refusal. Again, on the occasion of preparing for the contest in the House of Commons on the second reading, it was, after some objection on your side, agreed that a joint statement should be issued to the members of Parliament. Two whole days were spent in conference with you and your colleagues, and you unequivocally vouchsafed the opinion that, as prepared by us, the joint statement admirably covered the whole situation, and moreover you bound your clients that this should be the only statement issued. In contravention of this arrangement a separate statement for the Piccadilly Bill was immediately prepared without our knowledge and circulated by your agents in the lobby of the House, we only discovering the fact upon

> an MP handing the statement to us with a request for an explanation for one of the assertions contained therein—namely that the promoters of the Piccadilly and City Bill 'have nothing to do with the London United Tramways Company!' The patience of Mr Clifton Robinson and myself under the treatment we received was strained to breaking point on many occasions, but we have both persevered in the hope that, as the business was of such importance, wiser counsels would ultimately prevail.
>
> That it was absolutely necessary that we should insist on equal control in the management was made clear to us very early in the proceedings, for I need only to refer to the lamentable want of knowledge on all practical questions shown on your side on the occasion of the conference at Sir Clinton Dawkins' house (when we were actually in Committee of the Lords) and when we had to cut about the whole of your figures and enforce our view that you should not ask Parliament to grant you capital powers which were something like a million sterling in excess of the actual requirements for electrical equipment &c. In July we felt that the time had arrived when some definite action should be taken as to the proposed agreement, and accordingly again applied ourselves to thinking out a scheme for joint working, amongst other points suggesting that our proposed power station should suffice for the whole scheme and so obviate the wholly unnecessary expenditure of hundreds of thousands of pounds and a second power house which you proposed; and our suggestions further provided generally for the most economical and efficient installation and mode of working the whole through route from Hammersmith to City and Tottenham, and included a stipulation for an equal control of the joint working being given to each party. We submitted the draft agreement embodying all these matters to you with the natural feeling that it merited a careful and businesslike consideration by your clients. Judge then of our astonishment when within three days (i.e., 2nd August) you wrote that on reporting the scheme and terms of the draft agreement to Sir Clinton Dawkins 'he and his firm absolutely declined to discuss proposals on such a basis,' and you added 'I did not feel able to press them on their consideration.'
>
> No self-respecting man could tolerate a continuance of this treatment, and I immediately determined that I would make no further attempts to devise an agreement for your clients, who apparently overlooked the fact that it was our reputation for success in meeting public requirements (including the introduction of cheap fares which you objected to) which undoubtedly influenced the Lords Committee, and that we do not propose to be dominated in such a manner as would put it in the power of your clients to at any moment paralyse all our efforts to establish an important system of tube railways upon sound and economic principles.[212]

An attempt to negotiate was made by Dawkins's solicitor on 13 October, but White ignored it. With rather unfortunate timing, *The Railway Times* commented that the Morgan proposals had come off best before the House of Lords in the "three-cornered" fight between them, the CLR, and the Yerkes plans. They felt that the fight was likely to be interesting, but perhaps with a premonition, considered that in the interests of the existing companies the new lines would not be sanctioned.[213] Sir Henry Oakley of the CLR was still writing to *The Times* in defence of his company's circular scheme, noting that the Morgan proposal did not serve Oxford Street, and that only the NELR was required. However, the Morgan proposals were facing greater problems than the CLR could generate. The minutes of the LUT Board are very coy when they state:

> The position with regard to the Tube Bills and the course which had been taken during the vacation by the Chairman [George White] after consultation with and the approval of the other Directors was considered and arrangements made as to the course to be adopted before the House of Commons Committee.[214]

The meaning of this was soon to become clear.

Matters came to a head on 21 October 1902, when a letter informed Balfour Browne that instead of representing the LUER and PC&NELR, he was only to represent the latter company. Explanation for this was soon forthcoming. Sir Edward Clarke, Counsel for the LUT, revealed to Morgan that White had sold his interest in the LUT in the previous month. This would not necessarily have been an intractable problem, had he not sold it to the rival financial house of Speyer Brothers, who were the financiers to the Underground Electric Railways of London, run by Charles Yerkes. In an editorial the following month, *The Railway News* commented that if the LUER promoters had simply needed better terms from the Morgan group, there was no reason for them to sell their shares. However, their first thought was probably on obtaining "a powerful financial alliance somewhere". This they had certainly achieved.

The Yerkes group had had its eye on the LUT for a short while, considering it as being a suitable feeder of passengers onto its railways. A report was commissioned by Edgar Speyer into the condition of the LUT. Chapman, the UERL engineer, produced the report on 8 September, and it was positive about the state of the tramway company and its potential to feed passengers onto the underground railways of the UERL. White was only too happy to sell his holdings, due to his anger at the Morgan group, and had no qualms about them being bought by a rival to Morgan (although they had been offered elsewhere beforehand). The Imperial Tramways Company, another large shareholder of which Clifton Robinson was Managing Director, also sold its holding to Speyer at this time: Speyer (and the UERL) now held the majority of LUT shares. The deal with Speyer was completed in less than 24 hours.[215]

Speyer, of course, claimed that they had acquired the LUT because it was "a splendid property" (as shown by Chapman's report). Dunlop, writing in the *Railway Magazine*, stated that they

> knew that the Piccadilly and City Bill was practically defunct by reason of the disagreement, past healing, of the former allies.[216]

Since the UERL owned the rival Brompton & Piccadilly Circus Railway, which would be duplicated by the PC&NELR between Hammersmith and Piccadilly Circus, they were now in a position to stop the rival railway scheme — and the rival finance house. On 21 October the section of the LUER Bill between Sloane Street and Hyde Park Corner was withdrawn, since it duplicated the B&PCR, and was one of the most expensive sections to construct. Sir Edward informed the Commons that the UERL was unwilling to construct two tube lines under the same piece of street, for almost one mile.

It was immediately realized that the Morgan scheme was unravelling. The next day the *Financial Times* reported the "exceptional strength" of Underground stocks, which it claimed was due to the "somewhat startling developments" with the rival ventures. The newspaper saw from the start that this was some clever manoeuvring, writing in its editorial:

> Speyer, who being largely interested in the District line, had naturally no desire to see a competing line established such as the new scheme involved, and who consequently decided to frustrate the scheme by gaining a commanding interest in the London United Tramways.[217]

The trend continued, with CLR stock rising notably on 23 October. Two days later the same newspaper noted that the secrecy with which the transaction had been conducted was important, as it delayed the action to a time where submitting new Bills for the 1903 session would be almost impossible due to the very short time remaining. As well as thwarting the Morgan group, the CLR would also face difficulties getting their scheme re-introduced.

The deletion of the section from Sloane Street to Hyde Park Corner constituted an unacceptable alteration of the approved scheme, and so the entire LUER Bill was voluntarily withdrawn eight days later. This was the date that a statement was made by the Promoters to the evening sitting of the House of Lords, announcing the sale of interest. In the words of *The Railway Times*, "Yerkes had come out on top".[218] *Transport* noted that "for another year, at any rate, Mr Yerkes has succeeded in staving off from the District Railway the dreaded competition of a tube railway from Hammersmith under Piccadilly to the City."[219] Shares in both the MDR and the CLR rose in value upon announcement of the take-over.

The LUT had effectively been taken over by Speyer Brothers, which explains why they made no attempt to sell their interest to Morgan. Had he been given the chance, Morgan would undoubtedly have purchased the tramway company: in the event, he felt that a secret deal had been done.

The LUT claimed that the equal control of the combined railway had been "anticipated and arranged for"; reference to the Committee records from 22 April disproved this statement.

Needless to say, the House of Lords was most displeased with this turn of events. They responded by stating that it was the belief of the Lords that this represented a breach of faith with the promoters of the P&CR, and even more seriously, a breach of faith with Parliament itself.

Browne, for the Morgan railways, stated that he meant to proceed with the PC&NELR Bill, and that he would pledge the promoters to submit a Bill for the next parliamentary session that would sanction the construction of the line between Hammersmith and Hyde Park Corner. They were prepared to deposit security with Parliament, guaranteeing that a suitable Bill would be deposited.

The Bill for the PC&NELR that had been approved earlier in the year was dependent upon the approved LUER Bill. Since the latter had been withdrawn, the scheme approved by parliament differed from what would now be constructed and so the pre-amble of the PC&NELR Bill was found to be not proved on 23 October. In the words of McIver:

> The Committee are of the opinion that the scheme of your Bill as proposed in the pre-amble is the combined scheme which passed the House of Lords, and that you have

embodied in your scheme the result of the decision of the House of Lords. The scheme as it is now before us is no longer the scheme of your preamble ... The difficulty the Committee finds itself in is this – they would be very glad to get over it having regard to the expense and trouble which the promoters of the [PC&NELR] line have been at, and also to the public gain in getting this portion of the railway, but they are absolutely barred by the instruction of the House of Commons from proceeding any further with this Bill as it stands. Their intention was to give effect to the recommendation of the Joint Select Committee to secure through lines, and not to have piecework, and the result is that you cannot give the guarantees required by those instructions, and you cannot prove your preamble. We must find your preamble not proven, because it is not possible for you to prove three-fourths of it.[220]

In the absence of the Commons modifying or withdrawing their earlier instruction, it was suggested that the Committee should make a special report to the House, or suspend its decision. This would allow time for an independent motion to be made in the House, presumably to override the Commons instruction. The Committee did not find favour with either suggestion, believing them to be unwarranted and without precedent,[221] and so would not allow the Bill to proceed.

Yerkes took pains to point out that the acquisition of the LUT by his group did not mean the end of plans for a railway from Hammersmith to the City, stating in an interview with the *Daily Express* that

We intend to put in a Bill before Parliament that will take in the whole of the systems placed before Parliament, and advocated by the joint committee of last year. We feel that the last scheme we produced was too small, that we did not propose to do sufficient, and that this year or early next year we shall have a scheme before Parliament that will take in all that anyone else proposed to do ... That line, of course, will run from Hammersmith to the City ... Those lines for which we already have Parliamentary powers [i.e., the MDR and B&PCR] are not involved in this discussion.[222]

In other words, the Yerkes group were proposing yet another tube line to add to their combination, which would meet the requirements of the various Parliamentary Committees that had advocated a line on this route.

Not all possibilities for the Morgan group had been exhausted though, and there was some interesting legal manoeuvring in progress.

Recommittal

Balfour Browne requested that the LUER Bill be recommitted to Parliament but with original LUT promoters of Robinson, White, White, and Everard replaced with Dawkins, Morgan jr, Siemens, von Chauvin, and Mills, the PC&NELR promoters. Since the P&CR had originally promoted a section from Hyde Park Corner to Hammersmith, and only removed it following the entry of the LUER into the group, he felt that this would merely reinstate the original intention of the P&CR. The P&CR had an obvious interest in the whole line, and the LUER had behaved discreditably. The PC&NELR Bill would also be recommitted at the same time so that the complete scheme could be considered as one, with the two Bills probably being amalgamated.

This would have been an unusual but permitted legal manœuvre. A Promoters'

Statement recommended the recommittal to Parliament because:

- not to recommit was against public interest, and would "render difficult the honourable conduct of business before Parliament" if pledges could be disregarded;
- the scheme was of great public utility, and had received the approval of the Committee;
- great expense had been incurred thus far by Parliament; and
- the Promoters could not have foreseen or prevented the sale of the shares, and it is "neither in the public interest nor fair" that the MDR could wreck a competing scheme.

The Railway Times felt that if the recommittal was accepted it would set aside numerous Standing Orders of both Houses – in other words, whilst a legal manœuvre, it would be one without precedent. It commented that

> Messrs. Morgan and Co. were, in fact, beaten at their own game, and they must suffer the consequences. We have constantly argued that the exploitation of London transit facilities by American financiers augured well for nobody except themselves, and the latest developments confirm this.[223]

A motion for the recommittal was submitted by Thomas Ashton, the MP for Luton, and discussed on 27 October. Robert Perks, the MP for Louth, and also the Managing Director of the MDR, unsurprisingly objected to the motion, and it was set over for two days. Statements from both the LUT and the PC&NELR were issued on the intervening day. The LUT objected to the recommittal of their Bill, which had been done without their knowledge or authority. They described the breakdown in relations, and claimed that their connection with the UERL would provide better links between their tramways and the underground railways in London, thus providing a better system for the public. They noted the saving resulting from having only a single pair of tubes constructed beneath Piccadilly, and also that their scheme would be completed ahead of the Morgan tubes. To counter this, the PC&NELR promoters stated that the instruction from the House of Commons

> has been adroitly used by the District Railway group to secure, through the purchase of the London United interest, the destruction for the moment of the through route which it was the object of the House to ensure.[224]

They reminded readers that the LUT had sought a half-share in the control of the combine, even though they were putting up less than one-third of the capital, and when this was turned down, secretly made the deal with Speyer.

The next day the Speaker ruled the motion of two days previous out of order, presumably because it had been legitimately withdrawn by its promoters. Ashton then submitted a second motion, this time recommitting the PC&NELR Bill. The promoters wanted the remaining section of the PC&NELR from Hyde Park Corner to Palmer's Green to go ahead, and they promised to submit a Bill for the Hammersmith to Hyde Park Corner section in the next Parliamentary session.

In addition to the petition from the LUT, the CLR also opposed any reworking of the Bills, as they had an interest in seeing the PC&NELR fail. They noted that the line would not have through booking from the LUT, and so was not the scheme accepted by the Lords.

Ashton stated that the Committee had been "placed in a very awkward position" by the withdrawal of the LUER bill. He stated that "a very dishonourable transaction had taken place on the part of the promoters of the [L]UER", and that the latter railway had "taken advantage of the fact that their names alone appeared on the Bill". Other reasons for the recommittal were that:

- the scheme was not much altered if recommitted;
- the CLR scheme did not serve north-east London;
- Morgan deserved great consideration for the trouble that they had been put to;
- through fares from the LUT could be demanded from the Board of Trade under the Light Railways Act;
- he did not want to see a larger District monopoly;
- a large amount of money had thus far been spent by Parliament (in addition to the £50,000 – £80,000 spent by Morgan);
- nothing had been done on the B&PCR, and like the other unconstructed Yerkes railways it was a block line (i.e., one with the sole intention of thwarting other schemes, and which the promoters had no real intention of constructing).

The latter point was contested by Perks – work had started on the B&PCR, a fact conceded by Ashton. Perks also stated that he would not vote on the motion, even though he opposed it. Sir John Dickson-Poynder also opposed the recommittal, feeling that the scheme was no longer that approved by Parliament. Intriguingly, Claude Hay, who had opposed all tube railway Bills in July, spoke in support of the recommittal.[225]

The Chairman of Committees, J. W. Lowther[226] believed that the case for recommittal was not strong enough, and although he felt sorry for the Morgan group, it was the fault of their allies and not the House of Commons that the Bill had failed. He advised against the motion.

The final statement was from Sir Lewis McIver, who said that although it was "a scandal which had probably no precedent in the annals of their committee work upstairs" the House should not involve itself with the quarrel, and should relegate the Bill to the next session (i.e., 1903). Following this statement Ashton withdrew his motion.

It was the opinion of the House of Commons, as well as McIver, that the whole state of affairs was a scandal, but that it was to be expected given the American way of business. The railway press agreed with this view, with Dunlop commenting, "It was a very pretty and clever piece of manoeuvring on the part of the Yerkes combination, made possible by dissension in the enemy's camp".[227] Ashton was more forthright when he considered "whether, for a long time if ever, such a very dirty transaction was ever done by parties coming before Parliament". The November issue of *The Railway Engineer* commented that Morgan appeared to have been "dished", and, in a mildly xenophobic editorial, noted that there was satisfaction that, whilst the "two great Americans have been struggling for the upper hand, that Mr George White, of Bristol, ... seems to have been able so far to decide the matter to *his* way of thinking."[228]

Parliament did not allow the Bills to be remitted, and instead they were all withdrawn. An acrimonious exchange of letters between the Morgan group and George White took place in the columns of *The Times*, *The Financial Times*, and *The Railway Times* in the two weeks following the revelation about the sale of White's controlling interest in the LUT. Morgan alleged that the deal with Speyer had been kept secret because if it had been disclosed it would have seriously jeopardized the third reading of the B&PCR Bill in the House of Commons. Speyer, of course, denied that the purchase was done with the intention of defeating the LSR, and denied having anything to do with the breakdown in trust between Morgan and the LUT:

> The stock was offered to us long after the negotiations between those parties had been broken off, and had, in fact, been previously offered to other parties who were interested in another competing tube railway.[229]

Morgan retorted:

> Negotiations were not broken off by us at any time, nor had we any notice from our associates of their intention to break them off until the announcement of the withdrawal of the London United Bill ... A letter, full of calculated mis-statements, was received by us from the London United group, dated September 19, but it contained no notice of breaking off nor reference to arbitration.[230]

In turn, White of the LUT felt compelled to reply. He noted that Morgan had refused to consider the fine details of the agreement between the companies:

> If we had proceeded with our bill without the agreement and submitting to Messrs. Morgans' requirement of a majority in the control, we should have placed the whole future of our successfully established tramways undertaking — to say nothing of our own private fortunes — at the mercy of these people ... We determined that nothing on earth would induce us to continue business relations with that firm, but that, apart altogether from the possibility of an alliance elsewhere, when the committee again met we would withdraw our Bill.[231]

The rejection of 2 August was understood by White to be a breaking off of relations by Morgan.

The final public word on the matter came from Morgan, recalling the anger expressed in Parliament when the LUER withdrew their Bill:

> We can hardly think that anyone at all cognisant of the facts could expect us, after what has happened, to engage in controversy with the Chairman of the London United Tramways. We are perfectly satisfied with the opinions which have been expressed in Parliament and elsewhere on Mr White's proceedings.[232]

Arnold Hills, one of the original promoters, was in Cape Town at the time. He was informed about the collapse of the scheme on 16 November, and cabled Dawkins in London, urging him to resubmit the PC&NELR Bills for the next Parliamentary session. Dawkins replied, saying that he thought it was better not to go forward. After a further exchange of cables, in which Dawkins resolutely refused to resubmit the Bills, Hills cabled his own solicitor asking for the Bills to be resubmitted in his own name. He was just too late, however, to meet the Parliamentary timetable. Some three years later he was to describe the proceedings as "one of the most outrageous pieces of treachery that ever occurred in the history of American finance".

The London Suburban Railway scheme failed, and Morgan withdrew from promoting railways in London. J. Pierpont Morgan senior commiserated with Dawkins in a telegram of 24 October 1902, in which he described the actions of the LUT and UERL as the "greatest rascality and conspiracy I ever heard of". Depending on the source, either White or Robinson was later described as "the man who got the better of Pierpont Morgan". *The Railway Engineer* felt that the whole series of events showed that George White was the only character who knew what was going on.[233]

The original vision from when the LUER merged with the PC&NELR, of through bookings between the trams and the tube lines, was realized in a slightly different form. This feature was provided between the LUT and the Yerkes group of underground railways when the GNP&BR opened to Hammersmith on 15 December 1906. It ceased at some point during WW1, and then resumed in March 1922. Many of the tickets were withdrawn in 1935 due to low usage, and they were effectively scrapped in 1942.

Aftermath

The final outcome of what was seen by many as a giant game of chess played between the American financiers with Londoners as the pawns was that no new tube railways were authorized in 1902. Only extensions to the B&PCR, CCE&HR, and GN&CR were passed, in addition to a few minor works by the CLR.

As an interesting aside, it was noted by Perks at the MDR half-yearly meeting that had it not been for the intervention of Claude Hay, the Morgan Bills would have received their third reading in the Commons prior to the recess. One can only speculate on how Hay may have changed the face of London's tube railways through his ill-received interjection.

Yerkes was, according to a letter he wrote, not in favour of the system that had allowed him to win such a large amount of control over transport in London. He felt that allowing promoters to choose their own routes and then asking for Parliament's approval was wrong, and that a regulatory body should decide on routes to ensure that they were co-ordinated. However, as an outsider he did not feel in a position to ask for a change earlier, but hoped that the matter would be resolved faster than most Parliamentary Committees![234]

Lord Ribblesdale wrote to *The Times* on 31 October, with his views on the events of the year. He felt that "the fact that only 4 miles of tubing out of the 82 proposed last session should have been sanctioned is not a matter of unmitigated regret". He felt that the LCC should be responsible for tube railways, as they were the body with the best knowledge of London and its needs, and would be able to take a co-ordinated view of what is required. He was not sure as to whether the LCC should actually construct and run the tubes, but he was certain that it should act as a special adviser to Parliament with particular regard to unifying the tube railway schemes.[235]

The struggle between Yerkes and Morgan to control the tube railways of London was not well received in most quarters, and most commentators felt that some sort of action was required to prevent a similar situation from occurring again.

Dunlop wanted a Board of Control to be established

> consisting of expert engineers, electricians and traffic organisers, men versed in the financial, legal, and economical aspects of the question, not possessing interest in any of the present schemes nor in London's Tramways. The duties of this Board would not be to decide on the respective merits of various schemes promoted, but to reconstruct and complete the map of the transit of London from the point of view of passengers, inhabitants and workers.[236]

In order that such a scandal should not recur, the government decided to appoint a Royal Commission to investigate how traffic in London could be improved. Gerald Balfour, President of the Board of Trade, in response to a parliamentary question, agreed that such a commission "would be in all probability the best means of instituting inquiry into the key issues, including tube railways." The LCC concurred with this view, desiring that full enquiries should be held into tube railway Bills generally. After toying with the idea of promoting a tube railway themselves, they instead voted unanimously in favour of a Parliamentary Commission to investigate the problem first. The actions and report of this Commission are discussed in a later chapter.

Another proposal which went nowhere was that from the main line railways. The GER, LB&SCR, SE&CR, and GWR were reported in the *Financial Times* as discussing constructing a tube railway to unite their termini in London. Further enquiries by the *FT* found that the scheme was nothing more than a discussion on how to counter the threat posed by the tube railways. The failure of the 1902 schemes, together with the delays that would arise whilst a Commission considered matters ensured that this proposal came to nothing.

Of all of the railways which did not come to fruition, the London Suburban Railway was probably the one that had the most promise, and but for the inflexibility of the promoters, was the most likely to have been built. Had this happened, it would have probably opened around 1908 or 1909, and would almost certainly have been a success. It followed a key traffic artery across London, one that still has no railway surface over 100 years later. It would have connected Walthamstow with central London well before the advent of the Victoria Line. And given the congested nature of today's Piccadilly Line, the duplication of routes between Knightsbridge and Piccadilly would probably have been a blessing for passengers.

The presence of the Morgan line across London would have most likely changed much of the subsequent history of the Underground. The London Passenger Transport Board would still have been formed in 1933; not even the might of the MR prevented all of the underground railways being pulled into the new company. However, it is debatable as to whether the Piccadilly Line would have been extended north from Finsbury Park in the early 1930s, running parallel and close to the north-east section of the LSR; likewise, the construction of the Victoria Line to Walthamstow is unlikely, and funds may well have been focused on alternative routes to relieve traffic. Much of the history of the Jubilee Line was based on it connecting Charing Cross and Bank via the Strand route, which would not have been the case with a railway already there.

Speculation about what may have happened instead is fairly meaningless, and everyone will have their own view. Some minor changes to the line are easier to predict though. It is likely that the northern end would have eventually been extended to Southgate, in place of the Piccadilly Line, once the issues around the cricket pitch were overcome. In the west the line may have eventually been continued to take over one of the branches of the MDR.

Some of the stations in the central area would probably have changed their names to match those with which they interchanged: Law Courts would have become Strand; Knightsbridge would replace Sloane Street (or perhaps the other way around); Bishopsgate Street Without would certainly have become Liverpool Street. The station at Cannon Street, which would have been a very short distance from Monument (as with the stations on the MDR) would perhaps have closed in order to accelerate the service.

It is a tribute to the flexibility of the diagram developed by Harry Beck in the 1930s that the LSR can be easily fitted in with minimal disruption. Of course, the diagram was not introduced until 1933, but had it been around in 1910 it would probably have looked something like the diagram overleaf.

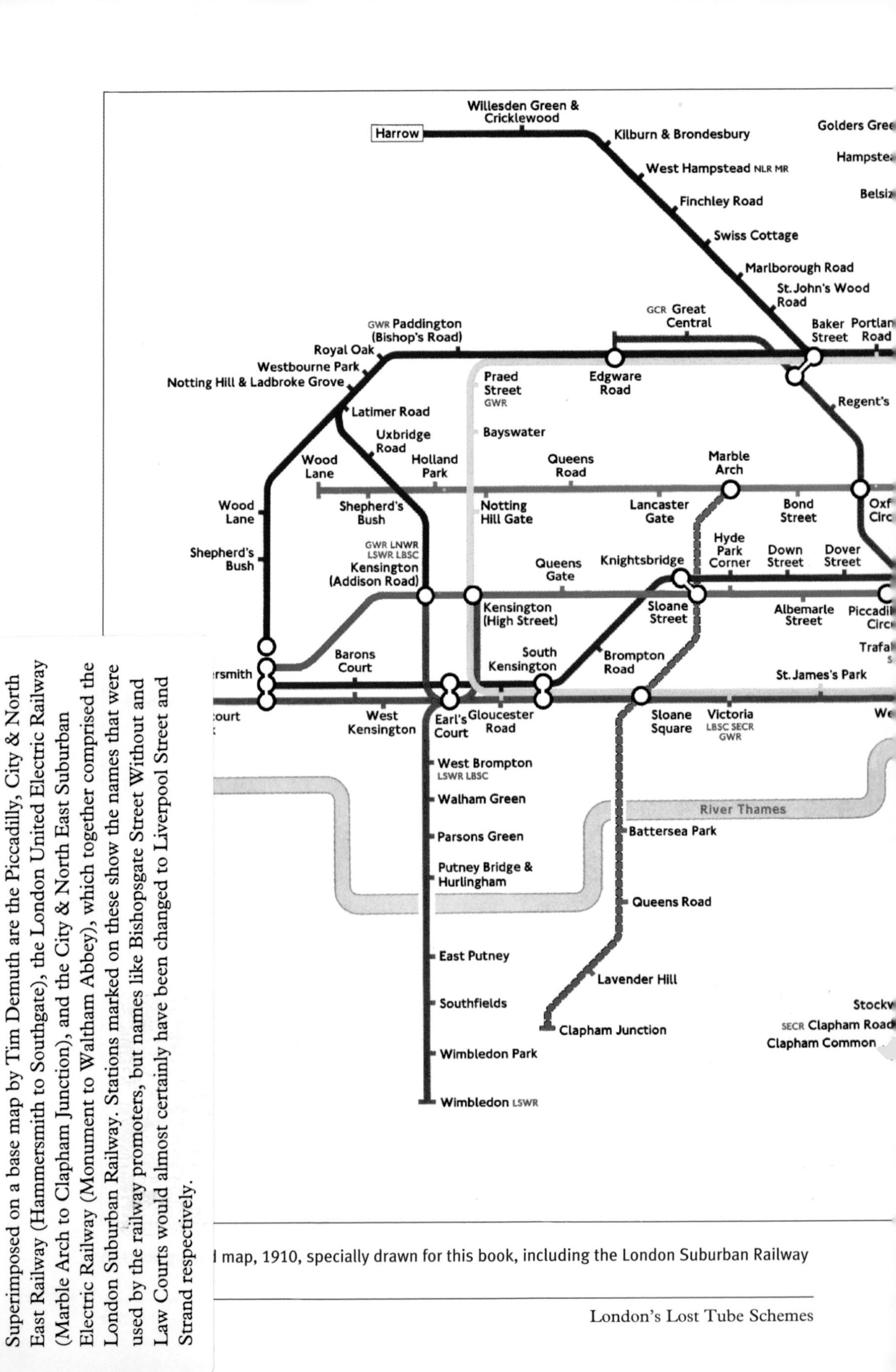

Superimposed on a base map by Tim Demuth are the Piccadilly, City & North East Railway (Hammersmith to Southgate), the London United Electric Railway (Marble Arch to Clapham Junction), and the City & North East Suburban Electric Railway (Monument to Waltham Abbey), which together comprised the London Suburban Railway. Stations marked on these show the names that were used by the railway promoters, but names like Bishopsgate Street Without and Law Courts would almost certainly have been changed to Liverpool Street and Strand respectively.

…d map, 1910, specially drawn for this book, including the London Suburban Railway

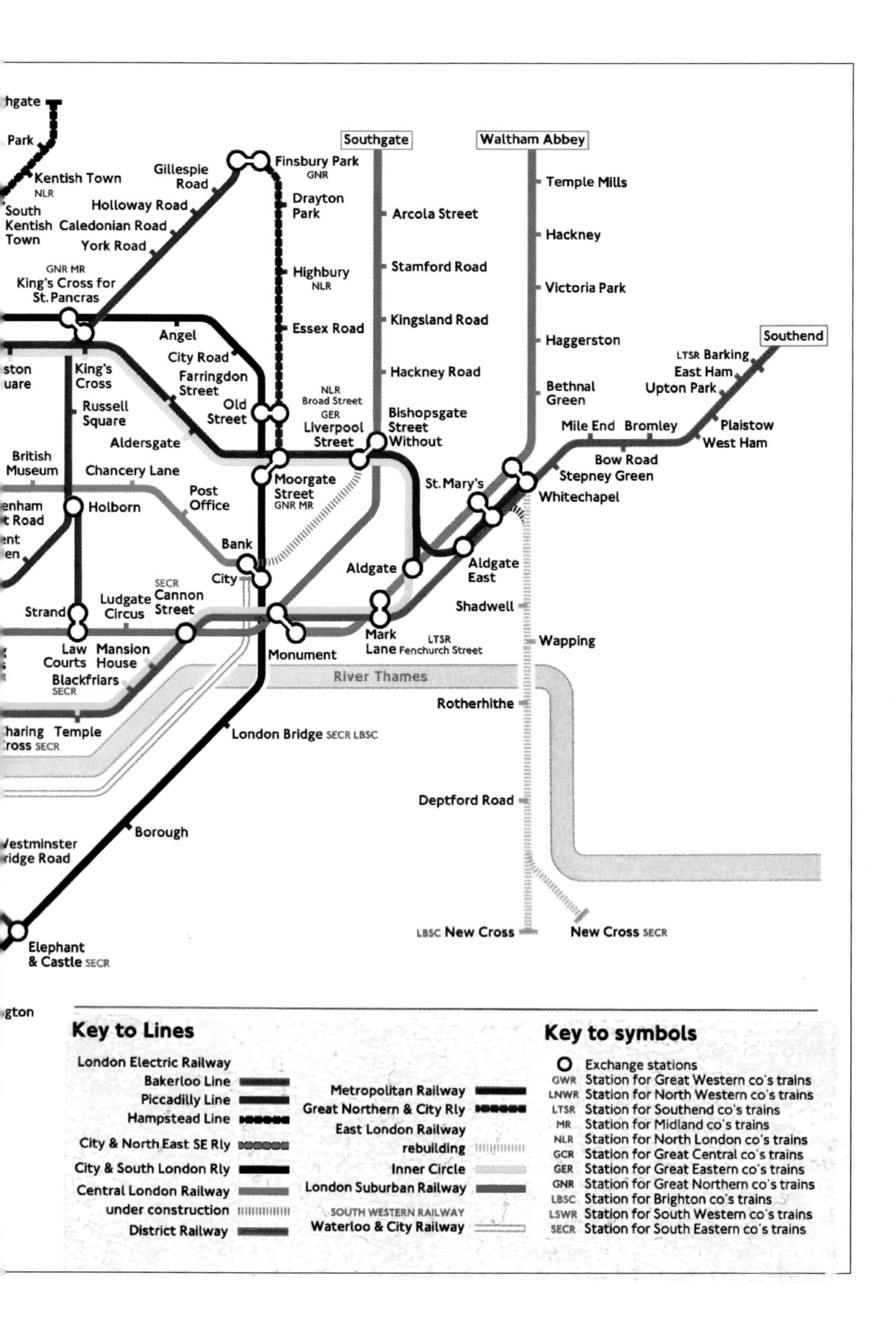

Southgate
Waltham Abbey
Southend
Finsbury Park GNR
Drayton Park
Highbury NLR
Essex Road
Arcola Street
Stamford Road
Kingsland Road
Hackney Road
Temple Mills
Hackney
Victoria Park
Haggerston
Bethnal Green
Mile End
Bromley
Bow Road
Stepney Green
Whitechapel
LTSR Barking
East Ham
Upton Park
Plaistow
West Ham
Kentish Town NLR
Gillespie Road
Holloway Road
South Kentish Town
Caledonian Road
York Road
GNR MR King's Cross for St. Pancras
Angel
City Road
Farringdon Street
Old Street
King's Cross
Russell Square
Aldersgate
British Museum
Chancery Lane
Post Office
Holborn
NLR Broad Street
GER Liverpool Street
Bishopsgate Street Without
Moorgate Street GNR MR
St. Mary's
Bank
City
Aldgate
Aldgate East
Shadwell
SECR Cannon Street
Ludgate Circus
Strand
Law Courts
Mansion House
Blackfriars SECR
Monument
Mark Lane
LTSR Fenchurch Street
Wapping
River Thames
Rotherhithe
Temple
London Bridge SECR LBSC
Deptford Road
Borough
Elephant & Castle SECR
LBSC New Cross
New Cross SECR
Key to Lines
London Electric Railway
Bakerloo Line
Piccadilly Line
Hampstead Line
City & North East SE Rly
City & South London Rly
Central London Railway
under construction
District Railway
Metropolitan Railway
Great Northern & City Rly
East London Railway
rebuilding
Inner Circle
London Suburban Railway
SOUTH WESTERN RAILWAY
Waterloo & City Railway
Key to symbols
Exchange stations
GWR Station for Great Western co's trains
LNWR Station for North Western co's trains
LTSR Station for Southend co's trains
MR Station for Midland co's trains
NLR Station for North London co's trains
GCR Station for Great Central co's trains
GER Station for Great Eastern co's trains
GNR Station for Great Northern co's trains
LBSC Station for Brighton co's trains
LSWR Station for South Western co's trains
SECR Station for South Eastern co's trains

Little Achieved in 1903

By comparison with 1902, there were relatively few tube railway Bills deposited in 1903. The table below gives a brief outline of all of them, completely new lines in bold:

Railway Name	From	To	Via
Baker Street & Waterloo	*Transfer of ownership to GNP&BR.* *Extension of time.*		
Central London (extension)	Shepherd's Bush	Bank	Hammersmith, Hyde Park Corner and Ludgate Hill (forming a large loop)
Charing Cross, Euston & Hampstead	*Transfer of ownership to GNP&BR.* *Additional stations at Charing Cross and North End.*		
City & Crystal Palace	Cannon Street	Crystal Palace	Peckham Rye
City & North East Suburban Electric	**Monument**	**Chequers Green & Waltham Abbey**	**Hackney**
City & South London	Angel	Euston	King's Cross
	Take-over of City & Brixton Railway.		
Clapham Junction & Marble Arch (No. 1)	**Clapham Junction**	**Marble Arch**	**Hyde Park Corner**
Clapham Junction & Marble Arch (No. 2)	**Clapham Junction**	**Marble Arch**	**Hyde Park Corner**
Great Northern Railway	*Construction of siding for GN&CR north of Finsbury Park.*		
Great Northern & City	*Changes to finances.*		
Great Northern, Piccadilly & Brompton (Various Powers)	*Additional land for stations.* Widening of Long Acre.		
Great Northern, Piccadilly & Brompton (New Lines & Extensions)	Knightsbridge	Goldhawk Road	High St Kensington and Hammersmith
	Piccadilly Circus	Mansion House	Fleet Street
Hammersmith, City & North East London	**Hammersmith**	**Palmer's Green & Walthamstow**	**City & Hackney**
Metropolitan District	South Kensington	Hammersmith	
	Mansion House	Stepney Green	
North West London	Marble Arch	Victoria	Hyde Park Corner
Paddington, Victoria & Kennington	**Paddington**	**Kennington Oval**	**Victoria**
Watford & Edgware	E&HR at Edgware	Watford	

One of the key reasons for the drop in number was the anticipation of the Commission; promoters were loathe to spend money promoting Bills which might be suspended whilst deliberations ensued. This was, in the event, a wise move, for a number of Bills were indeed postponed. The Royal Commission on London Traffic is examined in the next chapter. This chapter is concerned with the Bills as they were originally planned.

Two Bills were deposited for a Clapham Junction and Marble Arch Railway, from different promoters. The GNP&BR, CLR, C&SLR, and NWLR proposed extensions, which are examined in the following sections.

The BS&WR and the CCE&HR submitted Bills to allow them to be transferred formally to the GNP&BR. Both of these requests were ultimately refused by Parliament. The CCE&HR also wanted to construct two additional stations, abandon the section of line into the proposed depôt at Kentish Town, alter the vertical levels of the line at Golders Green, and take over the E&HR. They eventually withdrew the latter part of the Bill, but the new stations and Kentish Town changes were given Royal Assent on 21 July. The extension of time sought by the BS&WR in their Bill was likewise approved on 11 August.

The GNR Bill was for the construction of a siding tunnel to the north of Finsbury Park station, which they were also constructing for the GN&CR. Although the Bill received the Royal Assent on 21 July 1903, the siding was never built.

The City & Crystal Palace scheme from 1902 was redeposited by its promoters in December, but by 24 January the Bill was dead, with the promoters deciding not to proceed.

The Paddington, Victoria & Kennington Railway was remarkably similar to the failed West & South London Junction Railway from 1901–2, and in the end was never even deposited.

The City & North East Suburban Electric Railway

Although the London Suburban Railway had been scrapped, part of it was revived the following year. A completely different set of promoters had taken the scheme and modified it using parts of the NELR and the C&NESER. They proposed a tube railway running from the City north to Chequers Green, and north-east to Waltham Abbey, which was to be called the City & North East Suburban Electric Railway. An end-on connection was proposed with the deep level MDR line, but by 12 March this had been dropped.[237]

The proposals were considered before the Select Committee on Private Bills (Group 3), which had J. Compton Rickett as Chairman. Not all of the characters associated with the London Suburban Railway had retired; Balfour Browne was once again acting as Counsel for the promoters, and Sir Douglas Fox was the engineer for the line.

On 24 March 1903 Browne opened by explaining to the Committee that although the previous year's proposals had been rejected by Parliament, this was due to the instruction of 1902 that the approved railway had to run from Hammersmith to the City and be built in its entirety. The current railway was not using this route, and the instruction no longer existed in 1903.

The company was looking to raise £6 million of capital, of which £4.5 million was

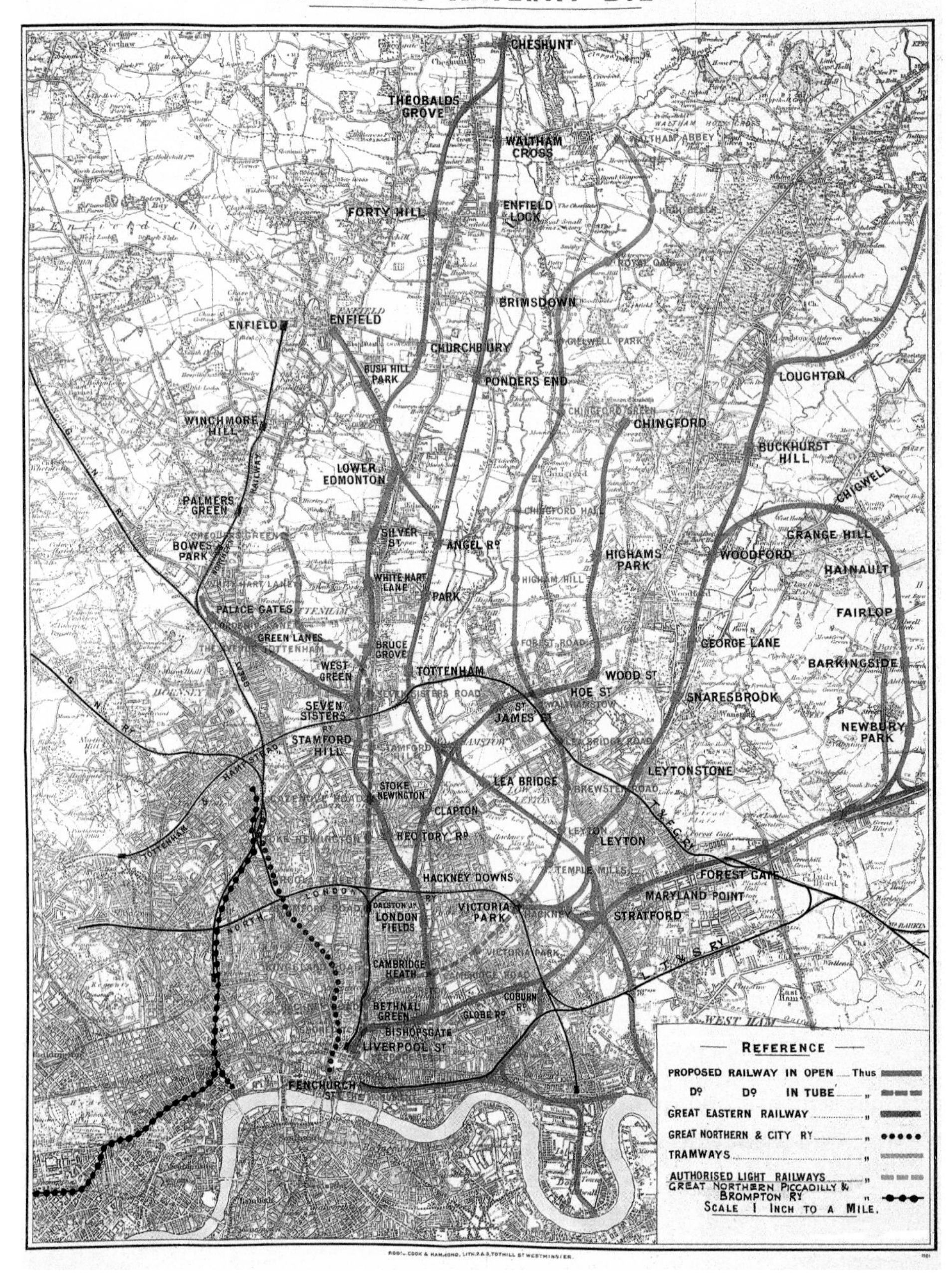

City & North East Suburban Railway

to be in the form of shares with the remainder as debenture. Some investment was to come from the principal promoter of the line, the Traction and Power Securities Company Ltd, a finance company of which Joseph Lukach was Managing Director. Lukach was also a director of British Westinghouse Electric and Manufacturing Company Ltd, one of the largest electrical concerns in Britain. Westinghouse were hoping to get the contract for the rolling stock and other electrical equipment.

Lukach had a history of promoting tube railways. He had been one of the promoters of the City & West End Railway in 1896, as well as the Central London Railway, opened in 1900.

The Route

The C&NESER was to run from a station at **The Monument**, close by the deep-level line of the MDR (still unconstructed). A running connection with this line had been originally proposed, and was shown on several plans, but had been abandoned at the request of the MDR, who harboured plans to extend to Whitechapel. Interchange with the original MDR line would be provided at Monument, as well as the C&SLR station at Bank (which would have led to the complications of having two names for a single station complex almost thirty years before Monument and Bank were joined with an escalator link). The station was to be located below the street, with five stairwells giving access to the booking hall. This arrangement was described as being similar to that proposed for the GN&CR extension station at the junction of Lothbury and Prince's Street, also with Fox as the engineer. The stairwells would be at the corner of Eastcheap and King William Street, on the west and east sides of Gracechurch Street, and in Eastcheap itself. The stairs at all sub-surface stations were to be 5 feet (1.53 m) wide, and required a width of 5 ft 9 ins (1.75 m) of pavement in order to accommodate the railings. Concerns as to the narrowing of the pavement in the vicinity of the stairwells led to the suggestion that the public toilet situated on an island in the centre of the road could be removed and replaced by a similar facility in the subway. The Metropolitan Police were not keen, but this was the agreed solution, as it would allow the removal of the island and widening of the pavements.

Beneath the road six lifts were to lead to the platforms. It was stated that there was to be no crossover tunnel beyond the platforms since this would obstruct the most convenient routeing for a passageway to the MDR.

The line would swing north below Gracechurch Street to a station at **Cornhill** (occasionally referred to as **Threadneedle Street**). The Colonial Bank, Mr Gibbs, Barings, and the Cordwainers Company all lodged petitions against this station, due to the land required. These objections were removed by again siting the station beneath the roadway with staircases from the pavements. Continuing north, the GER had agreed that a subway connection could be made between its main line station and the next tube station at **Liverpool Street**, where passengers would also be able to connect with NLR and MR trains. The station was to be sited in Liverpool Street, because the high cost of property on Bishopsgate precluded the company from purchasing a site there. This had the unfortunate effect of providing a less convenient interchange with the main line station, but did allow for convenient subway interchange with the Metropolitan Railway. There were to be two entrances and one large exit to the station in Liverpool Street, and four lifts descending to the platforms.

This section of the route caused a lengthy debate about the number of stations to be located within the City of London. The City Corporation was minded to permit just two stations; if so, the Company was prepared to drop Cornhill, but obviously preferred to leave it in the scheme. The Corporation was concerned as to the location of Cornhill station, and proposed moving it to the south, away from the road junction. The Committee was unhappy about the crossover to the north of Monument, feeling that it was better to reverse trains south of the station in a shunting neck. However, the tunnels could not be extended south of the platforms because of the planned deep-level MDR. The only way to meet the objection would be to move the platforms about 600 feet (183 m) further north. This would place them so close to the platforms at Cornhill station that as the final car of a train was leaving the platform at Monument station its front car would be entering the platform at Cornhill, a clearly ludicrous situation. Cornhill station would be dropped from the scheme if this proposal was enforced. In defence of the original scheme it was noted by Fox that similarly located crossovers were in use at the City station (now Bank) of the Waterloo & City Railway, and at Moorgate and Lothbury on the GN&CR, to which the Board of Trade had given their consent.

The main route of the NELR was to be followed from Liverpool Street to Chequers Green, although the locations of some of the stations were different. The first station north of Liverpool Street was to be at **Shoreditch**, located on the west side of Shoreditch High Street, opposite Bethnal Green Road. This would have been followed by **Hackney Road** station, immediately prior to which the Waltham Abbey line would diverge. Both Hackney Road and Shoreditch stations were to have been constructed on two levels. This was to allow for the junction to be provided without conflicts in opposite directions, since it too could be on two levels. A pair of platforms would be provided for each branch at Hackney Road. Southbound trains arriving at the station could therefore wait in the comfort of a platform if they were delayed by a train on the other branch. It was also felt to be safer, since trains would arrive at the actual junction 250 feet (76 m) south of the platforms travelling slowly following their halt at the station.

As a further safety measure, trap points and overrun tunnels containing hydraulic buffers were to be provided, into which trains would be diverted if they approached the junction without permission. The trap points would only allow a train to reach the junction if a signal was cleared. Colonel H. Yorke, the Chief Inspecting Officer of Railways, also required a method of cutting off the power of a train running into the dead end. It was not explained how this was to be accomplished.

Kingsland Road station was to be on that road just south of the Regent's Canal at Wilmer Gardens. **Stamford Road** and **Arcola Street** stations were in the same locations as previously proposed, but the next station, **Stoke Newington**, was to be located at the junction of Stoke Newington Road and Evering Road, some 500 m to the south of the Church Street site of 1902. An apparent improvement over the 1902 proposals was to have interchange with the GER station at Stoke Newington, although the C&NESER station was to be titled **Cazenove Road**. The station at Amhurst Park was to be in a similar location, but called **Stamford Hill**, followed by **Seven Sisters Road**. Beyond this station the line swung to the north-west, emerging from the tunnels as before, just to the south-east of a station at **The Avenue, Tottenham**. The three final stations on the line would have been at **Lordship Lane**, **White Hart Lane**, and **Chequers Green**, all located in approximately the same locations as in the 1902 plans. A depôt was to be located between the latter two stations.

The branch to Waltham Abbey would have diverged from the Tottenham branch at **Hackney Road** station, as previously described. The southern routeing to the City of London, introduced in 1902 at the behest of the original 1901 Committee had been dropped. It was explained that this would reduce the amount of tunnelling, and therefore the costs, since only one pair of running tunnels would be constructed south of Hackney Road. In addition the districts to the east of the City were now being served by the Whitechapel & Bow Railway, which was owned and operated by the MDR.

Beyond Hackney Road station the line would have curved north-east beneath the road of the same name, with its first station at **Haggerston**, located at the junction of Hackney and Queensbridge Roads. Another possible interchange with the GER lines from Liverpool Street would have been at **Cambridge Road**, where the station was to be adjacent to the existing Cambridge Heath station.

The line would have followed due east, beneath Bishop's Road to Victoria Park. **Victoria Park** station was to have been just to the north of the park on Grove Road, which bisects the park in a north-south direction. As with the original 1901 plan the railway was to travel below the north-west boundary of the park in tunnel, although the 1903 proposal included a station at **Hackney**, which appeared to be an interchange with the North London Railway station of Victoria Park (now Hackney Wick). Shortly beyond this station, somewhere just to the east of the greyhound stadium that existed until the 1990s, the line would have surfaced, heading in a north-easterly direction and gently swinging further north on an embankment across the marshes.

The first surface station was at **Temple Mills**, in the vicinity of Quarter Mile Lane. Part of some playing fields would need to be used for the railway, but the company stated that it would make up the land by providing some elsewhere on the site. A siding would also have been provided to connect to a siding belong to the GER.

Leyton station was next, probably in the region of today's Ruckholt Road. By now the railway would have been pointing due north, and on the approach to **Brewster Road** station would have entered a built-up area, thus involving some property purchase and clearance. This was the town of Walthamstow, which would have two further stations, the first on **Lea Bridge Road**, in the vicinity of the Tottenham & Forest Gate Railway (now the Gospel Oak – Barking line), which would have been crossed below, and the second at **Walthamstow**. This station may have been intended to have interchange with the GER Hoe Street station (today called Walthamstow Central).

To the north of the built-up area the railway would have entered open countryside, ripe for development. The first station would have been just to the north of **Forest Road**, followed by **Higham Hill** some 900 m to the north, probably on a site that today is located between the Banbury Reservoir and the Lee Valley Park sports grounds. **Chingford Hall** station was to be situated on Hall Lane in South Chingford, and **Chingford Green** would have been on Kings Head Hill just east of its junction with Sewardstone Road.

Gilwell Park station would have been sited at a kink in Sewardstone Road, on land that is still completely rural today. The only nearby building is the Fox & Hounds public house. Gilwell Park is an area of woodland located to the east of the station site.

The railway would then have swung north-east, roughly following around Barn Hill, before reaching **Royal Oak** station, somewhere to the west of the junction of Mott Street and Lippitts Hill. Curving back to the north the next station would have been **High Beech** (an area now spelled as Beach), and would have been located at the south-west corner of Beech Hill Park.

The final section of line was to run in a north-westerly direction, terminating on Farm Hill Road in **Waltham Abbey**, opposite the Green Man public house.

Technical Details

The line was to be constructed with 12 ft 6 ins (3.8 m) tunnels between the city and the tunnel mouths in Tottenham and Hackney. This was slightly smaller than the London Suburban Railway had proposed, principally to save money, but partly because improvements in electrical equipment meant that they could use smaller electric motors on the rolling stock. Fox explained that he felt that the tunnels would be better able to resist vibration than the 11 ft 6 ins (3.5 m) tunnels being used by the Yerkes consortium. If the Committee was to insist on the 13 ft 6 ins (4.1 m) tunnels that were originally proposed by the P&CR being constructed, then this would add some £220,000 to the costs. Col Yorke, whilst giving his evidence, preferred the 12 ft 6 ins tunnels to those of the Yerkes tubes. Stations would have 35 feet (10.7 m) tunnels.

Refuges would be provided in the tunnel every 200 yards (183 m), and there were no proposals for side walkways. A single fireproof walkway was to be constructed between the rails, and not below rail level. Tunnel lighting, activated by the signalmen, was also to be provided.

The construction costs were estimated at between £40,000 and £47,500 per mile for the open section. The tunnelled sections ranged from £522,000 per mile in the suburbs to £976,000 in the City of London, reflecting the cost of purchasing easements below the expensive City property.

The steepest gradient on the line was 1 in 50 (2%), and the sharpest curve was to have a radius of 7 chains (140 m). Rails with a depth of 5½ ins (14 cm) were to be used. By comparison, the rails on the CLR were only 3½ ins (9 cm) deep. The conductor rail was to be 1 ft 7¼ ins (49 cm) from the running rails.

Absolute Block Signalling

Block signalling is an arrangement where each line of railway is divided into a number of sections and no train is permitted to enter any section until the previous train has been proved to have left it without having become divided. Where the movement of trains is governed entirely by signalmen the system is called Absolute Block. Track Circuit Block automates the operation of the signals by passing small electrical currents through the rails to detect the presence of trains.

Absolute Block signalling was used on all early tube and sub-surface railways, but since 1905 new signalling on the Underground has always been track circuit block. In addition to red and green aspects, yellow is used as a preliminary warning where, owing to train speed or poor visibility, a danger signal might not be seen.

Signalling had to be on the absolute block principle, with blocks from station to station, or signal post to signal post. A discussion as to the feasibility of automatic signalling was held, and it was agreed that it may have to be a necessity on a line with an intensive service and a reversing point at its City terminus.

The rolling stock would have been of eight-car formation, this comprising two four-carriage units to allow for off-peak uncoupling. Each unit was to have a motor carriage at each end, and two trailer carriages in the middle. The capacity of such a train was to be 450 passengers.

One power station would have been built, although three possible sites were under consideration. They were at Kingsland Road, just south of the Regent's Canal (at a similar location to Kingsland Road station), at Temple Mills (beside the playing fields), and at Victoria Park (although no part of the park would have been used). The Temple Mills site was to be preferred, as it would have the best connections for supplies of coal.

Sidings and/or train depôts (the Bill did not distinguish between them) would have been provided at Kings Arms Lane, Blind Lane, and Pymm's Brook, all in the region of Chequers Green station.

Operations

As with its predecessors, the Bill proposed a 2½-minute service, but only between The Monument and Hackney Road. North of the latter station a 5-minute service would be provided on each branch. The superimposition of the running tunnels at Hackney Road to prevent conflicting train movements in opposite directions has already been described. At the outer reaches of the lines the trains would be uncoupled to provide four-carriage trains for greater economy. Trains were to average 18 m.p.h. between stations, increasing to 20 m.p.h. where the stations were further apart. The service would comprise at least 200 trains each day.

Unusually for an underground railway company, it was proposed that a goods service would be operated, but only on the surface sections of the line. (Temple Mills to Waltham Abbey).

The Bill introduced some unusual clauses relating to bridges on the line. No advertisements were permitted on the sides of the bridges, and the company was to prevent water from dripping from them as far as possible. The bridges at Tile Kiln Lane and Blind Lane were to be provided with lamps which the company had to ensure were lit from sunset until sunrise. These two bridges would have been of girder construction.

Costs

Fox gave the costs of the route as being £2,956,395 for the construction works (tunnels and surface lines, as well as stations and track) and £1,070,632 for the land required. The high costs of tunnelling in the City can be seen from the £1 million estimated cost of the line from Monument to Bishopsgate, over one-third of the total.[238] The generating station, rolling stock, and other electrical equipment would total £1,300,000. With the interest on the capital accrued during the construction period estimated at £270,000, the total required for the line was £5,597,027. The capital for the line was to be £6 million; the £400,000 difference between these two figures being for Parliamentary and other expenses, as well as contingency.

Rejection

The Bill for the C&NESER was read for the first time in the House of Commons on 24 February 1903. There was no major tube railway Committee sitting in 1903, as most other tube railways had been suspended by Parliament due to the sitting of the Royal Commission (see later), a fact which was not lost on opponents of this railway. These included the GNP&BR, unsurprisingly, who resolved at their Board meeting of 27 February to present petitions against this and other Bills. Indeed, in its editorial column on 7 March, *The Railway News* stated that it felt the C&NESER scheme should not continue, as it was an "ambitious" new scheme. Part of the opposition to it stemmed from the proposal of the company to take subsoil without any payment of compensation.

For the second reading in the Commons on 12 March the motion for the Bill was presented by David J. Morgan, MP for Walthamstow. He explained the proposal, and the advantages that it would bring. The overcrowding on the GER routes from Walthamstow was described, including a recent journey in which he had been forced to occupy the guard's van of a train, together with 22 workmen (and presumably the guard) due to lack of space anywhere else on the train.

The railway had very strong support from the local authorities for the areas through which the railway was to run. Resolutions in favour were passed by the Metropolitan Boroughs of Shoreditch, Bethnal Green, Hackney and Stoke Newington, and the Urban District Councils of Leyton, Walthamstow, Tottenham, Wood Green, Edmonton, Southgate, Chingford, and Waltham Holy Cross. However, these did not prevent the LCC from petitioning against the line. In briefing notes to the MP John Burns[239] they argued that no railway schemes should be considered whilst the Royal Commission was still investigating transport in London. Burns noted in Parliament that the length of the C&NESER was greater than all of the other underground railways being considered by the Royal Commission combined. Allowing it would remove the *raison d'être* for the Commission, and "they might as well open the door and let the others go through at the same time".[240]

The C&NESER had submitted a petition against an MDR (Works) Bill, which was proposing competing lines; the MDR Bill was postponed because of the Commission, so it did not seem fair that the C&NESER was allowed to progress. No provision for workmen's fares was given in the Bill. Most importantly, the LCC still wanted to see a through railway from the north-east to the west, through the centre of London, and felt that the C&NESER proposals would prevent any such line from being constructed in future. Burns presented this reasoning to the House in his case against the Bill.

The MP for St Albans, Vicary Gibbs, also opposed the Bill, and countered the accusations of GER overcrowding by informing Morgan that the day in which he travelled in the guard's van was exceptional — thirteen trains had been cancelled due to fog. He felt that Threadneedle Street would be become overcrowded with people flooding from the new station there, and then finally revealed the main cause of his objection. His City office, in Threadneedle Street, was to be purchased by the railway, presumably for the station.

Further opposition was voiced by Sir Frederick Banbury,[241] in anticipation of the Royal Commission:

> It seems to me that if the Royal Commission is not to be a farce it is most important a Bill to create new Railways should be referred to it, and not be passed by this house to-day.[242]

The Bill was eventually passed with 162 votes in favour, and 60 against. It then proceeded to the standard Private Bill Committee stage.

The finances of the C&NESER were scrutinized at length by the Committee, who were concerned about the stability of the company. Lukach stated that the scheme was financially sound, but was unwilling to name his fellow financiers who were to put up the money. The Traction Finance Company of New York, which was associated with the Traction and Power Securities Company, paid some £6,000 for the preliminary expenses. Once again, Lukach was sketchy on the details of this relationship. He did not want to suggest a figure that his company might invest in the scheme, and was unwilling to provide any guarantees (unlike Dawkins in the previous year).

It was noted that Lukach had been Managing Director of the Exploration Company, another finance company that had promoted the Central London Railway. He agreed that this was so, but pointed out that all association between him and the Exploration Company had now ceased. Sir Ralph Littler, Counsel for the NLR, asked if he was aware that the GN&CR was unable to raise the capital for its Lothbury extension, even with the supply of traffic from the NLR at Finsbury Park to sustain it. Lukach was not, and claimed to have no interest in things that were outside his sphere of business interest.

The Committee was not satisfied with the scheme, and a mass of evidence against it was collected. The recommendation of the 1901 Committee against junctions in tube tunnels had been ignored by the promoters, and there was no line further west than Monument. On 22 April 1902 Dawkins, giving evidence for the PC&NELR, had stated that the 1902 proposal would not pay without the section between the City and Charing Cross. Sir Lewis McIver had also stated that the London Suburban Railway scheme made sense only as a through route from Hammersmith, via the City, to the north-east — and the 1903 scheme was just a part of that route.

The North London Railway objected vigorously, and produced copious evidence showing the extensive network of trams and buses that were operated between the City and Stamford Hill, Victoria Park, and Clapton. These were in addition to the rail services offered by themselves and the GER — there was simply no need for a further railway in the district.

The promoters gathered statements from residents of the north-eastern suburbs, supporting the need for good rail transport so that they could live further from London and commute in. Those from the far reaches of the line beyond Chingford claimed that many of the men of the region worked in London and would benefit from the trains. This evidence was never used though, as the papers are annotated "These proofs were prepared but not used owing to collapse of the promoters' case".

On 30 April 1903 the Committee unanimously rejected the Bill. It was felt that the financial state of the company was unsound, and the evidence given by the promoters had given them no reason to believe otherwise. The refusal of the promoters to guarantee to find the necessary finances to construct the complete line was not appreciated by the Committee who, as in previous years, were concerned to ensure that the complete railway was built. The line in the north-west was the "poor" end; that in the City was the "rich" end, and it would be easy for the poor end to be abandoned, leaving north-east London without a service.[243]

The Hammersmith, City & North East London Railway

The origins of the HC&NELR are to be found in the failure of the C&NESER scheme of 1903. Arnold F. Hills, one of the original promoters of the Piccadilly & City Railway in 1901, and the North East London Railway in 1902 was still frustrated by the lack of progress in getting a railway to Walthamstow. Following the collapse of the London Suburban Railway scheme, he decided again to promote a tube railway to the north-east of London, with co-promoters James Worsfold and David Urquhart; the engineer was Robert Elliot-Cooper. The company was incorporated on 30 January 1903 with a share capital of £30,000.

The HC&NELR was a reprise of the original 1901 P&CR and NELR proposals. The line was to run from Hammersmith in the west, through the City of London, with two eastern branches terminating in Palmer's Green and Walthamstow. It is described fully in a later chapter.

The promoters prepared their Bill and announced on 14 February that it would be shortly deposited with Parliament, a long time after the standard Parliamentary deadline. *The Railway News* could not believe that this would be allowed, but hoped that the Standing Order Committee would permit it given that most tube railway Bills would be delayed by the proposed Commission.[244] Their hope was not met; in April the Standing Order Committee refused to allow the Bill to proceed.

The CLR Loop Again

The CLR decided that, in the light of the positive messages they had received the previous year, and the failure of the Morgan combine, their loop proposal would have a good chance of succeeding. They therefore redeposited the 1902 scheme as it had been the previous year.

The House of Commons announced on 2 March that because of the creation of the Royal Commission on London Traffic, the CLR Bill, as well of several of the others, would be postponed until the Commission reported. Consequently the CLR withdrew the Bill the following month; this was presumably to avoid paying for a Bill that might never see the light of day.

The C&SLR Goes to Euston

Although the Islington & Euston Railway Bill had been rejected in 1902, the C&SLR returned with a similar plan in their own name in 1903. Described as a "revival" by the press, the promoters were better prepared this year for the opposition of the MR, and the Bill received the Royal Assent on 11 August. This permitted the construction of 1 mile 60 chains (2.8 km) of twin tunnel extending their line from its terminus at Angel to Euston, following the Pentonville Road and via an intermediate station at **King's Cross for St Pancras**. The line would then pass under St Pancras station and follow the line of Drummond Street, terminating at **Euston**, with the platforms slightly east, and at a lower level than those of the CCE&HR. The station at King's Cross would have separate platform tunnels, whilst that at Euston was to have an island platform between the tracks in a single 30-feet (9.1 m) diameter tunnel, with sidings beyond. Included in the sidings tunnels was a locomotive traverser, allowing the locomotives to be slid sideways from one track to the other. As with the section from Moorgate to Angel, the running tunnels were to be of 10 ft 6 ins diameter.

Another part of the C&SLR Bill sought to resolve the situation with the City & Brixton Railway. This latter line, it will be remembered, had been authorized in 1898 to reuse the tunnels from the abandoned King William Street station in the City, and extend them south to Brixton. Further Bills in 1899 and 1901 had modified the scheme, but it still remained dormant, and in 1902 its promoters had proposed partial or complete abandonment of the line.

And so it was that the C&SLR Bill of 1903 included a proposal to take over all plans and powers of the C&BR, and dissolve that company. The general concept would be retained though: new tunnels, 11 ft 5 ins (3.5 m) in diameter were to be constructed beneath the Thames but at a higher level than the 1890 tunnels, thus easing the gradients. These would connect with the old tunnels under the south bank of the river, and cross the river upstream of London Bridge, and slightly downstream of the old tunnels. Passing under property to avoid the tortuous curve beneath Arthur Street West, the new tunnels would actually sever the old before they passed into Crooked Lane and then crossed under Cannon Street (and 48 feet below Monument MDR station) into a new station at **King William Street**. Access to the platforms would be via the original station (including a passageway across the eastern end of the old platform site), a new tunnel to the station at Bank, and a subway to Monument station. The platforms would be situated at a higher level and immediately to the south of the Bank platforms on the Islington extension, opened in 1900.

Interchange between the two C&SLR routes was to be provided at **London Bridge** and **Oval** stations. In March 1903 it was reported that the route of the C&BR was to be constructed in its entirety as far south as Brixton. The additional costs of this work resulted in the capital for the Bill being raised from its original figure of £600,000 (for the Euston extension) to a rather larger £1.5 million.

The powers were included in the C&SLR Act of 1903, but were never exercised. Competition from tramways was cutting into the revenue of the existing railway, and it was felt that constructing a parallel line would be a huge financial risk. It was decided by the railway to let the powers for the line lapse.

Clapham Junction to Marble Arch

As has already been noted, two separate proposals for railways connecting Clapham Junction to Marble Arch were made this year. They were known as the No. 1 and No. 2 Bills for the purposes of telling them apart in Parliament. The routes were practically identical, with the only discernible difference in the deposited plans being a 12-chain (241 m) variation in the stated lengths. They were also very similar to that of the LUER north/south line of 1902. The only notable difference from this line was that the 1903 railways were to run under the eastern edge of Battersea Park, rather than following Queenstown Road.

W. Abbott, C. J. Cater-Scott, and C. A. Spofford promoted the No. 1 Bill. Cater-Scott was associated with Yerkes, and it is presumed that, had this line been authorized and built, it would have joined the Yerkes conglomerate. The engineers were Sir John Wolfe Barry & Partners, and Harley H. Dalrymple-Hay, who had become associated with the Yerkes tubes in 1902. The capital was to be £2,720,000, and the estimated cost was £1,768,656.

The Yerkes standard of 11 ft 6 ins tunnel diameters would be adopted. Stations were to be placed on the south side of the Thames at **Clapham Junction**, immediately to the south of the main line station; **Latchmere Road**, on the north side of Lavender Hill; **Wandsworth Road**, on the north-west corner, where the railway curved north; and on the south-east corner of **Victoria Circus**. The line would cross the Thames just downstream of the Chelsea Suspension Bridge before following Chelsea Bridge Road and Lower **Sloane Street** to a station at **Sloane Square**. The buildings would be on the south-east corner of the Square, and interchange with the MDR station would almost certainly have been provided.

At the north end of Sloane Street the station would be on the north side of Knightsbridge; again, interchange with the GNP&BR was probable. The railway would continue northwards to Hyde Park, and then curve slightly to the right to its destination at **Marble Arch**. The station here would be aligned with Edgware Road, and a low-level interchange with the North West London Railway was planned.

The electricity for the line would undoubtedly have been supplied from the Lots Road power station being constructed to supply all of the other Yerkes railways. The depôt was to have been at the southern extremity, beyond the station at Clapham Junction. It would have a surface site bounded by Vardens Road, Strathblaine Road, and St John's Hill, and would have a steep 1 in 9 tunnel connection to the railway. It seems highly likely that trains would have been hauled to the surface using a winch mechanism, as used by the C&SLR at their Stockwell depôt.

The No. 2 Bill proposed a railway that was slightly shorter, at 4 miles 31 chains (7.1 km), and also slightly cheaper: its costs were said to be £1,384,231. This is slightly surprising, as its running tunnels were to be 13 ft 6 ins (4.1 m) diameter, which would have increased the costs of construction. It was promoted by A. J. Barker and J. W. Webb, and S. G. Fraser was the engineer. The reduction in length was at both ends; the station at Clapham Junction was a true terminus, with the tracks finishing at the south-western end of the platforms. At Marble Arch a running connection would be made with the North West London Railway, and so no separate platforms would need constructing. Presumably the NWLR depôt would be used for rolling stock maintenance as well, although electricity would be generated in their own power station on the banks of the Grosvenor Canal, to the north-east of the line as it curved into Chelsea Bridge Road.

The stations on this line would be in very similar positions to those for the No. 1 Bill, and so the list will not be repeated. Notable differences in the sites for buildings were at Sloane Square, where it would be on the west side of Lower Sloane Street a short distance south of the Square, and at Sloane Street, with buildings on both sides of Knightsbridge. Marble Arch would entirely use the facilities to be constructed by the NWLR.

Both Bills were postponed in the House of Commons on 2 March, and on 21 April the promoters of the No. 1 Bill withdrew it. The No. 2 Bill was never reinstated.

Growing the GNP&BR

The GNP&BR proposed in their Bill for 1903 to construct an extension of their line from Hammersmith to Knightsbridge via High Street Kensington. This would diverge from their existing route at Knightsbridge (immediately to the east of the existing station, to allow new platforms to be constructed on the extension). It would then follow Kensington Road and Kensington High Street, via the MR and MDR joint station, past Addison Road station, to Hammersmith. The line would continue by curving north from Hammersmith Broadway, beneath Hammersmith Grove, finally swinging eastwards to terminate at Shepherd's Bush. This entire extension would be underground.

At **Knightsbridge** the platforms on the extension would be at a slightly higher level that those on the existing line. The other stations would have been in similar locations to those on the Morgan tube, i.e., **Albert Hall**, **High Street Kensington**, **Addison Road** (actually sited at Holland Road), **Hammersmith**, and **Shepherd's Bush**. The terminal station would have been on the south side of Shepherd's Bush Green.

The same Bill contained details of another extension for the GNP&BR. A new pair of tunnels would diverge west of Piccadilly Circus, at Air Street, to a lower level than on the authorized line (which ascended slightly towards Covent Garden). It passed beneath Leicester Square to a station at **Charing Cross**, which was to be situated below King William Street, with its building on the north side of the Strand at the junction with Agar Street.

The station at **Strand** was unusual in that the two tunnels would diverge around the church of St Clement Danes, with one platform either side at a depth of 100 feet (30.5 m). The plans do not show an obvious station site, and it is likely that the existing station planned for the branch from Holborn would be used.

The railway would then continue under Fleet Street before curving south at **Ludgate Circus** under New Bridge Street (with the platforms beneath providing interchange with Ludgate Hill main line station), and then east again under Queen Victoria Street. Here the railway would join the deep level District line to Mansion House, with a running connection. An additional single running tunnel would be constructed between the junction and the terminal, with an extra platform at Mansion House. This would form an unusual triple-tube section of railway; regrettably the plans do not depict the track layout for this area.

The two extensions to the east and west would give the GNP&BR a line that effectively included the core of the Morgan route from the previous year.

One further provision of the Bill, connected to the proposed absorption of the BS&WR and CCE&HR, was the change in name to the Underground Consolidated Electric Railways Company.

In common with the CLR, the Bill was postponed and subsequently withdrawn because of the impending Royal Commission.

The agreement between the GNP&BR and the MDR relating to the construction and use of the deep-level MDR between Earl's Court and South Kensington was formally enshrined in the MDR (Various Powers) Act of 21 July 1903. This allowed the construction of deep-level platforms at Earl's Court station, with the tunnels reaching the MDR surface tracks at West Kensington, allowing it access to the existing station at Hammersmith.

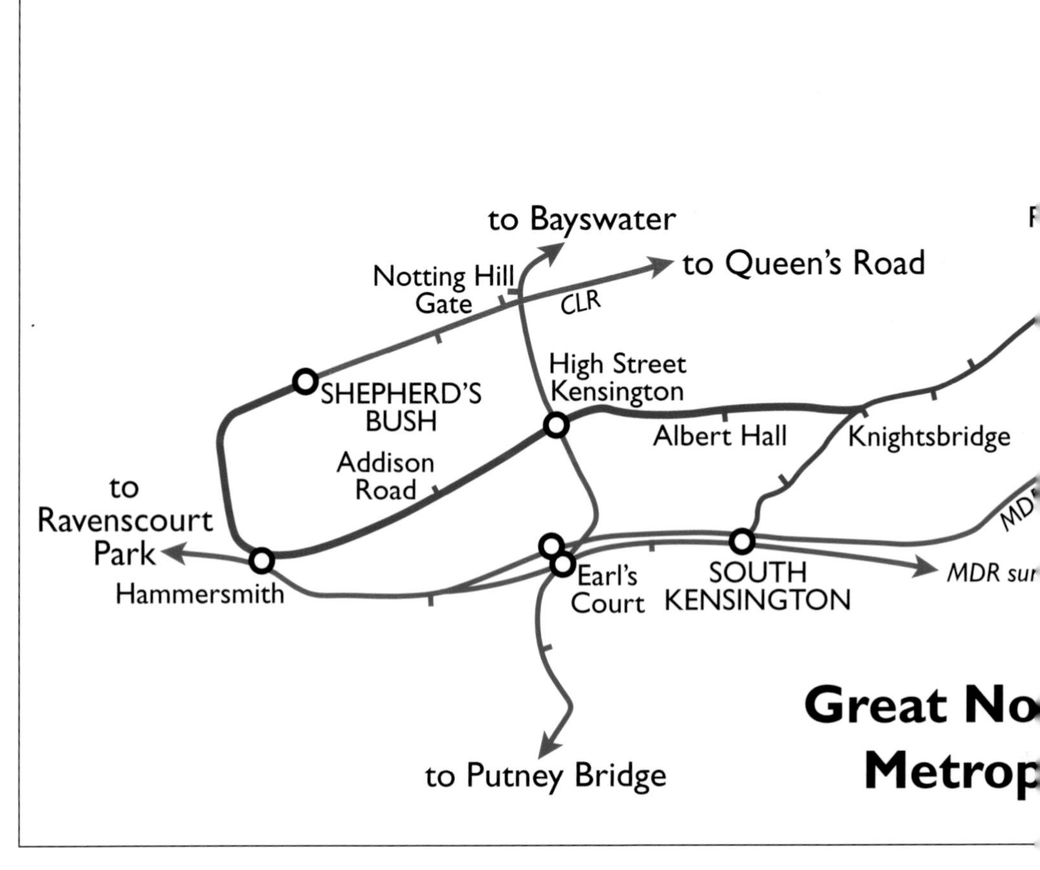

Another provision in the MDR Bill was withdrawn before Royal Assent, namely the construction of a pair of tracks west of Hammersmith, between Studland Road and Turnham Green Junctions. These would have been parallel to those of the L&SWR, which opposed this part of the Bill. An agreement was reached between the two companies: the MDR withdrew the relevant part of their Bill, and the L&SWR would allow MDR trains to use their tracks in exchange for an annual rental payment.

More for the MDR

The quiescent deep-level line of the MDR was still no nearer to construction than it had been in 1897, when first approved (with the exception of the Earl's Court to South Kensington portion that had been transferred to the GNP&BR). However, this did not curb the ambition of the MDR, and in 1903 they looked to extend their unbuilt railway both east and west.

The eastern extension was to take the line from Mansion House to Stepney Green, where it would rise to the surface and join the Whitechapel & Bow Railway. The W&BR was authorized in 1897 to extend the MDR eastwards to a junction with the main line London, Tilbury & Southend Railway (LTSR). It had opened in 1902, and

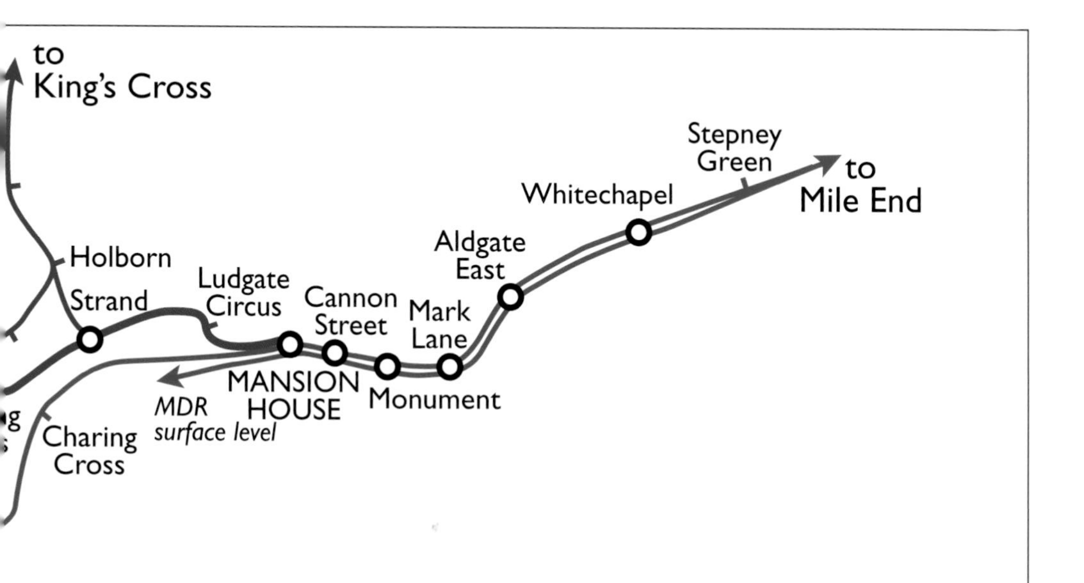

, Piccadilly & Brompton Railway 1903
District Railway (Deep Level) 1903

MDR trains had immediately started running over the LTSR to East Ham, Barking, and Upminster.

The tunnels of the deep-level MDR would be prolonged eastwards from their 1897 terminus at Mansion House, following under the surface level MDR with stations at **Cannon Street**, **Monument**, **Mark Lane**, **Aldgate East**, and **Whitechapel**. They would then join the tracks of the W&BR under the Mile End Road in the vicinity of its junction with Jubilee Street. [245]

To the west of Gloucester Road the line would remain in deep-level tube, with the station tunnels at **Earl's Court** being sited between Earl's Court Road and Knaresborough Place (east of the surface station), 37 ft 6 ins (11.4 m) below the existing tracks. Large crossover tunnels would be built either side of the station, allowing it to act as a terminus for trains from either direction. The line would then follow exactly under the surface-level MDR tracks as far as the bridge under Great Church Lane (which was considerably shortened following the construction of the Hammersmith Flyover in 1962, and no longer reaches the MDR). At this point they would form a junction allowing the existing MDR station at Hammersmith to be used for both the surface- and deep-level trains.

If constructed, these extensions would have allowed the MDR to operate express trains across London – at least as far as Mansion House. It seems strange, having planned an express line east of Earl's Court with intermediate stations at only South Kensington and Charing Cross, that this 1903 Bill contained closely-spaced stations in the City, mirroring those on the existing line. The retention of running powers over the deep-level section would allow it to interoperate with the GNP&BR between Hammersmith and South Kensington. The western extension proposed in this Bill contained a special clause allowing the GNP&BR to construct and maintain the new line between Gloucester Road and the tunnel portals at Great Church Lane.

However, times were changing for the District. The extension Bill was postponed because of the Royal Commission, and the MDR withdrew it on 21 April. The proposal was not made again. The improvements being made to their existing line through electrification and new signalling increased the capacity such that the deep-level line could not be justified financially.

The Works at South Kensington

Apart from the Piccadilly line between Earl's Court and South Kensington, constructed under the original 1897 District Railway powers, the only tangible trace of the scheme is at South Kensington station, where a limited amount of construction work took place. The station was from the outset an anomaly on the Piccadilly line – all of the other stations with two platforms had them both at the same level, whereas at South Kensington they were not. The lifts had two lower landings, and on descending would first stop at the eastbound level before descending a further 18 feet (5.5 m) to the level of the westbound platform.

Step-Plate Junctions

In order to merge two tunnels into one, a step-plate junction is sometimes constructed. This keeps the cross-section of the tunnel circular throughout. By constructing circular linings of increasing diameter, a stepped cone shape is formed, being at one end the diameter of a single running tunnel, and at the other of sufficient diameter to just encompass two adjacent tunnels.

It would seem, from the evidence available, that the Yerkes tubes did not use step-plate junctions, but instead constructed large cylindrical junction tunnels around 25 feet (7.6 m) in diameter.[246] These would have the advantage of being faster to construct (using a tunnelling shield), as well as using standard tunnelling segments throughout.

Step-plate junctions were used where a junction was being added to an existing line (e.g., Borough junction, where the Moorgate extension of the C&SLR branched from the line to King William Street). These junctions had to be hand-dug around the original tunnel, and so no shield could be used. It made sense to minimize the amount of digging, and a step-plate was therefore the best solution.

The first step-plate junctions on a Yerkes line were probably constructed at Camden Town around 1925, to connect the C&SLR with the Hampstead Tube.

See illustration on next page

The reason for this anomalous layout was that a junction was planned at the station, and the Piccadilly and District tubes would separate for their journeys east. Although the records are sketchy, it would appear that the eastbound platform would serve both lines with the separation occurring immediately to the east of the station, but westbound they would have separate platforms and the tunnels would merge to the west. The District platform would have been immediately to the south of that of the Piccadilly. A large cylindrical junction tunnel can be seen when departing for Gloucester Road; this is where the two lines would have merged. The Piccadilly line passes through this tunnel on a diagonal, giving the impression that a pair of step-plate junctions have been constructed. On the eastbound line the large-diameter platform tunnel continues past the eastern headwall, with the Piccadilly line immediately curving sharply left. The space remaining on the right would be ample for the District tracks to branch off on a slight right-hand curve.

A section of the westbound station tunnel 120 feet (37 m) long was constructed and even tiled at the same time as the GNP&BR station tunnels at South Kensington, using the original powers from 1897. It seems strange to go to the effort of constructing such a small fragment of platform, together with the junction sections, but its location is suggestive. It is immediately adjacent to the lift shafts. This would imply that it was constructed to avoid disruption or even damage to the shafts as and when the MDR finally decided to construct their deep-level line. It was noted some sixteen years afterwards that "it would have been difficult to carry out the work later." [247] Similarly the junction tunnels were constructed to avoid disruption to the Piccadilly line at a later date. [248]

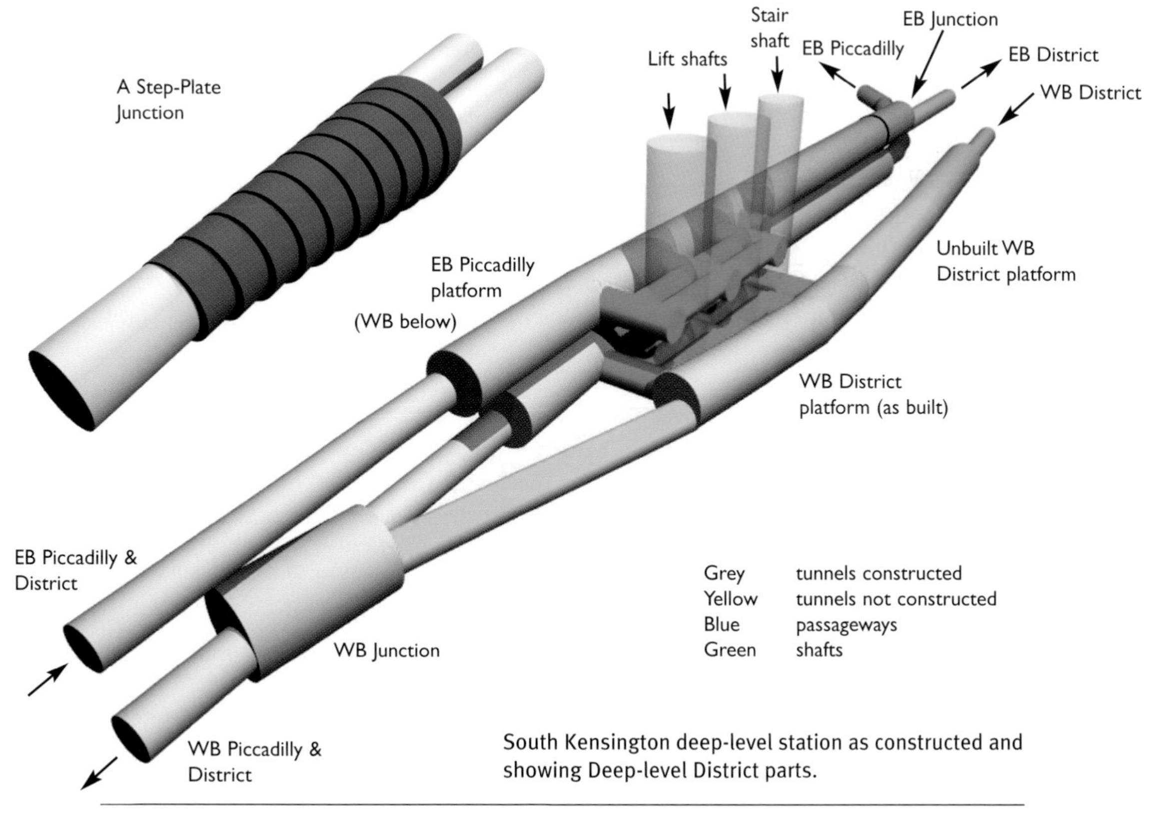

South Kensington deep-level station as constructed and showing Deep-level District parts.

Resignalling and electrification of the MDR increased the capacity of the line such that the deep-level line was not needed as urgently. The powers for the deep-level District railway between South Kensington and Mansion House were abandoned in the 1908 Act for the MDR. However, if the railway press is to be believed, plans for the District tube railway continued on-and-off for a number of years. For example, as late as 1916 it was noted that it "has not been abandoned altogether, and this problem will come up for examination as soon as there is a prospect of work of this character being undertaken."[249]

The platform tunnel was used during the First World War for storing treasures from the Victoria & Albert Museum and china from Buckingham Palace. It went on to be used as a signalling school from around 1927, for which it finally received track, including a set of points and a trainstop. It also had examples of all of the types of signalling that staff would encounter, including semaphores, colour-light signals, and fog repeaters, as well as signal cabin equipment. Demonstrations would be given to trainees on the equipment; once familiar with the operation of it, faults would be induced by the lecturers, and the task of the trainees would be to find the fault and rectify it. Part of the space was set aside for lectures, and had a seating capacity of 60, with desks, a blackboard, and a projector and screen.

The signalling school lasted until 1939. During the Second World War the tunnel became an emergency headquarters for the London Passenger Transport Board (LPTB)[250] engineering services,[251] and it was divided into two levels to increase the available space. It was also used to house equipment that would detect the landing in the Thames of bombs with delayed action fuses – which had the potential to breach the Underground tunnels. Hydrophones in the riverbed transmitted signals back to the equipment, and this was used to help decide whether to close the floodgates installed on some of the under-river tunnels at the start of the war.

Since the 1920s a rolling programme of lift replacement by escalators had been in operation, slowly converting the more heavily-used stations. In 1970 contracts were let for the £1.1 million reconstruction of South Kensington station with escalators. The scheme built a subway from beneath the District line platforms to an intermediate-level concourse. Two escalators from the reconstructed ticket hall also connected to this level. A further bank of three escalators descended to a concourse situated nine feet (2.75 m) below the eastbound Piccadilly line, which was linked by two sets of stairs. Another set of stairs descended to the level of the westbound line.

When the escalator shaft was dug it "intersected the headwall in a disused 21-feet diameter tunnel at the same level as the Piccadilly westbound"[252] – in other words, the disused District platform. The new westbound platform access subways are constructed within the space occupied by the disused platform. The new escalators and associated subways were opened to the public on 30 September 1973.

Changes to the North West London Railway

In 1903 the NWLR looked to extend their authorized line south to Victoria. Since their scheme was authorized in 1899 the CLR had opened, and the NWLR promoters had noticed the heavy traffic using the new tube. Marble Arch was quite congested, and they realized that their line would only add to this, especially since Marble Arch was their southern terminus. (It was subsequently revealed[253] that the NWLR had unsuccessfully tried to negotiate through fares with the CLR in 1901; the CLR had insisted on full payment of its flat 2d fare for each passenger.)

The new extension would be an additional 1 mile 51 chains (2.6 km) of railway running beneath Hyde Park, and then Grosvenor Place. This was similar to the suggestion from the 1901 Select Committee, which proposed connecting the southern section of the West & South London Joint Railway to the NWLR to provide a link to Victoria.

On 2 March the House of Commons announced that this was one of the Bills to be postponed for the duration of the Royal Commission; the promoters immediately withdrew the Bill. A note in a file from the Office of Woods comments that the Bill was withdrawn before their surveyor could assess the section through Hyde Park for the purposes of determining the easement to be paid to the Crown.

The Watford & Edgware Railway

The W&ER was similar in conception to the Edgware & Hampstead Railway of the previous year. It was intended to extend the reach of the CCE&HR further from London, but was independently promoted. Entirely on the surface, it was to stretch 6¼ miles (10.1 km) from the planned Edgware terminus, via a station at **Elstree**, to **Watford**, where the station would be sited to the east of the High Street.

This railway has been chronicled elsewhere;[254] suffice to say that after some modifications that removed the need for the CCE&HR to operate through trains on the line, it received Royal Assent on 11 August. Its powers were never used, and expired in 1911.

The Royal Commission on London Traffic

The Commission

On 10 February 1903 a Royal Commission on London Traffic was created, in part due to the London Suburban Railway debacle. It had the remit of investigating how transport could best be developed and organized in London, and it made its recommendations to Parliament in a report of 17 July 1905.

The number of tube railway schemes placed before Parliament whilst the Royal Commission was compiling its report dropped sharply. Indeed, warnings were given on 2 March 1903 in the House of Commons, 6 August 1903 in the House of Lords, and 4 November 1904 by public notification that no consideration could be given to any such scheme until the report was complete. The public notification quoted the Lord Chairman of Committees of the House of Lords: "It is impossible for Parliament to consider any new schemes for new tubes or large railway extensions through London until the Commission has reported". However, a few promoters submitted schemes in disregard of these warnings.

Thirteen Commissioners were appointed to create the report. The Chairman was Sir David Miller Barbour, with Lynden Macassey as Secretary. Notable amongst them were the engineer Sir John Wolfe Barry; Baron Ribblesdale (who chaired one of the 1902 Committees); Earl Cawdor, Chairman of the GWR; and George Gibb, the General Manager of the NER.[255] The Commission was asked to report

> (a) as to the measures which the Commission deem most effectual for the improvement of the same by the development and inter-connexion of Railways and Tramways on, or below, the surface; by increasing the facilities for other forms of mechanical locomotion; by better provision for the organization and regulation of vehicular and pedestrian traffic, or otherwise;
>
> (b) as to the desirability of establishing some authority or tribunal to which all schemes of Railway or Tramway construction of a local character should be referred, and the powers which it would be advisable to confer on such a body.

The Commissioners held 112 meetings, and examined 134 witnesses. Six of the members[256] visited New York, Boston, Philadelphia, and Washington on a fact-finding trip during September 1903, and one of them[257] made a further trip to Vienna, Budapest, Prague, Cologne, Dresden, Berlin, Brussels and Paris in the autumn of 1904. These visits allowed them to investigate how other large cities managed the planning, construction, and operation of their transport systems.

The Report and Recommendations

The report they produced was composed of eight large volumes that occupy a considerable amount of shelf space. In scope it covered the City of London and the Metropolitan Police District, defined as any borough wholly within 15 miles of Charing Cross, or which had part within 12 miles. This region covered an area of 692.84 square miles (1,794 square km), and held a population of over 6.5 million in 1901.

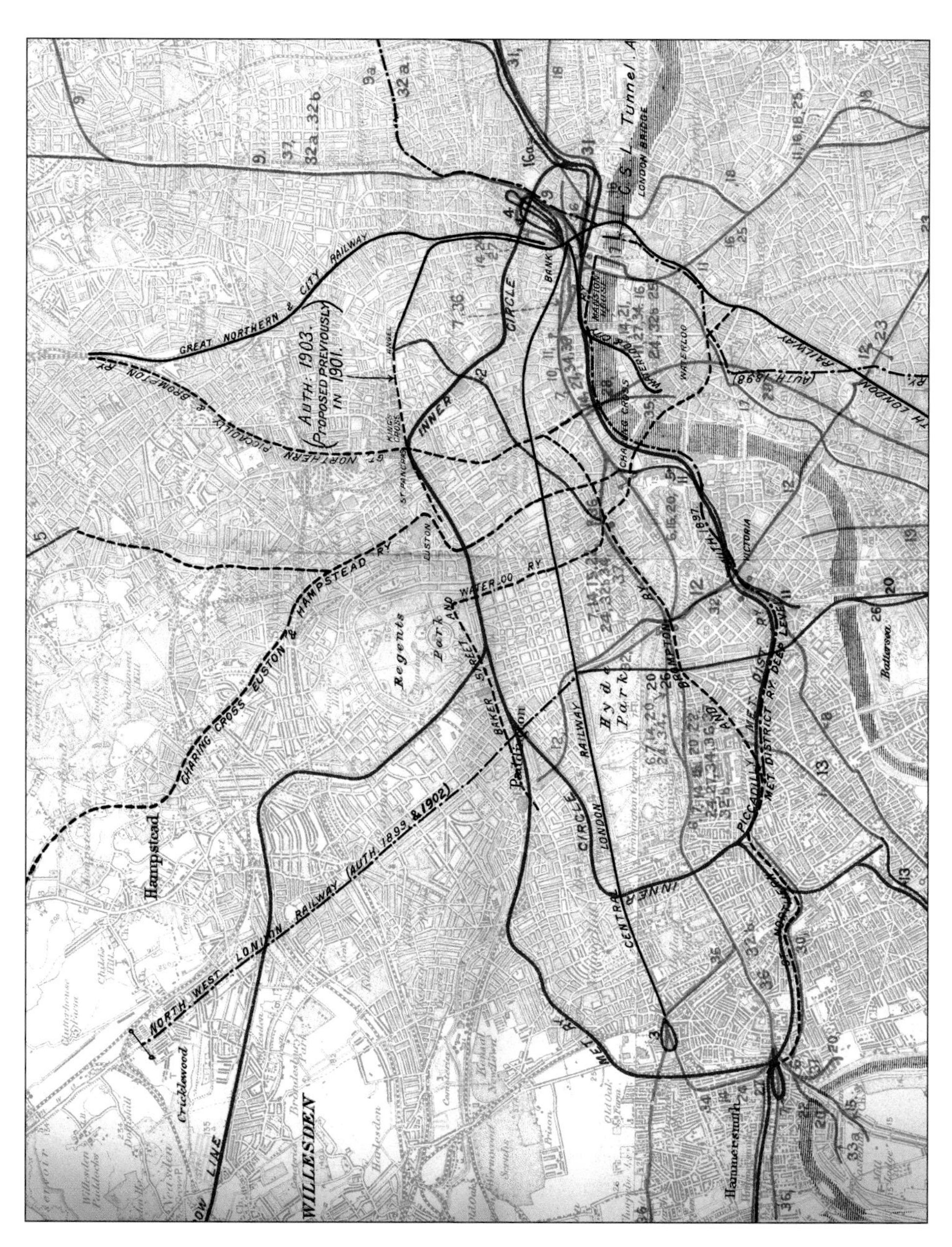

One of the Royal Commission maps, showing the plethora of new tube schemes proposed in the first few years of the 20th century (see Appendix 3 for key).

The Commissioners began their report by considering the work of previous committees that had looked at this problem, most notably in the field of the railways. These included:

- The Royal Commission on Railway Termini within or in the immediate vicinity of the Metropolis, 1846, which investigated whether the main line railways should be allowed to extend into central London. They concluded that on the north side of the Thames no railway should enter the area roughly defined by Edgware Road and Park Lane to the west; Marylebone, Euston, Pentonville, and City Roads to the north; Bishopsgate, Gracechurch Street, and London Bridge to the east, and Borough High Street, Lambeth Road, and Vauxhall Bridge to the south.[258] It was this recommendation that stopped the main line railways where they remain today, and indirectly caused the creation of the Metropolitan Railway.

- The House of Commons Select Committee on Metropolitan Communications, 1855, took this further, and actually recommended that a railway should be formed to link the main line termini with each other, the Thames, the docks, and the Post Office.

- The Select Committee on Metropolitan Railway Communication of 1863 – a Lords committee, which had recommended the creation of the Inner and Outer Circle Railways,[259] and favoured one management body for all railways existing in the London metropolis (which they termed the "Metropolitan Railway District"). They were also the first Committee to suggest that all railway Bills affecting the aforementioned District in a given year should be grouped together and be considered by a Select Committee, so that a comprehensive examination could be made.

- The Joint Select Committee on Railway Schemes (Metropolis) of 1864, which endorsed the Inner Circle proposal.

- The Joint Select Committee on the Electric & Cable Railways (Metropolis) of 1892. This Committee recommended that wayleaves should be purchasable where tube railways ran beneath private property; before this time, such railways were compelled to purchase the freeholds of all private property beneath which they ran. Wayleaves would allow them to reduce their costs, especially since the further recommendation was made that beneath public streets the wayleaves should be granted free of charge.[260] This explains why much of the London Underground from the early 1900s follows the pattern of the streets above. It also recommended a minimum tunnel diameter of 11 ft 6 ins (3.5 m).

- The report of the Central London Railway (Vibration) Committee appointed by the Board of Trade in 1901.[261] This investigation had led to the insertion of the special compensation clause into all tube railway Bills.

The Commissioners decided that there were three main questions for them to consider in respect of railways. Firstly, whether additional railways were required in central London, and if so where should they run, and the form they should take: deep tubes, cut-and-cover lines, or surface railways. Secondly, whether the existing facilities for suburban traffic were adequate, and thirdly, whether "special encouragement or assistance" was required for future railway construction. This last point was due to the concerns as to the finances of many of the proposed schemes, as shown by the rejection of the C&NESER proposal of 1903.

The key recommendation in the report was that a central Traffic Board should be established, which would have the task of examining all railway Bills before they were submitted to Parliament. This was to be a new body, rather than the existing local or municipal authorities; even the establishment of a new local authority just for this purpose was rejected by the Commissioners. The Board was to have limited powers and duties to avoid undue interference with the work of the existing local authorities, and was to report annually to Parliament.

The only new tube that the Commissioners saw fit to recommend (in answer to their first question) was a line between the north-west and Victoria. This could be achieved, in their view, by extending the authorized North West London Railway from its planned terminus at Marble Arch about one mile south, beneath Park Lane and Grosvenor Place. This small addition to the network of underground railways would, they felt, leave the central area of London well provided with by the tubes.

The route from Hammersmith to north-east London could be occupied by a shallow tram subway, similar to that under construction beneath Kingsway. This would allow trams to operate between Hammersmith and the London county boundary in Stamford Hill. This answered their second question.

In response to their third question, the Commissioners noted that there were difficulties in raising finance for tube railways. Construction costs were between £500,000 and £1 million per mile (1.6 km). This was not very different from the costs for cut-and-cover construction, but the two had different areas of spend. Tubes spent more on shafts and lifts, whilst cut-and-cover cost more because of the public inconvenience, the taking up of cellars, and the greater risk of damage to houses and public utilities. The other main cost for shallow lines was that of taking private land so that open stations could be constructed, allowing smoke and steam to disperse.

The Commissioners noted that shallow railways are more convenient for public access, and so they suggested that in future cut-and-cover work should be performed with minimal surface impact. This had been achieved in the City of London with the completion of the Inner Circle and in Paris with the construction of the Métro.

An interesting proposal that was unfortunately ignored by the promoters of new railways, probably on grounds of cost, was that railways should be of four-track construction, as with the New York subway. This would allow for local and express trains to operate, and give greater flexibility during engineering work.

With regard to the finance, the Commission recommended that railways should be allowed to purchase land in less densely populated areas into which they wanted to extend. This would then allow them to benefit from the increase in land values that the railways brought, and provide them with a better return on their investment. The raising of capital in the first instance would therefore be made easier for them.

The Commissioners also recommended that tramways should be constructed in central London, but that the various county councils and the City of London should have preferential rights for this.

The report was signed on 26 June 1905, but not by all of the Commissioners. Earl Cawdor had resigned from the Commission on 25 March, citing the pressures of his work as First Lord of the Admiralty. Bartley refused to sign and issued his own report. This was published at the end of the main report volume. He felt that the recommendations did not answer the great question of transport in the metropolis, and were just for small improvements that would achieve little. He wanted nothing less than the scheme of grand avenues recommended by the Advisory Board (see later).

Dimsdale did sign the report, but, like Bartley, added his own short report in which he rejected the recommendation for tramways in central London. Likewise, Gibb also signed the report, but appended a note in which he recommended the construction of a tube railway between Shepherd's Bush and the City, along the Strand axis, which would form a loop with the CLR. This was to be in a similar manner to that promoted in the previous years by the CLR. However, to avoid duplication with the GNP&BR, Gibb proposed that that company's line be used between Hammersmith and Leicester Square, with a loop in the west connecting to Shepherd's Bush, and an extension to the east to Bank via Liverpool Street. The remainder of the GNP&BR could, he suggested, be operated as a shuttle between Leicester Square and Finsbury Park. The reaction of Yerkes to this idea is not recorded!

The Evidence

As mentioned previously, a large volume of evidence was heard and collected by the Commissioners. This was compiled into the second volume of their report. Much of it has no bearing on the railway lines discussed here.

As one of Britain's eminent engineers, as well as someone closely associated with the recent tube railway proposals in London, it was not unexpected that Douglas Fox would be one of the first to give evidence. He believed that shallow subways cost around twice as much as deep level tubes, due to the engineering complexity necessary for underpinning the neighbouring buildings, as well as the need to re-route pipes and other subterranean services. He gave many details about the C&NESER proposals of 1903, which have been mentioned earlier. His brother Francis, also an engineer and a business partner, felt that the finance requirements placed upon that railway by the Committee were most unfair.

The evidence of Col. Yorke of the BoT supported the tunnel size suggested by Sir Douglas Fox in 1902. He suggested that 13 ft 6 ins (4.1 m) should be the minimum for tube railway tunnels, as this would provide better ventilation, and allow more space for both signalling equipment and escape routes in the event of an accident. However, for the route between Hammersmith and the City, still unbuilt despite the many proposals of previous years. Yorke favoured construction in a shallow subway of the sort favoured by the LCC. This would run between Hammermith and Hyde Park Corner before turning south-east under Green Park to Westminster, where the line would surface and join the proposed tramway on the Embankment. To avoid damage to the grass and trees in the parks Yorke recommended that the subway be positioned beneath the existing roads.

Arnold Hills, promoter of the NELR and P&CR, as well as the LW&EFR in 1898, gave a large amount of evidence. As Chairman of the Thames Iron Works he took considerable interest in the travelling conditions for his workmen. He also commuted to Blackwall from his home in Woodford Green, and so had first-hand experience of the overcrowding on GER trains. After the collapse of the LW&EFR he had studied the transport problem for a couple of years, before promoting the NELR and P&CR of 1901. He felt that the West End connection was important to the success of the railways. At this point he submitted a map of the Hammersmith, City & North East London Railway, a new scheme on which he was working. More details of this scheme are given in a later chapter.

Hills felt that the parliamentary procedure for gaining approval for railway Bills was too inflexible. Schemes had to be deposited in November, and once deposited, could not be improved or modified. They were considered by Parliamentary Committees who were not experts in the field of tube railways (or even railways). As seen with the proposals so far, the Committees could add instructions to the Bills that cause problems for them later. All in all, it was not a satisfactory state of affairs.

He proposed that an Authority should be formed to carry out ordinary administration in London, instead of this being done by the LCC or Borough Councils. In addition, there should be a development authority that would look at all major railway and tramway development schemes. Finally, the approving authority should remain as a Joint Committee of the Houses of Parliament.

An unusual suggestion came from Charles Scott Meik, the engineer involved with a number of earlier tube railway proposals. He told that Commission that road improvements were key to improving London's traffic, and that underground railways could not provide the answer. He presented detailed plans and drawings for wide avenues crossing London in the middle of each would be two lines of suspended monorail. Motor roads would be provided beneath the monorails, trams would run outside of these, and between the pavements and the trams, roadways would be provided for horse-drawn traffic. In some areas the motor roads would be sunk below ground level, and the monorail trains would be just above the surface — presumably this would make it easier for passengers to use the stations.

The surveyor for Shoreditch, J. R. Dixon, suggested on behalf of the Council that a railway from Piccadilly to the Tottenham and Walthamstow areas would be a very useful amenity. In addition to this, he also proposed a line from Shoreditch Church to Charing Cross, running beneath Old Street, Clerkenwell Road, and Bloomsbury Way. As with so many of these schemes, no money was provided – they were just another set of ideas. It is highly unlikely that both would have been constructed anyway, as they provided alternative routes between Charing Cross and Shoreditch. The second line might have been considered if congestion on the first had become too great through the City, but no speculator would have put up the money for it whilst the first was still just a proposal.

Another locality offering support, but not of the financial kind, was Hackney. Norman Scorgie, their Engineer and Surveyor, supported the C&NESER proposals, and opposed any delay in its construction. He was willing to give evidence to Parliament if it would secure the scheme.

Joseph Levy, Councillor for Hammersmith, requested that a tube railway between

Hammersmith and the City be provided. Other improvements for his locality that he suggested included extending the CLR to Hammersmith Broadway, and various extensions of the London United Tramways to make better connections. He also sought improvements to the main line railway services.

The General Manager of the CLR, Granville Cunningham, once again proposed the circular route for his railway (as promoted in 1902 and 1903), and also encouraged the revival of the C&NESER scheme of 1903. He suggested that at the southern end the C&NESER should be continued past Monument and below the river to London Bridge, before swinging south-east towards New Cross. This would obviously be favourable for the CLR. It would provide a new source of traffic for them at Liverpool Street, and prevent the C&NESER from being extended west where the two lines would be in competition. Other suggestions included the extension of the NWLR from Marble Arch, through Victoria, and south to Clapham Junction, and an extension for the CCE&HR from Charing Cross to Clapham via Westminster Bridge, Vauxhall, and Wandsworth Road stations. His final tube extension proposal was for the BS&WR to continue beyond Elephant & Castle to Denmark Hill station, passing through Camberwell.

The Underground Freight Railway

One of the more unusual proposals for the Commission to consider came from Henry Knight, an Alderman of the City of London, and former Mayor of London. He proposed a double loop of twin tubes to transport freight into the metropolis. The tubes would be placed one above the other, and stations would be placed about once every mile. These stations would have through tracks, with platforms on loop lines, so that trains could pass if required.

Shafts with hoists would allow wagons to be lowered or raised, removing the need to transfer goods manually. Surface depôts at each shaft head would act as distribution points for the businesses for about one-half mile around. Transfer points would be located on each main line railway where they intersected the goods railway, and the main line companies would be encouraged to transfer their freight to the new line.

Knight wanted to rid the streets of the many carts used to transport goods for miles across London. The only carts remaining would be making short journeys to the goods depôts, or transporting coal. Coal would not be permitted on the underground railway on account of its weight, and the dirt it would bring.

The estimated cost of the 40 miles of tunnel required was tentatively estimated at £20 million by Knight. This was a conservative estimate, based on the existing tube railways; given that he wanted 17-feet (5.2 m) diameter tunnels, the cost would most likely have been a lot higher.

An interesting proposal was placed in front of the Commissioners by Maurice Fitzmaurice, the Chief Engineer of the LCC.[262] This was for a tram subway along the route of the PC&NELR (an enlargement of the subway scheme proposed earlier by Yorke). This was to run from Hammersmith to the London County boundary, and would be very similar to the LCC tram subway that was under construction between Holborn and the Strand, underneath the new Kingsway road.[263] The width is given as 20 feet (6.1 m). If we can assume that the construction would be similar then the new subway would be designed for single-deck tramcars, and would have had a headroom of about 11 ft 6 ins (3.5 m). Short platforms would be constructed at each subway station, as the service was to be composed of short, frequent trams. Through Hyde Park the subway would run directly beneath the park roads, thus avoiding both damage to the trees of the park, and excavation of more heavily used public roads.

Fitzmaurice gave costs of £862,348 from Hammersmith to Walsingham House, Piccadilly; £2,514,628 from there to Bishopsgate; and £1,789,986 for the final portion to the county boundary. This gave a total of £5,166,962, which was almost £1 million more than the estimated cost of constructing the same in a deep level tube of 13 ft 6 ins in diameter with normal platform lengths. The additional cost of the subway reflected the difficulties, already mentioned, of cut-and-cover construction, and the need to acquire almost all of the cellars in Piccadilly. Like many roads in London the cellars extended beneath the streets, almost to the point of touching those of the properties opposite in some cases. Further costs were due to the necessity of making a half-mile section through the City as a deep tube, probably to avoid the deep cellars and vaults.

James Clifton Robinson also appeared before the Royal Commission. He continued to support the extension of tramways into central London, and felt that because of street widenings the Hammersmith to City route via Hyde Park Corner and the Strand would be ideal. Another proposal was for a line from Shepherd's Bush to St Paul's or St Martin's-le-Grand. This latter scheme would undoubtedly have been opposed by the CLR, as it would have duplicated almost the entire length of their route, as well as removing the need for passengers to interchange from the LUT trams at Shepherd's Bush.

The Advisory Board of Engineers

The Commissioners recognized that, whilst they had been tasked with reporting on a technical matter, they were not engineers. They therefore sought expert and technical advice by forming an Advisory Board of Engineers whose remit, as far as railways was concerned, was to examine

- the type and direction of railways required in addition to those already existing or authorised.
- the cost of construction and the practicability in London of underground railways other than "tube" railways on the routes which have been suggested in evidence before the Commission or such routes as may appear preferable.

The Board consisted of the eminent engineer Sir John Wolfe Barry, who was also one of the Commissioners; Sir Benjamin Baker, who had worked on many of London's underground railways;[264] and William Barclay Parsons, Chief Engineer to the Board of Rapid Transit Railroad Commissioners of the City of New York.

This eminent trio issued their own report, as the seventh volume of the overall Commission Report, with its voluminous appendix as the eighth. They confirmed the view of the LCC engineer Maurice Fitzmaurice, who greatly favoured the construction of shallow tram subways. They felt that the satisfactory construction of the pedestrian subways at Bank by the CLR demonstrated that this was a practical means of providing the necessary tunnels.

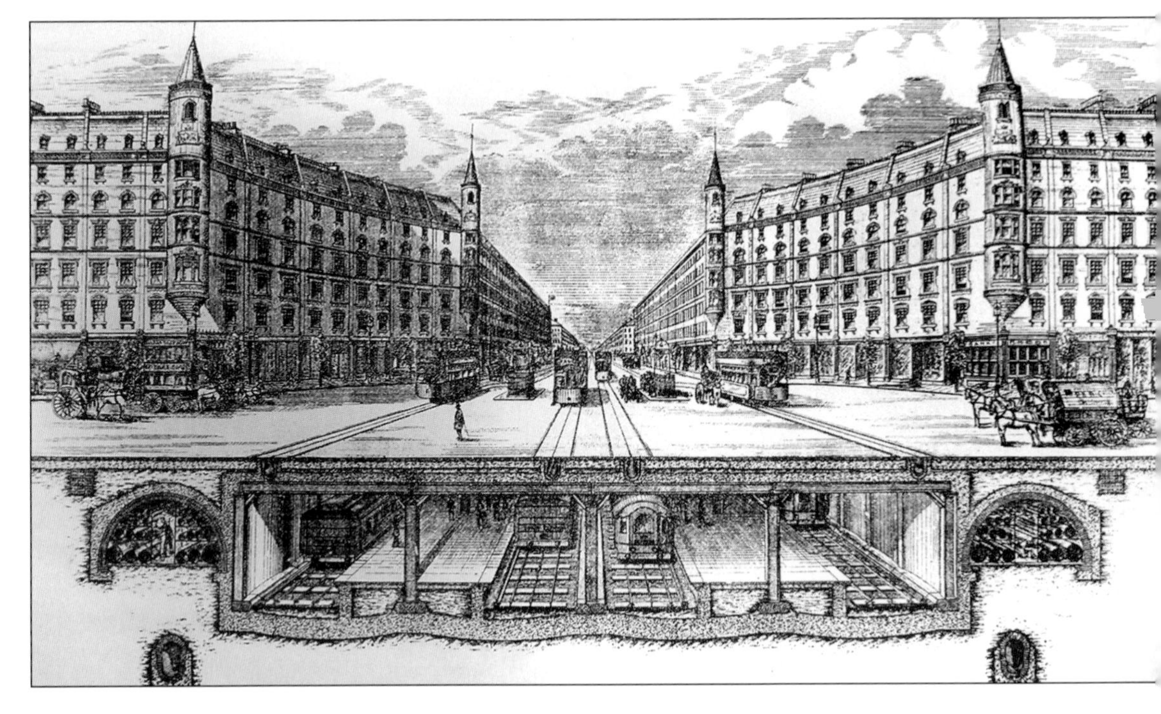

Underground railway beneath one of the two proposed new avenues.

The most dramatic proposal was for the creation of two new avenues across London. One was to run from Holloway Road in the north to Elephant & Castle south of the Thames, crossing the river on a new bridge to the west of Blackfriars Bridge. To the north of the river it would follow the course of Gray's Inn Road and Caledonian Road (but avoiding King's Cross by keeping east).

The other avenue was to run east-west from Whitechapel Road at its junction with Commercial Road, to the Victoria Gate of Hyde Park, on Bayswater Road. This would cut through Portman and Russell Squares, and then follow the course of the MR between Farringdon and Liverpool Street. The two new avenues would have crossed at Gray's Inn Road.

The avenues were to be 140 feet (42.7 m) wide, with four lines of tramways. The middle of the street could have express trams; towards the edges (but leaving enough room for parked vehicles) would be slower trams. Conduit pick-up, as used by the LCC trams, was to be used. Pavements would be 23 feet (7 m) wide, with cellars of houses beneath them (where these were provided).

They recommended that subways should be constructed at the same time just beneath the new avenues to accommodate railways. These would have four tracks, providing express and local services in each direction. This suggestion comes from the New York Subway, where such lines were often provided. Following the practice adopted for the construction of Shaftesbury Avenue and Kingsway, utility subways would be built along both sides of the road, either side of the train subway. This would allow the gas, water, and electricity supplies to be maintained without the inconvenience of digging up the road.

Other recommendations made by the Board included:

- Spacing stations out – closely spaced stations increased the cost and decreased the average speed on railways.
- Making shallow stations, as this provides easier access with shorter stairs or lifts. Hump profiles, as used on the CLR, assist in this, as well as in the running of the trains. The rising gradient on the approach to the stations assists with braking, and the falling gradient upon departure aids rapid acceleration.
- Providing free easements under private property. Baker in particular believed that the construction of tube railways caused little problem to buildings above, and so the provision of free easements would prevent the difficulties seen so far in constructing railways directly beneath public streets.
- No general rules for the design and equipment of railways.
- Separate train services should be provided for long-distance, suburban, and urban services.
- Through running from one side of London to the other was better than circular lines within the metropolis. Through lines would provide transport to the suburbs, and railways across London would take a balance of traffic from each side.
- No new tube railway lines should be sanctioned until the existing ones had been tested and proved their worth.

1904: Treading Water during the Commission

Tinkering Around the Edges

Bills for the 1904 session of Parliament had to be deposited by December 1903 at the latest. Given that the Royal Commission was still in progress it was to be expected that very few tube railway Bills for London would be promoted.

Four of the Bills can be discussed in a few lines. The BS&WR wanted to increase their capital, and add stations at Edgware Road, Regent's Park, and Lambeth,[265] so the Bill was for land for the station buildings, and enlargement of the tunnels.[266] Their Bill received Royal Assent on 22 July 1904.

The CCE&HR similarly sought to raise additional capital, and to add a station at Mornington Crescent, again by acquiring a surface site and enlarging the running tunnels. They also needed to take more subsoil for their station at Tottenham Court Road, and route the line slightly closer to the church of St Martin-in-the-Fields at Trafalgar Square. With the exception of the capital, which was opposed by the LCC, the Bill also became an Act on 22 July. The LCC's opposition to the increased capital requested by both this line and the BS&WR was on the grounds that the capital authorized previously had not been completely raised. As has been seen earlier, the LCC kept a close eye on the amount of capital that the companies sought to raise, believing that "excessive capital was not conducive to low fares".[267] The BS&WR argued that there had been no provision in their capital for the construction of Edgware Road station, or for the fireproofing work that was essential for stations and rolling stock following the disaster on the Paris Métro the previous year.[268]

The BS&WR reduced the capital request in their Bill from £440,000 to £384,000, which the LCC accepted.

The Great Northern & City finally opens

The GN&CR asked for a further extension of time in their 1904 Bill. This was to allow completion of a small portion of the original line at Moorgate, which apparently could not be completed except in conjunction with the Lothbury extension. This Bill received Royal Assent on 24 June.

The line finally opened on 14 February, with the exception of Highbury station, the last to be approved. This was opened on 28 June. The GNR totally ignored the event, and did not advertise the existence of the line. Unsurprisingly, the line was not a great success, and passenger numbers were about 60% of the original forecasts. However, it was not totally without impact, as a year later an indebted umbrella salesman who was before Clerkenwell County Court blamed it for the falling off in sales.[269]

The low revenues meant that the Lothbury extension plans remained in abeyance.

The MDR asks for more time

An extension of time was also requested by the MDR for their deep-level scheme. Their Bill included measures to form agreements with the other Yerkes railways, and to take additional land between Hammersmith and West Kensington to accommodate the tracks of the GNP&BR trains that would soon arrive. Royal Assent was received on 1 August.

The HC&NELR returns

The only other railway that was actively promoting itself was the HC&NELR, which was ignominiously rejected in 1903. Taking heed of the warning from Parliament not to deposit tube railway Bills before the report of the Royal Commission was produced, the Bill was deposited *pro forma* for the 1904 session, i.e., declaring intent without actually seeking to start the Parliamentary procedures. In these circumstances the promoters did not have to make a financial deposit with Parliament.

Since Hills had been called to give evidence before the Commission at around the same time, he used this as a further opportunity to stake his claim to the Hammersmith to Walthamstow route across London, as mentioned above.

A Couple of New Ideas

Whilst the Royal Commission was in progress, very few people were prepared to promote new tube railways in London. Only two such schemes were put forward in 1904.

The North & South Woolwich Electric Railway

Only one entirely new tube railway was contemplated for the 1904 session of Parliament, and this was not for central London. The North & South Woolwich Electric Railway (N&SWER) was to be a short line connecting the opposite sides of the Thames at Woolwich, for which capital of £240,000 was required. The Mayor of Kensington, Major Lewis Isaacs, was promoting it, together with Sir Robert Dashwood. The engineer was Sir James Szlumper, who was also responsible for the GNP&BR.

The N&SWER was a short line in the tradition of the schemes promoted in the 1880s: passing under the river, with a station at each end. The main tunnel under the Thames would be bored conventionally, and the stations and approaches would be constructed using the cut-and-cover principle. The subsoil in North Woolwich was particularly unfavourable, and particular care would be needed not to damage sewers, buildings, or the river bank.

The station on the north side would be at the junction of Albert Road and the High Street;[270] that on the south, at Beresford Square, outside the Arsenal. A single tube about ¾-mile (1.2 km) long and 11 ft 6 ins diameter would connect the two. One train would operate in each direction every 6 minutes (presumably the same train shuttling back and forth). The train would have six cars, and have a capacity of 330 passengers, each paying a fare of 1d. The electricity for the line would be generated on the north side, on a site bounded by Francis Street, Blois Street, and High Street. This site will not be found on modern maps, as it has been lost beneath the King George V Dock and its warehouses on the south side of the dock, opened in 1921.

The railway had the support of the Arsenal authorities, as well as the Borough

Councils of Woolwich and West Ham. As usual the water companies nearby sought clauses protecting them from electrolysis. Chief opposition came from the LCC, which wanted some 27 clauses adding to the Bill. The LCC had started a free ferry service across the river nearby in 1889, to link the two halves of the Borough of Woolwich. However, the thick fogs that blanketed London brought the service to a halt, as crossing the river perpendicular to all of the other shipping was inviting an accident when visibility was poor. Such a collision could cost the lives of 800–1000 people. During the winter months the fogs were so frequent that the ferry could be suspended for days at a time, with the only alternative being to charter small skiffs, which were frequently overloaded. Some employers would lay off all staff who lived across the river for the duration of winter. It was not surprising that a tunnel was seen as the solution, and indeed the LCC had been considering constructing a tunnel itself, either for pedestrians, or both pedestrians and vehicles.

The Council considered requesting a clause be added to the Bill allowing them to purchase the railway in the future, with the intention of connecting it to the tramways either side of the river. In particular linking the tramway along Plumstead High Street with the north bank was considered desirable. Such a connection would also make the railway's own power station unnecessary.

They then felt that the single tunnel would be too restrictive and decided that a double tunnel was necessary to handle peak-hour traffic. Maurice Fitzmaurice, the LCC's Chief Engineer, estimated that a ten-minute service would be operable with just the one tunnel, but the promoters demurred and stated six. This was rather optimistically based on a single trip running time of 2½ minutes, plus 30 seconds to unload and load at each end – rather unfeasible for moving 660 people in the peaks! This evidence would suggest that two platforms were intended at each station, with three trains in operation, although no documentary proof of this can be found. One train would be in motion, and the other two would be at opposite stations loading and unloading.

Eventually all of the LCC clauses were agreed with the promoters, except for one about future tunnels and compensation. This clause would forbid the promoters from opposing the LCC constructing any similar tunnels nearby; also that if such a tunnel was built the railway company would not be eligible for any compensation. The LCC insisted upon this clause as it had already compensated the Thames ferrymen when it had started the free ferry, and it felt that it should not be obliged to pay any more compensation to private companies when it provided free public access across the river. It was not surprising that the promoters objected to this clause.

The preamble of the Bill was proved on 16 March 1904, but the Committee included the final LCC clause. On 22 March the promoters stated that they did not wish to proceed under such terms, and thus the Bill was killed.[271]

Waterloo to Ludgate Circus

The engineer for the N&SWER, James Szlumper, proposed another tube railway in 1904, and contacted the London & South Western Railway to see if they were interested. The line was to be similar to the W&CR, in that it would connect the LSWR terminus at Waterloo with Ludgate Circus. Unusually the line was to have just a single tunnel. It was estimated to cost £253,000, and Szlumper wanted to know if the LSWR would undertake to the work the line once it was constructed.

The Traffic Committee referred the matter to the Board. After putting the matter off for a couple of meetings it was finally reported in October 1904 that the scheme would not proceed. In a short article about the proposal, Peter Bancroft considered that perhaps three tube railways from Waterloo were thought too many.[272]

The LUT Again

Another tube railway was proposed by the LUT in 1904, similar to the Castelnau spur of the original LUER scheme. This was again to get around the LCC, who had changed their minds following the earlier agreement, and once again refused to allow them to construct a tramway across Hammersmith Bridge.

The proposal was for a short line between Lonsdale Road in Castelnau, where the LUT had an authorized scheme to terminate a tramway, and The Grove in Hammersmith. Trams would reverse in Hammersmith MDR station, this providing cross-platform interchange with the railway. Twin tunnels beneath the Thames, just downstream of the bridge, would be used to connect the ends of the line, and would be spacious enough to accommodate double-deck trams and overhead wiring.

The LCC defeated this scheme on a number of legal technicalities. These included the issues that the Bill had been submitted as a Railways Bill, but part of the line was to be constructed on a public street and was therefore a tramway; also that the correct maps had not been provided. The submission as a Railway Bill would have allowed the LUT to get around requirements for obtaining local consent. Unfortunately for them, this was also a breach of Standing Orders, and so the Bill proceeded no further. Robinson, the LUT Chairman, was not impressed with the LCC opposition, given that they were constructing their own tram subway along Kingsway at that time.[273]

An Unusual Map

A map published in 1904 in a journal called *The World's Work* (reproduced overleaf) shows the electric railways of London, together with their planned extensions. Of interest is a proposed extension of the GNP&BR. This was to be from Knightsbridge station running west to Addison Road, where it diverged. One branch curved north-west to Shepherd's Bush, and then west to Acton, whilst the other continued along the line of the Hammersmith Road to Hammersmith and Chiswick.

This is a very puzzling map, as it shows the extensions to the west as proposed in 1905 (see below). However, it omits the other changes proposed in the GNP&BR Bill for 1905. The C&BR is shown as sanctioned as far south as Brixton (which was true, as the powers were taken over by the C&SLR). However, the CCE&HR is indicated as under construction as far north as Highgate Archway (and beyond), a section of line that was struck out by Parliament in 1902, with the Victoria extension, which the map does omit. Most intriguingly of all, it shows the NWLR forming a junction with the BS&WR at Edgware Road, and not extending south to Marble Arch. Such a junction was only proposed in the BS&WR and NWLR Bills of 1909.

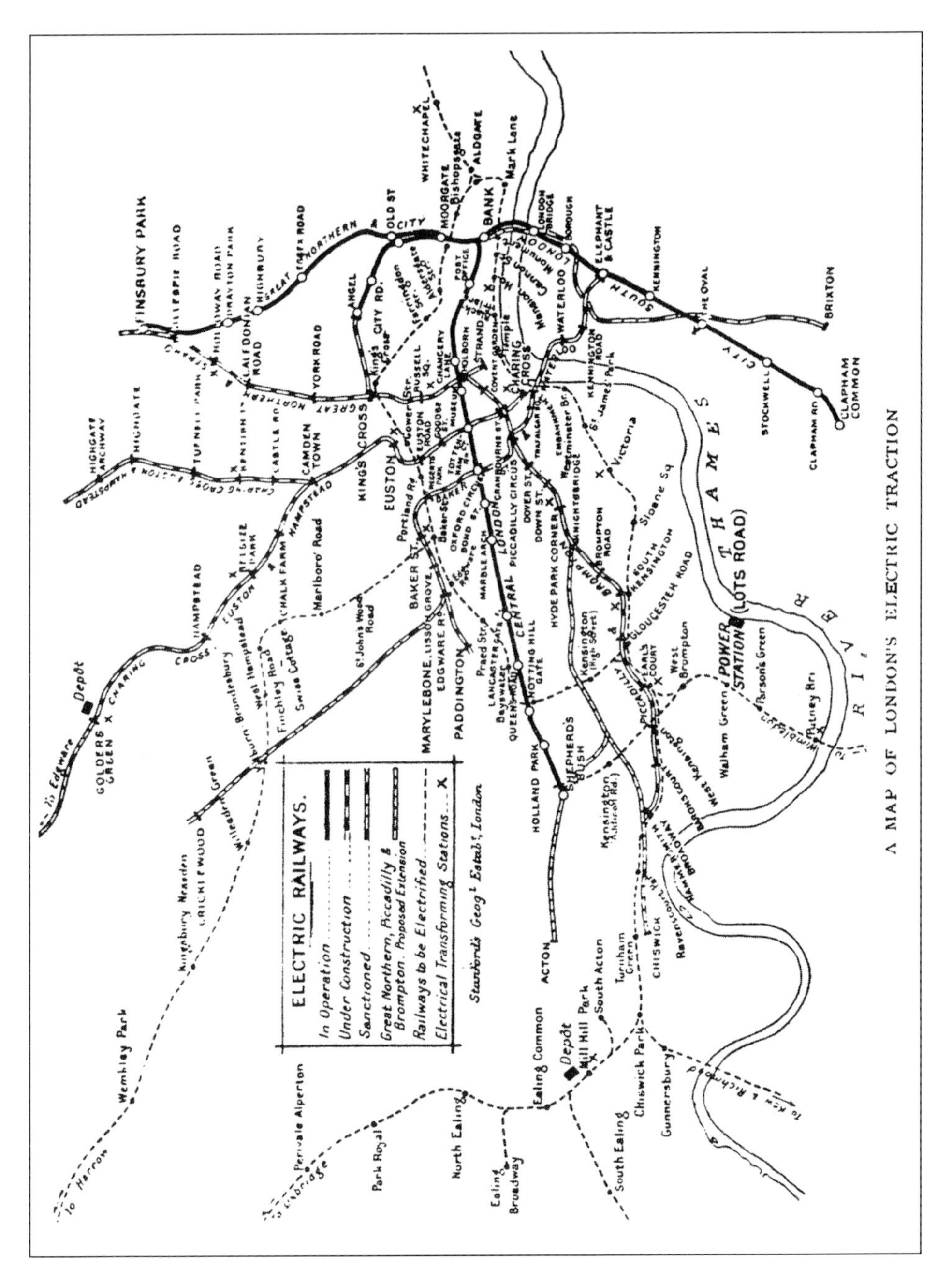

The map published in 1904 in *The World's Work* showing electric railways in London and their planned extensions.

The 1905 Rivalry

The year 1905 had two new railway schemes submitted. These were the Hammersmith, City & North East London Railway (HC&NELR), and the North East London Railway (NELR); the latter was not to be confused with the plans of the same name from 1901 and 1902. The GNP&BR looked to make a number of new extensions, some similar to those in their 1904 Bill.

As well as these Bills, there were the usual smaller Bills for modifications to existing schemes. The CLR rather tediously submitted their Bill for a large loop, as they had in 1902 and 1903; as in the latter year, the Bill was again withdrawn, for reasons that are explained later. An agreement was reached in October with the Yerkes group for neither company to submit a Bill for an east-west line in the 1906 session. This was the last time the CLR was to propose such a line.

The Edgware & Hampstead Railway, now under Yerkes control, deposited a Bill for the modification of the line at Golders Green, where it would join the CCE&HR. In a separate Bill, the latter company sought, and gained approval to expand their station at Charing Cross. Previous approval had allowed them to use the eastern half of the SER station forecourt; this Bill permitted them to use the western half as well, as far as Brewers Lane, which ran along the western edge of the main line station. They were still not allowed to disturb the surface of the forecourt, as this would disrupt the cab traffic to the station, and so planned to tunnel the lift shafts from platform level upwards, and then create the ticket hall under the forecourt. All of this changed when the roof of the main station collapsed on 5 December 1905. During the period of closure and rebuilding, the CCE&HR obtained permission from the SECR to work from the forecourt for six weeks. This allowed one shaft to be completed, as well as the ticket office walls. The site in the station forecourt was then roofed over, and the rest of the work continued beneath the surface.

The CCE&HR's sister railway, the BS&WR, submitted a Bill for the modification of the four passenger subways at Charing Cross.

Finally, the Whitechapel & Bow Railway of the MDR put forward a Bill allowing it to form agreements with certain other railways.

All four Bills received the Royal Assent on 4 August.

The Ealing & Shepherd's Bush Railway

One other railway with Underground connections, although entirely on the surface, was approved the previous month. The Ealing & Shepherd's Bush Railway was promoted by the GWR to connect Ealing Broadway on their main line with the West London Railway at Shepherd's Bush, as well as providing a terminus at the latter point adjacent to the CLR premises. Six years later the CLR promoted a Bill to extend their line beyond the western terminus at Wood Lane to connect with this railway, giving them access to Ealing. This was finally brought into use in 1920, having been delayed by the First World War.

GNP&BR Extensions

The GNP&BR submitted two Bills for the 1905 session. The first was to make more of the vestigial GN&SR line between Holborn and Strand. **Strand** station would be relocated from the junction of Kingsway and Aldwych to a site on the corner of Strand and Surrey Street, passing under the LCC's crescent-shaped block of new buildings between Aldwych and Strand.[274] A southward extension under Surrey Street would merge the twin tunnels into a single line via a junction beneath where Surrey Street met Howard Street.[275] The single tunnel would then pass under the MDR line at the west end of Temple station, followed by the Thames, and would be running due south. A gentle curve to the right would bring the line under York Road, adjacent to **Waterloo** station, where the two-platform terminus would be lower than that of the BS&WR.[276] All of the platforms on the branch would be the standard length of 350 feet (106.8 m). The extension was estimated to cost £450,000, and would be constructed from staging in the river, as used by many of the other tube railways.

The BS&WR station would be used for access, and an additional shaft containing two lifts would be sunk. Three trains would operate the branch, with two passing at Strand station whilst the third loaded at Waterloo. Yerkes appeared before the House of Commons Select Committee, and estimated that trains would take five minutes to run between Strand and Waterloo. He noted that the GNP&BR would be charging a flat fare of 2d between all stations, except Waterloo: an additional 2d would be charged to cross the river. The Committee were slightly incredulous of this, asking if that meant a 4d charge for the short journey between Holborn and Waterloo: Yerkes agreed that this was exactly what he meant.

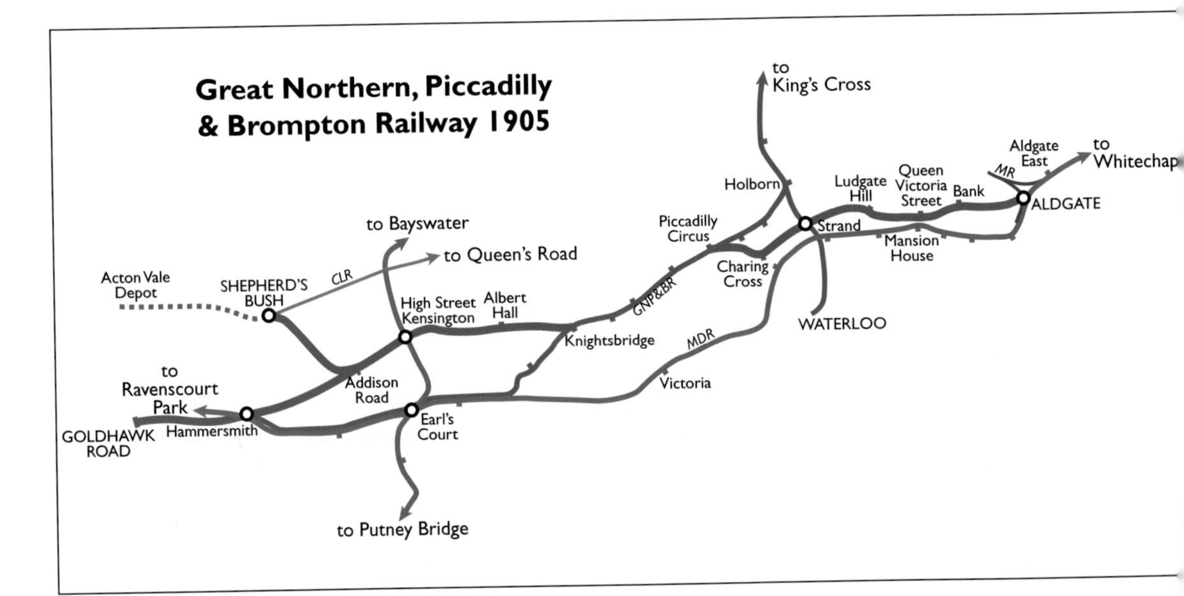

The CLR opposed the extension; they were still hoping that their plans for a large loop would be achieved, and worried that the line under the Strand would block them. Yerkes dismissed this concern, noting that the CLR had ample room to pass under his branch.

The Holborn Junction

The connection between the main Piccadilly line and its branch to Aldwych has been a source of interest for many years, principally because of the peculiar nature of the junction as constructed. The 1903 plans provided a junction on both northbound and southbound lines, but with the southbound platform being shared by the main line and the branch. Had it been built as shown on the 1905 plans (see main text), a short length of tunnel could have been added at a later date to provide a junction between the southbound running tunnels. This would have permitted a through service to operate between Aldwych and stations north of Holborn.

The 1905 plans included an extension to Waterloo, and so the shuttle would operate from the dead-end platform only, Northbound trains would operate onto the 'main line' if required. With the rejection of the Waterloo extension it made more sense to rearrange Holborn, as the only alternative was to add a crossover north of Aldwych. Since the track layout forced the operation of independent shuttle trains in both tunnels to Aldwych, the Holborn arrangement allowed both branch platforms to be more conveniently sited for southbound travellers. It also provided a better same-level interchange with the 'main line' for northbound passengers for Aldwych.

Of course, this was at the expense of operational convenience and future adaptability. To access the branch, trains had to reverse north of Holborn, as there was no southbound connection. Suggestions to allow southbound services throughout the years[277] have all floundered because of the complexity of rearranging the tunnels at Holborn: a new platform on the 'southbound' branch tunnel would almost certainly be required.

The other provision of the Bill was for the junction of the Strand branch with the main line. The GNP&BR had never resolved how to connect the tubes satisfactorily. The engineer's report to the Board on 31 December 1904 had noted that tunnelling east of Covent Garden had been stopped, pending alterations. In part this was because of the LCC refusing to allow construction at Holborn until they had completed their new street (Kingsway), but it was also because of the difficulties in deciding how Holborn station should be laid out.

The problem was that originally only two platforms were planned at Holborn; when the Brompton & Piccadilly Circus Railway was connected the junction was placed to the south of the station. This would undoubtedly cause problems with a frequent service operating on the 'main line' being interrupted by shuttle trains from Strand. In 1903 plans were prepared by the GNP&BR that proposed an extra platform on the northbound line of the Strand branch. The single platform serving both the branch and the main line was lowered so that southbound trains would pass beneath the new northbound branch platform. At the south end the large-diameter station tunnel would continue beyond the platform giving room for a set of points and the divergence of the branch line.[278] The southbound platform would also be moved northwards, placing it under the Central London Railway tunnels that crossed almost perpendicularly. This was a very similar arrangement to that planned (and partially constructed) at South Kensington for the junction of the Piccadilly and deep-level District tube railways.

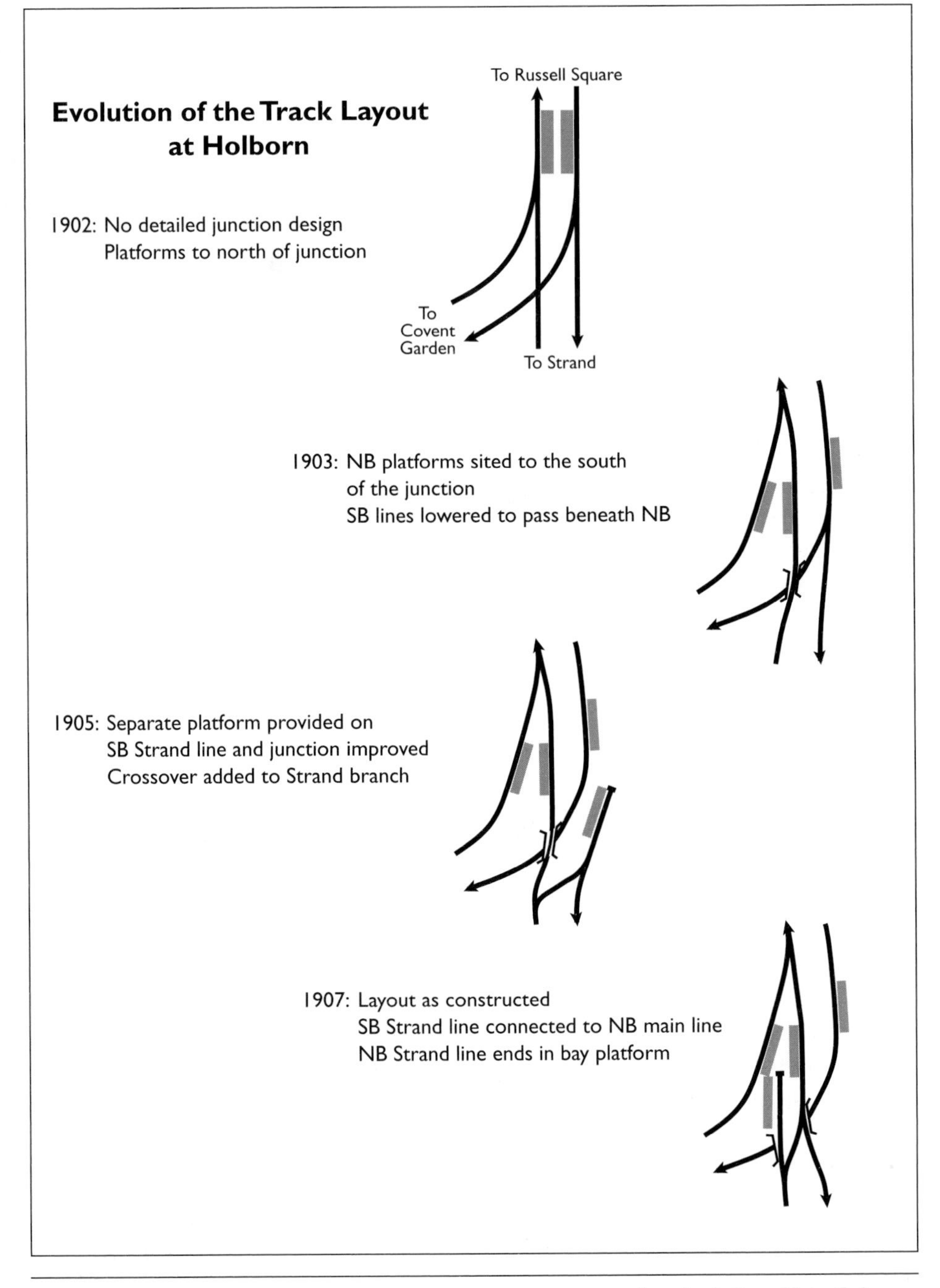

At the north end of the station the northbound branch and main lines would be merged in a junction sited within a large cylindrical tunnel. Catch points would be placed on the main line to protect the passage of trains from the branch. Another junction on the branch line, immediately to the south and in a similar tunnel, would house catch points whose purpose was to protect the main line trains when they had the through route. A short stub tunnel (i.e., a dead end) would probably have housed a sand drag for trains that were re-routed by the catch points.

These plans were marked "Approved 6th May 1903" — presumably by one of the GNP&BR company officers — but no Parliamentary powers were sought to authorize them. It was two years later in the 1905 GNP&BR Bill that detailed plans for the changes were submitted. The cost for the changes was calculated to be £102,616.

The plans deposited with the Bill showed that space had been made for the northbound branch platform by moving the southbound main line slightly west, and its northbound counterpart east under the property along Kingsway. The lowering of the former line was also included. However, the junction on the southbound line that was shown on the 1903 plans was dropped, and in its place was a dead-end platform tunnel on the southbound branch line. This was positioned so the line could theoretically have been extended northwards at a later date to allow a connection to be made with the southbound main line north of Holborn. It also permitted the two branch lines to be at the same level as the northbound main line, rather than at different depths.

The changes to the branch are more interesting, as they do not correspond to the line as constructed. In fact it was the northbound branch line that terminated in a dead-end bay platform, and the southbound line that joined the main route north, in a large cylindrical (rather than step-plate) junction tunnel. The plans deposited at the London Metropolitan Archive[279] confirm this; they have been amended following a Ministry of Transport Inspection Plan made in November 1927, and show the changes.

The Committee were not keen on the single line to Waterloo. In response, the promoters estimated that the cost of doubling the extension would be £120,000. The promoters added a clause to the Bill on 29 March to meet the concerns of the Committee by stating that the extension was not to be opened until a second tunnel was constructed.

The second Bill proposed a number of extensions both east and west. To the east, a branch diverging at Great Windmill Street, to the east of Piccadilly Circus, would pass under Leicester Square and continue to the Strand with a station at **Charing Cross**, sited under King William Street with the building on the east side of Agar Street. Gradients and curves were less severe than on the 1902 proposal, as this time they were not trying to link to the embankment line. At the eastern end of the Strand an interchange would be provided with the **Strand** branch from Holborn, using the same station. The line would then follow the course of Fleet Street. Interchange with the LC&DR would be provided through a station beneath **Ludgate Hill**. Rather than curving south, it would cross under the main line station diagonally, and pass east into Carter Lane, on the same alignment as the Piccadilly & City Railway in its 1901 Bill. In a similar manner to the P&CR the tunnels would be superimposed under Carter Lane due to the narrowness of the street.

It would then progress beneath Cannon Street to a station at **Queen Victoria Street**, which would have street access at the junction of Queen Street and Watling

Street, just east of Mansion House MDR station. **Bank** station would provide interchange with the C&SLR and CLR, before the line followed Cornhill and Leadenhall Street to the terminus at **Aldgate**, in the High Street on the eastern side of the MR station. This line was seen by *The Railway News* as "a defensive measure directed against the other promoters who wish to occupy the Strand route".[280]

The western branch would run from **Knightsbridge**, where two new platforms would be provided immediately west of the junction with the main line as for the unsuccessful 1903 westward extension. A flying junction, similar to that at Holborn, would be constructed, with the westbound branch line passing beneath the main route to South Kensington. The first new station on the branch would be at **Albert Hall**, sited in the block immediately west of the hall itself. Continuing west through **High Street Kensington** (with the station opposite that of the MR and MDR), **Addison Road**, and **Hammersmith**, the line would terminate under Chiswick High Road at its junction with Homefield Road (about mid-way between Stamford Brook and Turnham Green stations). The final station would be provided at **Goldhawk Road**, on the south-eastern corner of the junction with Chiswick High Road and British Grove.

This branch would have been very similar to the 1903 plans. However, a new branch would diverge at Addison Road, leading north through Shepherd's Bush to Acton Vale. **Addison Road** station would have two eastbound platforms, one on each branch, and a single westbound platform sited just east of the junction. The westbound Acton line would then diverge and pass under the Hammersmith route as it curved north into Holland Road. **Shepherd's Bush** station would be located at the east end of the Green, opposite the CLR station, and on the site currently occupied by the shopping centre. Continuing west under Uxbridge Road, the line would terminate by rising to the surface at a depôt sited on the south side of Acton Vale, between David Road and Agnes Road. There does not appear to be a station situated between Shepherd's Bush and the depôt; certainly the plans do not show the enlargement of tunnels required for a tube station, although a surface station might have been built.

This Bill had an initial problem with complying with the Standing Orders. Some rapid negotiations resolved the problem, and it was agreed that it could proceed. Additional capital powers of £4.2 million were included in the Bill, to pay for the considerable additional length of railway that it sought to authorize.

The Committee considered that whilst the Royal Commission was sitting, the second Bill should wait, and it was duly reported in the press on 27 May that both the CLR and GNP&BR No. 2 Bills were "hung up in Parliament" pending the report of Royal Commission. On 26 July both Bills were withdrawn. Although the report from the Commission had been issued, it was too late in the Parliamentary session for these complex Bills to have a hope of success. It was unlikely that Parliament would allow them to be suspended until the 1906 session, as the promoters had been fully aware of the situation when they deposited the Bills back in December.

However, the first GNP&BR Bill was allowed to proceed, and was partly approved. The extension south of Strand station was not permitted, and the remainder of the Bill gained Royal Assent on 4 August.

One final point about the station at Strand. This was constructed with three lift shafts, each capable of taking two lifts – a somewhat generous provision for the end of a short spur line. Indeed, the report prepared by Yorke of the Board of Trade sanctioning the opening of the branch to public traffic noted that

> the design of this station is suitable for a very much larger traffic than is likely at the present time to use it, and only so much of it is completed and brought into use as is required for present conditions.[281]

Of course, it was originally intended to be the southern terminus of the GN&SR, which would explain the original design. However, the 1905 Bill may explain the fact that the station was actually built with all three shafts, as had the Bill been passed then the station would have seen much additional traffic from the new line to Aldgate, as well as the extension south to Waterloo. Station construction started in the latter half of 1905, and although the Bill had been withdrawn by the time that the shafts were sunk, it could be that the company felt that it would be cheaper to construct the shafts in 1905 than risk disruption later (similar to the situation with the deep-level MDR platform at South Kensington). The intention was, of course, to resubmit the Bill in 1906.

The Hammersmith, City & North East London Railway

At the end of 1904 the Board of Trade had again reiterated their warning to potential tube railway promoters, instructing them not to deposit Bills before the report of the Royal Commission was produced. Because of this, the HC&NELR Bill was left in Parliament in 1905 without the deposit money being paid.

The Route

The HC&NELR was to adopt for its main line an almost identical route to the PC&NELR of 1902, running from Hammersmith to Palmer's Green. The cricket pitch at Southgate was not to be touched, recalling the difficulties caused in 1902 by the Walker family. A branch to north Walthamstow was added, reminiscent of the original NELR branch proposed in 1901.

From west to east,[282] stations were to have been situated at **Hammersmith Broadway**, adjacent to the MDR station, followed by **Brook Green** (on the Hammersmith Road) and **Addison Road**, at the junction of that road with Kensington High Street and Warwick Gardens. **High Street Kensington** would again provide interchange with the MR and MDR, and was to be sited opposite the existing station on the corner of Hornton Street. Running beneath Kensington Road and Kensington Gore, **Albert Hall**, in the immediate neighbourhood of the Albert Memorial, would have been followed by **Knightsbridge**, and then **Hyde Park Corner**, where the station buildings would be at 15/17 Knightsbridge, slightly further from both Apsley House and St George's Hospital than previous schemes had proposed.

The next station was to be halfway along Piccadilly, at the junction with **St James's** Street.[283] At **Piccadilly Circus** the line would diverge from the route of the GNP&BR, and would be located at a higher level. The latter railway was now nearing completion, and was to be paralleled by the HC&NELR between Knightsbridge and Piccadilly Circus.

East of Piccadilly Circus the tunnels would realign so that one was above the other; this formation would remain, with at least 20 feet (6.1 m) height difference between the rail level in the tunnels, until east of Ludgate Circus.

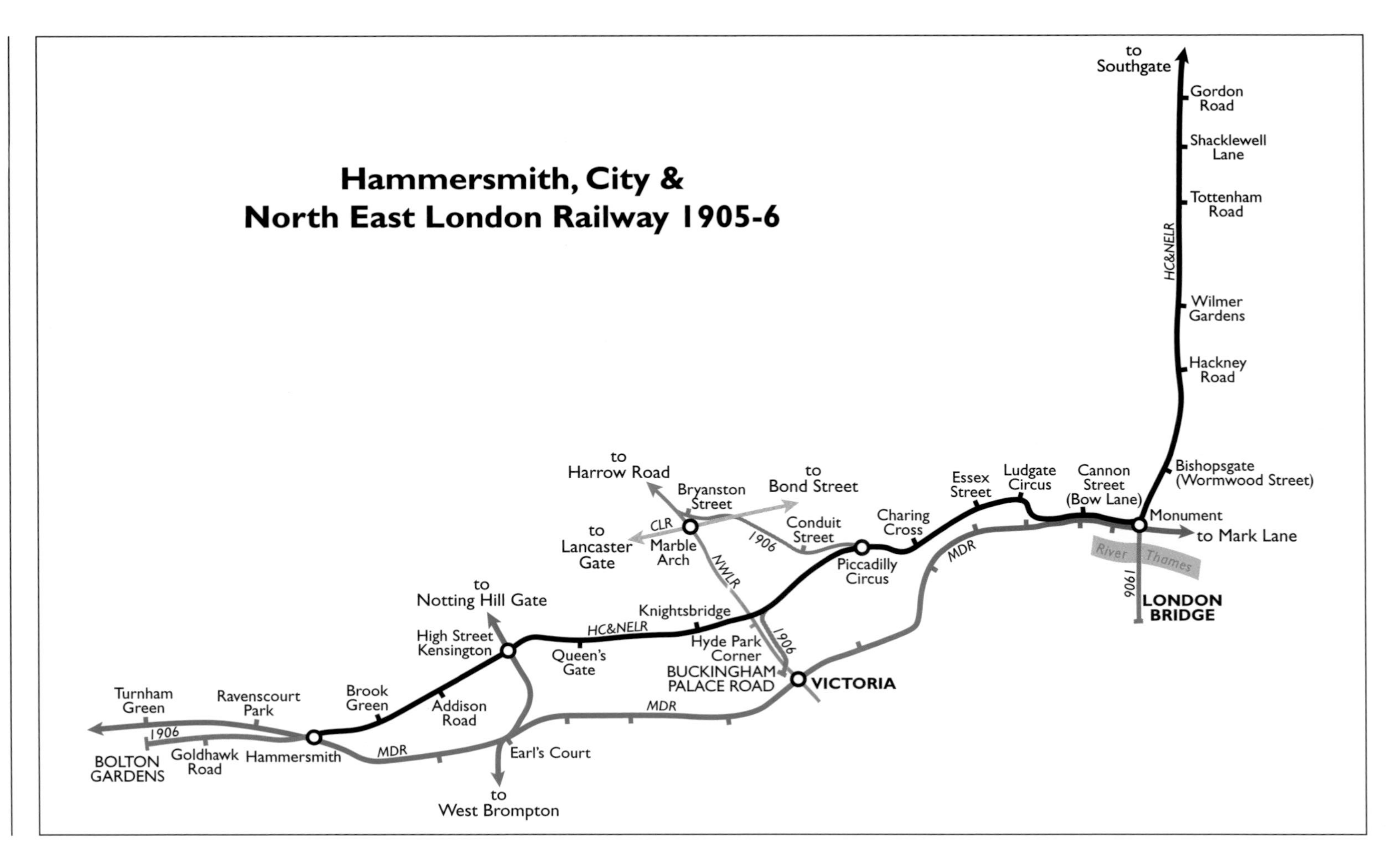
Hammersmith, City &
North East London Railway 1905-6
to Southgate
Gordon Road
Shacklewell Lane
Tottenham Road
HC&NELR
Wilmer Gardens
Hackney Road
Bishopsgate (Wormwood Street)
to Harrow Road
Bryanston Street
to Bond Street
Essex Street
Ludgate Circus
Cannon Street (Bow Lane)
Monument
to Mark Lane
CLR
to Lancaster Gate
Marble Arch
1906
Conduit Street
Charing Cross
Piccadilly Circus
MDR
River Thames
1906
LONDON BRIDGE
NWLR
to Notting Hill Gate
Knightsbridge
HC&NELR
High Street Kensington
Queen's Gate
Hyde Park Corner
1906
BUCKINGHAM PALACE ROAD
VICTORIA
Turnham Green
Ravenscourt Park
Brook Green
Addison Road
MDR
1906
BOLTON GARDENS
Goldhawk Road
Hammersmith
MDR
Earl's Court
to West Brompton

Charing Cross was to provide connections to other railways, both in operation and planned. The surface station was to be constructed between Agar Street and Bedford Street.

A station at the western end of the Aldwych, provisionally entitled **Wellington Street**, was a new addition to the various schemes on this route, and was to be positioned below the centre of the Strand. The line would then curve to the south of St Mary-le-Strand, and to the north of St Clement Danes, producing a rather ugly S-shaped curve. The station at **Law Courts** would have been better sited for the courts than the proposals of previous years, being somewhat to the east of the Aldwych at the junction of Chancery Lane and Fleet Street. The building would have been on the north-east corner of this junction.

A deviation to avoid St Paul's Cathedral similar to those introduced in previous plans was proposed from the next station at **Ludgate Circus**, swinging the line south and closer to the Thames. The next six stations were identically named to those of the NELR proposal of 1902, being at **Cannon Street**, **Monument**, **Bishopsgate Street Without**, **Hackney Road**, **Kingsland Road** (located at the junction of that road with Laburnum Street), and **Stamford Road**. No details have come to light to suggest any differences in the actual locations for these stations. However, Monument would have had an additional pair of platforms running north/south to the east of the main line. These would act as a city terminus, allowing trains from the north to be reversed away from the main line, and providing additional capacity at one of the key stations.

The next station was to be at **Shacklewell Lane**, probably at the junction of that road with Stoke Newington Road. Further north was **Gordon Road** station, the last station before the line split into two branches. Gordon Road has today been renamed Beatty Road.

The Tottenham branch continued north beneath Stamford Hill to a station at **Amhurst Park**, another station from the 1902 NELR. Next would come a station just to the north of the junction of **High Road** and Broad Lane. The line turned north-west, emerged from the tunnels at Napier Road, and headed towards a station at **Lordship Lane**. Beyond this station it would curve north to **Chequers Green**. The final station was to be at **Palmer's Green**, sited on Green Lanes. These final three stations were to be again at similar locations to those proposed in 1902.

The Walthamstow branch swung east at a junction to the north of Gordon Road, with its first station at **Upper Clapton**. This would have been on Upper Clapton Road, near the junction with Mount Pleasant Lane. The line would then surface, and there was to be a long stretch across the Walthamstow marshes devoid of stations before arriving at a station at the junction of **Manor Road** and Lea Bridge Road. Here the line would start to swing in a curve to the north, with a station at **Leyton**, situated at the junction of High Road Leyton and Leyton Green Road. Continuing north, the next station was to be at the junction of **Grove Road** and Lea Bridge Road. North from here near to where **Shernhall Street** and Addison Road met was the penultimate station. The line then travelled north-west to its terminus on the **Chingford Road**, near the current site of some playing fields.

The railway was to be constructed in 11 ft 6 ins (3.5 m) diameter tubes, widening to 12 ft 6 ins (3.8 m) at curves. This was in line with the tunnel sizes in use on the Yerkes tubes. A covered way was to be used for the railway where it passed through "the best parts of Leyton and Walthamstow" to keep the trains out of sight. It would also have the advantage of reducing the noise (and, presumably, the petitions against it).

Electricity for the railway was to be generated at two power stations: one at Hammersmith, beside the Thames, and the other at Shoreditch, beside the Regent's Canal. One depôt was to be at Hammersmith, with a short single-track line rising to the surface to meet it. The other was to be at Chequers Green, on the same area of land proposed by the NELR in 1902.

Middlesex County Council felt that the proposed amount of land required was an excessive amount, and petitioned against it. They also voiced objections to the proposed bridge over Lordship Lane in Tottenham, which was in their opinion too low to accommodate their new tramways.

The costs for the railway, as estimated in 1904,[284] totalled £7,232,947 excluding trains. As can be seen, the support of the Local Authorities had been sought by the inclusion of improvements to streets. In Hammersmith, Bridge Street (now Hammersmith Bridge Road) and Sussex Place were to be improved, and Southgate was to get new roads constructed by the railway company.

Not everyone was pleased by the prospect of the railway. The Phillimore Estate in Kensington was situated just to the north of the proposed line along Kensington High Street. It petitioned against the line, arguing that the vibration caused by tube railways would damage the properties. It also claimed to own a share of the subsoil beneath the High Street, and objected to the easement being granted. The proposed station site at Hornton Street was also their land, and they did not want it to be compulsorily purchased.

The promoters also upset the Office of Woods, which looked after the parks and gardens owned by the Crown, by refusing to supply them with plans of the railway. The Office of Woods official handling the matter noted, "I have not known a case of an absolute refusal to supply us with plans ... These people are new to the work and we had better try them again with a little gentle persuasion."[285] The matter was swiftly resolved, and the plans were issued.

It will be recalled that no deposit was paid at the end of 1904 for the 1905 session of Parliament, because the Board of Trade warned potential promoters to wait until the report of the Royal Commission. The North East London Railway however had ignored the warning and deposited their Bill, which started to proceed through the House of Commons.

This understandably upset the promoters of the HC&NELR. A rival company, having ignored a parliamentary instruction, was about to usurp them in getting a railway to Walthamstow. They immediately reported the situation to the Standing Orders Committee in order to get their Bill accepted.[286] At around the same time they also decided to drop the section between Hammersmith and Monument to make their Bill more comparable with that of the NELR.

The competition, in the form of other tube railways, was also upset (but with the HC&NELR), and led by the GNP&BR proceeded to deposit memorials with Parliament complaining about the situation with the Standing Orders. As well as the lack of deposit from the HC&NELR, it emerged that the Orders had been breached in other ways: apparently no plans had been deposited with the Borough of Chelsea for the route of the line through their area.

In early May 1905 the Committee reported that the Bill had failed Standing Orders for a number of reasons, not least because no deposit had been paid. Sir Edward Strachey[287] proposed a motion asking that the Standing Orders be dispensed with, thus allowing the Bill to proceed. His argument was that the Bill had failed because of the Board of Trade repeating the Parliamentary warning, and that this had been ignored by the North East London Railway. The two Bills, for similar railways, should be compared side-by-side. His fellow MP, Dr John Shipman[288] noted that the promoters were perfectly capable of paying the deposit. A debate ensued, in which the Committee Chairman noted that the missing deposit was a very serious matter, and that it was not the only fault, explaining that normally cases of non-compliance were on technicalities and took up half a sheet of paper. "In this case, however, it occupied three full foolscap sheets of print".

A vote was taken, and the introduction of the HC&NELR Bill was rejected by 133 votes to 71.

The North East London Railway

In 1905 the North East London Railway was proposed, along an identical route to that proposed by the C&NESER for their Waltham branch in 1903. This was, however, a completely new scheme put forward by unrelated promoters, including several Members of Parliament. Ironically, Claude Hay, the MP who had sought to reject all tube railway proposals of 1902 was amongst them. The engineer was again Sir Douglas Fox, together with S. G. Fraser (engineer to the LUER of 1902) and Messrs. Hassard and Tyrrell.

The line was to run between termini at Monument and Waltham Abbey. The key differences between this railway and the C&NESER of 1903 were the omission of Shoreditch, Haggerston, Temple Mills, and Gilwell Park stations (to reduce costs), and the straightening of the route beyond Chingford Hall, so that it would run almost continuously in a north-north-easterly direction. Beyond Waltham Abbey, the line was extended in a curve to the east. A north-facing connection would be made to the Hertford line of the GER just to the north of Cadmores Lane. This would allow the line to act as an alternative route into the City for GER trains.

Minor changes from the 1903 scheme included Higham Hill station becoming Highams Hill, and Cornhill station being renamed Threadneedle Street (Gresham House). All remaining stations were to have identical names to those proposed two years earlier. Stations would have platforms 400 feet (122 m) long.

Two power stations were to be located on the Hackney Marshes. The first was to be just to the north of the tunnel mouths, on the south-west boundary of the marshes, with the second approximately one-half mile north-east, at Temple Mills. The company promised to compensate the owners of the marshes, the LCC, by purchasing land of an equivalent area adjacent to the marshes and donating this to them.

Eight-car trains were to be used.

The company sought powers to raise capital of £3 million, with additional borrowing of £1 million. The railway was estimated to cost £271,000 per mile; this was explained as the average over the line, with a mile of tunnel costing £400,000 and a mile of open line £80,000. The cost of the tunnels was kept low by adopting the standard diameter of 11 ft 8¼ ins (3.56 m) that was being used by the Yerkes tubes, although the Act permitted a maximum diameter of 13 ft 6 ins. Neither would have been large enough to allow main line trains, and so it must be assumed that had through working from the GER been instituted, passengers would have been required to change trains somewhere to the north of Victoria Park. The alternative would have been the provision of a special fleet of smaller GER carriages that would operate on the main line and could run through the tunnels following a change of engine.

Before the Committee, Fox declared that Price & Reeves, and Walter Scott & Co (both firms of contractors involved with earlier tube railway construction) were prepared to build this line. One-third of their payment would be in NELR shares.

The proposed fares from Monument would have been:

- Hackney Road – 2d;
- Walthamstow or Leyton – 3d;
- Waltham Abbey – 3d.

The LCC had a long debate about the possibility of being paid by the company for an easement beneath Victoria Park. Unfortunately for them, it transpired that the park was Crown land, in which the LCC only had an interest. Since the railway was not to disturb the surface of the Park it was felt that there was no case for compensation.

The Statistical Officer of the LCC was very concerned as to the effect of discharging all passengers into the City, and would have preferred a through line to the West End, if not beyond. However, the LCC Engineer felt that with three City stations within the space of one-half mile the passenger dispersal rate would be sufficient. This debate led to the LCC requesting a clause insisting on construction of all three stations.

In the House of Commons the LCC petitioned against the railway, wanting protection for their sewers and other subterranean utilities. They asked that all booking offices and station accesses be above ground, to prevent them interfering with subways or sewers in future. They also felt that unnecessary passenger subways should not be provided, as they would increase congestion below the streets, and would potentially hinder other subterranean schemes. Finally, since the railway was substantially the same as the 1903 scheme, they felt that it should not progress until the Royal Commission had reported. If it was to progress, the Council objected to any trial borings interfering with their tramways, and insisted that stations should be set back where they deemed that this would allow for street widening, either at the time or in the future.

Hills submitted a petition against the Bill, claiming that the new Company was adopting the name of earlier Companies in order to mislead both Parliament and the public. As promoter for the HC&NELR it was understandable that he would object. Notwithstanding the petition, he claimed that he had no objection to it though, as long as it did not interfere with his own scheme. He believed that the NELR route was poorer because of the reservoirs, marshes and parks through which it would run.

The southern part of the line, between Monument and Temple Mills was on an alignment already rejected twice by various Parliamentary committees, Hills continued. It was claimed in his petition that the route beneath Bishopsgate and Shoreditch High Street had been "specially allocated by Parliament to [the] Petitioners" — no evidence for this can be found, and it seems unlikely. He also alleged that the Bill was of a speculative nature, and once passed would be sold to the highest bidder.

Nevertheless, the Bill reached its second reading before the House of Commons on 1 June 1905. The statement in favour of this, issued by the promoters, claimed to have the support of the Metropolitan Boroughs of Shoreditch, Bethnal Green and Hackney, and Urban District Councils of Leyton, Walthamstow, Chingford and Waltham Abbey.

The HC&NELR once again opposed the Bill, claiming that no tube railway Bills were to be approved until the Royal Commission on London Traffic had reported. This opposition "was rejected by the Select Committee on Standing Orders chiefly on the ground that the money deposit of 5% [for the HC&NELR] on the estimate of expense had not been made".[289] Dr John Shipman, who had favoured the introduction of the HC&NELR Bill (see above) gained agreement that the petitioners against that railway would also be heard against the NELR, since they were such similar routes.

Balfour Browne reiterated Shipley's view on 29 June, claiming the HC&NELR petition to be untrue, especially as they did not even have a Bill before Parliament. The next day, Fox explained that the Hackney Road route was chosen over the 1902 more southerly route via Whitechapel in order to reduce costs. He also discussed the reservoirs being constructed to the north-west of Walthamstow by the Metropolitan Board of Works, and claimed that these did not affect the scheme, even though they would lie immediately to the west of the line between Highams Hill and Royal Oak stations. Plans were in place for a new road to cross the River Lea and bring traffic from the west, and besides, having the railway on one side of the remaining land was good, since it would not sever the district. The area was changing, and far end of line was now good for building (unlike nine years before, when the LW&EFR was sanctioned).

The GER was very much opposed to the NELR, and Mr Gooday, their General Manager argued that the NELR would not be profitable, as they would not be able to charge more for their trains than the GER or else risk losing traffic. He also noted that all of the NELR trains would have to stop at all of their stations, therefore they would take longer to reach the City than the GER trains from comparable areas. He then produced detailed calculations demonstrating how the NELR would lose over £26,000 per annum, based on the traffic levels seen on the GER, and allowing for some new traffic. This was refuted by the promoters, who claimed that much new traffic would arise.

A minor concern that arose was about electrical interference with other railways. Clauses protecting the MR and NLR had been struck out from the Bill, but one for the GER was left in. The Board of Trade felt that the same protection should be given to all of the railways, especially as tests on the GER had shown "almost daily" interference with signalling equipment following the electrification of the MDR.[290]

The Committee passed the preamble of the Bill, but on a number of conditions. Firstly, the tube tunnels were to be constructed deep enough between Monument and Hackney Road to allow another pair to run above them (because of concerns from the HC&NELR that they were being blocked out). Secondly, half of the share capital was to be raised within one year of the Bill passing, and the construction work was to start within two years of the same date. Thirdly, the fares to Walthamstow were not to exceed those of the GER – forcing the NELR to offer a 2d fare. Balfour Browne, for the NELR, claimed that a 2d fare would kill them. With smaller trains, constrained in length, they would have a smaller traffic capacity than the GER, and so would not be able to run as cheaply. The Committee were not swayed, and the conditions remained. Royal Assent for the Bill was granted on 11 August 1905.

London's Tube Railways Take Shape

Although the Royal Commission had reported, and the three Yerkes tubes were nearing completion, the rush to deposit tube Bills as seen in 1901 was not to be repeated. Times had changed, and the dream of huge returns on money invested in tube railways was proving to be somewhat elusive. Only one serious attempt at a completely new scheme emerged after 1905; all of the rest of the tube Bills were for changes to previously authorized railways.

The Yerkes Tubes Open for Business

The main events of 1906 from a tube railway perspective were the openings of the first two Yerkes tubes. The BS&WR was the first, opening to the public between Baker Street and Kennington Road (as the station at Lambeth was known) on 10 March. The southernmost portion of the line to Elephant & Castle followed on 5 August, by which time the railway had been named the 'Bakerloo' by the *Evening News*. Although deplored by the railway press, the name caught on, and remains to this day. The initial passenger numbers were disappointingly low, and in its July issue *The Railway Engineer* described the line as "a beautiful failure". Within a few months the numbers picked up in a more satisfying manner. In 1907 the line was extended first to Marylebone (then called Great Central) on 27 March, and then to Edgware Road on 15 June.

The second opening was that of the GNP&BR. In order to make the most of the Christmas traffic it was opened on 15 December, before it was fully ready. South Kensington, Dover Street, and Covent Garden stations remained closed, and opened in the first three months of 1907. The short branch to Strand was finally opened in the same year on 30 November, thus completing what the public was calling the Piccadilly Tube. As with the Bakerloo, the passenger numbers were low to start with, and short trains were run for a few months until the numbers picked up.

The third Yerkes tube railway, the CCE&HR, also opened in 1907 and was promptly dubbed the "Hampstead Tube". The big day was on 22 June, and travel was free throughout the line for the day. The slogan used on the posters and publicity dubbed the line as "The Last Link" – and indeed it was, until the opening of the Victoria Line in 1968. All of the stations opened on the same day, with one exception. North End station, only authorized in 1903, remained unfinished and closed to this day. The station was to be sited in tunnel between Hampstead and Golders Green. The extension of Hampstead Heath reduced the commuter traffic potential of the area, and around the middle of 1906 it was decided to abandon work on the station, leaving just the platform tunnels and stairs to the lower lift landing. No connection to the surface was made.[291]

The HC&NELR Again

In 1906 the HC&NELR Bill was reintroduced, with some modifications. Hills had reverted to large tunnels of 15 ft 6 ins (4.7 m) that would be able to accommodate main-line rolling stock. Consequently a number of connections to other railways had been added, and in the light of the approval of the NELR, the Walthamstow branch was dropped. Unfortunately no record has been found of the proposed station names, and the ones given here are a best guess based on the location of the station sites in the plans. The power stations at Hammersmith and Shoreditch were to remain, but another one in Battersea was added to the plans.

To the west, an extension had been made from Hammersmith to Dukes Avenue at Turnham Green, under Chiswick High Road. Stations would be located at **Bolton Gardens** and **Goldhawk Road**, and would both be 40 feet (12.2 m) below the surface. The next stations would be at **Hammersmith Broadway**, **Brook Green**, **Addison Road**, **High Street Kensington**, **Queen's Gate**, and **Knightsbridge**.

Another southward branch would diverge at Hyde Park Corner, terminating at a station under **Buckingham Palace Road**, sited between Lower Belgrave Street and Eccleston Street. This was presumably to add traffic to the railway from those arriving at the main line stations at Victoria.

Unusually there was to be no station at Hyde Park Corner; only junction tunnels for the line to Victoria. This was by agreement with Apsley House, the former home of the Duke of Wellington. Indeed there were to be no intermediate stations between Knightsbridge and **Piccadilly Circus**; perhaps they were relying on the Great Northern, Piccadilly & Brompton to carry passengers intermediately. This omission would undoubtedly have reduced the construction costs for the railway. The junction at Hyde Park Corner would be made easier by the positioning of the running tunnels for both lines one above the other.

The HC&NELR proposed a connection from the as-yet-unbuilt North West London Railway just north of Marble Arch, with a station at **Bryanston Street**. (Douglas Fox, engineer to the NWLR, fiercely opposed this connection, describing it as "most objectionable"[292]). The line would then follow along Granville Place and Somerset Street before curving south across Oxford Street (and below the CLR) to South Molton Street and New Bond Street, with the tunnels moving onto different levels. Another station would be sited at the junction with **Conduit Street** and Bruton Street. From here the line would have curved to the east beneath Burlington Gardens, Vigo Street and Glasshouse Street. It would then reach a junction with the main route. As with Hyde Park Corner, the running tunnels at Piccadilly Circus would be on different levels to facilitate the junction, which was to be at the east end of the station. Platform tunnels would exist on both routes.

On 27 January the solicitors wrote to the relevant government department explaining that the promoters would prefer to construct subways under Piccadilly Circus for the railway, with various entrance stairwells. They asked for details of any proposed changes to the area so that they could be accommodated in the new plans.

East of Piccadilly Circus, stations were to be sited at **Charing Cross** (junction of Strand and Agar Street), followed by one at the junction of Strand and **Essex Street** (beside St Clement Danes). In the City, they were proposed for **Ludgate Circus**, **Cannon St (Bow Lane)**, and **Monument**.

A branch from the latter station would lead south parallel to London Bridge and into platforms beneath **London Bridge** main line station. This branch would terminate at Great Maze Pond, beside Guy's Hospital. The station buildings on this branch were to be on the south side of Denman Street[293] (although the plans indicate an alternative on the north side). The platform tunnels were to be located between Duke Street and St Thomas's Street, directly below the main line station. Again, this was an attempt to attract extra passenger traffic that the previously proposed lines would not have been able to get.

Back on the 'main' HC&NELR line, the next station north of Monument would be at **Bishopsgate (Wormwood Street)**, which would have been the closest station to Liverpool Street GER terminus. Heading north through Shoreditch, a station was to be near the junction with **Hackney Road**. Kingsland Road was to have stations at its junctions with **Wilmer Gardens** and **Tottenham Road**. Stations at **Shacklewell Lane**, and then **Gordon Road** (now Beatty Road) followed this. The final two stations in the County of London were to be at **High Street Stoke Newington** (near Abney Park), and on Stamford Hill, at **Amhurst Park**.

Continuing through **Chequers Green** and **Palmer's Green**, the line was extended back to **Southgate**, as with the NELR of 1902. However, a more northerly route was proposed, avoiding the cricket pitch, and with its terminus at the junction of Chase Side and Chase Road. Some 27 years after this Bill was being debated, an underground railway finally made it to this road junction. The Great Northern, Piccadilly & Brompton Railway (since renamed as the Piccadilly Line) opened its northern extension to Cockfosters, including a station called Southgate, in a short section of tunnel at this location.

On 28 March 1906 Hills wrote to the LCC asking for their support, claiming that

> a serious effort is being made by what may be termed the vested interests of existing tube railways to hang up the important scheme of tube extension which I have the honour to represent as long as possible in the hope that procrastination may in some way prove to their advantage.

The LCC resolved not to oppose the second reading, and to not intervene further. The Bill passed its second reading in July, but a new twist emerged. The Board of Trade had written to the promoters of the HC&NELR and an unnamed rival scheme in the previous year. This letter had been interpreted differently by the two companies, with the result that the former had deposited their Bill, and the latter not. The Chairman of the Commons Ways and Means Committee, Mr Alfred Emmott,[294] moved that the promoters of the HC&NELR Bill should have leave to suspend their Bill and proceed with it next session. He had met with the BoT and the Chairman of the Lords Committee, and they had decided that the Bill should not be allowed to proceed this session, claiming that this would save the promoters the expense and trouble of new plans and petitions.

This seems particularly unfair on the promoters of the HC&NELR, given that they had been in a similar situation in the previous year (but had not been shown any favourable treatment by Parliament). However, Parliament reluctantly agreed to the suspension of the Bill (one MP describing it as "a piece of special indulgence") and created a new Standing Order to that effect. Both Houses confirmed this new instruction, and the fact that it would not give either promoter an advantage, on 4 July.

The Phillimore Estate still had concerns about the HC&NELR, but had decided by early 1907 that having a station on or adjoining their estate would be advantageous, and so decided to petition for protective clauses, rather than outright rejection. However, in February their Parliamentary Agent informed their solicitors that the promoters had decided not to proceed with the Bill. It is most likely that after almost a decade of setbacks Hills had lost the will to continue with his vision of a railway to Walthamstow. In 1906 he had become paralysed, perhaps as a result of overwork, and it is plausible that this had a major influence on the decision.

The company continued in existence until 1921, with the directors and share owners remaining unchanged. Returns were filed with Somerset House every six months until 1922. In February of that year the solicitors for the HC&NELR wrote asking for the company to be struck off the list of registered companies, as it had neither assets nor creditors, and had carried out no business. It was dissolved on 9 February 1923.

The NELR

As with so many schemes before, capital could not be raised for the North East London Railway, even though it had been authorized in the previous year. In 1906 the companies responsible for arranging the underwriting wrote to the LCC. They were having problems raising the £2 million, due to unfavourable market conditions, and notified the LCC that they would be submitting a new Bill, which would ask for an extension of time for the powers.[295] LCC had no problem with the time extension, but submitted a petition against the proposed closure ('stopping up') of Swiss Cottage Passage, between Lauriston and Wetherell Roads. This was just to the north of Victoria Park, on the site of the station.

The new Bill gained Royal Assent on 20 July 1906, extending the time by one year and permitting the closure of the passage.

The NELR submitted Bills seeking extensions of time in 1907, 1908, and 1909, but still the money could not be found. In 1908 the Chairman of the LCC's Ways and Means Committee had stated that this was to be the last extension permitted by the Council. It was therefore rather embarrassing for the NELR to have to write to the Council one year later requesting yet another extension. The condition of the money markets had continued to be most unfavourable for British railway capital, the promoters explained. They also reminded the LCC that even the mighty LNWR had had to postpone the issue of capital for its tube line to Watford (see below). They also pointed to the £151,685-worth of 2½% consols[296] deposited with Parliament as a sign of their good faith in building the line.

In 1910 a Bill proposing that the Metropolitan Railway work the line was thrown out by Parliament. Viscount Hutchinson, speaking on behalf of the Select Committee that examined the Bill, said in his report of 7 July

> The preamble is not proved; that the Committee were unanimously of the opinion that the Great Eastern Railway Company had been vexatiously subjected to expense by the promoters of the Bill, and were entitled to recover from the said promoters, namely the North East London Railway Company, the costs incurred by them in respect of their opposition to the Bill.[297]

With this, the scheme collapsed, and no more was heard of the North East London Railway.

The GN&CR

In 1907 the GN&CR revived its 1902 Bill for a southward extension to Lothbury. The powers granted previously were due to expire, and there was still hope that the short piece of tunnel that was necessary could be built.

The plans were slightly altered, in that a circular subway was planned beneath the road junction at Lothbury, similar to that at Bank. This would make it easier for pedestrians to cross the road, as well as providing access from a number of points. The promoters noted that their Moorgate terminus was already overcrowded in the peaks, Lothbury would be a more convenient City terminus, and that it would permit a better connection to be made with the other tube railways. They had not already constructed it because of the unfavourable conditions of the money markets, conditions that were improving in 1907. It was also noted that the company had already underpinned part of the Bank of England in readiness for the railway, and had constructed their Moorgate Street terminus so it could be used as a through line.

The Corporation of the City of London opposed the plan, feeling that such a short extension was unnecessary. They stated that it would interfere with street traffic, and that their ratepayers would be put to considerable expense. Quite why they felt this was not explained. The LCC was in more of a quandary. Their Chief Engineer was concerned that the station at Lothbury might make it impossible to construct a sewer along Lothbury in the future. However, at the same time, their Statistical Officer wrote that

> it would be a convenience to the great majority of the passengers on the railway to have the terminus at Lothbury, instead of, as at present, near Finsbury-circus, and the construction of the line is, on that account, desirable.[298]

A solution was arrived at, whereby the GN&CR were compelled by a new clause in their Bill to construct a length of sewer at the same time as the station, ready for connection at some later date. The LCC specified exactly where the sewer was to lie.

At the same time that this was being debated, the LCC and the GN&CR were in court on a separate, but related matter. It may be recalled that the LCC had a *locus standi* to oppose any tube railway Bill affecting London. The GN&CR were arguing that it did not apply to their Bill for a number of reasons:

- The LCC did not own any of the land affected by the Bill;
- No rights of the LCC would be affected;
- The LCC itself was not affected by the Bill and had no control over Lothbury.

The case came before the Court of Reference on 5 March, and the GN&CR lost the case. The following month their fortune changed, when the Bill was passed by the House of Lords, and on 26 July their Bill was granted the Royal Assent. It made no difference to the line however; the money was not forthcoming, and the extension remained unbuilt. Competition from the tramways cut the passenger numbers on the line by 25% between 1907 and 1908, and so it became harder for the railway to persuade people to invest in it. A Bill to extend the available time was deposited in 1909, for the 1910 session of Parliament, but this was withdrawn in January of that year. In the same month the Directors of the company reported that the extension plans had been dropped because of their financial position.

C&SLR to Euston

It will be recalled that in 1903 the C&SLR finally managed to get an Act authorizing an extension from Angel to Euston. The line included an intermediate station at King's Cross for St Pancras, which had two separate platforms in adjacent tunnels. As with their other terminal stations, the C&SLR's Euston had one large tunnel 30 feet (9.15 m) in diameter that contained an island platform flanked by the tracks. These continued beyond the station, where an engine traverser was situated in a 25-feet (7.6 m) diameter tunnel, allowing trains to be slid from one track to another. A crossover and siding were to the east of the platforms. The site was under Drummond Street and the westernmost corner of the main line station. It had its own building in Seymour Street (since renamed Eversholt Street), which most unusually was clad in white and green Carrara-ware faience.[299]

The extension opened on 12 May 1907, just over a month before the CCE&HR reached Euston. It demonstrated its utility to the travelling public, but one thing that it did not do was improve the finances of the C&SLR.

The CLR's First Extension

The CLR had proposed a number of extensions since it was originally authorized, but the only one that had received Royal Assent was the extension to Liverpool Street. The powers for this had since expired, and the line had remained its original length for over six years.

An opportunity arose in 1906. The Franco-British Exhibition was to be held in west London, opposite the CLR depôt. The Uxbridge Road station of the West London Line was adjacent to the site, and the Hammersmith & City route of the MR already passed by (although no station was provided); the CLR could not pass up this traffic opportunity, and anyhow, the projected traffic was sufficient for all three.

The westbound line of the CLR already reached the surface depôt, and their Bill for the 1907 session proposed the construction of another tunnel from the eastbound line, which was just a reversing siding west of Shepherd's Bush. By continuing this in a northward curve to the west side of the depôt site, and then looping it through 180° to connect to the original access track, they could provide a through passenger service. The topology of the loop thus formed would mean that trains would pass around it anti-clockwise. The total length of new railway was 4 furlongs 5 chains (905 m).

There was one other item of work in the Bill. This was the construction of a subway from the west end of Bond Street platforms to the north side of Oxford Street. No reason was given for the subway, which perplexed the LCC. On 24 January the *Daily Telegraph* revealed that it was to connect directly into the new department store being constructed by Harry Selfridge, and "would be a great boon to ladies when shopping in bad weather". Lifts would connect the subway to all floors in the building. Steps would lead from the platforms to a long inclined subway that would connect into Selfridge's basement 40 feet (12.2 m) below ground level.

The LCC could not decide whether to oppose the subway; they decided that although they objected to it linking directly into the store, this was not reason to oppose, and there were no engineering grounds either. Other shop owners and traders did protest most strongly, believing that they would be deprived of custom if the public could enter Selfridge's store without ever passing them by in the street. They raised a petition against the Bill in Parliament, but it was not necessary. By the time they did so, the subway provision had been dropped.

The Corporation of the City of London opposed the Bill as well. Mr Morton, speaking on their behalf in the House of Commons, spoke in opposition because the Bill did not include provision for a subway from Bank station to King William Street. This annoyed other MPs, who pointed out that the Bill had nothing to do with the City, and was entirely concerned with Shepherd's Bush. Morton rapidly withdrew his opposition.

The Bill was given Royal Assent on 26 July 1907, and construction must have started shortly afterwards, given that there was less than a year before the exhibition opened.

The new station was at the north-west corner of the depôt site, with its entrance across **Wood Lane** from the exhibition. To make access even easier, steps within the station led up to a footbridge that passed across the road into the exhibition site. A platform was provided either side of the single track, allowing arriving and departing passenger flows to be separated.

The Kearney High-Speed Railway

Elfric Wells Chalmers Kearney (1881–1960)

E. W. C. Kearney was an Australian inventor whose early years seems to have been spent devoted to promoting his unusual monorail. His interest was sparked around the turn of the century, and he remained devoted to it until beyond the Second World War. Another of his creations, in a rather different vein, was a work of science fiction called *Erone*, published in 1950.

An idea for a rather unconventional form of railway emerged in 1905. Invented by the Reverend R. Riach Thom, and further developed and promoted by E. W. C. Kearney, it placed one rail below the train, and one above. The trains would have four doubly flanged wheels on the underside of each carriage, with each axle powered by two motors, giving a high rate of acceleration, and a low centre of gravity. Two roof-mounted wheels would use the upper rail, which would be flanged for guidance. At speed they would barely touch the rail, as the gyroscopic effect and low centre of gravity would stabilize the car on the lower rail. Power would be supplied from the two rails, with a trolley wire on top of the car to make contact with the upper rail. Ball bearings were used extensively in the design to minimize friction; Kearney claimed, "Their use reduces rolling friction to one-sixth that of the best anti-friction bearing metal used on ordinary railways".[300]

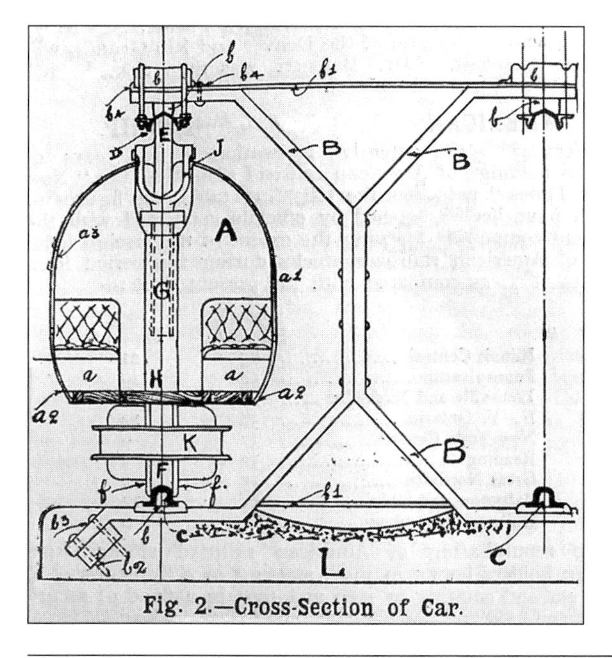

Fig. 2.—Cross-Section of Car.

Cross-section of a Kearney railway and car

Kearney (who was at pains to point out that the first syllable of his surname rhymed with "pear") had been developing the idea since 1902, and filed patent number 17,583 in 1907. The rights to this patent were transferred to the Kearney High-Speed Railway Company, which he founded in the same year. Kearney was the managing director, and received £1,500 of fully paid-up shares in return for the patent. A prospectus was issued in June 1908, offering 9,500 £1 shares to the public. Few were sold.

Kearney published a booklet in 1907, describing his invention. In it he explained how trains were safe from derailment, and that the single rail would allow for a smoother ride. The key selling point for the High-Speed Railway was its low cost: although it required the structure to support the upper rail, with supports every 60 feet (18.3 m), this was similar to the supports required for a standard line with an overhead power supply. A cost of £6,050 for a mile of double-track line ("first class main-line railway") was quoted, comparing most favourably with the £40,000 cost of a conventional railway.

The key selling point was the reduced costs of both construction and operation. In his 1907 book Kearney published the following table, demonstrating the alleged cost differences when compared to a normal surface railway between Herne Hill and Crystal Palace. The ordinary railway would have to be constructed on a viaduct for much of the distance, and would be about half a mile (800 m) longer that the Kearney line in order to detour around the hill at the Crystal Palace end. By comparison his railway could cope with steeper gradients and would not require viaducts or deviations.

	Ordinary Line	**Kearney Line**
Permanent way	£22,000	£20,000
Bridge over SE&C Rly	£8,000	£7,000
Grading	£107,000	£23,000
Two stations	£5,000	£5,000
Rolling stock	£10,000*	£5,000
Electrical equipment	£15,000†	£10,000
Land	£22,000	£20,000
Total	£189,000	£90,000
Contingencies 10%	£18,900	£9,000
Total	**£207,900**	**£99,000**

* Slower trains means twice as much rolling stock required

† Electrical equipment costs more for the ordinary railway as more power is required, and supports are required for the overhead wire.

A model of such a car was made in 1905, and made available for press viewing. The model was based on a double-track surface railway, in which T-supports would be used to hold the upper rail. The cars had a streamlined appearance, not dissimilar to the prototype 1935 tube stock developed by the LPTB. The top speed on the surface was estimated at between 120 and 150 m.p.h. (193 and 241 km/h).[301]

The 1905 model car

Kearney's Plans for Tube Railways

Although Kearney proposed designs for surface and overhead versions of the railway, a tube was the ideal form for such a line, and in London Kearney proposed the construction of two lines. The first would follow the route of the NWLR from Cricklewood to Victoria, and continue south-east to the Oval. The second would connect the Strand (near Aldwych) with Crystal Palace, interchanging with the first line at Oval. Both would be constructed in 14ofeet (4.3 m) diameter tubes.

Stations would have been located on the first line at **Cricklewood**, **Brondesbury** (for interchange with the MR and NLR), **Quex Road**, **Carlton Hill**, **Lords**, and **Edgware Road**, where passengers could change for the MR and BS&WR. Continuing south, interchange with the CLR would be provided at **Marble Arch**, the GNP&BR at **Hyde Park Corner**, and the MDR at **Victoria** (as well as the main line services). On the north side of the Thames a station would be provided at **Pimlico**, and on the south side at **Vauxhall** and finally **Oval**. There was a possibility of extending this line to Camberwell Green and Peckham.

The other line would start at the **Strand**, where interchange with both the GNP&BR station of the same name and the MDR's Temple station would be provided. The next stations would be at **Waterloo** (for the main line, BS&WR, and W&CR), **Kennington Road**, and **Oval**, where passenger interchange with the C&SLR would have been provided. The spacing increased between the next stations, at **North Brixton**, **East Brixton** (with interchange to the main line railways: the station closed on 5 January 1976), **Herne Hill** (again with main line interchange), and finally **Crystal Palace**. Unfortunately the exact locations for these stations have not been determined.

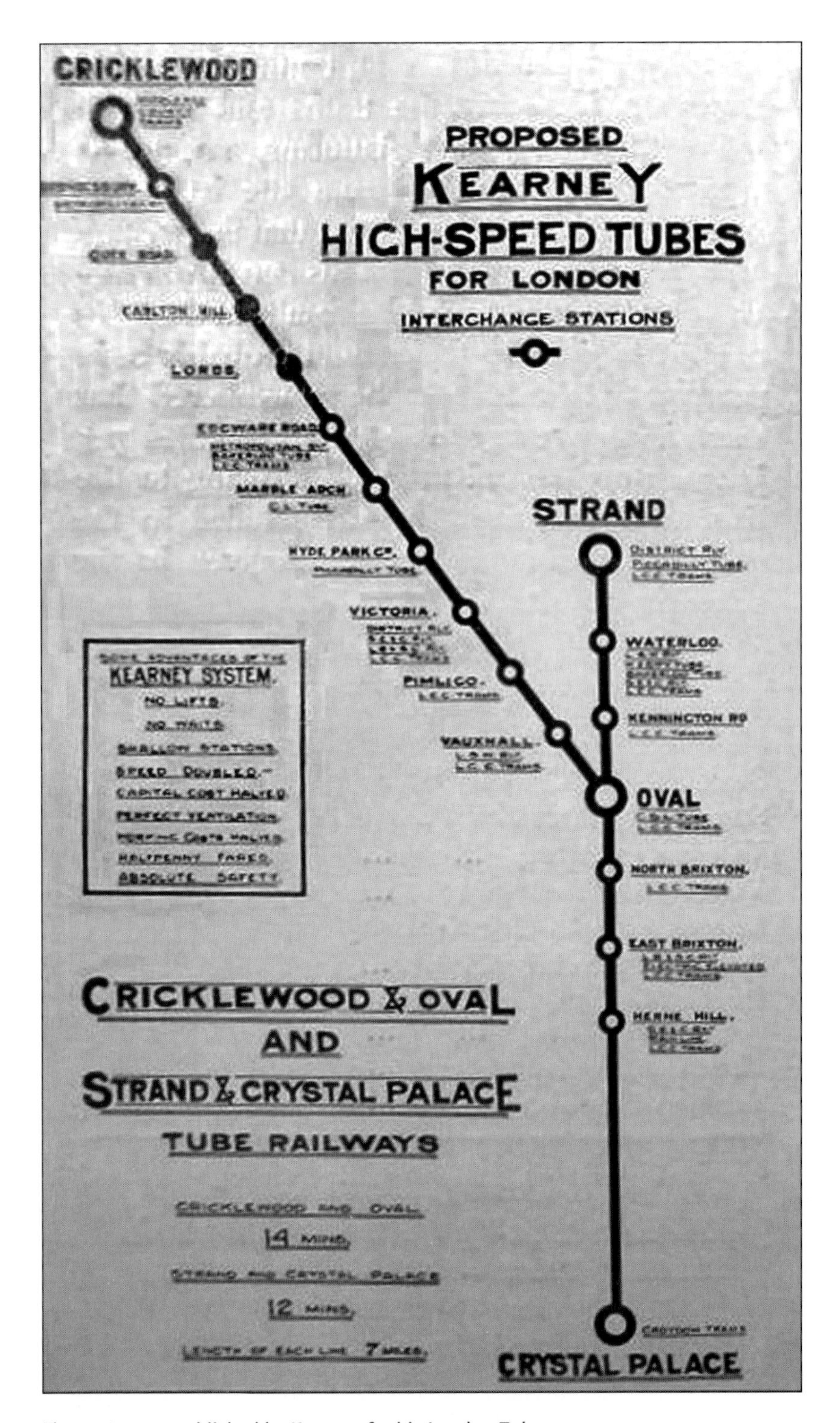

The route map published by Kearney for his London Tubes

In order to emphasize the express nature of the railway, Kearney quoted sample times in minutes between stations on his proposed lines:

Strand – Oval	3
Strand – Brixton	4½
Strand – Herne Hill	7
Strand – Crystal Palace	10
North Brixton – Cricklewood	14
Victoria – Cricklewood	10
Victoria – Marble Arch	3

He noted that trains on the existing tube railways averaged 15 m.p.h. (24 km/h), and if the time taken for passengers to wait for and use the lifts was included, this would drop to between 5 and 12 m.p.h. (8–19 km/h). However, the absence of lifts on his railway combined with the faster trains would mean that the speed would average 30 m.p.h. (48 km/h).

The Kearney High-Speed Railway would have similarities with the schemes promoted briefly in 1885, in that the stations would be located just below the surface, with deep-level tube connecting them. If surface stations were not possible then the platforms could be about 14 feet (4.3 m) below the street, with short flights of stairs. The stations would have access at both ends, and each track would have a platform on each side, one for boarding and one for alighting. Passenger flows would be speeded up because passengers could board and alight simultaneously. One door per eight seats on each car would allow station dwell times to be 15 seconds at most.

Either side of the stations the line would consist of a single tube, dividing into two platforms at stations to allow trains to pass. Points at each end of each station would be fail-safe, operated by the passage of the trains, and catch points would prevent a train from entering an occupied tunnel. The tunnels would drop away from the stations at a gradient of 1 in 7, to assist acceleration. Twenty seconds after leaving the station, the train would be at a speed of 50 m.p.h. (80 km/h), and a depth of 80 feet (24.4 m). Speeds of up to 60 m.p.h. (97 km/h) would be achieved before the trains were decelerated by the incline on the approach to the next station. It was claimed that an average speed of 40 m.p.h. (64 km/h) could be attained if the stations were sited about a mile apart. The effect on the passengers would have been interesting to consider – the line would have been perhaps more akin to a roller coaster! However, no adverse sensations would be felt, according to Kearney. The gradients would have to be 1 in 3.3 before the passengers would notice anything, allegedly.

If a train broke down between stations then the line would continue to operate in two sections, either side of the obstruction. Another advantage was that the ventilation was claimed to be better than on the existing deep tubes, because the stations were close to the surface and air could easily flow into the tunnels. Each pair of trains arriving at a station would force air out of the tunnels via the station, and would then pull in fresh air as they departed.

The power consumption of the railway would also be low, as no lifts would be required at stations, and the motors on the trains were required to accelerate them briefly from the station to the incline, and then to assist up the slope into the next station. Single- and multiple-car trains were proposed, and to reduce the effect of air resistance they would have pointed ends, rather like the prow of a ship.

A large working model, at a scale of ¾-inch to the foot (1 to 16), and around 200 feet (61 m) long was presented in 1908, and formed the basis of the report in *The Railway Engineer*. The wheels on the roof were described as being on "a telescopic adjustment controlled by compressed air".[302] This allowed for variation in the distance between the upper and lower rails, without danger to the train. The single car that operated back and forth between three model stations was 44-inches (112 cm) long, and, according to the advertisement for its manufacturer, contained nearly 6,000 parts. The construction of this model cost the company over £535.

The stations on the model were 90 feet apart, with the middle station being twin-track. It included S-curves, and the track dropped at 1 in 3 away from the stations to demonstrate Kearney's idea to the extreme. He calculated that the scale running speed of the model trains (both of a single-car) was 400 m.p.h.!

Kearney continued to promote his ideas by publishing leaflets and giving lectures. In 1913 he announced that his line from Strand to Crystal Palace would cost £2.5 million for double tube construction, and that the journey would take 10 minutes. He believed that he would see the day when it was possible to travel from London to Paris in an hour.[303] The City of London Tradesmen's Club, whom he was addressing, unanimously agreed to press Parliament to give facilities for building a Kearney line.

Despite all of his efforts, no Bill was ever deposited for this interesting variant on a monorail.

Other Kearney Plans

In 1920 the *Railway Magazine* reported that Kearney was preparing to construct a demonstration line on the surface between Brighton and Rottingdean, on land loaned by the Brighton Corporation. This would connect two hills, and would include gradients of 1 in 7, thus proving that his tube scheme would work. A single car would be used; this had already been built to gain more publicity.

Another Kearney tube was planned between North and South Shields, but after several years of planning was repeatedly rejected by the local councils, which wanted a road tunnel. Kearney kept the plans alive, principally through the means of regular pamphlets exhorting people to support him. In 1938 he published a history of the scheme, together with plans. He noted that the LNER had approved the line on a route linking their stations at North and South Shields, and pointed out the benefits of constructing the line, at no cost to the Councils, and with the cast iron lining being made in Tyneside. It finishes "A SQUARE DEAL for the Kearney Tube – NOW!"

During the Second World War he spent his time planning tube railways around Britain that could be used to provide deep shelters. Although he and his friends wrote many letters to government officials, including Winston Churchill, nothing came of this. A fundamental flaw in adopting his tubes as shelters was felt to be the shallowness of the tunnels in the vicinity of the stations.

Kearney continued to refine and promote his system after the Second World War, including suggesting a line in Italy between Venice and Venice Lido. Sadly he never succeeded in getting a railway built.

Further Tube Plans

In 1917 Kearney presented the evolution of his work to the Institute of Civil Engineers. He explained that constructing and leasing offices over the stations would offset the cost of acquiring the land for the surface stations. With a single tube between stations, Kearney estimated the costs as 40% of the price of constructing either a typical London tube, or a New York subway. If twin tubes were provided between stations then this figure would be 60%.

Unfortunately, the necessary finance was not forthcoming, and other than the 1908 model, no Kearney tubes were ever built. It remains an interesting example of what may have happened in the history of London's tube railways.

London was not the only city in which Kearney looked to build his tubular monorail. His company prospectus of 1908 noted that negotiations were underway with the transit authorities in New York and Boston. In 1909, the Toronto *Evening Telegram* reported that Kearney was in discussion with the City Engineer, and was offering to build two lines at a cost of $1 million per mile. However, he lost interest when informed that any franchise awarded would expire in 1921, the year that the City authorities planned to take responsibility for all public transport.

The Railway Magazine, in answer to a correspondent's query, discussed the concept again in 1919.[304] It also noted that a Kearney tube was likely to be constructed between Beresford Square, Woolwich, and North Woolwich station. This line, just under 0.75 mile long, would have a single tube, and would allow passengers to cross the Thames in 1 minute. It was on a very similar alignment to the North & South Woolwich Electric Railway proposed in 1904. The schemes shared another common trait in that neither was built.

The sumptuous interior proposed for the Kearney High-Speed Railway cars.

More Extensions to the North-West

A number of railways proposed extensions from central London to the north-west, where suburbs and towns provided the prospect of commuter traffic. The main line railway from Euston did not serve much of this district, as when it had opened in 1844 its first two stations were at Harrow (now Harrow & Wealdstone) and Watford (now Watford Junction).

The NWLR, extending as far as Cricklewood, had been approved in 1899 but still remained on the drawing board, and the Bakerloo Tube seemed incapable of deciding how to reach the important main line station at Paddington, let alone the districts beyond.

The NWLR takes up the Royal Commission's Suggestion

The North West London Railway, although still unable to start construction, were buoyed by the suggestion from the Royal Commission that their line should be connected with Victoria, and in 1906 put forward a Bill for such an extension. This was essentially the same as their 1903 Bill, which had been postponed in the face of the impending Royal Commission. The additional funding sought totalled £1.4 million, of which £1,050,000 was to be raised through shares, and the remaining quarter through borrowing.

The 1906 railway was principally a southward extension from Marble Arch, under Hyde Park and via a station at **Hyde Park Corner**, thence under Grosvenor Place and to a terminus at **Victoria**. The tunnels would be below the MDR, and above the authorized deep-level MDR. The terminal station would be situated at the north end of Vauxhall Bridge Road, with the surface station on the west side and also facing onto Wilton Road.

An adjustment would be made at Marble Arch, raising the level of the authorized line so that it would pass over the CLR, rather than beneath it. As part of this re-planning the connecting subway to the CLR platforms was also moved to pass over the CLR tunnels.

One of the more unusual features of the line was to be four surface connections for the railway, all in double tunnels, and allowing eventual connection to the surface tramways. The plans deposited with Parliament also showed that the tunnels were to be 16 feet in diameter, allowing passage of larger trains (perhaps including trams). The connections were to rise to the surface on 1 in 15 gradients, and would actually surface alongside the road, on sites that the NWLR would purchase and clear. Their locations were to be as follows (listing from south to north):

Main Road Connection	Location on surface	Direction
Vauxhall Bridge Road	N corner with Francis Street	SE
Edgware Road	S corner with Cambridge Street (now Kendal Street)	NW
Kilburn High Road	N corner of Kilburn Square	NW
Cricklewood Broadway	Opposite Mora Road	NW

A rather cryptic statement concerning the tunnels was published, noting that "It is also intended to construct some short branch lines to facilitate intercommunication with the tramways. The actual lines will not, of course, be joined, but subways will be built leading to the existing tramway route."[305] Was this suggesting that the trains would run up the steep inclines to deposit passengers adjacent to the tram stops? Or were the tunnels to be for pedestrians – in which case, did they need to be double?

In early May, shortly before the Committee sat to consider the Bill, all of these connections were dropped from the Bill. Presumably the absence of surface tramways with which to connect, and the costs of construction (totalling over £225,000) made their deletion the obvious way to cut costs. The diameter of the running tunnels was also dropped to the more standard 11 ft 8¼ ins (3.6 m); another large cost saving, as this would reduce by almost half the amount of clay to be removed to form the tunnels.

The LCC opposed the Bill, and sought to employ Balfour Browne as their Counsel. They were somewhat upset to discover that he had already been retained by the promoters! The Council claimed that their permission had not been sought for tunnelling under the streets. It transpired that their chief objection was that they wanted a shallow subway. The Royal Commission, whilst recommending the NWLR extension, had muddied the waters by also recommending the construction of a tramway from Cricklewood to Victoria, on the surface as far south as Marble Arch, and then to Victoria partly in a subway. The LCC naturally seized upon this idea, and claimed that it obviated the need for the tube railway. Their Chief Engineer proposed extending the tramway on Vauxhall Bridge Road (which terminated at Victoria Street) in a subway beneath the MDR, and then continuing north to Marble Arch. He wanted an agreement with the NWLR that they would not interfere with such a scheme.

The Council also noted that the tube promoters would have difficulty raising capital given the competition from the tramways. Their statistical officer produced detailed tables demonstrating that the tube railway would have to carry 30,967,742 passengers annually in order to cover the running costs and pay 4% interest on the capital, even before a profit was turned. This was based on the operating costs of the CLR, and their average fare of 1.86d.

The HC&NELR raised further opposition. They were promoting a branch from Victoria to Hyde Park Corner, following the same route as the NWLR between these locations. This opposition could be seen as somewhat mean-spirited, since they were not running further north, nor were they providing a station at Hyde Park Corner, so the competition would be very limited. A charitable view is that the promoters of the HC&NELR were concerned about the engineering challenge of placing four tube tunnels between Victoria and Hyde Park Corner.

The Bill was passed by Parliament and received Royal Assent on 4 August. However, some additions to the Bill were to make life awkward for the promoters.

The Brush Electrical Engineering Company had agreed to subscribe £100,000 to the NWLR if they were given the contract for electrical equipment. The Bill confirmed this arrangement, and obliged the Brush Co to pay should it receive the contracts (which was a far stricter legal condition than they had envisaged). However, the price for the electrical equipment was to be agreed by arbitration. This was to prevent them kick-starting the railway finances, and then making a large profit by charging inflated prices for their products. Of course, the new provision of the Bill now made the NWLR a less attractive proposition for Brush.

Additional costs were imposed on the railway by demanding the provision of extra interchanges, i.e., proper subway connections to other railways. These were to be at Edgware Road (for the BS&WR), Hyde Park Corner (for the GNP&BR), and Victoria (connecting to the subway between the MDR and the main line station). The time permitted for the compulsory purchase of land and the completion of construction was limited; these had to be completed by 1908 and 1910 respectively.

The NWLR Seeks a Link with the Bakerloo

These onerous conditions included in the NWLR Act deterred any work being carried out. The British Electric Traction Company, which had previously supported the scheme, took it over entirely, and looked at how to make it succeed. They decided in 1908 that this would be achieved by connecting it to the BS&WR (since opening known as the Bakerloo Tube). The desire of the latter company to extend their railway to the north-west has already been mentioned; by the simple expedient of a connection at Edgware Road they would have a ready-authorized line. The only drawback was that Paddington would not be on the main line, but the company saw a shuttle service between Paddington and Edgware Road as an acceptable solution.

The NWLR Bill for 1909 therefore included powers to construct 3 furlongs 7.6 chains (756 m) of connecting tunnel at Edgware Road; to abandon the line south of the connection, including the 1906 line to Victoria; and to allow the Bakerloo to construct, maintain, manage, and operate the line. The time for the construction of the line was also extended again. A separate BS&WR Bill was promoted, allowing for the connection, and extending the time for the construction of the 1906 Paddington extension (described in the next section).

Edgware Road station would have four platforms, allowing the Paddington shuttle to operate without interfering with the main route. Additional provision for stations was included at **St John's Wood Road**, and **Abercorn Road**. It can be presumed, but is not stated in the records, that these stations would replace the station originally planned at Maida Vale (thus increasing the catchment area of the line). A change to Brondesbury was also made, placing the station slightly further north – perhaps for better interchange with the MR.

According to their evidence the NWLR had found it "impossible from a financial point of view to arrange for the construction of the line between Edgware Road and Victoria".[306] The shortening of their line reduced the required capital from £3 million to £1.2 million. The annual passenger receipts of the NWLR section of railway were estimated at £96,000, and with estimated expenses of £52,000 it was predicted that the line would turn a profit. The Bakerloo would receive 25% of the gross receipts, with a minimum payment of £25,000 per year. The British Electric Traction Company claimed that they had £220,000 ready to invest in the construction of the line, and were also prepared to accept £400,000 of NWLR shares as deferred payment.

Middlesex County Council (MCC) originally opposed the Bill, citing interference with the main roads and with property. They also noted the failure to raise any capital to date, stating that the proposals "have from the first been of an entirely speculative character". The MCC felt that the company should not be entrusted with any new powers, especially as they were now effectively on behalf of another company (the Bakerloo). The failure of the latter to complete its own line was also mentioned by the MCC.

Following discussions between the Council and the company the opposition was removed, and by the time the Bill was debated in Parliament it counted on the MCC as a supporter. The Council's tramways terminated at Cricklewood, and it now saw the line as a benefit to its citizens, who could be transported into the metropolis with ease. However, this benefit was rather reduced when the Bakerloo admitted that they had no interest in building the line north of Brondesbury.

As usual, the MR put up strong opposition. This scheme was now in direct competition with their trunk line between Baker Street and Brondesbury. The GWR also objected to Paddington being relegated to a branch from the main Bakerloo line. To add to the insult the Bakerloo had proposed that the GWR should contribute to the cost of the Paddington extension.

Once again the NWLR was not to be, although for the first time it was due to rejection of their Bill. The crucial point for the Committee was the abandoning of the section between Marble Arch and Victoria that the Royal Commission had recommended. The other opposition just added to the sense that this was not the best of schemes, and so on 14 May the NWLR Bill was thrown out. As a direct result, the BS&WR Bill was withdrawn shortly afterwards.

The Bakerloo tries to reach Paddington

The BS&WR was in a quandary about reaching Paddington. An extension had been vetoed in 1899, but was approved the following year. This had been constructed between Baker Street and Edgware Road, but no further. The problem lay in deciding where to go beyond Paddington. The 1900 alignment would have passed to the north of the GWR main line station, with a long passageway provided for interchanging passengers.

The 1906 Bill continued the line west beyond Edgware Road station, cutting under property, and curving to a route beneath London Street adjacent to Paddington station and opposite South Wharf Road, with the tunnels terminating at the junction of Devonport Street and Grand Junction Road (now Sussex Gardens). Twin sidings 120-yards (110 m) long would lie beyond the station tunnels, as at Elephant & Castle, with a crossover situated under Norfolk Square. The station platform tunnels would be adjacent to the GWR station concourse, with subways under the concourse linking the platforms and the western side of the concourse; these would also connect into the MR subway under the front of the station into their Praed Street station.

This would make interchange easier, but would leave the line pointing south-east —

a very awkward direction for future extension. Whilst the Bill was approved on 4 August, nothing was done by way of construction, and the west end of the tunnels remained firmly at Edgware Road.

Following the failure of the 1909 plans for the link to the NWLR, the Bakerloo took stock of its position. In 1911 it promoted (under the auspices of the London Electric Railway Company) another Paddington extension Bill, on yet another alignment which would leave it pointing north-west. Forgetting its previous dispute the GWR had agreed to contribute £18,000 to the costs. The Bill was successful, and gained Royal Assent on 2 June of that year. Construction started four months later, and on 1 December 1913 the Bakerloo finally reached Paddington.

Since an acceptable route had been agreed the Bakerloo wasted no time in extending further. A Bill of 1912 prolonged the line beyond Paddington to Queen's Park, where it met the rails of the main line LNWR, and used the local tracks of this company to reach stations as far north as Watford Junction. As part of the agreement between the two companies the main line gave a loan of £1 million at 4% in perpetuity to the Bakerloo, to pay the construction costs of the extension.

A Southwards Extension is Proposed

Although this section is primarily about the extension of the Bakerloo to north-west London, it is worth recording that the other end of the line was also receiving attention. The terminus at Elephant & Castle was (and remains) very close to central London, and has long appeared ripe for extension.

In 1913, the Lord Mayor of London announced that the Underground Railways of London were prepared to continue the Bakerloo Tube to the south-west.[307] Its terminus at Elephant & Castle was never particularly convenient, and pointed towards tempting commuter districts. The destination proposed would be, as for the Kearney line, Crystal Palace, which would be reached via Camberwell Green, Champion Hill, Dulwich, Lordship Lane, Sydenham Hill, and West Hill. The terminus was to be under the Crystal Palace. This was not the same route as planned by Kearney, and would run about a mile (1.6 km) to the east. The Mayor continued to explain that the extension depended on the support of the districts through which the line would pass. As with all subsequent proposals to extend the Bakerloo line from Elephant & Castle, this vanished into obscurity.[308]

The LNWR 'New Line' to Watford

The main line company operating services to the north of England from its terminus at Euston was, like many other railways in the early years of the twentieth century, considering how it could benefit from electrification. The plan that it started to discuss publicly in mid-1906, and put forward in 1907 was for a new pair of tracks alongside its existing line. These new tracks would start at Watford Junction, and would run south via Willesden Junction and Queen's Park. To the east of this station they would dive into tunnels (with the portals near to the bridge under Kilburn Priory), and follow under the main line all the way to Euston. These would then pass through two intermediate tube stations at **Loudon Road** and **Chalk Farm** before arriving at Euston, where they would terminate at a platform on a single-line underground loop. The loop was situated directly below the existing main line terminus station, at a depth of 55 ft 6

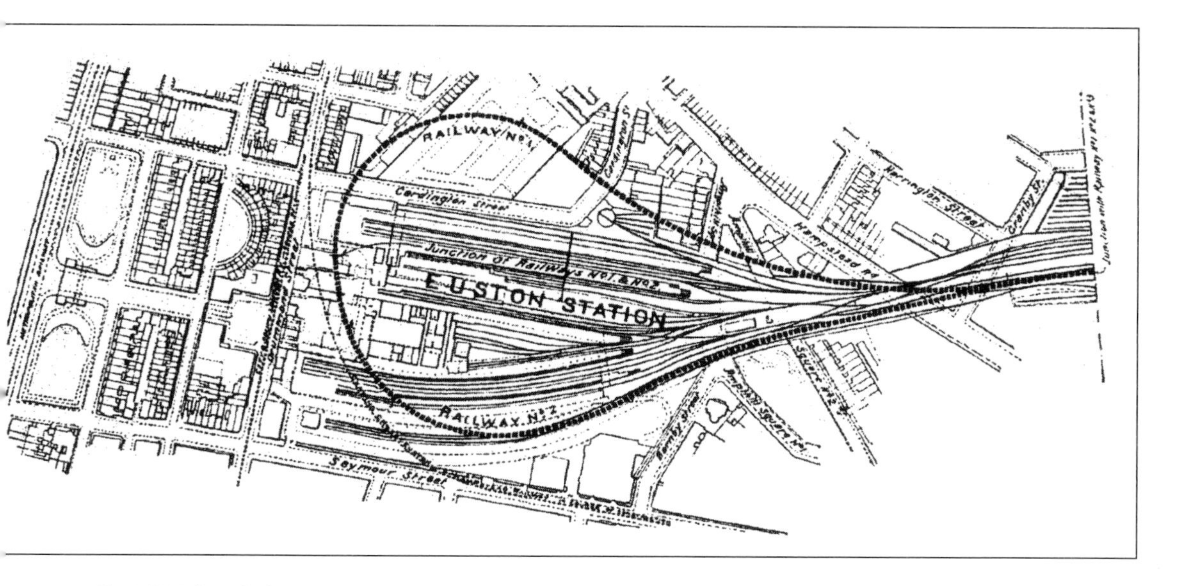

The LNWR loop below Euston, with the CCE&HR immediately to its left.

ins (16.9 m) with the platform in the eastern corner near to those of the CCE&HR. It would then continue to curve back on itself, passing under Cardington Street twice before rejoining the main line alignment at Hampstead Road. The total length of the loop was 7 furlongs 2.2 chains (1,452 m).

Stairs and lifts were to be used for passenger access to the stations, which would have their platforms in tunnels not more than 30 feet (9.15 m) in diameter. The running tunnels would be 13 ft 6 ins (4.1 m) in diameter; new rolling stock would therefore be required for the line. The Act did not authorize construction of a power station, or connection to a power station; a separate Act was required for this. This may have made the Bill easier to pass, whilst allowing the LNWR to consider all of its options for electrical power, on this and other lines. One interesting report stated that Elfric Kearney was hoping to get his monorail technology adopted by the LNWR for the line.[309]

The Bill was opposed in the House of Commons by Mr Morton, on behalf of the Corporation of the City of London. The opposition was not well received, and the MP Hudson E. Kearley stated that

> persistent opposition like this from a great Corporation was not paying the proper deference to Parliament that it ought to receive. The Corporation had fallen into the hands of bad advisers in this matter, and was abusing its privilege.[310]

The line received Royal Assent on 26 July 1907, and was to require the company to raise an additional £2.7 million of capital, with the usual proportion of borrowing giving an additional £900,000. As was noted by the promoters of the NELR in 1909, the main line company had difficulty raising the money to pay for the scheme in the financially difficult years of 1907 and 1908. Indeed, less than a month of their success, the half-yearly Board meeting of 16 August 1907 noted that the raising of capital for the work would be delayed until "better terms" could be reached.

In 1909 the LNWR took over the working of the North London Railway (NLR), and as a result began to rethink their previous plans. The surface section was to be constructed first, and the expensive loop under Euston left until last. Construction was to permit steam operation, which would allow the cost of electrification to be deferred as well.

In 1911 it was announced that the subterranean loop had been dropped from the plans. The new proposal was to extend the two new tracks on the surface to Camden, and then connect them to the existing lines from Euston via a complex series of burrowing junctions (i.e., where the line would pass beneath other tracks to avoid conflicts between trains). This section was forever known to the LNWR as the 'New Line'. The NLR was to be electrified from its Broad Street terminus to the Camden junctions, and from Camden to Richmond, Kew Bridge, and Earl's Court (via the West London Railway). To connect with central London, the Bakerloo would be extended from Paddington to Queen's Park. This was authorized by the London Electric Railway Act of 1912, described in a previous section.

A number of new stations would open on the new tracks, and platforms would be provided on the new line at the existing stations. From south to north they were (with the completely new stations in bold): Queen's Park, Willesden Junction, **Harlesden**, **Stonebridge Park**, Wembley for Sudbury,[311] **North Wembley**, **Kenton**, Harrow & Wealdstone, **Headstone Lane**, Pinner & Hatch End, Carpenders Park, Bushey & Oxhey, Watford High Street, and Watford Junction. At the existing stations new platforms were constructed to take the electrified services.

The line was opened in sections. Willesden Junction to Harrow & Wealdstone opened on 15 June 1912. The northernmost section from Harrow to Watford Junction was opened next, on 10 February 1913.

The Bakerloo was extended to Queen's Park on 11 February 1915. Three months later, on 10 May, the final section of the 'New Line' between Queen's Park and Willesden Junction was opened. This section included twin tunnels west of Kensal Green that were dug using tunnelling shields. At the time they were the largest tube tunnels ever made, being 16 ft 4 ins (5.0 m) in diameter.

Extensions, Not New Lines

The Hampstead Improves its Connections

The LER Act for 1911, as well as authorizing the Bakerloo extension to Paddington, included another extension. This was to continue the CCE&HR southwards from its terminus at Strand to a station at Charing Cross,[312] where it could provide interchange with both the MDR and the Bakerloo Tube. This extension was 4 furlongs 4.25 chains (890 m) long, and was in the form of a single track loop extending below the Thames. One platform was provided, and was located directly beneath the MDR station, and adjacent to the main line railway bridge.

A large rectangular excavation 65 feet (19.8 m) deep was made immediately north-west of the MDR station entrance, and from this the loop was excavated. A long pedestrian subway connecting the platform to those of the Bakerloo Tube was also made, and four escalators were installed to link both tube railways with the District Railway. The loop was opened for passenger traffic on 6 April 1914.[313]

The CLR Reaches Liverpool Street and Ealing

In the 1909 session of Parliament the CLR promoted another Bill that would take them to Liverpool Street. It will be recalled that the previous attempt had ended in failure when negotiations with the GER broke down. This time the GER had agreed to the construction of CLR platforms beneath their main line station. Like the GNR at Finsbury Park they imposed conditions on the tube railway: it was to be extended no further. The Bill received Royal Assent on 16 August, and construction began the following year. The sidings beneath Old Broad Street were extended to the north-easternmost corner of the main line station site, following the line of the road until the station was reached.

Crossover tunnels were provided either side of the platforms at Liverpool Street, to give maximum operating flexibility. The actual crossovers were electro-pneumatically operated, and had movable diamonds and spring frogs. The original plan to remove the scissors crossover to the east of Bank was changed in 1912, and this was merely reduced to a single trailing crossover. The line was resignalled with automatic signalling as far west as Post Office station (now St Paul's); this was the beginning of a plan to resignal the entire railway. The running rails on the extension were welded together using the new "thermite" process.

The platform tunnels were more widely separated than for most stations, allowing for the lift shafts to descend to platform level without the need for any stairs. However, in November 1911 the CLR wrote to the Board of Trade asking to make some changes to the plans for the station. These changes involved substituting escalators for the lifts. The Board agreed in the same month, and the connections to the main line stations at Liverpool Street and the adjacent Broad Street were each constructed with two escalators.[314] Lifts were also provided to the latter station (although were reportedly out of use by 1915). At Liverpool Street station a single lift shaft was provided, but fitted with a spiral staircase. If traffic was too heavy for the escalators then a lift could always be installed. A spare escalator shaft was also dug on the south side of the others; this was also fitted out with a staircase. More innovation was to be found above the escalators and stairs: an experimental lighting installation was installed. This was the Moore Vacuum Tube System, a forerunner to the fluorescent tubes that are ubiquitous in today's Underground stations. An operating mechanism for this was placed in the ticket hall; this is likely to have been the transformer to generate the several thousand volts required, and the gas replenishment reservoir.

The Moore Gas-Discharge Tube

The American inventor Daniel McFarlan Moore developed the first commercial gas-discharge tube lamp in the 1890s. It was not a great success because the gases in the tube (carbon dioxide and nitrogen) reacted with the metal electrodes, burning them out and depleting the gases. Moore developed an automatic refilling valve, allowing the gases to be replenished, and substituted graphite electrodes, thus improving the lifespan. His lamps gave three times as much light as an equivalent incandescent bulb, and were the predecessor of today's fluorescent tube lighting. The first installation was in 1898, and it was used in an illuminated advertising sign for a hardware store in New Jersey in 1904.

The Liverpool Street installation predates the provision of fluorescent lighting on the westbound Piccadilly line at Piccadilly Circus by 33 years. However, it can also be assumed that it was not a great success, as it does not appear to have been installed at any other tube station in London.

The extension opened to the public on 28 July 1912, although passengers wishing to use the Broad Street facilities had to wait until 10 October.

The next extension proposed by the CLR was to the west. In 1905 the Great Western Railway had received authorization to build a line between their existing station at Ealing Broadway and a site at Shepherd's Bush (not surprisingly called the Ealing & Shepherd's Bush Railway – E&SBR). The latter station was to be adjacent to that of the CLR, on the eastern side. The First World War delayed construction, and the line was only opened in 1917 for freight, and 1920 for passengers.

The CLR saw an opportunity to reach Ealing, and in its Bill of 1911 sought and gained approval for a short connection to this new line. The MR opposed the Bill on the grounds of competition with their Hammersmith & City Railway, but lost the argument. The CLR explained that when the E&SBR had originally been designed it was intended that passengers would transfer between the two stations at Shepherd's Bush on foot. However, there was a difference in level of 30 feet (9.2 m), and a subway of some 450 feet (137 m) would need to be walked. Sir Henry Oakley, Chairman of the CLR, described this as "quite impracticable", and hence the railway link was suggested. The planned E&SBR station at Shepherd's Bush was subsequently dropped.

The line connected the loop at Wood Lane to platforms at **Ealing Broadway** that were placed between the GWR main line platforms and those of the MDR. A small intermediate station was built at **East Acton** to serve a housing estate.[315] The only feature of interest on the line was a fly-over constructed to switch the position of the CLR tracks, which operated right-hand running from Wood Lane because of the anti-clockwise nature of the loop. The line was opened to the public on 3 August 1920.

The final CLR extension that was mooted prior to 1914 was again in the west, but this time to Gunnersbury. Shepherd's Bush station was not far from this location, and there was a road running almost directly between the two points. The CLR Bill of 1913 proposed a branch extending west from Shepherd's Bush Green, under the Goldhawk Road, with stations provided at **The Grove** (now Hammersmith Grove), **Paddenswick Road**, and the junction with **Rylett Road** and Stamford Brook Road. This latter road would be followed, together with Bath Road, via a station at **Stamford Gardens** to **Turnham Green** station. This would be sited just north of the identically named District Railway station, at the west end of Bath Road and adjacent to Acton Green.

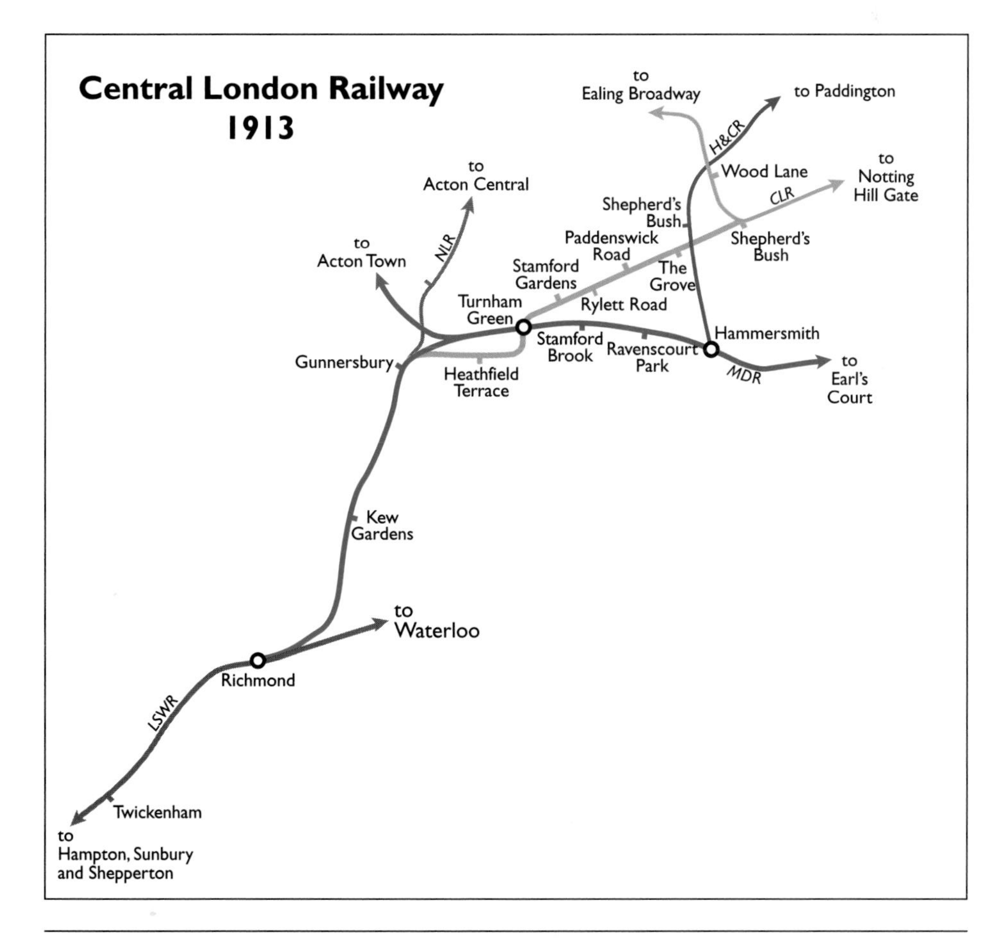

The railway would then curve south under Turnham Green Terrace (and the line of the District Railway) to the Chiswick High Road, where it would regain its westward course. One further station would be provided at **Heathfield Terrace** (arguably a better candidate for the name Turnham Green, given that it would be at the north-east corner of that location). It would continue west, before looping slightly to the north to ease the curve into the LSWR station at **Gunnersbury**. The line would reach the surface just north of the station, but for the rest of the extension it would vary in depth between 35 and 50 feet (10.7 – 15.3 m), making it relatively shallow. During the construction of the railway additional shafts would be sunk on both Acton Green and Turnham Green, but the Middlesex County Council was satisfied that these would be restored once the works were complete.

A running connection would be made with the LSWR, allowing the CLR trains to reach Kew Gardens, Richmond, and on to Twickenham, Hampton, Sunbury, Shepperton, and other districts, according to the directors at their meeting on 20 February 1913.[316] Quite how much of the LSWR they proposed to electrify using the CLR's central third rail was not made clear.

Their engineers Mott & Hay estimated the cost of the section between Shepherd's Bush and Gunnersbury at £759,072. In order to finance this the company sought to issue a further £750,000 of shares in their Bill, together with borrowing powers of £250,000.

The LCC insisted on its usual provisions to protect its sewers and provide workmen's trains; a fare of 2½d return from either Bank or Liverpool Street to Turnham Green was set in the Bill. Since the LCC was planning to purchase the LUT's Hammersmith tram lines, they also included a clause to protect these from the tube construction works. One point on which they had to back down concerned widening of streets: they wanted to compel the CLR to widen the roads outside their new stations (mostly in Goldhawk Road). The CLR refused, but as a trade-off agreed to sell any unnecessary land at the station sites to the LCC for widening purposes. This satisfied the Council, and on 17 April they withdrew their petition against the Bill.

This left the Bill unopposed in Parliament, and it received Royal Assent on 15 August 1913. As with the E&SBR, the start of construction was suspended because of the First World War; however, the difference was that this extension was never built. The CLR Board minutes note that extensions of time were sought in 1916 and 1917, as the original Act gave three years for them to purchase the necessary land.

Tentative plans along similar lines were drawn up in 1920, but with the line routeing via Hammersmith instead. However, it was decided to project the Piccadilly Line from its terminus at Hammersmith along the LSWR route to Acton and Ealing instead, using powers that were also acquired in 1913.

Bills for 1913

The year 1913 was one of the busiest for a while for tube railway Bills. We can skip over two related Bills for the MDR and the Wimbledon & Sutton Railway, as they are both for surface railways; the former sought to operate the latter as an extension of its branch through Putney to Wimbledon.

Two Bills of some interest were those of the C&SLR and LER. The C&SLR had been purchased by the LER on 1 January 1913, and as part of the deal the newly-purchased company now sought authority to widen its tunnels to allow larger trains to be operated. Although authority to widen them to the same size as the LER tubes was sought in the 1913 Bill (in fact, a maximum diameter of 13 feet was permitted), ways of saving money on the work were considered. One possibility was just to enlarge the section between Elephant & Castle and Borough junction, where the running tunnels had a diameter of 10 ft 2 ins. These would be expanded to 10 ft 6 ins, the same as the section south of Elephant & Castle, and between Angel and Euston, but still narrower than the other London tubes. The LER engineers had designed a train that allegedly had the same seating capacity as those operated on their other lines but which would fit into the smaller tunnel. The disadvantage for passengers was that the headroom was 4 inches (10 cm) less, which would have been rather claustrophobic.[317] The seating claim proved to be an exaggeration — a motor car would actually seat 36 as opposed to 42 on the existing, larger LER cars. According to the minutes of a meeting of the UERL Executive Officers, a mock-up of a single car was constructed in 1916 and was to have been exhibited at Ealing Common depôt, alongside a standard C&SLR car and a normal LER car (sometimes known as 'gate stock'). The car was almost exactly the same length as one of the LER cars, but the floor was one inch lower.[318] Access was via a platform with lattice gates at one end, plus a central swing door on either side. Tentative plans were made to order 78 driving motor cars, 19 double-ended control trailers, 20 single-ended control trailers, and 74 trailer cars.

Another experiment in 1914 was made to determine the ease of expanding the tunnels to 11 ft 8¼ ins, and it was decided that the larger tunnel size was more practical. The First World War delayed the enlargement works and they only began in the summer of 1922.

For its part, the LER Bill proposed extending the C&SLR from Euston to join the Hampstead tube at Camden Town, thus giving passengers from Golders Green and Highgate the option of a City route through London. Had the C&SLR been widened on the cheap then this would have severely restricted the ability of trains to be transferred via this connection. It is likely also that the Board of Trade would have raised objections on safety grounds, and required some form of protection device where the narrow tunnels connected to prevent larger trains from entering.

The LER Bill also sought to connect the Piccadilly Tube at Hammersmith with the L&SWR to the west of the station, as mentioned earlier.

The Metropolitan's Plans for the GN&CR

The MR purchased the GN&CR in 1913, following the unanimous decision by the tube railway's shareholders to accept the offer. The defunct GN&CR shares were exchanged for a set amount of Metropolitan stock. The take-over date was agreed for 1 July 1913.

However, the GN&CR was of no use to the MR as an isolated railway. The situation was described by *The Tramway and Railway World* on 8 May 1913: "Clearly if the MR are to get any benefit from acquiring the GN&C line a physical junction must be provided between the two railways". This is precisely what the MR promoted in its Bill of 1913, alongside the acquisition of the GN&CR.

Two short extensions were described. The first linked the southern end of the tube to the MR just west of Liverpool Street station. The extension would branch off the GN&CR tracks to the north of its Moorgate terminus in a rather strange way. Both

The proposed connection between the GN&CR and MR (extension to Bank omitted for clarity)

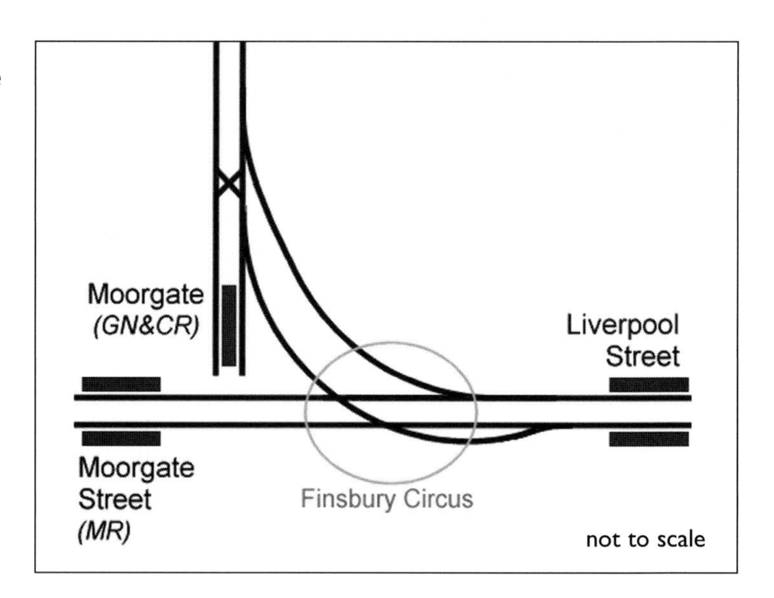

connections would diverge from the southbound tunnel of the tube railway; however, that for westbound/northbound trains would connect south of the crossover, allowing the trains from Liverpool Street access to the northbound GN&CR. This was a practical solution to the problem posed by the C&SLR tunnels being directly below those of the GN&CR, preventing the connecting tunnel from passing beneath.

The new tunnels would rise steeply (1 in 34 up; 1 in 30 down) to the MR, joining its tracks at the east end of Liverpool Street station. East of Finsbury Circus they would be constructed in a cut-and-cover trench. The MR foresaw trains using this link to run from Finsbury Park, via Liverpool Street, onto the recently-electrified East London Railway to the station at New Cross, and thence onto the tracks of the SER and LB&SCR. Another possibility was the reconnection of the MR to the GER at Liverpool Street, allowing the GN&CR trains onto the eastern main line tracks.

There was a lot of opposition to this connection, in particular from "people interested in the buildings and garden at Finsbury Circus",[319] i.e., the residents and property owners, who undoubtedly felt threatened by the prospect of a large-diameter tube running just below their fine houses, and the disruption of cut-and-cover construction work on the east side of their Circus. A meeting was held between the locals and the MR management to discuss their concerns, and in April it was reported at a Metropolitan Board meeting that the line would be so close to the station that the cellars of buildings would be affected. The Metropolitan's engineers suggested lowering the existing railway between the west side of Finsbury Circus and Blomfield Street, by a maximum of 12 feet. However, in discussion with their Parliamentary Counsel it was agreed that these works could not be covered by the Bill as it stood, and there was no way of modifying the Bill this late into the Parliamentary session. Counsel also advised that there was "no hope of obtaining Parliamentary sanction to the construction of the junction lines as deposited", and that the rejection of the junction part of the Bill might jeopardize the entire Bill, including the take-over of the GN&CR.[320] The offending section of line, and the connection to the MR was therefore withdrawn from the Bill, a better scheme being planned for the following year.

The second extension would connect the GN&CR to the W&CR at its City terminus. An extension of 502 yards (459 m) southward would take the GN&CR to a new station at **Lothbury**. This was almost identical to the proposed Lothbury extensions of 1902 and 1907. However, a further extension would prolong the line by another 250 yards (229 m) to join the eastern end of the W&CR station tunnels, just beyond the platforms at City station. The new southbound tunnel would cut through the existing eastbound overrun tunnel, which continued beyond the platform in a straight line. The tunnelling of this section would have to be done in compressed air because of the water-bearing ground: the ancient Walbrook stream was known to run through the area, and had caused the previous tunnellers difficulties.

Of course, the GN&CR had running tunnels 16 feet in diameter; the W&CR tunnels were just 12 feet across. Expanding the tunnels of the W&CR was not proposed. Instead, the line to Lothbury would be built to match the existing GN&CR, but south of that station the new tunnels would have a diameter of 12 feet. A crossover tunnel would be built immediately to the north of Lothbury. Small-size trains that could fit the W&CR tunnels would operate between Waterloo and Finsbury Park, but the larger trains of the GN&CR would be confined to the section north of Lothbury. This would allow passengers from the north to be brought into the heart of the City. Quite how large trains were to be prevented from entering the smaller tunnels was not explained.

The Bill contained a third short extension that had nothing to do with the GN&CR. A 5-furlong (1 km) connection was proposed between the Hammersmith & City Railway (H&CR), just west of Latimer Road station, and the E&SBR. The new line would join the latter railway on the west side of Wood Lane, after passing over the CLR link to the E&SBR via an arched bridge. This connection was dropped early on in the history of the Bill, because of opposition from the GWR, owners of the E&SBR, who were concerned about congestion on their new railway with both MR and CLR trains operating to Ealing. The MR gave up the extension in return for taking "practical control" of the H&CR services and maintenance from the GWR at the start of 1913.[321]

The MR was also exploring a partnership with the GNR, who had caused so many problems for the GN&CR initially. The GNR had proposed a partnership in owning the tube railway as early as April 1913, and for the connections to the main line at Finsbury Park to be constructed. Within three weeks of this suggestion agreement was reached with the MR, and the GNR withdrew its opposition to the MR Bill. A formal agreement between the two companies was made in June of the same year.

When the Bill came before a Select Committee of the House of Lords the Corporation of London objected to the station at Lothbury, arguing that it was unnecessary with stations at Moorgate and Bank (City). They did not object to the extension *per se*, but the station tunnels would risk causing subsidence to the Bank of England and other heavy buildings in the vicinity of the Lothbury interchange. They suggested that the extension be built entirely in tunnels of 12-feet diameter. The MR argued that allowing the large trains from the north to disgorge their passengers at two City stations would reduce the congestion at Moorgate, and passengers from Waterloo would have a choice of three City stations.

The problem with the section between Lothbury and the W&CR was that it was forced to run quite shallowly for a tube railway. Below, the C&SLR tunnels prevented it from descending too much; above, a sewer was proposed. The angle of the road

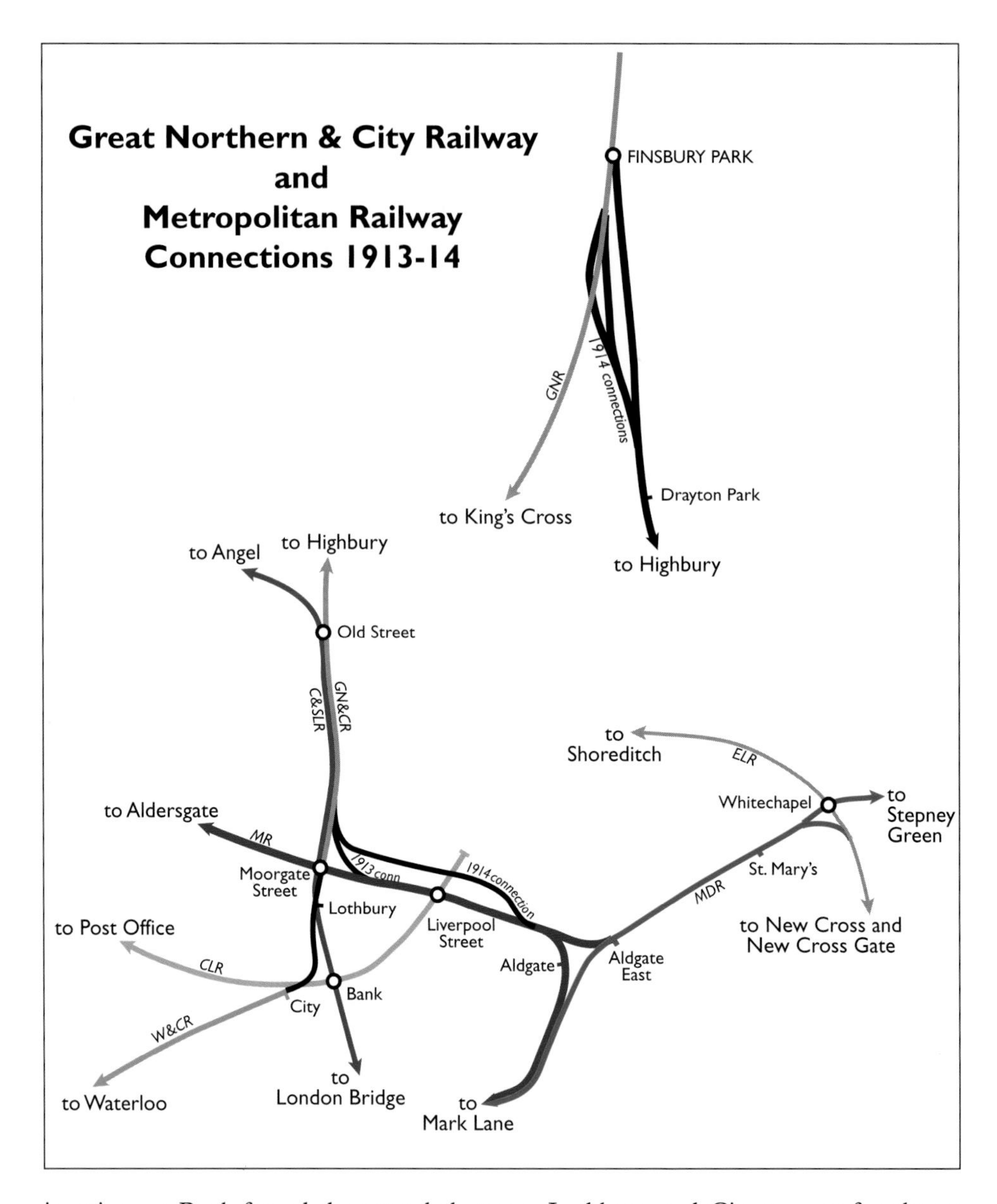

junctions at Bank forced the tunnels between Lothbury and City to pass for almost their entire length beneath property belonging to the Grocers' Company on the west side of Princes Street. A further restriction on their depth was posed by the CLR running tunnels at Bank, above which the new tunnels would pass with a gap of just 1½ feet (46 cm).

The LER did not object to the extensions. This may seem surprising, but was the result of an agreement dating back to 20 November 1912. This allowed the LER to pursue the acquisition of the C&SLR (but not to link it to the BS&WR through extensions to either), and if successful, to link it to the Hampstead tube. In return, the MR would be free to purchase the GN&CR, and to connect it to the W&CR. The owners of the latter railway, the LSWR, were also amenable to the connection.

By the time the Bill was passed it was very different from its original form. The MR was permitted to acquire the GN&CR, but the only authorized extension was to Lothbury. The tunnel to the W&CR had caused too much concern and opposition to be allowed. Some MR shareholders were not happy with this result; they saw the MR getting no benefit from its acquisition of the tube line at all. Capel George Pett Pownall, who owned MR shares worth £11,000, petitioned against the reduced Bill. He argued that the acquisition of the GN&CR would be "injurious to the property, rights and interests of himself and other shareholders of the Company" due to the poor financial state of the GN&CR.[322] The Metropolitan claimed that the GN&CR could be made to pay through operating efficiencies, and the lack of connections was not a problem. However, Pownall believed that the Bill being approved was different from that presented to the shareholders for approval (which was true, with the MR and W&CR connections removed). The Committee politely listened to his arguments, and then unanimously found in favour of the Bill. Royal Assent was given on 13 August 1913, over a month after the nominally agreed date for the acquisition. The MR started operating the GN&CR with effect from 1 September.

The next year a Bill was promoted to enact the proposed partnership between the MR and GNR, and for the construction of a number of connecting lines. A joint committee of the two railway companies would be formed, to which each would appoint three directors. The MR would lease the GN&CR to the committee for 900 years, starting on 1 July 1913, for rent equal to the interest and dividend on the stock they had issued to pay for the railway. In other words, once the joint committee took over, the MR would no longer be paying its shareholders for the purchase directly, although it would be contributing via the committee.

The southward extension to the W&CR at **City** was included, but without a running connection. The plans from the previous year had the extension passing closely above the CLR's running tunnels, bringing it closer to the surface, and this was one reason for the Bill's rejection. Now the plans were for it to pass below the CLR tunnels, making the new line run deeper (allaying concerns about subsidence). However, it would terminate in platforms under those of the W&CR, forcing passengers to change trains at Bank.[323]

This year, all but one objection to the Bill had been withdrawn, even though the tunnels had been increased to 16 feet in diameter. Escalators would be used to connect the platforms of the two lines at Bank. Street access to the W&CR, which was via a long, sloping tunnel that wearied its users, would be replaced with more escalators. West of the station platforms the tunnels would continue beneath Queen Victoria Street as far as the junction with Friday and Knightrider Streets.[324] This would allow the locomotives on the GNR trains to shunt around the carriages in readiness for their return journey north.

One side effect of making the line deeper between Moorgate Street and Bank was the deletion of Lothbury station from the plans. The additional depth would have increased the cost of the station, as well as making construction more difficult, as it would be closer to the tunnels of the C&SLR. With a full-size connection to Bank, Lothbury was seen as unnecessary; Bank had better interchange with other underground railways, whereas Lothbury would have none. It also removed the chief objection from the Corporation of London.

The connection to the MR was again proposed, but with the MR junction near to Aldgate, making the connection over 5 furlongs (1 km) long. The connections to the southbound track of the GN&CR would be the same as planned in 1913, but with the tunnels remaining at depth until they rose to join the Inner Circle just west of Aldgate Junction, where the Inner Circle split from the line to Whitechapel. This was the "better scheme" planned in 1913. There did not appear to be a station planned at Liverpool Street, which seems at first glance to be a glaring omission. However, it is likely that it would have been too shallow to be sanctioned by the GER, which would have objected to large platform tunnels being constructed under its station buildings and hotel; the gradient may also have been off-putting.

In his evidence to Parliament the MR's General Manager, Robert Selbie, explained that congestion on the western part of the Inner Circle meant that they could not connect any further west. Some MR trains terminated at Moorgate Street and Liverpool Street, giving capacity on the line to the east. Hence the MR proposed to connect near to Aldgate Junction, allowing trains to run through and onto the East London Railway.[325]

At the northern end of the GN&CR two single track connections would be constructed just north of Drayton Park station, linking to the GNR main line, allowing through trains to operate to the surface station at Finsbury Park as originally planned in 1892. The GNR would pay for, and own, these connections (allowing it to retain control over them), and the other costs would be split equally with the MR, which would own the other links. Whilst the GNR could pay from its existing capital, the Bill authorized the MR to raise £480,000 in shares and £160,000 through borrowing to finance its half.

It was agreed that the new joint committee would be responsible for maintaining the entire line, except for the GNR connections, and would construct the connections to the Inner Circle and the W&CR. The committee would maintain the junction at Drayton Park at the expense of the GNR. The electricity supply would come from the Metropolitan.

An interesting angle, which would have been obvious to the promoting companies, was that the GN&CR would be used for goods trains as well as passengers. The Metropolitan was used to operating goods trains, and the GNR saw the benefit of being able to operate its trains from the north through to south of the Thames via the East London Railway (ELR). Indeed, it is possible that it considered the link to the Inner Circle to be more valuable for goods than passenger traffic, which could also explain the lack of a station at Liverpool Street.

The fears of subsidence presented the previous year for both the Inner Circle and W&CR link lines were allayed by the depth of the tunnels proposed in 1914. This placed them for almost their entire length within the London clay.

As usual, the petition from the LCC sought protection for its sewers, and for a proposed new street between Liverpool Street and Aldgate, and the usual provision for workmen's trains. The Metropolitan Borough of Islington raised similar objections, because of their sewers. Willesden Urban District Council and the Metropolitan Borough of St Marylebone objected on the rather more irrelevant grounds that the MR were allowed to own property not relating to the railway, and that they were supplying electricity to buildings that were not used for railway purposes.[326]

The North London Railway felt threatened by the new plan, believing that its running powers over the GNR would be withdrawn. These dated back to 1874, when the Great Northern had sought to relieve congestion at its King's Cross terminus by routeing some of its suburban trains to the North London's Broad Street station, via a recently opened link line between Finsbury Park and Canonbury, called the Canonbury Curve (or Spur). The LNWR, who held a majority interest in the NLR, blocked this, and "in desperation the Great Northern invited the NLR to run trains from Broad Street out to its suburban stations."[327] However, the powers remained fairly informal, and the NLR was greatly concerned that, with a direct route to the City, the GNR would block any more of their trains.

Once they had proved at an initial hearing that they had a valid objection, Counsel for the NLR presented their petition. Their evidence was obviously convincing, and the Parliamentary Committee, whilst passing the Bill on 23 June 1914, added the following conditions:

- The NLR was to be granted running powers over the GNR in perpetuity, between Canonbury and Barnet (its existing route).
- The tracks between Finsbury Park and Canonbury were to be electrified at the same time as the GNR lines used by the NLR, allowing NLR electric trains to run over the GNR. If this was not done then it would condemn the NLR to using steam trains on its services over the GNR.
- The GN&CR was only to be used for passenger and parcels traffic, thwarting the plans to operate goods trains.

The MR and GNR felt unable to accept these conditions, and immediately withdrew the Bill. It must be suspected that the goods traffic was the main reason: electrifying the Canonbury Curve would not have been a huge cost. Although the capacity south of Finsbury Park would be increased with the GN&CR link, there would be a limit to the number of passenger trains that the GNR would want to run through to the ELR. After all, trains using the link would run non-stop between Old Street and Aldgate East, which would have been rather less attractive to the City commuter than Broad Street.

Henceforth the MR had to make do with its first and only investment in tube railways as it was, the authorized extension to Lothbury not being attractive enough to pursue on its own.[328] In July Selbie sought the authorization of the Metropolitan Board to repaint the GN&CR stations, noting that no restoration work had been carried out since the take-over. Presumably the MR had been hoping to split the costs of any work with the GNR through the joint committee, had that been created.

The full story of the GN&CR is documented elsewhere;[329] suffice to say here that the MR effected economies and improved the line, to the point where 20 million passengers were being carried each year by 1920, an increase of over 7 million from 1912. Unusually, and in accordance with the practice of the MR, the GN&CR also became the only tube railway in London to offer first- and third-class accommodation to its passengers.

Epilogue

The golden age of promoting tube railways in London was over by 1907. The high hopes of the promoters, and the thousands of speculators who eagerly advanced their money in the hope of making a fortune, had been brought rudely to earth by the meagre returns. The far greater numbers of people who had refused to invest (and caused such problems for the tube promoters) had had their fears justified. The passenger numbers on the Yerkes tubes (which jointly became the London Electric Railway Company by Act of 1910) were significantly less than predicted. Indeed, even in 1909 the Hampstead Tube was struggling to reach 60% of the figure confidently predicted some four years earlier.

The £5 million raised by the UERL in 1902 had proved insufficient as early as 1903. Only two-fifths of another batch of £2 million worth of shares were raised, and so Yerkes resorted to another financial instrument: the profit-sharing note. These would be sold at a discount of 4%, and by paying interest of 5%, would be more attractive to investors than shares. They had a life of five years, as the company confidently expected to be making a healthy profit in 1908, and would be able to redeem them. Another £7 million was raised, and again these were mostly sold to Americans. Over £3 million of additional shares were sold in 1904 and 1905, bringing the UERL's capital to over £15 million.

Needless to say, by 1908 the company's finances were in no suitable state to pay back the original £5 million from 1902, and after an attempt to sell the company to the LCC was rebuffed, the notes were exchanged for bonds and preference shares, redeemable in 1933 and 1948. Bankruptcy had been held off.

We have already seen that raising the capital was a major problem for many of the tube railways in the early years of the twentieth century. The CLR, which had started so well, suffered greatly from competition with the new motor buses. The opening of the Piccadilly Tube, and the electrification of the MR and MDR all served to decrease passenger numbers, and the railway sought to reduce their operating costs and improve traffic by modifying the ticketing system. First to go was the flat 2d fare: journeys greater than seven or eight stations henceforth cost 3d. Books of tickets (similar to today's 'carnets') were also introduced. Notwithstanding all of this, the dividend on its shares had slipped to 3%.

The C&SLR had fared even worse. Its route was paralleled by tramways, which sought to steal its traffic, and its services were still hampered by its small tunnels and trains. The 1907 extension to Euston, whilst adding 1¾ miles (2.8 km) and two important main line stations to its route, had not improved the passenger numbers.

Closer co-operation between the tubes was inevitable, and a number of fare agreements were put into place from 1907. Joint publicity under the banner of the name 'Underground' commenced in 1908, so that a united front could be presented to passengers. Finally, in 1912 the LER announced that it was to purchase both the C&SLR and the CLR. This was approved and enacted the following year, with LER stock being substituted for that of the older railways. The MR, not wishing to be left out, bought the GN&CR in the same year; as shown in the previous chapter, this did not dramatically improve the situation of the latter railway, which continued to suffer from its isolation from the main line at Finsbury Park. However, it did eliminate a potential threat to the MR, which had long worried that the railway would be bought or taken over by the GNR. This would have allowed the latter company to route its trains directly to Moorgate, instead of using the 'City Widened Lines' that paralleled the MR between King's Cross and Moorgate. The GNR traffic over the Widened Lines brought the MR an income of £38,000 each year, which it was keen to keep. Whilst the GN&CR remained independent, the MR had considered it to be "a menace".[330]

It was therefore not surprising that, with the opening of the three UERL railways, the interest in promoting new lines dried up. No one was prepared to promote new lines whilst those in existence could not meet the optimistic passenger figures predicted in 1905. The negligible returns on the stock deterred investors, and if a financial titan like Yerkes could not make the tubes pay, what chance did anyone else have? Had Yerkes lived to see the opening of his lines even he may have realized that extensive experience in US tramway operation did not mean that the construction of tube railways in a different country would be assured of success.

London continued to grow in size and population, but this growth was met by providing extensions to the existing underground railways (for the most part these extensions were on the surface), and increasing the network of trams and buses.

A few people believed that they could cut the high costs of tube railway construction by inventing radical improvements, such as Kearney's tubular monorail, but still the investors stayed away, and it was not until 1968 that the next completely new tube line (as opposed to an extension) was opened, in the shape of the Victoria Line. Times had changed by then and this was funded by the Government, since the tube railways had been nationalized in 1948 along with the main line railways.

By 1914, tube railway speculation in London really had come to a close.

Appendix 1: Parliamentary Procedure

It is worth explaining in a few words how the UK Parliament works with regard to the authorization of railways. Note that the details in this section are given with particular relevance to the period covered in this book.[331]

In order to construct any railway that is not to be entirely located on land already owned by the promoter, an Act of Parliament is usually required. However, with the agreement of landowners it was sometimes possible to do without the Act. The logic behind going to Parliament is that once enshrined in law, the Act confers statutory powers for the compulsory purchase of land, and allows diversion, obstruction and closing ('stopping-up') of public streets.

Since the Act will be deposited with Parliament for a private body (the railway company), it is called a Private Bill. The Bill should contain the complete text describing the works to be carried out. This is just concerned with the site of the railway works: details of stations, rolling stock, and other items are not required (although the means of locomotion is usually specified in the case of underground railways). An accompanying set of plans will also be deposited. These show the exact line of the railway plotted onto detailed maps, together with the limits of deviation, outside of which construction may not stray. Gradient profiles are also required, showing the depth below the surface (or height above, in the case of embankments and viaducts) of the line. Each site or building that will be taken by the company (e.g., for stations) is numbered and cross-referenced in an accompanying Book of Reference, which lists the owner of each building.

There is limited time available for depositing Bills, as Parliament works on the basis of annual sessions. Bills must be deposited late in the calendar year (which is early in the Parliamentary year), and must gain Royal Assent before the end of the session, otherwise it will fail. Such failed Bills have to be reintroduced in the following session, and start all over again. Only in exceptional circumstances, such as those surrounding the tube railway Bills of 1901, can a Bill be carried across between sessions of Parliament.

The Bill must comply with the Standing Orders of Parliament, and a financial deposit originally had to be made, of 5% of the cost of the works. This was to prevent, as far as possible, the submission of bogus or blocking lines that had no intention of being constructed. The deposit was refunded when the railway was completed, or if the scheme was withdrawn. By 1914, the requirement for a deposit was relaxed, and the *bona fides* of the promoting company could be accepted instead.

In order to become an Act, the Bill must be read three times before both the House of Commons and the House of Lords, and it must pass a vote in both Houses. In different years tube railway Bills were started in different Houses, which appears to be

Parliamentary whim. The concept of "reading a Bill" does not imply that it is read out loud, although this was done until Stuart times, and made for very dull affairs. The first two readings are, in general, matters of formality, and are separated by about seven days. During this time an Examiner checks that the Bill complies with all relevant Standing Orders. After the second reading the Bill will be referred to a Select Committee. This comprises a number of members of the House (four in the case of a Commons Committee; five for a Lords Committee; all Committee members must declare that they have no personal interest in the Bill) in front of whom the Bill was being read, who will scrutinize it line by line. Those opposing the Bill submit petitions explaining their reasons, which are considered at this stage as well. Promoters and petitioners may engage barristers to argue their cases. All petitions must be submitted to Parliament by 12 February, and the promoting company receives copies.

Counsel for the promoters opens the committee stage by describing generally the new works, and addressing the points of objection from the petitioners. Supporting witnesses are then called, followed by the company engineer, who gives the technical detail. The General Manager of the company is then often called to describe the benefits and opportunities of the scheme.

This stage is then followed by the petitioners, who will in most cases each have appointed their own Counsel. Mr F. H. Graveson, of the North Eastern Railway described this part of the proceedings in an article of 1914:

> ... this stage is most interesting from a spectators point of view. Imagination is freely drawn upon and amusing descriptions of potential disasters which the proposed scheme will cause to social, moral, and industrial progress are often heard.[332]

After these stages are complete, the Committee then deliberates and debates the scheme in private, before reporting their conclusions. If they reject the Bill then it cannot proceed in that session of Parliament. If successful then it generally results in a number of amendments being made to the Bill. Sometimes these are agreed between the promoters and the petitioners independently, and other times the Committee imposes them. Once the Committee work is complete, the amended Bill is returned to the House for its third reading, at which no amendments may be made. If successful, it is then sent to the other House for consideration. The process just described occurs again, with the first reading occurring shortly after the second House receives the Bill (sometimes it is the same day). Finally, if successful at this third reading, the Bill becomes law (and therefore an Act) by gaining Royal Assent.

If it can be shown that a petitioner has been vexatious with its opposition, then the promoter may claim the costs of defending it from the petitioner, by making a request to Parliament. Similarly, if a scheme is shown to have been promoted unnecessarily then the petitioners may claim their costs from the promoters.

As can be imagined, the cost of promoting a railway Bill can be very high, and the legal profession can do very well from the process. In 1914 it was estimated that, even discounting the failed Bills, the railways of Great Britain cost £4,000 per mile in promotion costs.[333]

Appendix 2: **Stations on the London Suburban Railway**

PC&NELR and LUER Combined Scheme (1902)

Station Name	Station Location	Depth m (ft)	Distance from previous station in metres	Interchanges	Notes
Hammersmith Broadway	North side of the Broadway, at No. 32	16.8 (55)	–	MDR MR London United Tramways	
Shepherd's Bush	East end of Shepherd's Bush Green	14.6 (48)	–	CLR Tramways	Deleted by the Windsor Committee 16 May 1902
Addison Road	Addison Road station	16.5 (54)	1,066 (from Hammersmith)	WLR	Renamed Warwick Road in April 1902
High Street Kensington	High St Kensington station	20.4/27.8 (67/91)	1,448	MR MDR	
Queen's Gate	Junction of Kensington Gore and Queen's Gate	19.5 (64)	845		Renamed Albert Hall in April 1902
Sloane Street	Junction of Sloane Street and Knightsbridge	31.4 (103)	1,126	Marble Arch - Clapham Junction LUER line B&PCR (authorized)	Renamed Knightsbridge in April 1902
Hyde Park Corner	West side of Hyde Park Corner	33.9 (111)	603		Unlikely to have (or require) B&PCR interchange
Albemarle Street	Junction of Albemarle Street and Piccadilly	27.5 (90)	1,086		Unlikely to have (or require B&PCR interchange. Station tunnels to be 23 ft (7 m) diameter
Piccadilly Circus	East side of the junction of Haymarket and Coventry Street	32.6 (107)	643	B&PCR (authorized) BS&WR (under construction)	
Charing Cross	East side of Adelaide Street	19.5 (64)	503	CCE&HR (authorized) SER	
Law Courts	East end of the Aldwych island	20.7/28.4 (68/93)	845	GN&SR (authorized - Strand station)	
Ludgate Circus	West side of New Bridge Street, south side of Fleet Street	13.7/18.9 (45/62)	764	LC&DR (Ludgate Hill station)	
Cannon Street	Cannon Street station	23.2 (76)	1,046	MDR MDR Deep Level (authorized) C&NESER (proposed)	
City & Crystal Palace Railway (proposed)					
Monument	Monument station	25.0 (82)	503	MDR C&SLR (Bank station) City & Brixton Railway (proposed)	
Bishopsgate St Without	East of Liverpool Street station; corner of New Street and Bishopsgate	17.7/25.0 (58/82)	664	MR (Liverpool Street station) GER (Liverpool Street station) NLR (Broad Street station)	
Hackney Road	Junction of Old Street, Shoreditch High Street, Kingsland Road and Hackney Road	17.1/24.4 (56/80)	1,106		

Kingsland Road	On Kingsland Road, to the south of Regent's Canal	18.0 (59)	905		
Stamford Road	Junction of Stamford Road and Kingsland Road	17.1 (56)	1,206		
Arcola Street	Junction of Arcola Street and Stoke Newington Road	15.9 (52)	704		
Church Street	Junction of Stoke Newington Church Street and Stoke Newington High Street	15.6 (51)	1,106		
Amhurst Park	Junction of Amhurst Park and Stamford Hill	20.4 (67)	1,247		
Seven Sisters Road	Junction of Seven Sisters Road and High Road	10.4 (34)	1,106		Known as High Road in May 1902
The Avenue	The Avenue, Tottenham near to the junction with Gloucester Road	-	1,607		
Lordship Lane	Junction of Lordship Lane and Westbury Avenue	-	804		
White Hart Lane	On White Hart Lane, between the junctions with Rivulet and Fenton Roads	-	905		
Chequers Green	Near the junction of Tottenhall Road and Pasteur Gardens	-	804		
Palmer's Green	Green Lanes, between Hazelwood Lane and Lodge Drive	-	945	Tramways	
High Street, Southgate	At the site of Ash Lodge	(20) *	1,408	Deleted by the Windsor Committee 12 May 1902	
Chase Side, Southgate	Near the junction of Chase side and Chase Way	(20) *	1,347	Deleted by the Windsor Committee 12 May 1902	

* Station situated in cutting

LUER North/South Line (1902)

Station Name	**Station Location**	**Depth m (ft)**	**Interchanges**	**Notes**
Marble Arch	South side of Oxford Street, west of Park Street	27.8 (91)	CLR NWLR (authorized)	
Sloane Street	North side of Sloane Street and Knightsbridge junction	25.9 (85)	Main route of LSR B&PCR (authorized)	Named Knightsbridge in April 1902
Sloane Square	South-east corner of Sloane Square	26.5 (87)	MDR	
Battersea Park	South-east corner of Queen's Circus	18.3 (60)		
Queen's Road	Junction of Lavender Hill and Queen's Road	13.7 (45)		
Lavender Hill	Junction of Lavender Hill and Latchmere Road	23.5 (77)		
Clapham Junction	Under St John's Hill, south-west of the main station	15.6 (51)	LSWR	

Appendix 3

The table below is the key to the Royal Commission map reproduced on page 223

No.	Colour	Railway	Details	Year
1	Red	B&PCR	Fulham extension	1901
2	Blue	B&PCR	Angel extension	
3	Blue	CLR	Shepherd's Bush loop	
4	Blue	CLR	Alternative Bank/Liverpool Street loops	
5	Blue	CCE&HR	Victoria / Highgate extensions	
6	Red	CCH&DR		
7	Red	C&WER		
8	Red	KRR		
9	Green/red	NELR		
9a	Red	C&NESER		
10	Red	P&CR		
11	Blue/red	VC&SER		
12	Green	W&SLJR		
13	Red/blue	B&PCR		1902
14	Red	CLR		
15	Red	CCH&DR		
16	Red	C&CPR		
16a	Blue	C&NESER	No.2	
17	Green	CW&WR		
18	Red	ELC&PR		
19	Red	L&BE	London & Brighton Electric	
20	Red/blue	LUER		
21	Red/green	NELR	No.2	
22	Red	P&CR	No.2	
23	Green	VK&GR		
23a	Red	KRR	No.2	
24	Red	CLR		1903
25	Red	C&CPR		
26	Blue	CJ&MAR		
27	Red	GNP&BR		
28	Red	L&BE		
29	Green	MDR		
30	Green	MDR		
31	Green	MDR		
32	Red	NWLR		
32a	Red/green	C&NESER		
32b	Green/red	HC&NELR		
33	Red	N&SWER		1904
33a	Red	LUT	Railway Bill	
34	Red	CLR		1905
35	Green	GNP&BR	Waterloo extension	
36	Red	GNP&BR	Acton & Chiswick extension	
37	Red/green	HC&NELR		

Appendix 4: **References**

Primary Sources

Where possible the original documents produced by the railway companies themselves have been consulted. These records are to be found in the House of Lords Records Office, the National Archives, and the London Metropolitan Archives. The records include the Acts of Parliament, draft Bills, deposited plans, books of reference, company accounts, meeting minutes, and letters. As can be expected, the amount of material held varies considerably from company to company. All of the archives have on-line search facilities that allow the researcher to browse the record indices at their leisure.

Other primary sources that have been used, but which do not originate from the railway companies include:

- Hansard (Proceedings of the Houses of Parliament) 1889-1910
- The Journals of the House of Commons
- The Journals of the House of Lords
- Transcripts from the many Select Committees that considered the various Bills
- The Royal Commission on London Traffic 1905
- Metropolitan Board of Works Minutes of Proceedings
- London County Council Minutes of Proceedings
- Various Waterworks Company Records

London's Transport Museum

Joint Select Committee of the House of Lords and House of Commons on London Underground Railways 1901

The Royal Commission on London Traffic 1905

The Kearney High-Speed Railway, ICE reprint, 1917

Maps

Historic information has been greatly assisted by the republication of Old Ordnance Survey Maps by Alan Godfrey Maps. Both the 1894 and 1913/14 series have been used.

Collins Greater London Street Atlas and the *Geographers' London A-Z* have been invaluable for checking modern place names.

Secondary Sources

Books

The key books used in the research are listed below. A number of other publications were used to check facts or confirm evidence; where appropriate the details of these may be found in the notes.

Bancroft, P., *The Railway to King William Street*, (P. Bancroft 1981)

Barker, T. C. & Robbins, M., *A History of London Transport Vols. 1 & 2* (Allen & Unwin 1963 & 1974)

Borley, H. V., *Chronology of London Railways* (Railway & Canal Historical Society 1982)

Bruce, J. G., *The Big Tube* (London Transport 1976)

Bruce, J. G. & Croome, D. F. (*The Twopenny Tube*, Capital Transport 1996)

Chrimes, M., *Taking the Railway Underground: The Work of Benjamin Baker and his Contemporaries* (Institution of Civil Engineers 1999)

Clout, H (Editor), *The Times London History Atlas* (Times Books 1997)

Connelly, B., *The London United Tramways: A Short History* (Tramway and Light Railway Society 1964)

Connor, J. E. & Halford, B. L. (*The Forgotten Stations of Greater London*, Connor & Butler 1991)

Croome, D. F. & Jackson, A. A., *Rails through the Clay* (Capital Transport 2nd Edition 1993)

Croome, D. F., *The Piccadilly Line* (Capital Transport 1998)

Day, J. & Wilson, B. G., *Unusual Railways* (Frederick Muller Ltd 1957)

Douglas, H., *The Underground Story* (Robert Hale 1963)

Edmonds, A., *History of the Metropolitan District Railway to 1908* (London Transport 1973)

Edwards, C., *Railway Records* (Public Record Office 2001)

Follenfant, H. G., *Reconstructing London's Underground* (London Transport 1974)

Gillham, J. C., *The Waterloo & City Railway* (Oakwood Press 2001)

Halliday, S., *Underground to Everywhere* (Sutton Press and London's Transport Museum 2002)

Holman, P., *The Amazing Electric Tube* (London Transport Museum 1990)

Jackson, A. A., *London's Termini* (David & Charles 1969)

Jackson, A. A., *London's Metropolitan Railway* (David & Charles 1986)

Jackson, A. A., *London's Local Railways* (Capital Transport 2nd Edition 1999)

Kearney, E. W. C., *Rapid Transit in the Future – The Kearney High-Speed Railway* (1907)

Klapper, C, *London's Lost Railways*, (Routledge & Kegan Paul 1976)

Kynaston, D., *The City of London: Golden Years 1890–1914* (Chatto & Windus 1995)

Lee, C. E., *Fifty Years of the Hampstead Tube* (London Transport 1957)

Lee, C. E., *Sixty Years of the Bakerloo* (London Transport 1966)

Lee, C. E., *Sixty Years of the Piccadilly* (London Transport 1966)

Lee, C. E., *The Tower Subway: The First Tube Tunnel in the World* (Institute of Mechanical Engineers 1970)

Pennick, N., *Tunnels Under London* (Fenris-Wolf, 2nd edition 1981)

Pond, C. C., *The Walthamstow and Chingford Railway* (Walthamstow Antiquarian Society 1982)
Sinclair, A., *Corsair: The Life of J. Pierpont Morgan* (Weidenfeld & Nicholson 1981)
Smeeton, C. S., *The London United Tramways Vol. 1* (LRTA 1994)
Various, *London's Tramway Subway* (LRTL, date unknown)
White, H. P., *A Regional History of the Railways of Great Britain Volume 3 – Greater London* (Phoenix 1963)
Wallace, D., *It Ain't Cricket: Tales of the Tube* (D. Wallace 2000)
Wilson, B. G. & Haram, V. S., *The Central London Railway* (Fairseat Press 1950)
Wilson, G., *London United Tramways* (Allen & Unwin 1971)
Who Was Who
Chambers Biographical Dictionary
Dictionary of National Biography

Periodicals, Journals, and Magazines
The Engineer
The Financial Times
The Railway Engineer
The Railway Gazette
The Railway Magazine
The Railway News
The Railway Official Gazette
The Railway Times
The Times
The Tramway and Railway World
Transport
The London Railway Record (Connor & Butler)
Railways South East (Capital Transport)
Underground (The London Underground Railway Society)
Underground News (The London Underground Railway Society)

Notes

References to specific files are listed in the format *archive: reference*, where *archive* is NA for the National Archives, LMA for the London Metropolitan Archive, and HLRO for the House of Lords Records Office.

1. *The Times* on 30 November 1861 wrote that "it seemed an insult to common sense to suppose that people ... would ever prefer, merely as a quicker medium, to be driven amid palpable darkness through the foul subsoil of London."
2. Quoted in *Tunnels Under London*, p3.
3. Westminster Bridge was renamed Westminster in 1907.
4. A vestry was the smallest unit of local government, originally based around the church after which it was named.
5. Duke Street is now John Adam Street.
6. Portland Road was renamed Great Portland Street on 1 March 1917.
7. *The Railway Times*, 28 February 1885
8. *The Railway News*, 11 May 1872
9. W. H. Smith had taken over the newspaper-distribution and railway bookstall business started by his father, also called W. H. Smith. In 1868 he became the liberal-Conservative M. P. for Westminster.
10. It is not permitted to accuse another Member of Parliament of lying.
11. *The Railway Times*, 13 May 1882
12. An electrically-powered car had been used some four months earlier on a new railway in Portrush, Northern Ireland, but this was for part of one day following a breakdown of the steam locomotive, and was not a scheduled public service.
13. NA: T 1/13326 mentions the use of pneumatic power.
14. *The Railway News*, 28 March 1885
15. Castle Street was in roughly the position occupied today by Charing Cross Road. Dudley Street became the eastern end of Shaftesbury Avenue.
16. Charing Cross in the context of many of the railways in this book refers to the street of that name, sited between Trafalgar Square and Whitehall, rather than the railway station opened by the South Eastern Railway. This station has a replica of the original Charing Cross in its forecourt (completed in 1856 by E. M. Barry).
17. The southern Regent Circus later became Piccadilly Circus. Richmond and King Streets were removed when Shaftesbury Avenue was cut through Soho in the late 1880s.
18. Little Queen Street was removed to make way for Kingsway; it occupied roughly the same position as the north end of that road.
19. Until 1941 the MR station at King's Cross was parallel to the current Thameslink station, and to the east of today's platforms. The station entrance was in King's Cross Bridge. The disused westbound platform can still be seen from passing trains, but the adjacent King's Cross Thameslink station has absorbed most of the eastbound platform.
20. NA: ED 27/1987. The Charities Commissioners were contacted again in 1899 by the Skinners' Company, this time in relation to the Great Northern & Strand Railway passing under the Sandhills Estate, of which they were also governors.
21. Today these are Monmouth Street and Shorts Gardens.

22. Scott, C., *The Design and Construction of the IRT: Civil Engineering*, (US Department of the Interior: Historic American Engineering Record, unknown year). This book, now available on the web at http://www. nycsubway. org/irt/irthaer/design-civil–2. html, describes in detail the early history and construction of the Interborough Rapid Transport in New York.
23. LMA: LRB/LD/P/22/1
24. A concept known as 'articulation', and experimented with by London Underground in 1970.
25. LCC Board Meeting minutes, 28 May 1899.
26. The Shortlands & Nunhead Railway was being opposed because it would sever a projected recreation ground in Lewisham.
27. *The Times*, 10 February 1863
28. Opposition from property-owners prevented the more obvious route under Southampton Row from being used.
29. The section of tunnel under Tottenham Court Road is still in use for this purpose.
30. More information about the PDC Railway can be found in Stanway, L. C., *Mails Under London* (Association of Essex Philatelic Societies 2000)
31. A detailed history of the Crystal Palace Pneumatic Railway can be found in *The London Railway Record* 37 and 38.
32. W&WR prospectus 1865. NA: RAIL 1075/361
33. *The Railway News*, 28 March 1885
34. Bancroft, P, *The Proposed Hyde Park Tube Railway*, London Railway Record 39, p47
35. The details of this railway are to be found in LMA: Acc/1297/MET10/674.
36. *The Standard*, 12 July 1876, and *The Echo*, 3 August 1876
37. 20 January 1883
38. *The Railway News*, 12 December 1885
39. A station at London Bridge main line station had been originally proposed as well. The failure of the C&SLR to agree with the London, Brighton & South Coast Railway about a passenger subway between the two stations led to this being dropped. In their report for the latter half of 1886 the C&SLR Board put the blame firmly on the shoulders of the main line company.
40. Renamed Clapham North on 13 September 1926.
41. According to Greathead, in his evidence to Parliament for the Central London Railway in 1890, tunnelling on the C&SLR progressed at a rate of roughly 16 feet (4.9 m) per day in London clay, which corresponded to 10 steps forward of the tunnelling shield. In gravel this was reduced to about 5 feet (1.5 m).
42. The use of steam trains was explicitly forbidden in the original Act of Parliament.
43. A crossover siding linking the two running tunnels was provided to the north of Elephant & Castle, requiring the platforms to be on the same level.
44. *Rails Through the Clay* (Croome and Jackson) is the definitive history of London's tube railways.
45. The northern Regent Circus was renamed Oxford Circus at a later date.
46. At St Martin's le Grand, the tunnels would be at the even steeper gradient of 1 in 15. By comparison, the steepest gradient used by passenger trains on the Underground today is 1 in 32, just east of Bow Road on the District Line.
47. *The Railway Times*, 3 January 1885

48. LMA: LRB/LD/P/23/1. The promoters' statement did not name the newspaper.
49. *The Railway Times*, 19 July 1890
50. The formal opening of the line, attended by the Prince of Wales and many other distinguished guests, took place on 27 June 1900.
51. The District Railway Act 1906 authorized extension of this subway to the north west corner of the Royal Albert Hall courtyard; needless to say, these works were never carried out.
52. Anonymous letter to *The Times*, published 26 February 1891.
53. 2 March 1891
54. Webber had served previously in the Royal Engineers, was a Vestryman for Kensington, and had been Chief Engineer to the City of London Electric Lighting Company, hence his interest in the railway.
55. This was a response to the action of the C&SLR, which constructed its Kennington station up to the edge of its property, and in doing so brought forward the building line, because it built over the area of the front garden. The LCC took the company to court, and lost. Thereafter it took great care to ensure the sanctity of the building line.
56. Trafalgar Square was combined with the Strand station of the CCE&HR when the Jubilee Line was opened on 1 May 1979; the whole complex was renamed Charing Cross from the same date.
57. Euston Road was renamed Warren Street on 7 June 1908, less than a year after opening. The original name can still be seen in the tiling on the platform walls.
58. Drummond Street used to pass across the front of Euston station, before the station was expanded southwards across it. Doric Way, to the east of the station, is a remnant whose name recalls the massive Doric portico that used to stand in front of the station.
59. Tottenham Court Road station was renamed Goodge Street, and Oxford Street renamed Tottenham Court Road on 9 March 1908. This was to avoid confusion with the CLR station at St Giles Circus, which was called Tottenham Court Road from opening.
60. Chalk Farm station was renamed Primrose Hill on 25 September 1950, and closed 28 September 1992.
61. *The Railway News*, 11 March 1893
62. This extension was granted after it was revealed in January 1897 that only 401 shares had been sold.
63. The Canonbury spur was opened in 1874, and links Finsbury Park with Canonbury station on the North London Railway. Passenger services ceased in 1976.
64. NA: RAIL 1066/1073
65. City Road station did not see a great deal of traffic, and closed permanently on 8 August 1922.
66. Kilburn & Maida Vale was renamed Kilburn High Road from 1 August 1923.
67. The island concerned is not the same as the large roundabout that exists to day at Hyde Park Corner. A number of small traffic islands existed at the site long before the massive traffic works of the 1960s marooned the Wellington Monument in the middle of the junction.
68. High Beach is the currently used name, but contemporary sources also shown it as High Beech, Highbeach, and Highbeech. A long debate about the name, including the origins, took place in the pages of *Underground News* from May until October 1995.

69. More about the history of the GER line can be found in *The Walthamstow and Chingford Railway* (Pond).
70. The northern end of Pitfield Street, between New North Road and Hyde Road was called St John's Road in 1902.
71. NA: BT 285/726
72. *Ibid.*
73. Dover Street was renamed Green Park on 18 September 1933.
74. Not to be confused with the 1877 scheme of the same name, described earlier.
75. The station on the West London Railway was called Kensington (Addison Road) until 19 December 1946, when it was renamed Kensington (Olympia) for the adjacent exhibition halls.
76. This site is now occupied by the Lanesborough Hotel.
77. NA: MEPO 2/241
78. All station names given for the C&BR are taken from the map presented to the Royal Commission on London Traffic. No other maps of the line give names.
79. The C&SLR depot site is now occupied by Stockwell Gardens.
80. This station was actually called Old Kent Road & Hatcham and closed on 31 December 1916.
81. *The Railway News*, 4 December 1897
82. Kilburn & Maida Vale was renamed Kilburn High Road on 1 August 1923.
83. No names for stations were listed in NWLR documents for 1899. The names given here are those supplied by Douglas Fox to the Royal Commission on London Traffic in 1905.
84. For more details of the Glasgow Subway, see Wright & Maclean, *Circles Under the Clyde* (Capital Transport 1997)
85. *The Engineer*, 24 November 1905. This was discussing the NWLR 1906 Bill.
86. NA: BT 31/8107/58481
87. Great James Street is now the eastern end of Bell Street.
88. Seymour Street has since been renamed Eversholt Street.
89. Cranbourn Street was renamed Leicester Square before the station opened.
90. Renamed South Kentish Town before opening; it was closed on 5 June 1924 following a strike at Lots Road power station, and never reopened.
91. This was to reduce the cost of the line, as explained in the booklet issued to celebrate the reopening of the line following its reconstruction in the early 1920s.
92. *The Railway Times*, 11 June 1898
93. *The Railway News*, 16 January 1897
94. *The Railway News*, 2 December 1899
95. *The Railway Times*, 16 June 1900, p738.
96. *The Railway News*, 2 June 1900
97. It was reported in *The Railway News* on 24 November 1900 as being one of the Bills for the 1901 session.
98. MP for Chippenham, and one of the Commissioners on the Royal Commission for London Traffic (see later).
99. MP for Leeds Central.
100. *The Tramway and Railway World*, 11 April 1901, p207.
101. MP for Wigan.

102. MP for Kent St Augustine's.
103. Their meetings were held on Tuesday and Friday mornings at 11.30.
104. Brecknock Road was opened as Tufnell Park; Archway Tavern as Highgate.
105. The Business Design Centre now occupies the site of the Royal Agricultural Hall.
106. This referred to the subway built under Exhibition Road, opened in 1885, and closed at the end of 1886, charging pedestrians a toll of 1d. It was only opened occasionally after that date, until 1908, when it was reopened free of charge.
107. British Museum closed on 24 September 1933, and was replaced by new Central London Railway platforms at Holborn station the following day. This provided far better interchange than the 170-yard street-level walk between the two stations previously.
108. The CCH&DR was sometime referred to as the Charing Cross, Hammersmith & District Electric Railway, or CCH&DER.
109. This was the first tube railway of the session against which the Grand Junction petitioned; all of its other petitions exist in draft form based around that for the CCH&DR.
110. Thanet Place has disappeared from the 1914 Ordnance Survey map. See London Sheet 62 from *The Godfrey Edition* of Old Ordnance Survey maps.
111. Carter Lane was used instead of the more obvious route along Ludgate Hill to place the railway further from St Paul's Cathedral. This helped to remove the opposition raised by the St Paul's authorities.
112. Much of the information about the stations comes from the evidence of Sir Douglas Fox to the Committee on 24 May 1901.
113. Balfour Browne gave his evidence to the Committee on 7 May 1901.
114. Evidence given on 10 May 1901.
115. NA: RAIL 227/26.
116. This detail was found in a sketch added to the copy of the plans deposited with the East London Waterworks. LMA: ACC/2423/PP/17.
117. Greenleaf Road & Bemsted Road, and Melville Road & Mersey Road.
118. Fortescue was one of the representatives for Walthamstow on Essex County Council.
119. Hassard gave his evidence on 14 May 1901.
120. Also shown as Hazard in some publications, but not related to Colonel Rowland Hazard.
121. *The Tramway and Railway World*, July 11 1901, p385.
122. The Regent's Canal & Dock Railway was a scheme that had emerged in 1882 to drain the canal and replace it by a railway that would connect together a number of the main lines out of London. Despite a number of successful Acts in the 1880s and 1890s, nothing ever came of the scheme.
123. Editorial, *The Tramway and Railway World*, 8 August 1901, p423.
124. The World's Progress in Electric Traction, *The Railway Magazine*, December 1901, p558.
125. *Transport*, 24 May 1901
126. *The Sydney Morning Herald*, 29 January 1904
127. *The Railway News*, 12 April 1902, p563.
128. Published in *The Tramway and Railway World*, 11 January 1906, p33.
129. See *Corsair: The Life of J. Pierpont Morgan* (Sinclair), p29.
130. Written (incorrectly) as McAllister in some accounts
131. NA: RAIL 1066/691, and RAIL 1066/1420

132. Fordyce Sheridan, together with three family members, was a director of the *Financial Post*, a newspaper which allegedly threatened to print damaging articles about companies unless those companies paid up. In August 1897 Sheridan had tried this on with a Manchester-based finance company called Commerce Ltd, whose Managing Director went to the Police claiming that Sheridan had requested £50,000. On 26 and 27 August 1897 the newspaper did print damaging articles about Commerce Ltd, and Sheridan worked hard to ensure maximum distribution in Manchester. This all emerged at his trial, and despite pleading not guilty he was sentenced to six months in Lancaster prison. Sheridan was qualified as a barrister (although he had never practised as such), and was disbarred from the Inner Temple at his own request in January 1899.
133. NA: RAIL 1066/691
134. The information and invitation to request a prospectus was printed in an advert in the *Financial Times* on 21 July 1902, p7.
135. *Transport*, 25 July 1902, p108.
136. This has been quoted as £5,000 for an Earl and £10,000 for a Duke.
137. To ensure positive media coverage, he allegedly issued a press release claiming the run was a success – two days before the run took place!
138. Some accounts state that other companies were involved in the charges, including the Electric Tramways Construction & Maintenance Company Ltd.
139. According to *The Tramway and Railway World*, the inconsistent Bills of the C&BR were to give the promoters a choice in deciding what length of line to abandon.
140. Although 23 new Bills are shown in the table above, the City & Old Kent Road Railway Bill was never deposited with Parliament – see below for more details.
141. NA: CRES 35/4171. The table was compiled as part of a 1906 report to the Treasury.
142. Strangely, although the subway was authorized to the Embankment, the tramway was only authorized to the north side of the Strand. It took the LCC another four years to get permission to continue the tramway south onto the Embankment.
143. Stepney East was renamed Limehouse in the 1980s following the opening of the Docklands Light Railway station.
144. NA: RAIL 1066/78
145. *Ibid.*
146. The following year the latter company obtained powers to take over the E&HR, which was done swiftly afterwards.
147. *The Railway News*, 10 May 1902, p722.
148. Penge station was opened by the London, Brighton & South Coast Railway, and renamed Penge West on 9 July 1923.
149. NA: RAIL 1066/691. The notes were a briefing for their Counsel.
150. Schenk was also part of the syndicate that had promoted the City, Wandsworth & Wimbledon Railway unsuccessfully.
151. *The Financial Times*, 8 August 1902.
152. NA: RAIL 1066/650
153. NA: RAIL 1066/628
154. This had been agreed by the B&PCR Board at their meeting of 23 December 1901.
155. This was explained to the Committee by Yerkes on 30 April 1902.
156. Walham Green was renamed Fulham Broadway on 2 March 1952.
157. The Brompton Consumptive Hospital, the Chelsea Hospital for Women, the Guardians

for the Poor for the St George's Union (a workhouse), and the Cancer Hospital all presented evidence against the Bill.

158. This deviation was first reported in *The Railway Times*, 25 January 1902.
159. See *London United Tramways* (Wilson), p84.
160. See *A History of London Transport Vol. 1* (Barker and Robbins), p305–8.
161. The London News Agency reported the amalgamation on 26 April 1902.
162. Report of Hugh Godfray to LUT Board on 30 April 1902.
163. *The Railway Magazine*, May 1902, p494; originally quoted in the *Morning Leader.*
164. Brereton, the B&PCR engineer, also estimated the cost of 13 ft 6 ins diameter tunnels as £48 per yard, compared to £40 per yard for 11 ft 6 ins diameter tunnels.
165. An article in the *Financial Times* on 31 October 1902 explained the division of capital and control for the various sections of line.
166. Fox had originally wanted to oppose the C&NESER in favour of the NELR Walthamstow branch. He then became convinced of its importance, and recommended that it be brought into the combine, and the NELR branch be dropped.
167. *The Railway Times*, 2 August 1902.
168. This locomotive was called the *Decapod*, named for its ten wheels. It never entered public service, and as such had a very short life (operating for a just a few months in 1903) due to it breaking the track and bridges beneath its vast weight. The large estimated cost of reconstructing the bridges on the GER to support it was not justifiable, and so it was eventually rebuilt to a smaller size. The *Decapod* is mentioned in a number of sources; see Allen, C. J., *The Great Eastern Railway* (Ian Allen 1955).
169. *The Railway Times*, 26 April 1902
170. *The Engineer*, 23 May 1902, p502.
171. NA: RAIL 1066/1940
172. It was stated that the electrification would be complete in eighteen months. In fact, electric services on the District main line were not introduced until June 1905.
173. This was Clause 53k in 1901, and clause 30b in 1902. It was also allowed to inspect the workings and to claim compensation if any damage was caused. Electrical interference with their signalling, telegraphs, or telephony equipment was also to be prevented.
174. Minutes of the CCE&HR Board Meeting of 24 January 1902.
175. See *It Ain't Cricket: Tales of the Tube* (Wallace), p22.
176. One of the criteria for the names, approved by the LCC meeting of 10 February 1903, was that they be single words. Aldwych was chosen for its long historical association with the area, once Aldwych fields. Prior to the improvement works the only sign of the name was in Wych Street, which was entirely obliterated by 1905.
177. Ironically, the crescent remained a building site until well into the 1920s; it took rather longer than the LCC anticipated to construct the buildings.
178. The Third Schedule (for an agreement of 22 May) was an agreement with Charles Eley, an Edmonton landowner, specifying the land permitted to be taken and the nature of the works. The Fourth Schedule to the Bill was added on 25 August, which was very similar in nature to the Third Schedule and was with a group of Tottenham landowners.
179. *The Railway News*, 17 May 1902, p775.
180. *The Railway Engineer*, July 1902, p194.
181. *The Engineer*, 13 June 1902, p583.
182. Sloane Street was the original name proposed for the GNP&BR station at this location

as well, and was still in use for it as late as 1905. See the District Railway map, 6th edition, c. 1905. *London Passenger Transport*, No. 7, p394.

183. The generating station for the C&NESER at Hackney Marshes is not shown; nor is one of the NELR proposals at the Regent's Canal in Hackney Road.
184. Low-level ticket offices were provided in subways connecting the Yerkes tubes with the C&SLR at Euston, King's Cross, and Elephant & Castle, and the CLR at Oxford Circus and Oxford Street/Tottenham Court Road.
185. Edwards D. & Pigram R., *London's Underground Suburbs* (Bloomsbury Books 1986)
186. Victoria Circus has been subsequently renamed Queen's Circus.
187. St Mary's was officially called St Mary's (Whitechapel), and was closed on 1 May 1938 due to the eastward resiting of Aldgate East station.
188. Much of the information about the stations comes from the evidence of Fraser to the Committee on 28 April 1902.
189. Derek Wallace, personal communication. The archivist at the Institute of Civil Engineers informed him that "it appears Sir Douglas Fox's drawings were destroyed during the 1st World War".
190. HLRO: HLplan1902/L26
191. Interestingly, Douglas Fox was the engineer for this railway. It will be noted from the description below that the machine was more like the moving walkways at Bank station, installed in the 1960s and called Trav-o-lators by Otis, rather than a true escalator.
192. The word 'Escalator' was coined by one of the original pioneers, Charles Seeberger, who sold his designs to the Otis Elevator Company. They trademarked the word in 1911, and had a monopoly on its use until 1950.
193. *Financial Times*, 15 July 1902
194. The only place that this arrangement is described is *The Railway Magazine*, August 1902, p154.
195. Jenkin originally stated that they would be of seven cars, but corrected this subsequently.
196. Canal Road is today called Orsman Road.
197. The original figures come from the evidence presented to the Joint Select Committee. The later fare revisions were reported in *The Railway Times* on 26 July 1902, and were also mentioned on 1 May 1903 by W. Dickinson in the Minutes of Evidence to the Royal Commission on London Traffic.
198. Campion was one of three Examiners for Standing Orders in the Lords.
199. Reported in *The Railway Times*, 12 July 1902.
200. MP for Shoreditch, Hoxton.
201. *The Railway Times*, 19 July 1902
202. MP for Peckham.
203. MP for York.
204. MP for Hammersmith.
205. MP for Battersea.
206. MP for Manchester South.
207. MP for Luton.
208. Reported in *The Financial Times* on 31 July 1902.
209. McIver appears in some publications as M'Iver.
210. "That it be an Instruction to the Committee on the Bill to take security from the

Undertakers for the completion of the whole Scheme of Railways comprised in the Bill, either by making the rights of the Undertakers under the Bills conditional upon the due performance of their whole Undertaking, or otherwise as the Committee may think fit."

211. This was reported in *The Railway Times* on 9 August 1902, and noted at the meeting of the B&PCR Board on 28 August.
212. Letter from George White to Mr Gray, quoted in the *Financial Times* on 22 October (p3).
213. *The Railway Times*, 18 October 1902
214. This is the only minute of the LUT Board meeting held on 17 October 1902.
215. Noted by D. N. Dunlop in *The Railway Magazine*, January 1903, p27.
216. *The Railway Magazine*, January 1903, p28.
217. *The Financial Times*, 22 October 1902
218. *The Railway Times*, 25 October 1902. The commentary also predicted the failure of the (then) proposed motion of recommital.
219. *Transport*, 24 October 1902.
220. This was also reported verbatim in *The Railway Times*, 25 October 1902, p417.
221. Journal of the House of Commons, 23 October 1902, p447.
222. *The Railway News*, 25 October 1902, p592.
223. *The Railway Times*, 1 November 1902, p443.
224. Circular issued by the Morgan group on 28 October 1902.
225. Reported in *The Railway* News, 25 October 1902, and *The Tramway and Railway World*, 13 November 1902.
226. MP for Penrith.
227. *The Railway Magazine*, January 1903, p 28.
228. *The Railway Engineer*, November 1902
229. Letter of 30 October, published in *The Financial Times* on 31 October 1902.
230. Letter of 30 October, published in *The Financial Times* the following day, and in *The Railway Times* on 8 November 1902.
231. Letter of 3 November, published in *The Financial Times* the following day, and in *The Railway Times* on 15 November 1902.
232. Letter of 4 November, published in *The Financial Times* the following day.
233. *The Railway Engineer*, November 1902, p323.
234. Letter of 12 November, published in *The Railway Times* on 15 November 1902.
235. *The Railway News*, 8 November 1902, p662.
236. *The Railway Magazine*, January 1903, p29.
237. Reported in MDR Board minutes of 12 March 1903.
238. This figure was given in evidence to the Royal Commission on London Traffic on 14 January 1904.
239. MP for Battersea.
240. Hansard, Volume 119, p657.
241. MP for Camberwell, Peckham.
242. Hansard, Volume 119, p657.
243. More detail about the rejection of this scheme can be found in the evidence of W. H. Dickenson to the Royal Commission on London Traffic, given on 1 May 1903.
244. *The Railway News*, 12 March 1903
245. Jubilee Street has since been cut back so that it no longer joins the Mile End Road, but

instead ends at O'Leary Square.

246. I am grateful to Mike Horne for bringing this observation to my attention.
247. *The Railway Magazine*, January 1919
248. Over ninety years later similar work was done at North Greenwich on the Jubilee Line. Junction tunnels have been constructed at the north-east end of the station box to allow for easy connection to any eastward extension of the line via the Royal Docks or Thamesmead.
249. *The Railway Gazette*, 24 November 1916
250. The LPTB was the statutory authority created by the government in 1933 to run public transport in London.
251. This was connected to the Civil Defence Headquarters, situated beneath the Geological Museum, by cables that passed via the public subway under Exhibition Road.
252. *Reconstructing London's Underground*, p97.
253. In 1906, as part of the evidence given by the promoters for the NWLR Act of that year.
254. See, for example, Beard, T., *By Tube Beyond Edgware* (Capital Transport 2002), for the definitive history of the proposed railway beyond Edgware.
255. The other Commissioners were: Viscount Cobham, Sir Joseph Dimsdale, Sir John Dickson-Poynder, Sir Robert Reid, Sir Francis Hopwood, Sir George Bartley, Charles Murdoch, and Felix Schuster.
256. Barbour, Ribblesdale, Dickson-Poynder, Bartley, and Gibb, with Macassey.
257. Sir George Bartley.
258. See *London's Termini* for more details about this and the other Committees.
259. The Inner Circle, linking most of the main line termini north of the Thames was finally completed in 1884. The Outer Circle was not a complete circle, but a service of trains operated from 1872 by the LNWR between Broad Street and Mansion House, via Willesden Junction, Addison Road, and Earl's Court.
260. However, wayleaves had not been introduced even in 1895, when a Mr William Farmer informed the Waterloo & City Railway that they had no right to enter the subsoil beneath his house. The dispute went to court, where Justice Kekewich ruled that the railway company had to either purchase the entirety of his property, or pay him substantial compensation for the right to tunnel. The compensation was set at £750, which was finally paid in September 1896.
261. An interim report was published in May 1901, and the final report in February 1902.
262. Fitzmaurice took over from Binnie in January 1902.
263. This subway was opened on 24 February 1906 between Theobalds Road and had subway stations at Holborn and Aldwych (at the junction with Kingsway). It was extended to the Embankment on 10 April 1908. For more information about this subway, see *London's Tramway Subway*.
264. Baker acted as engineer or consultant to the MR, MDR, C&SLR, CLR, and BS&WR.
265. The surface site for the station at Lambeth was approved in the 1903 Bill. However, this may have been intended for the electricity substation that is adjacent to the station buildings.
266. The tunnels were enlarged for a length of 318 feet (97 m) at Lambeth, 311 feet (95 m) at Regent's Park, and 540 feet (165 m) at Edgware Road. The widened section at the latter station was presumably for the crossover required at the line's terminus.
267. LCC Board Minutes, 29 March 1904.

268. A short circuit caused a fire on a wooden-bodied train. Whilst attempting to get it to a siding the fire broke out with great strength, filling the tunnels with smoke. The station lighting at Couronnes failed, and 84 people died in the resulting mêlée.
269. Quoted in *Reconstructing London's Underground*, p30.
270. High Street has since been renamed Pier Road.
271. The LCC eventually obtained powers to build a foot tunnel at Woolwich in the Thames Tunnel (North & South Woolwich) Act of 1909. The tunnel that was constructed is 1,655 yards (505 m) long, and has a diameter of 12ft 8 ins (3.86 m). It is slightly upstream of the tunnel proposed by the N&SWER, and was opened to the public on 26 October 1912.
272. Bancroft, P, *The Waterloo to Ludgate Circus Tube Railway*, London Railway Record 40, p85
273. Noted in *London's Tramway Subway*.
274. In 1915 the railway company was forced to pay the LCC the sum of £1,355 for damage caused by their railway passing beneath the set of buildings between Aldwych and Strand. (*Railway Gazette*, 28 May 1915, p562).
275. Howard Street linked Surrey Street to Arundel Street about halfway between the Strand and Temple Place. It was built over as part of the Arundel Great Court development between the latter four roads.
276. The deposited plans do not show two platforms at Waterloo, but when the Bill was considered by the House of Commons Select Committee this detail came to light.
277. See, for example, *Underground* No. 92, p121 and response in No. 94, p154.
278. NA: MR 1/2028
279. LMA: LCC/CL/PARL/3/22
280. *The Railway News*, 26 November 1904, p763.
281. NA: MT 6/2466/24
282. Some of the detail in this section comes from the evidence given by Cooper on 11 March 1904 to the Royal Commission on London Traffic.
283. The word 'Street' was omitted from the station name.
284. These figures come from the evidence given by Cooper on 11 March 1904 to the Royal Commission on London Traffic.
285. NA: CRES 35/2621
286. This led to the GNP&BR Board agreeing to deposit a petition against the Bill at their meeting on 12 January 1905.
287. MP for Somersetshire South.
288. MP for Northampton.
289. NA: RAIL 1066/2278
290. NA: MT 6/1384/4
291. In the 1950s stair and lift shafts were sunk, allowing the station to be equipped as a floodgate control room.
292. *The Railway News*, 24 March 1906
293. Denman Street is now called London Bridge Street.
294. MP for Oldham.
295. Letter of 11 May 1906 from Foster & Braithwaite, and Linton Clarke & Co., to the LCC.
296. According to the Oxford English Dictionary, consols are undated government stock,

representing the consolidated annuities of the UK (part of the National Debt).

297. HLRO: HL/PO/JO/2/142
298. LMA: LRB/LD/P/40/5
299. This building was closed in 1914 when the underground stations were joined to the main line station. It was demolished in 1934.
300. Much of this section uses Kearney's book of 1907 as its source.
301. *The Railway News*, 8 July 1905, and *The Railway Engineer*, August 1908.
302. *Monorails*, H. S. D. Botzof Jr (Simmons-Boardman Publishing Corp. 1960)
303. One wonders how deep and fast he intended his tubes to go, given that the Eurostar trains travelling at up to 186 m.p.h. (300 km/h) take over two hours to make this journey.
304. *The Railway Magazine*, January 1919 (Answers to Correspondents).
305. *The Railway News*, 25 November 1905
306. LMA: MCC/CL/L/LR/2/109
307. *The Railway Times*, 1 November 1913
308. An estimate of the costs of extending to Camberwell was prepared in 1921, but the first real push to make the extension was in 1931, when Parliamentary powers were obtained. These were used in 1940 to reconstruct the sidings south of Elephant & Castle on the new alignment. Further plans were made in the late 1940s, with powers again being obtained in 1949. More planning work was again undertaken in the early 1970s, but all petered out on cost grounds.
309. *The Railway Engineer*, August 1908
310. *The Railway News*, 11 May 1907
311. Wembley for Sudbury was renamed Wembley Central on 5 July 1948.
312. Charing Cross was renamed Charing Cross Embankment on 4 August 1974, and then Simply to Embankment on 12 September 1976.
313. The loop was subsequently severed when the Hampstead tube was extended southwards to link with the C&SLR at Kennington in 1926. Fortunately the disused tunnel was completely sealed off, as it had the dubious honour of being the only tube railway tunnel under the Thames to be breached by a bomb in World War II. The Tower Subway was damaged by a bomb in December 1940, but was not actually breached (although the tunnel diameter was reduced in the region near the bomb site).
314. This was the first Underground station to be designed with escalators. The first pair to be used on the Underground had come into service the previous year at Earl's Court.
315. The stations at North and West Acton were opened on 5 November 1923.
316. *The Railway News*, 22 February 1913
317. *The Railway News*, 14 February 1914
318. Detailed dimensions for the experimental car are given in *Underground* No. 77, May 1968, p69. If the exhibition at Ealing Common depôt ever took place then it seems not to have been recorded in the railway press, as no reports have come to light.
319. *The Tramway & Railway World*, 8 May 1913
320. LMA: ACC 1297/MET1/32
321. *London's Metropolitan Railway*, p203 and note 3, p347
322. LMA: ACC/1297/MET10/627
323. In its issue of 29 November 1913, describing new Bills for the 1914 session, *The RailwayTimes* claimed that a junction would be made between the GN&CR extension

and the W&CR, and that trains of the latter will run through to the GN&CR. They did not care to explain how the larger GN&CR trains would fit into the smaller platforms of the W&CR.

324. Knightrider Street has since been cut back to less than half its length, and no longer meets Queen Victoria Street.
325. A further connection was included in the Bill, although it had nothing to do with the GN&CR. The MR wished to build a link between its stations at West Harrow and South Harrow, in effect forming a triangular junction at Rayners Lane.
326. Most railway companies were legally compelled to dispose of land not required for their operations. Unusually the Metropolitan was exempt from this requirement, and used it to great effect, with the rising land values helping to pay for the railway. It is this provision that Willesden and St Marylebone objected, and especially the supply of electricity – at the time, the municipalities were monopoly suppliers to their areas.
327. *A Regional History of the Railways of Great Britain Volume 3 – Greater London* (White), p157–8.
328. However, the MR kept the powers for the extension to Lothbury alive until the end of October 1932.
329. See *The Big Tube* and *Rails Through the Clay*.
330. LMA: ACC/1297/MET10/627
331. I am indebted to the transcript of a lecture *The Evolution of Parliamentary Procedure*, given by Maurice Bond in 1966, and printed by the House of Lords Record Office for some of the details in this appendix.
332. *The Railway News*, 24 January 1914
333. *Ibid.*

Index

Notes:

There may be more than one reference on the page indicated.
Under major entries (in capitals), subheadings, where appropriate, are in alphabetical order of railway, or approximate chronological order.
Station names are cross-referenced, as different names may have been applied to stations proposed at the same site by different railway companies.
Entries in italics are or include a map.